Serving the Web

Robert Mudry

CORIOLIS GROUP BOOKS

Publisher	Keith Weiskamp
Editor	Jeff Duntemann
Managing Editor	Ron Pronk
Cover Design	Gary Smith
Interior Design	Bradley Grannis
Layout Production	Rob Mauhar, Jenni Aloi, and Michelle Stroup
Indexer	Diane Cook
Publicist	Shannon Bounds

Library of Congress Cataloging-in-Publication Data

Mudry, Robert
    Serving the Web/Robert Mudry
        p. cm.
    Includes index.
    ISBN 1-883577-30-6: $39.99

Printed in the United States of America

10 9 8 7 6 5 4 3 2 1

To my wife Ginger.

*Without her love, patience, and understanding,
this book would not have been possible.*

Contents

Introduction .... **xv**

Chapter 1   How May We Serve You? **1**

Client/Server 101   1
Scenario 1: Your Personal Home Page   3
Scenario 2: A Web Site Hosted by Your Internet Service Provider   4
Scenario 3: Leasing Space for Your Machine at a Provider's Location   5
Scenario 4: Your Own Server Computer with a Low-Speed Dedicated Connection   7
Scenario 5: Your Own Server Computer with a Dedicated High-Speed Connection   8
Scenario 6: Your Own Minicomputer and Multiple High-Speed Connections   9
Setup Considerations   10
Static Versus Dynamic HTML Documents   11
Interaction with CGI Scripts   12
CGI Considerations   15

Chapter 2   The Web from the Client Side **17**

Getting on the World Wide Web   18
   Uh oh! I Don't Have an Internet Connection!   18
   No, I Really Don't Have Internet Access!   19
I Have Internet Access. What Now?   20
   Fully Graphical Internet Access   20
   Netscape Navigator   20
   NCSA Mosaic   22
   The Many Faces of "Mosaic"   23
   Kiosks and Presentations   23
Text-Only Access   26
   Lynx: A Full-Screen Text-Only Browser   26
   A Line-Mode Browser   27
   Email Browsers   27
   TIA and SlipKnot   30
Life Behind the Firewall   31
Surf and Take Notes!   32
Summing Up   33

Chapter 3   Hardware and Network Connections **35**

How the Network Works   35
   Connecting to the Internet   36

Low-Speed "Serial Line" Connections 37
56 K Leased Lines 38
56 K Frame Relay 41
T1 42
FRACTIONAL T1 43
ISDN—Integrated Services Digital Network 43
T3 45

Getting Your Web Pages on the Internet   45
  So What Is Your Goal? 46
  Renting Space and Services 46

How to Find ISPs to Carry Your Pages   47

Selecting an ISP   48
  Gauging the ISP as a Company 48
  Do They Offer What You Need? 50
  The Bill, Please 51

Owning Your Own Equipment   53
  The Computer 53

The Network Connection   54

So Where Do I Start?   59

Connect and Prosper!   61

Chapter 4   Choosing Your Server 63

Which Server Is for You?   64
  Web Server Features 65
  SSL and S-HTTP Support 67
  Graphical Setup and Maintenance 67
  Gopher Server Capability 67
  User Directories 68
  Price 68

A Little More about the Servers   68
  Unix Servers 69
  Windows NT Servers 70
  Macintosh Servers 71
  Windows 3.1 Servers 71
  OS/2 Servers 71

So You Want to Take Credit Cards...   72
  Public Key Cryptography 73
  Your Certificate, Please 74
  The Certificate Authority 75
  RSA Data Security 75

Advanced Information   76
  Log Formats 76
  Server-Side Includes 77
  Access Control 79

Other Security Concerns   79

Firewalls   79
Which Side of the Wall?   80
Some Unix Security Tips   81

Server Choice Summary   82

Chapter 5   HTML 101 85

Hypertext and Markup Languages   85
Markup and Markup Languages   86
SGML   87

Basic HTML Markup   88
The Document Head   89
The Document Body   90
Paragraphs   92
Logical and Physical Styles   92
Section Headings   95
The Horizontal Rule   97

Blockquotes, Addresses, and Linebreaks   98
Address Formatting   98
Line Breaks   100
Lists and Menus   101
Directories and Glossaries   103

Preformatted Text   104

Chapter 6   Anchors Aweigh! 107

HTML Levels   108

Linking Documents Together   109
Relative URLs   110
Slash and Dots   110

Linking to a Specific Point within a Document   111
Fragment Navigation   113
Escaping "Bad Characters" within URLs   113

External Images, Sounds, and Movies   116
Warning: Monster File Coming!   117
Linking to Nonstandard Files   118

Inline Images   118
Alternate Text for the Graphically Challenged   119
Inline Image File Types   121

Mastheads, Icons, and Fancy Rules   121
Fancy Horizontal Rules   123
Icons from Inline Images   123

Icons Inside of Anchors   128

Finding and Using Existing Icons and Images   129

Transparent GIFs   130

Don't Foresake "Manual" HTML   133

Chapter 7   Authoring Tools 133

Editors   135
    WYSIWYG Editors   136
    Raw HTML Editors   137
    Test Driving an HTML Editor: HoTMetaL by SoftQuad   137

Templates   142
    Test Driving a Template: Internet Assistant   142

Butterfly Times   147
    Joyride in the Park   147

Converters   149
    Test Driving a Converter: rtftohtml   149

Leveraging Your HTML Skills   150

Chapter 8   More HTML, Style, and
a Sample Home Page 153

Advanced and Obscure HTML   153

Comments in HTML   154

Things That Go in the Document Head   155
    <BASE>   156
    <LINK>   158
    <NEXTID>   161
    <ISINDEX>   162
    <META>   162
    More Attributes for Anchors   162

Optional End Tags   162

General Style Guidelines for Web Page Design   163

Guidelines for Designing Your Home Page   164
    Your Organization's Image   164
    Graphics Anyone?   164
    The Layout of Your Home Page   166
    Things You Should Keep in Mind   167

A Sample Home Page   171

Substance and Style   173

Chapter 9   HTML Forms and Simple CGI Scripts 175

The Form of Things to Come   176
    Static and Dynamic HTML   176
    Scripts for Generating Dynamic HTML   177
    CGI Scripts   178

Designing a Simple Form   180
    The <INPUT> Tag   180
    The SIZE and MAXLENGTH Attributes   183

Check Boxes   184
A Simple CGI Script for Processing the Form   186
To POST or to GET?   186
Obtaining and Preparing Form Data   187
Environment Variables Used by CGI Scripts   188
A Simple CGI Script in Perl   188
How the Script Works   190
Associative Arrays in Perl   191
The Great Unescape   191

Talking Back to the Browser   192
MIME's the Word   193
Sending Dynamic HTML Back to the Web Browser   194
Things That Can Go Wrong   197

More Advanced HTML Forms   198
Radio Buttons to "Choose One of the Above"   200
Radio Buttons Versus Check Boxes   201
OPTION Menus and <SELECT>   202
<SELECT> and Scrolled Lists   204
Multiple Selections with <SELECT>   205
A Two-Dimensional Text Box   205
Text Defaults   206
The "Infinite Input Flaw" and Its Solution   208
How They Faked <TEXTAREA> in Olden Tymes   208
A CGI Script for the Custom User-Feedback Form   209
Handling Multiple <SELECT> Selections   211
Storing Data Submitted by the User   215

Some Notes on Script Security   215
So What Can I Do about It?   217
Following the Script   218

Chapter 10   Image Maps 219

Image Maps   219
So How's It Done?   223
Paint Programs   224
Hotspots and Scripts   225

Step 1: Designing the Image   225
Keep an Eye on the Overall Size of Your Image Map   226
Identify Your Hotspots Clearly   226
Avoid the "Because It's There" Trap!   226

Step 2: Defining the Hotspots   227
Map Configuration Files   227
The CERN Map Format   229
The NCSA Map Format   229
NCSA's IMAGEMAP.CONF File   230

Step 3: Write the HTML   231
The Action at Click-Time   232
A Quick Note on Style   232

The INPUT vs. ISMAP Methods   232
    You Can't Use Pre-made Scripts!   233
    What Your Script Sees   235
    Image Maps as Submit Buttons   235

Using the MIME Location Header   239

Hotspots in INPUT-Method Image Maps   241

Following the Map!   245

Chapter 11   Advanced CGI 247

Scripts Generating Forms   247

The Art of Keeping State: A New Mailing List Script   248
    Another Use for VALUE   248

Environment Variables with CGI   256
    SERVER_NAME   258
    SERVER_PORT   258
    SERVER_SOFTWARE   258
    SERVER_PROTOCOL   259
    GATEWAY_INTERFACE   259
    REQUEST_METHOD   259
    QUERY_STRING   259
    CONTENT_LENGTH   260
    CONTENT_TYPE   260
    SCRIPT_NAME   260
    PATH_INFO   261
    PATH_TRANSLATED   261
    Request Headers and the HTTP_ Variables   261
    Variables that Identify the User   262

Server-Side Includes   264
    Configuring NCSA HTTPD 1.3 for SSIs   264
    SSI Syntax   265
    Executing Commands and CGI Scripts   275

Using <ISINDEX>   279
    <ISINDEX> and Server-Side Includes   282
    How about some ACTION?   283

Indexing and Searching Your Web Pages   284
    SWISH- "Simple Web Indexing System for Humans"   286

The Uncommon Gateway Interface   293

Chapter 12   The Mozilla Extensions and "Things Netscape" 297

The Mozilla Extensions   298

Improving on Inline Images   298
    ALIGN attribute   299
    VSPACE and HSPACE Attributes: "Keep your distance!"   301

The BORDER Attribute   302
The WIDTH and HEIGHT Attributes   303
Inline JPEGs   307
The LOWSRC Attribute   308
Interlaced Inline Images   309

New Attributes for the
 Element 310

New Attributes for Horizontal Rules 311
Setting Horizontal Rule Thickness   312
Setting Horizontal Rule Width   312
Aligning Rules Left, Center, or Right   314
Solid Rather than Shaded Rules   315

Changes to Lists: New Attributes for
    <UL>, <OL>, and <LI> 315
Unordered Lists   316
Ordered Lists   318
Warning on the Use of These Extensions for Lists   320

Changes to <ISINDEX> 321

Brand New Elements 321

Centering Your Text 322

Changing Your Font Sizes 323
Changing the Base Font   323
Overriding the Base Font Size   324

To Break or Not to Break 327

The Dreaded "Blink" 329

Tables 329
A Simple Table   329
Cells that Span Rows and Columns   332
Header Cells   337
Aligning Text within Cells   340
Text Wrapping inside Cells   341
Adding Captions   344
Things about Tables that Are Netscape-Specific   346
How NCSA Mosaic Handles Tables   355

"Things Netscape" 355

Chapter 13   More From Mozilla 357

Changing Colors 357
How Computers See Color   358
Background Colors   358
Foreground Colors   363
Background Patterns   363

Client Pull 367
HTTP Response Headers: The Short Story   367
The <META> Element   368
The Response Header and Client Pull   369

Client Pull in CGI   371
Things Not To Do With Client Pull   372

Server Push   374
Oh No! More MIME!   374
Applying Multipart MIME Messages to Server Push   375
How Not to Write a Server Push Script   376
No-Parse-Header (NPH) Scripts— Bypassing the Server   383
Implementing an Effective Server Push Script   385
Server Push and the "Poor Man's Animation"   387

Mozilla Swings!   389

Chapter 14   After Your Documents Are Written...... 391

Marketing and Promoting Your Web Pages   392
Internet Newsgroups   392
Internet Directories   395
For-Pay Internet Marketing   396
Trading Links   397

Working With Your Marketing Department   398
Helping Marketing Promote Your Web Server   399

Making Sense of Your Logs   399
The Common Log Format   400
Analyzing Your Logs with "getstats"   403
Back To Reality: The Dazzling Stats Syndrome   405
Making Your Statistics Publicly Available   406
Archiving Your Logs   407

There Be Robots A'roaming   407

General Web Server Maintenance   408
Robert's Eight Rules of Web Server Maintenance   409

Dealing with Problem Reports and Suggestions   411
Solutions to Common Problem Reports   412
"mailto:" is Your Friend   414

Some Concerns About the Law   414

Conclusion   417

Chapter 15   Future Directions 419

HTML 3.0   420

VRML—Virtual Reality on the Internet   421

Helper Apps That Control Your Browser   424
CCI—The Common Client Interface   424
JAVA   425

RealAudio   426

Cash and Security   427

Spinning the Future   428

Chapter 16   Using the CD-ROM 431

Audio, Video, Animation, and Clip Art   432
   Audio   432
   Images   432
   Video and Animation   432

Slackware 2.2.0   433
Internet Chameleon with Instant Internet   434
Internet Documentation   434
HomePage Creator   435
Microsoft Internet Assistant for Word 6.0   435
HotMetal   436
HTML Assistant   437
HTMLed   438
HTML Writer   438
RTF2HTML   439
MPEGplay version 1.65   439
Paint Shop Pro version 3.0   440
ViewSpace   441
Web Spinner   442
DOSPERL   442
Web4ham   443
Windows httpd 1.4   443
Win32 and WinG   443
Book Examples   444
Microsoft Video for Windows 1.1e   444
NetSeeker   444
   Running NetSeeker   445
   Using the NetSeeker Interface   447
   Using NetSeeker to Download Resources and Software   447
   Selecting Installation Options   448
   Getting More Help and Information   449
   Getting a Report of Your Activity   449
   Quitting NetSeeker   450
   Troubleshooting NetSeeker   450

Appendix A   HTML Reference 453

Appendix B   ISO-Latin-1 Coded Character Set 459

Appendix C   The Common Gateway Interface and Server-Side Includes 465

CGI Environment Variables Reference   465
Server Side Includes (SSIs) Reference   466

Appendix D   Decimal to Hexadecimal Conversion 469

Index 471

Introduction

One weekend in late spring of 1994, Bob Smith of Qualitas, Inc. came to visit us in the high desert north of Phoenix, and he brought the Internet with him. Astonished that I was not yet "on the Net," he installed a suite of Internet apps on some loose megabytes of my hard disk, and gave me a grand tour. I had read plenty about the Internet, of course, and "real soon now" I was going to get an account of my own. So I sat back and watched with interest.

E-Mail and NetNews were nice, but seemed only a variant on CompuServe, which I had used for many years. Telnet was better—we logged into someone's machine somewhere and perused a database of audio CDs in realtime—but it had the same feel of logging into a mainframe, which I had done for a living long before there were desktop computers. Gopher—*now* we were getting somewhere. Cool! Then he loaded a utility called Cello and launched off into the World Wide Web....

Egad! Now that...yessiree, *that* could change the world.

Like ripples in a calm pond, the success of the Web and utilities like Cello and Mosaic and Netscape has been radiating farther and farther afield from the core of Internet fanatics that created it. First, the mainstream computer press discovered it, then the electronics magazines, and eventually the "Computer Sunday" supplement of major newspapers. Now even as I write, the cover story on *Time* Magazine is "Cyberporn," and the dark underside of the Net is riling people nationwide and stirring a fanatical reaction in Congress that will be fought for years to come.

Like I said, Egad.

So the world of online communications is changing, and the Web is definitely one hand—perhaps one of the most important hands—on the crank. The Internet is now a household term, and Internet books outnumber books on any other single category in the computer field. Web books, which were unknown a year ago, are now the single biggest category of Internet books.

The term "home page" is now commonplace—but where only recently a "home page" meant a Web site belonging to any person or organization, a home page is now something that individuals set up as part of their Internet accounts, to contain pictures of their cats and lists of their favorite rock bands. Companies and institutions are now abandoning the term "home page" for "Web site" as quickly as they can. The difference is now perceived as a matter of professonalism. The Big Secret has been broached—that writing enough HTML to create a home page is actually a snap—and now everybody is doing it, and doing it about as well as everybody does it when everybody does anything, which is to say, well, so-so...unless you're really into cats or rock bands.

The Web has done some world-changing, and will almost certainly do some more. But the home page people won't do it. There's a tremendous need for professionals in the Web community, where by "professional" I don't mean people who get paid for their work (getting paid is still a pretty exotic idea on the Internet) but people who take it as seriously as they take making a living doing whatever it is they do.

There is a tendency in our business to equate professionalism with a sort of technical wizardry, the focus of which is pulling miracle after miracle out of the protean hat of globally networked computing. Don't make that mistake. Wizardry is the first and most necessary ingredient of any kind of success in computing, and wizardry can be accomplished in a professional manner if done by professionals. But there is nothing inherently professional in working miracles of any stripe. *Professionalism is the art of pursuing one's line of work in such a manner as to serve the best interests of the surrounding community.*

This is a little more than just doing something to demonstrate that it's possible. It's the major difference, in fact, between just having fun and actually making a difference.

This book is in large measure a quest for professionalism in creating Web content and maintaining Web presence. There is plenty of wizardry in these pages, but in every case Robert attempts to advise not only on how things work and how to do them, but how to put them together in accordance with evolving Web standards, and with consideration for the people who actually use the Web.

This can be a tough business when the HTML 3.0 spec, holding in its hands as it does the future direction of the Web and all its wonders, changes radically from week to week. Robert explains his best vision of where things are going, but he remembers to advise that he's as likely to be wrong as not, and that using "upstream" features of the Web can leave the users of your Web site in a lurch if their browsers have headed in a different direction.

He is unafraid to declare that one feature or another is simply a bad idea—blinking text, for example—and that even though it's a legal construct, it does more harm than good. That's a difficult sort of advice to give, because people are going to argue with you over it, but such advice gives those of us framing members a grasp of what "professionalism" means in a Web context.

So study HTML, CGI, server-side includes, client pull, server push, and all the rest of the technical wizardry that makes the Web happen, but also be aware of the polish, sense, and consideration that makes the Web serve the higher cause of education and (increasingly) polite commerce. This book will provide a firm grounding in both. The professionalism...well, you'll have to add *that* on your own.

Do your best. Tens of millions of people may be watching. (Egad!) We'll try our best to help.

Jeff Duntemann
Scottsdale, Arizona

Acknowledgments

Special thanks to Vince Emery, Jeff Duntemann, Ron Pronk, and all the staff at Computer Literacy Bookshops: Jay Michlin, for his patience and understanding; Dan Dornberg and Rachel Unkefer, Computer Literacy Bookshops' founders, for giving me the opportunity to shine; Tracy Russ, Cherrie Chiu, and Claire Collins, for all their support and encouragement; and Penny Wendland and Sean Mick—"Soon. Soon." I'd also like to thank Steve Ruben of Exodus Communications for his help with my networking questions, and my best friend George Starcher, who I met over the Internet and promise to visit "real soon now!"

I should also thank plenty of Mountain Dew, coffee, and caffeine in general; occasional sleep; the Internet; and the World Wide Web.

How May We Serve You?

All of the many things to be found on the World Wide Web come from somewhere—and this book is about how you can become that "somewhere." I'll be covering content creation in detail, in the form of HTML, but HTML is only part of the picture. The content has to be created, but then it has to be served, and what this means is that you must become the server portion of a true client/server architecture.

Like a lot of mystical magical jargon that people in our industry use without necessarily understanding it, client/server is both more and less than it appears. It's less because it's not magic at all, nor even rocket science. Mostly, it's badly documented (otherwise, there'd be very little reason for this book), and was, until very recently, not something that an ordinary individual could hope to do on his or her own—that is, at least not without the resources of a university or major corporation behind them.

And a client/server is more than it appears because it has the potential to completely recast the role of information in a global society. A client/server system is *way* more than COBOL programs pulling data out of mainframes with a pair of tweezers, which is how a lot of otherwise knowledgeable individuals see it.

Client/Server 101

In fact, it's just this simple: A client/server system consists of two programs that communicate across a network of some sort. The client program asks for information, and the server program provides it. The conversation between the two programs follows a predesigned plan called a *protocol*, which is nothing more than a template for legal questions and answers, and a sequence to be followed in asking and responding to them.

For our needs in connection with this book, the network is the Internet, and the protocol is called *HTTP*, for Hypertext Transport Protocol. (More on HTTP later.) The client program is called a *Web browser*, and the most popular are the original Mosaic, and the current market leader, Netscape. A Web browser called Lynx is also used for text-only applications, but those are certainly not where the action is today.

The server program is by no means as glamorous as a Web browser. Most people never see it—but there isn't much to see. Several leading server programs exist, and I'll discuss them in detail in Chapter 4. Server programs are often free for the downloading, but the more advanced server programs, especially those designed for electronic commerce, can cost many thousands of dollars.

What the server program does is, in a sense, act as a database manager. The data are the HTML files that Web content creators create. They're stored on the machine that runs the Web server program, and the Web server program knows how to find them by name. So when a client program (a Web browser) requests a particular HTML file, wham! The server program loads it from its disk and begins stuffing HTML out through the Internet pipe to the client browser.

The devil is in the details, of course. But from a height, there's really nothing more to Web servers than that.

At this point, your impulse might be to take pen in hand and begin jotting down your shopping list. You'll need a Web server program, and a machine to run it on, and a fast connection to the Internet, and....

Stop!

You may not need all of that. In fact, you may not need *any* of that. I'm reminded of the old *National Lampoon* cartoon showing a hot dog sifting the mail beside his mailbox, and turning up a junk-mail postcard reading "*You may already be a weiner!*"

You may already have everything you need to serve up content on the Web. You may, in fact, be doing it already. There's more than one way to deliver

Web content, and you can approach it at many different levels. Certainly, before you go out and buy anything, you should have a solid idea of what those different levels and approaches are, and which ones make sense for what it is you're trying to do.

For the rest of this chapter, I'm going to lay out all of the major scenarios for serving content on the Web. I'll start with the simplest and least expensive, and end with all stops pulled out. Somewhere in the middle is an approach that will enable you to do what you want to do on the Web, and knowing what approach that is will help you *a lot* in getting your money's worth from the rest of this book.

Scenario 1: Your Personal Home Page

Most people don't think of it in quite those terms, but if you have a personal home page somewhere on a university or an Internet service provider (ISP) machine, then you are truthfully serving up content on the Web.

Offering a home page along with personal Internet accounts was almost unheard of even a year ago, but now it's commonplace, often at no extra charge. The fact that most people don't use their personal home page ability (or fill it with banalities like pictures of their cats) doesn't make such home pages any less valuable for simple Web serving. There's no law stating that your home page has to be exclusively about you. In fact, you'll recieve many oohs and ahhs if you can provide your site visitors with any sort of useful and interesting information.

You may already have everything you need to create Web content for your personal home page. HTML documents can be edited in simple ASCII text editors like Windows Notepad, and viewed from local disk through the same Web browser (Netscape or Mosaic, typically) that you used to surf the Internet.

Some minor knowledge of the Unix shell (the equivalent of the DOS command line) may be necessary to get an HTML document from your desktop machine to its proper place on your school's or provider's machine, but that and a working familiarity with HTML (which I will provide in this book) are literally all you need.

Personal home pages are appropriate for serving relatively simple HTML documents with only a few images. Most service providers place a limit on the amount of space that personal home page content can occupy. More significantly, content placed in a personal home page generally cannot return information to you. That is, you cannot place fill-out forms or buttons in your Web content. What you serve up is for Web browsers to read, and that's that.

However, for publishing such extensive reading materials as FAQ (Frequently Asked Question) files, newsletters for wide distribution, or (as is frequently done) directories of links to other interesting places on the Web, a personal home page may work very well—and it's a perfect place to get your feet wet and see whether this field is really for you.

Scenario 2: A Web Site Hosted by Your Internet Service Provider

The defining characteristic of a personal home page is that it's one-way (that is, no forms or buttons in the content) and set up in a standardized fashion. Many providers will (sometimes at additional charge) give you a spot on their "big" system for a full-fledged Web site supporting advanced HTML features like fill-out forms and buttons.

What you get with this approach is essentially a subdirectory on the provider's system, plus the use of whatever Unix utilities pertain to Web work, along with permissions to set up and use Common Gateway Interface (CGI) scripts. CGI scripts are the only way to obtain data from the person reading your Web content. To use them, you'll need some familiarity with a programming language. (I'll describe their nature briefly toward the end of this chapter.) The server program is the same one that the provider uses to serve *all* Web activity originating at that location.

This is, in many respects, the best way to start out if you have ambitions to run your own Web server. The really big plus is that you don't have to buy, install, or configure any Web server hardware or software, or high-speed connections to the Internet. The provider has already done that. An associated plus is that your provider may be able to provide technical support in getting your Web site up and running.

This will almost certainly cost you money beyond what it costs for a simple Internet account. It will also require that you become familiar with the provider's Web software, which is typically operated under the Unix operating system. Learning Unix can be infuriating (especially in this era of GUI dominance) and takes significant time. Of course, if you already know Unix, you're time and effort ahead. You will also need to have a good grasp of HTML and CGI, both of which I'll cover in detail in this book.

The primary disadvantage here is the lack of control. You typically can't choose which Web server software to use, and you can't necessarily set your site up the way you like. If your Web site becomes very popular, it may overload your provider's capacity to provide connections. Many Internet service providers, remember, are nothing more than three people, a husky Unix workstation with a big disk, and a cable to the Internet. Such systems have finite throughput, and if your Web site starts to strain your provider's resources, you may well be shown the door. So much for your success!

If you intend to operate a business through your Internet site, there may be legal consequences as well, especially if you'll be accepting credit-card orders. Many providers will not allow you to solicit or accept credit card numbers through their system, justifiably fearing liability if card theft is claimed.

Setting up and running a Web site on someone else's machine for awhile, however, is an excellent exercise in prototyping, and if your intent is eventually to have a really flashy Web site on your own hardware, it will let you get an early start in developing your content.

Scenario 3: Leasing Space for Your Machine at a Provider's Location

This scenario is fairly uncommon, but it has been done and can be very effective. What I mean here is that you negotiate a lease agreement to place your own computer in the same office where your Internet service provider has their equipment. This approach allows you to share your provider's high-speed connection to the Internet without having to physically share their computers.

The reason to do this is simple: The *really* tough part of setting up a world-class Web site on your own is obtaining a high-speed connection into the

Internet. Such connections are expensive. (A fast connection, called a T1 line, which runs at 1.5 million bps, may cost $18,000 or more per year!) More important, they are not available at all locations. Such fast connections are available most commonly in large, fairly recent industrial parks, or in the central business districts of medium-to-large cities. If your office is off the beaten path, or if you wish to operate your site from your home, it may be physically impossible to obtain a fast connection at any price, because the infrastructure (that is, the special cabling) does not exist in your area.

If you place a computer at your provider's site, you can simply run a cable across the room or over an office wall and plug into their high-speed connection hardware, which is something like a big (and expensive) modem. Apart from that, you're not dependent on the provider in any way.

But does this mean you have to traipse down to the provider's physical location every time you need to maintain your computer there? Not at all. You can dial in to your machine using a simple phone line and auto-answer modem (and not even an especially fast modem, either!), and control the system remotely. Unix implementations are very good at this, and Unix software—Linux is an excellent recent implementation for Intel-based PCs—can be very inexpensive.

In this scenario, you must buy a server-class computer (and I wouldn't recommend anything short of a 66 MHz 486 with at least 16 MB of RAM) and obtain all software yourself, either "freeware" from the Internet or purchased commercial software.

The upside to this arrangement is that you can get to the high-speed connection easily; in fact, such a connection may not be possible any other way. Apart from the way the connection mates with your computer, you have complete control over the hardware, software, and configuration of your server machine and programs.

The downside is that many providers won't consider doing this; you would be, after all, competing with them to a degree. The cost can still be considerable, since high-speed lines aren't cheap by any measure. The only reason a provider would be willing to set up such an arrangement would be to reduce their cost for the high-speed connection, so you can be sure they will bargain with you aggressively. Unless the top people in the provider organization are your personal friends, you're unlikely to get much technical assistance from them, either.

Finally, as bizarre as it sounds, your computer is at the mercy of the provider who owns or rents the physical space. If the provider was to go out of business and lose possession of their assets to creditors, could you prove that your machine located at their site belonged to you and not to them? (This has happened!) As I said earlier, this is an approach you should consider only if you *must* have a fast physical connection to the Internet and can't obtain it elsewhere.

Scenario 4: Your Own Server Computer with a Low-Speed Dedicated Connection

If you're providing content on the Web, you need to provide it 24 hours a day. You can't just shut down at arbitrary times of the day; the Internet is a global entity, and it's always nine in the morning *somewhere*. A fast connection is ideal, but a slower connection may do (perhaps just barely) if it's dedicated to the Internet and connected all the time.

You can obtain an always-connected phone line by special arrangement with your local phone company. With that available at your home or office, you just park your server computer in a quiet corner and let it use the phone line 24 hours a day. Everything is under your control, but everything is also your responsibility: The machine, the software, the connection, maintenance, physical security, and so on. That's a lot of work, and a fair amount of expense, for a line that can at most run at 28.8 Kbps. Multiple connections are possible through even a connection as slow as this, but two people sharing a 28.8 Kbps line will see performance typical of a 14.4 Kbps modem—with predictable slowing as more people attempt to connect. This is not something you want to do if you expect a great many people to connect to your Web server (which is what you hope for, after all).

On the other hand, this might be an option if you're a company's IS person supporting a handful of service or sales people around the country, and need to distribute centrally-maintained information of a textual nature. If no more than two or three of them are likely to dial in at once, throughput across a 28.8 Kbps line may be sufficient. And such a system allows connection to your central office over the Internet, through local service providers around the country. Each service rep would have, say, a $22/month account and never have to dial long distance to access the central server.

There is a middle ground that might be available in your area. It's called ISDN (Integrated Services Digital Network), and it's a medium-speed connection that falls between standard phone lines and T1. ISDN operates at 128 Kbps, and will support a reasonable number of connections (five or six simultaneously) to a Web server. ISDN service is remarkably inexpensive—where it exists at all. Some operating companies like Pacific Bell offer the service for under $50 per month. However, ISDN requires special connection hardware that still costs over $1,000 in many places.

But the big gotcha is that outside major metropolitan areas, ISDN often isn't even on the drawing boards. Contact your local phone company to see what the situation is in your area.

A slow, dedicated line to a Web server will work, and it gives you complete control, but it gives you no room to *grow.* If people can't log into your site, word will get around, and you won't really accomplish much. Publishers wouldn't truly be publishers if they only distributed ten or fifteen copies of their books. To be taken seriously as a Web content provider to the general Internet public, you had better be able to service *at least* twenty or thirty people connecting at once. And for that, a fast, dedicated connection like T1 is almost essential.

Scenario 5: Your Own Server Computer with a Dedicated High-Speed Connection

This scenario was until recently beyond the individual Web author. The cost of high-speed connections is coming down, but the price of a T1 connection is still frighteningly high ($1,200 per month in the Phoenix metropolitan area, for example). However, if you can implement a viable Internet-based business through your server, the price may be considered a perfectly reasonable cost of doing business.

T1 connections can be had through your local phone company, or through national connection firms like Sprint and PSI. Recently, Internet providers have begun allowing "pass-through" service, whereby your T1 connection goes to the provider, and the provider "passes you through" to the Internet. It's a little like Scenario 3, except that your server computer is at *your* site, and connected to the provider's Internet gateway via a fast dedicated connection. The cost may come down some if you can locate your office in a building already wired for T1; then all your building's owner has to do is bring a cable through the ceiling plenum to your office.

This is definitely the "high road," and requires a muscular machine (100 MHz Pentium, 32 MB RAM, and 1 GB hard drive), good software, and a highly knowledgeable individual to configure and maintain it—working mostly full-time. Unix is the traditional operating system for installations like this, although Windows NT is perfectly capable and is coming into this use more and more frequently. Unix still has a richer tool set for Internet work, however.

With such high up-front and continual maintenance costs, and a full-time person to maintain the system (assuming this won't necessarily be you), this scenario requires careful research and some experience in the technology going in, or you *will* waste money on a heroic scale. Numerous on-line businesses are already on the Web and making money, but it isn't something done overnight and without committed capital.

Scenario 6: Your Own Minicomputer and Multiple High-Speed Connections

If you pull out all the stops, the scenario becomes one in which you basically duplicate the typical provider setup: A Unix-based RISC workstation or minicomputer and multiple high-speed connections, along with support hardware and staff to keep it all running. Certainly, becoming a provider yourself and reselling slices of the connection is one way to finance such a high-end Web publishing engine, but the provider business is fiercely competitive today and is not necessarily the best way to use a setup like this.

Rather, you might wish to become a Web site agency (providing full-service Web page creation and server capabilities) for large firms who don't wish to acquire the equipment or staff to do it themselves. This would require some art/design talent on staff and some fairly sophisticated efforts to obtain and keep clients. I suspect it would require a capital investment of $75,000 or more to open the doors and keep them open for a few months.

This would be an interesting side-business for an established and successful advertising agency or marketing firm with the capital to commit. In the fairly near future, this is how a lot of marketing and advertising is going to be done, and the experience and expertise to be gained in such a venture could pay off handsomely in the long run.

Setup Considerations

With all of those scenarios fresh in your mind, there are some questions you should begin to ask yourself about the nature of your Web publishing mission:

• *How much material do you intend to publish? And how many documents and images, comprising how many megabytes, will your material require?* HTML files are very compact (they are, after all, simply ASCII text files), but bitmapped graphics images can be bulky, and if you have a lot of them, the space adds up fast. Because many providers have limits on the amount of room your Web material can occupy on their servers (especially for personal home pages), this is an important question to nail down early in the game.

• *Will you be needing to request information from people who will be reading your Web pages?* If your customers are going to be performing online searches, or filling out questionnaires, order forms, and items like that, you will be heading into the realm of CGI, which requires knowledge of CGI scripting and the ability to run CGI scripts. Not all providers give you access to CGI.

• *How broad will the interest in your published material be?* Are you going to publish the definitive Web page on restoring Nash Metropolitans of the late Fifties? Or are you going to create a fan site for the Grateful Dead? The question is pertinent because you should be able to provide enough connections to your server to satisfy demand, and if fifty or a hundred people consistently want to access your server at the same time and most can't get in, people will become unhappy with you. Perhaps it's best to start small, which in this context means start *narrow*.

- *Will you be handling electronic funds transfers over the Internet?* If so, this opens up a host of other difficult questions, mostly regarding security and privacy. New Web server software is being developed that will handle many of these concerns and handle them well—but at a cost that could run into the low five figures. When you begin asking people for money, a whole raft of government regulations and other considerations come to the forefront, and you had better be aware of them long before you put anything online.

I don't expect you to know all the details before you read the rest of this book. I simply want you to realize that these questions will to some extent govern the shape of what you do to publish on the Web. If you think about them now, you'll almost certainly avoid some mistakes along the way that would have cost you time, money, and an unhealthy share of frustration.

Static Versus Dynamic HTML Documents

As I described a few pages back, simply handing out HTML documents from a Web server is easy: The server locates the requested document file by name and sends it to "standard output"—which on a server is connected to the Internet interface. It's no different conceptually from reading a text file from disk and sending it to the printer.

Such HTML documents are considered "static" because they're written entirely ahead of time and never change. Because they never change, they do not allow any interaction with the Web user at the other end of the client/server connection across the Internet. Nor do they allow the transmission of updated information automatically, without having someone re-edit the HTML document for the update.

Setting up *dynamic* HTML documents opens a new universe of possibility. A dynamic HTML document is generated *at the moment the Web browser requests it*, which provides the browser with up-to-the-minute information.

The process is not difficult at all. When a dynamic HTML document is requested, a program called a *script* is executed at the behest of the Web server. The script generates an HTML document (which, remember, is simply ASCII text) "on the fly" and feeds it to the Internet connection.

A simple example would be an automated weather report Web page. Electronic sensors feed continually changing information on wind speed and direction, temperature, and barometric pressure to the server machine. When a Web browser requests the weather report page, the server launches the weather report script program. The script program takes a snapshot of the weather readings at that very second, and merges the numbers with "boilerplate" HTML text before sending the finished HTML document down the line to the requesting Web browser. Such a script need not be elaborate or tricky; it could be done, in fact, in less than a hundred lines of C code, or much less in a "script-friendly" language like Perl.

Interaction with CGI Scripts

A dynamic script like our instantaneous weather report generator is certainly a step forward, but it doesn't really interact with the user—and it certainly tells the owner of the server nothing useful about the user or anything else. Going the rest of the way to interaction requires dynamic HTML and a more sophisticated script—and something called CGI.

CGI stands for Common Gateway Interface, and the scripts that follow CGI specifications are called *CGI scripts*. Don't make the mistake of assuming that CGI is a programming language of some sort, like C or Pascal or Perl. It's not—rather, it's a *protocol*; that is, a set of conventions through which some sort of conversation happens. The script itself may be written in almost any programming language you choose. In this book, that will generally be Perl, because Perl is the de-facto standard CGI scripting language. But CGI scripts can be written in C, C++, Basic, REXX, Pascal, or almost anything else that can read and write from an operating system's standard input and standard output devices.

CGI, if you will, is a collection of rules that govern the way the Web client program interacts with the Web server program and your scripts. It defines what the data stream looks like, tells how to identify fields within fill-in forms, and other things of that nature.

A CGI system works something like this: An HTML document is written to contain controls like data entry fields, check boxes, or push buttons. A Web browser requests this document, and a copy is sent down the line by the server to the browser. The user interacts with the HTML document by entering data in fields, pushing buttons, or clicking check boxes. Input to the HTML document is sent to the server, which passes it on to the CGI script, according to the CGI rules.

The CGI script accepts data that came from the Web browser, and can react to that input by creating a dynamic HTML document and returning it to the browser. This dynamic HTML document can be customized to incorporate some of the entered data or some calculated or looked-up response to the entered data.

An excellent example is the well-known Web Crawler Web index site. The Web Crawler is a very sophisticated database of Web content. It is searched by means of an HTML form and a CGI script. When the user requests the Web Crawler's query page, the form shown in Figure 1.1 appears on the browser screen.

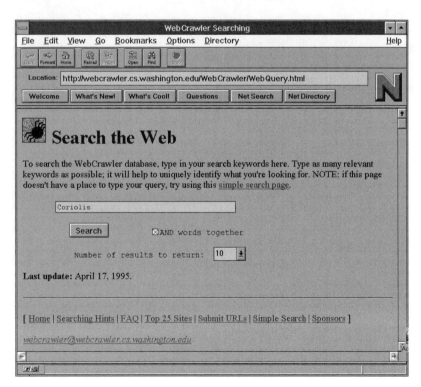

Figure 1.1   The Web Crawler query page

There are several controls on this page, any or all of which may be changed by the user. When the button marked "Search" is pushed, the current "state" (that is, the contents) of the other controls is transferred to the Web server according to the CGI rules. The Web server hands the data over to the CGI script implementing the actual search for the keyword, which in this case is "Coriolis."

The CGI script performs the search in the Web Crawler database, and then creates a dynamic HTML document containing the results of the search. This document is then transmitted back to the Web browser. The search results page is shown in Figure 1.2.

Similar form-and-feedback systems are now very common on the Web, at least since the majority of Web browsers became equipped to handle fill-in forms. You can create such systems too, and a good part of what this book is about is explaining how to do just that.

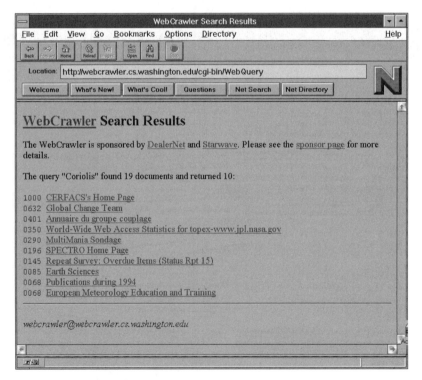

Figure 1.2   The Web Crawler results page

CGI Considerations

Currently, CGI is perhaps the least-understood aspect of the Internet—and the one people are curious about the most. With the emergence of the World Wide Web as the single platform of choice for accessing the Internet, CGI will play an extremely important role in the future evolution of the Internet and how we use it. Becoming familiar with CGI is a good idea, even if you do not intend to become a large-scale Web content provider.

Here are some points to keep in mind regarding CGI:

• *CGI is a data transfer specification, not a language.* It defines a protocol by which data is passed among the client, the server, and your script in an interactive Web transaction.

• *A CGI script is simply an executable program that understands the CGI specification.* It is called by the Web server when an HTML document associated with it returns data to the server.

• *CGI scripts can be written in virtually any programming language.* The sole requirement is that the language in question be capable of reading from the operating system's standard input device, and writing to its standard output device. Being able to read environment variables (if the operating system supports them) is also useful.

• *Most CGI scripts operate under Unix, and are written in Perl.* Unix has long been the host operating system of choice for Internet systems, and Perl, being the most popular Unix scripting language, works extremely well for CGI scripts running under Unix. Newer Web servers running under Windows NT might use scripts in Basic or C++. Web servers running under OS/2 often use scripts written in REXX.

• *Not all Web browsers support CGI fill-in forms.* Most early versions of Mosaic, Cello, and other graphics browsers do not support forms, nor do some of the makers of newer browsers who are still trying to iron the bugs out. The majority of current Web users with graphics browsers now have forms-capable browsers, however.

With all of that in mind, you're ready to begin a detailed look at the Web, its machinery, and how you can put it to work serving *you*.

The Web from the Client Side

The noise being made about the power of the Web has gotten so intense that people in many areas of commerce and government are investigating how to create Web servers without necessarily having ever seen the Web with their own eyes. For those of us who have been in the trenches all along this may seem odd, but it's the way many larger organizations work: A manager inside MIS reads an article about the Web in ComputerWorld, and thinks, *Well, we can do that!* Next thing you know, he's assigned one of his people to scope out the cost of a server installation without knowing anything special about the Web or even the Internet.

So on the outside chance that you may be one of those people, I thought it prudent to include a brief chapter on the Web from the client—that is, the browser—side. Alas, I have to assume something as a starting point, so I'll assume that you're at least cognizant of what the Internet is. And while this book is designed to teach anybody, regardless of their Web experience, the technical aspects behind designing a Web site, I hold that without at least a working knowledge of client-side tools and the culture of Web surfers themselves, you will waste precious time, and run the risk of creating a site that is nowhere near as effective as it could be. With this in mind, I strongly recommend you read this chapter carefully, and get yourself on the Web as a user *first*.

I made two other decisions as well, mostly for my sanity and any hope of a timely release for this book. First, I would be focusing on the two most popular and widely available *free* browsers, NCSA Mosaic and Netscape. Second, I would try to stay as platform *unspecific* as possible, at least on the client side. I'm a Unix guy at heart, and nobody but other Unix people want to even think about that operating system. As long as you're just browsing the Web, the platform under which the browser is operating doesn't matter much at all. Platform issues don't arise at all until we start setting up the server software and doing the much more advanced stuff, like CGI scripting. So, with all that said and done with, let's get up to speed with current Web browser technology.

Getting on the World Wide Web

There are a lot of different ways to get on the Web—too many, in fact, to actually list here. But thankfully, for browsing purposes at least, there are a couple of options which should be available to just about everyone and aren't too expensive.

I'll simply assume that you already have a computer available to you. Your home computer will do just fine. It's even better if you have access to a university or business computer system. Whatever your situation, if that computer has a direct Internet connection, you're all set. If you don't know whether or not you have an Internet connection and your computer is a university or business computer, ask your resident computer guru, usually the network or system administrator. If you're on your own, and you have a *SLIP* or *PPP* connection, this will also do just fine. If you don't know what SLIP and PPP are, don't worry about it for now. I'll explain all that later. If this is your own computer and you have this type of connection, you'll know it!

Another type of Internet access is called a *dial-up shell* account, virtually always on a Unix machine. If you have to call another computer using a modem, and enter obscure Unix commands to send email and read netnews, you probably have this type of account. If you can also use telnet and FTP, then it's official. You have Internet access, and the ability—within some limitations— to use the Web!

Uh oh! I Don't Have an Internet Connection!

Don't panic. Maybe you do! If you subscribe to an online service, such as CompuServe, GEnie, America Online (AOL), or Prodigy, you may have an option for Internet service and not even realize it. As the Internet gets more media coverage, and Al Gore continues to wax poetic about the "Information Superhighway," most of the major online services have started offering various Internet services, such as Internet email and Usenet newsgroups. And now that the Web has become such a media buzzword, Web access is just around the corner for many of these services! For example, CompuServe recently released its new "Internet Club," with fully graphical access to the Web. AOL has also announced Web service, as well as Prodigy.

No, I Really Don't Have Internet Access!

There are several quick and inexpensive ways to get Internet access if nothing we have discussed so far applies to you. The good thing about the methods described below is that they are fairly non-committal, so when it comes time to expand to a more robust Internet connection, you won't have a ton of time and money invested into your current access method.

CompuServe's new "Internet Club" now offers low-cost access to the Web, and a plethora of other Internet services. If you are using Microsoft Windows, a Macintosh, or OS/2, you may want to check them out. If you are out of the United States, CompuServe may be the way to go, for now at least, since they have many international access points. In the United States, give them a call at 1-800-848-8990, or you can fax them, from anywhere in the world, at +1-614-529-1611. While you are at it, ask them for their closest 14.4 K modem number. Browsing the Web at anything slower is the definition of frustration!

Netcom Online Communication Services, Inc. also offers a low-cost Web (and full Internet) access package, called Netcruiser, for Windows users. If you are in the United States and want to give them a try, call 1-408-983-5950 to see if they have a number local to you, and for more information on Netcruiser.

If you're *not* a Windows person, call Netcom anyway. But don't get a Netcruiser account, since you won't be able to use it except under Windows. Instead, specifically ask for a *Unix shell account*. Don't cringe yet! First of all, prices on such accounts are *extremely* reasonable. A Netcom Unix shell account, also known as a *dial-up shell account*, will at least give you text-based access to the Web. And as you'll find out a little later in this chapter, this may not be the ultimate Web browsing environment, but there is some software you can get which can start from there and take you the rest of the way.

I Have Internet Access. What Now?

It's time to pick a Web browser. But which one? If your current Internet access is through CompuServe, Netcom Netcruiser, or one of the other online services mentioned previously, then the choice has already been made for you. What you'll use is what they give you. But if not, there is still one more important question to answer: Do you have text-only or fully graphical Internet access?

Fully Graphical Internet Access

If your computer is running Microsoft Windows, Windows NT, MacOS, X Windows, OS/2, or another graphical user interface, *and* it has a direct Internet connection, you're in luck! All that's left now is choosing a graphical Web browser and exploring the Web.

Even though you might feel like you're on the other side of the client/ server equation, one of your most important tools as a webmaster is your Web browser. Your Web browser allows you to view your work, and in many ways the particular browser you choose will *affect* your work and the way you do it as well. Since every browser will display your pages in a slightly different manner, what looks good in one browser may not look as good in another, and your work will change to reflect those differences.

 In the interest of brevity, and for the purely practical reasons of serving the majority market, I've decided to focus on what most people consider the two best browsers available: Netscape Navigator and NCSA Mosaic.

Netscape Navigator

Netscape Communications' Netscape browser (nicknamed *Mozilla* by its creators, after the cartoon mascot appearing on many of their Web pages) is available for almost every computing platform in wide use. If you own a computer that can't run Netscape, you're using an odd platform indeed. See Figure 2.1 for Netscape's home page.

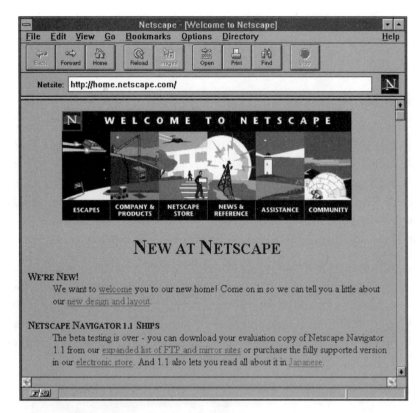

Figure 2.1   The Netscape Navigator's home page

Netscape has three major things going for it. First, it is free for personal use. Second, it is a good, solid browser that is constantly being upgraded and improved. These two points alone combine to make it one of the most popular and widely used browsers on the Web. According to Netscape Communications, Netscape accounts for over 75% of the browsers currently in use on the Web, and a little research on my part seems to confirm this claim. But there is one more reason it is so popular, perhaps the most important reason: Netscape has addressed businesses' need for secure, encrypted transactions, and has built security features directly into the browser. At the time of this writing (as best I'm aware) no other Web browser supports secure transactions. You'll learn more about Netscape's security technology, called the *Secure Socket Layer* (SSL), a bit later.

You can get your own copy of Netscape via anonymous FTP at *ftp.mcom.com.* Binary files are available for Microsoft Windows, Macintosh, and all major

Unix operating systems running X Windows. The latest version is 1.1N, but that is likely to change at least a half dozen times before you read this. Be sure to get the latest version!

NCSA Mosaic

The National Center for Supercomputer Applications (NCSA) released one of the first widely available graphical browsers for the Web. And for quite awhile, NCSA Mosaic was *the* Web browser to have. It runs on Microsoft Windows, Macintosh, and X Windows, just like Netscape, and it is also free of charge for private use. An added bonus with NCSA Mosaic is the availability of the browser's C source code under license, for people who want to develop derivative products. Figure 2.2 shows the NCSA Mosaic home page.

NCSA Mosaic had not had a new major release for a very long time, until very recently when they perhaps realized that Netscape had completely surpassed them in popularity and utility. The latest release is 2.0.0b3. One of the biggest differences between Netscape and NCSA Mosaic is Mosaic's lack of commerce-secure transactions. Most assuredly, this will change someday,

Figure 2.2　NCSA Mosaic's home page

and when it does Mosaic may begin to approach Netscape's popularity again. The binaries for NCSA Mosaic are available via anonymous FTP at *ftp.ncsa.uiuc.edu,* along with information on obtaining the source code.

The Many Faces of "Mosaic"

Since NCSA Mosaic was, for all intents and purpopses, the first graphical browser widely available, it is no wonder that the name "Mosaic" has become synonymous with the World Wide Web. But Mosaic is *not* the Web. It is the name of a Web browser, just like Netscape is the name of another, different, Web browser. It is something like calling facial tissues "Kleenex," regardless of the actual brand.

Adding considerably to the confusion is the fact that there are several completely different browsers in existence, all named "Mosaic." There is Spry's AIRMosaic, AMosaic, Quarterdeck Mosaic, and probably a half dozen others I don't even know about. These are all different browsers, with different features and written by different companies. (Many are loosely based on some version of the original NCSA Mosaic.) And in some cases, their relationships to one another seems almost like a soap opera, as certain companies acquire the rights to browsers, adding features and modifying them. For example, AIRMosaic, originally distributed by Spry for O'Reilly and Associates in their "Internet in a Box" product, has been acquired by Compuserve and is now the browser used with CompuServe's new Internet access program.

Kiosks and Presentations

As an interesting sidenote, NCSA Mosaic has a very nice feature, called *presentation mode,* which Netscape lacks. When in presentation mode, all the buttons, switches, and pull down menus that are ordinarily on display are removed. (See Figure 2.3 for an example.) The browser window is enlarged to its maximum possible size, filling the entire screen, which is wonderful for public kiosks and presentations, where a very large display area is important. The user can use the mouse to follow hotlinks that are displayed on the screen, but there are no menus for entering arbitrary URLs. Thus, by being careful what hot links you place in your kiosk pages, you can retain complete control

> over where the user of a kiosk or presentation can wander. This prevents users at your unattended kiosks from pulling up "morally objectionable" subject matter, or your competitor's home page, or from exiting out of the browser and playing with your configuration files. Yes, take it from me, that sort of thing happens!
>
> Beware of including other people's pages in a such a presentation or kiosk, however—you never know when those pages might vanish or link to things that you don't want seen as part of your own material.

Of course, there *are* other browsers. Plenty of them. And you may find one more to your liking than NCSA Mosaic or Netscape. If so, by all means, grab a copy! Like I said, choosing a browser is all a matter of personal taste. Just remember that I will be focusing on NCSA Mosaic and Netscape in this book. Table 2.1 lists all the browsers I am personally aware of, as well as any comments I may have about them.

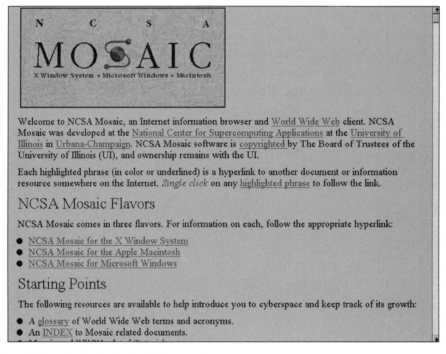

Figure 2.3   Mosaic in presentation mode

Table 2.1 Currently available Web browsers

Browser	Platform	Available from	Notes
Albert	VM/CMS	gopher.ufl.edu/pub/vm/www	Text
Amosaic	Amiga	max.physics.sunysb.edu/pub/amosaic	
Arena Testbed	X Windows	ftp.w3.org/pub/www/arena	HTML 3.0
BookLink	MS Windows	ftp.booklink.com/lite	Demo version only
Cello	MS Windows	ftp.law.cornell.edu/pub/LII/cello	
CERN WWW	NeXTStep	info.cern.ch/pub/www/src	Outdated
Chimera	X Windows	ftp.cs.unlv.edu/pub/chimera	
DosLynx	MS DOS	ftp2.cc.ukans.edu/pub/www/DosLynx	Full-screen text
Emacs-W3	Unix, VMS, MS DOS, Mac, Amiga, or any machine with EMACS	ftp.cs.indiana.edu/pub/elisp/w3	
For VMS	VMS	vms.huji.ac.il/www/www_client	Text
Lynx	Unix	ftp2.cc.ukans.edu	Full-screen text
MacWeb	Mac	ftp.einet.net/einet/mac/macweb	
Midas WWW	X Windows	ftp.slac.stanford.edu/pub/midaswww	
NCSA Mosaic	MS Windows, Mac, X Windows, VMS	ftp.ncsa.uiuc.edu	
Netscape	MS Windows, Mac, X Windows	ftp.mcom.com	
OmniWeb	NeXTStep	ftp.omnigroup.com/pub/software	
QuarterDeck Mosaic	MS Windows	Email for more info: lfeldman@qdeck.com	Commercial Beta pre-release
Samba	Mac	info.cern.ch/ftp/pub/www/bin	
SlipKnot	MS Windows	ftp.netcom.com/pub/pb/pbrooks/slipknot	Dial-up shell access
Spider Woman	NeXTStep	sente.epfl.ch/pub/software	
Spry Mosaic	MS Windows	ftp.spry.com/AirMosaicDemo	Demo version only
tkWWW	X Windows	harbor.ecn.purdue.edu	WYSIWYG editor
Tom Fine's perlWWW	Unix	archive.cis.ohio-state.edu/pub/w3browser	Text, requires Perl
Viola	X Windows	ora.com/pub/www/viola	
WebExplorer	Native OS/2	ftp01.ny.us.ibm.net/pub/WebExplorer	
WebWorks Mosaic	Mac, MS Windows, X Windows	Email for information to: info@quadralay.com	Commercial software
WinWeb	MS Windows	ftp.einet.net/einet/pc/winweb	
WWW Linemode	Unix	info.cern.ch/pub/www/src	Line-mode (text)

Text-Only Access

Even though you may have access to the entire Internet, you may not have *graphical* access, and instead are stuck with text-only access; for example, you might have a dial-up shell account on a Unix system, or a text-only terminal in the university lab or your office at work. If this is your situation, you have three, maybe four possibilities: a text-only, full-screen browser, a line-mode browser, or an email browser, in that order of desirability. In fact, you have several more options like SLIP emulation through a program called SlipKnot, but we'll come back to that.

Lynx: A Full-Screen Text-Only Browser

Lynx is a freely available, full-screen, text-only browser written by Lou Montulli. It is a fast, free, solid item which runs on just about any computer platform you can dream of, and is the best you can get without having a graphical browser. To see if you have it, type *lynx* on your command line and cross your fingers. If you can't find it, ask the nearest computer guru, probably your system administrator. If it isn't on your computer, but the computer does have Internet access, go fetch a copy. The latest version is available via anonymous FTP at *ftp2.cc.ukans.edu*. If you can't convince your system administrator to install it for you, do it yourself! The help files that come with it should be good enough to get you going.

Figure 2.4 shows the Lynx text-mode browser in action.

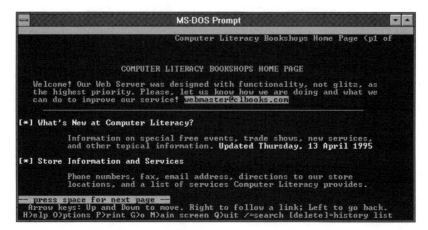

Figure 2.4   The Lynx browser in action

Table 2.2 Web browsers available through telnet

Telnet To:	Login Name	Location	Notes
www.cc.ukans.edu	www	Kansas	
www.njit.edu	www	New Jersey	
www.huji.ac.il	www	Israel	Both Hebrew and English language
sun.uakom.cs		Slovakia	
info.funet.fi	www	Finland	
fserv.kfki.hu	www	Hungary	

If you at least have access to telnet (which is a remote command line allowing you to log into and execute commands on other people's Unix machines), you can try out Lynx without actually getting a copy of the program and installing it. Telnet to one of the machines listed in Table 2.2 and you're on your way! But get your own browser as soon as possible. When you use the browsers at one of these machines, you are using someone else's resources.

A Line-Mode Browser

If Lynx doesn't work for you—if, for example, you're using a *really* dumb terminal without the capability to even control the cursor position on your screen—your next shot is a *line-mode browser* available free of charge at CERN. A line mode browser is an absolute bare-bones, no fancy graphics, non-full-screen, no-frills whatsoever browser. All I can say is, it works. Barely. A copy can be had via anonymous FTP at *info.cern.ch* in the directory */pub/www/src*. Figure 2.5 shows the generic line-mode browser at work. Instead of "pointing and clicking," you select a link by typing a reference number, which the browser assigns to each link.

Email Browsers

Yes, as bizarre as it sounds, you can browse the Web through email. Any Internet-connected email system, even a UUCP connection, will work. Send email to *server@mail.w3.org*, with nothing for the subject and the following as the first line of the message body:

```
send http://www.earn.net/gnrt/www.html
```

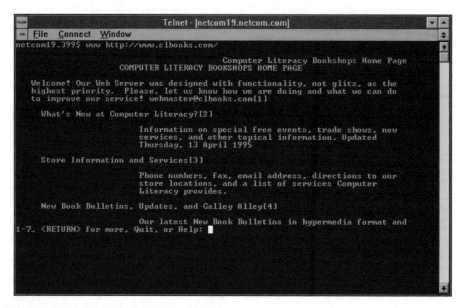

Figure 2.5   The generic line-mode browser

The server will send back further instructions on the mechanisms and methods of browsing the Web through email. This is definitely *not* the way to travel the Web, but it demonstrates the lengths that can be traveled to receive information from a service like the Web. Listing 2.1 is a text listing of my company's home page fetched and returned via email.

Listing 2.1   A Web home page as email

```
Return-Path: <server@www10.w3.org>
Date: Sat, 22 Apr 1995 08:19:43 +0500
Errors-To: agora-bugs@www10.w3.org
Reply-To: agora@www10.w3.org
From: agora@www10.w3.org
To: robert@somewhere.com
Subject: Computer Literacy Bookshops Home Page (URL: http://www.clbooks.com/)
content-length: 2535


To get help, just send a mail with the body WWW
Please mail to agora-bug@mail.w3.org if you have a problem


COMPUTER LITERACY BOOKSHOPS HOME PAGE

Welcome! Our Web Server was designed with functionality, not glitz,
as the highest priority. Please, let us know how we are doing and
```

what we can do to improve our service! webmaster@clbooks.com[1]

_____

[*] What's New at Computer Literacy?[2]

Information on special free events, trade
shows, new services, and other topical
information. Updated Thursday, 13 April 1995

[*] Store Information and Services[3]

Phone numbers, fax, email address, directions
to our store locations, and a list of
services Computer Literacy provides.

[*] New Book Bulletins, Updates, and Galley Alley[4]

Our latest New Book Bulletins in hypermedia
format and various related files, including
an interview with Donald Knuth, and a list of
some hot forthcoming titles in Galley Alley
(sm)!

[*] Browse our full database[5]

Search for books by title or author, look up
book reviews, and other neat features! Your
web browser must have forms support. If you
have problems accessing this service, try
reading our problem list[6].

_____

All material Copyright © 1994 Computer Literacy Bookshops,
Inc. All rights reserved. "Computer Literacy" and "Computer
Literacy Bookshops" are service marks of Computer Literacy
Bookshops Inc.

webmaster@clbooks.com[7]

*** References from this document ***
[orig] http://www.clbooks.com/
[1] mailto:webmaster@clbooks.com
[2] http://www.clbooks.com/news/newatclb.html
[3] http://www.clbooks.com/clbinfo/aboutclb.html
[4] http://www.clbooks.com/nbb/nbbindex.html
[5] http://www.clbooks.com/cgi-bin/browsedb
[6] http://www.clbooks.com/browse/browsebugs.html
[7] mailto:webmaster@clbooks.com

Of course, none of the text-only methods mentioned are going to get you anywhere *really* exciting. Or is there yet *another* option?

TIA and SlipKnot

Actually, there are *two* other options, but only if you have dial-up shell access. The first option is a software package called *The Internet Adaptor* (TIA), and the second is called *SlipKnot*. Both options may be able to give you access to a fully graphical Web browser like Mosaic, instead of one of the text-only mechanisms just described.

TIA is a nifty little program which works through a dial-up shell account but emulates what is called a SLIP (Serial Line Internet Protocol) connection, allowing you to hook up almost any computer to the Internet. Because Web browsers like Mosaic and the Netscape Explorer require one of the more advanced Internet connection mechanisms like SLIP, TIA will allow you to use any of the fully graphical Web browsers on your regular dial-up shell account. It's also reasonably fast, *very* inexpensive, and if SLIP is unavailable in your area, it may be your best option. For information on obtaining, trying out, and installing TIA, send an email to *tia-info@marketplace.com.* One caution: Using TIA requires the cooperation and permission of the agency providing your shell account (TIA is basically a Unix program that translates a shell account data stream into a SLIP data stream), so if your provider wants nothing to do with TIA, TIA is not an option.

SlipKnot is another innovative program that allows you to run a graphical Web browser on a dial-up shell account, but it is quite different in operation from TIA. Instead of emulating a SLIP connection and allowing you to run any graphical Web browser, SlipKnot uses the copy of Lynx on your shell account to access the Web, but displays the output, including graphic images, in a "nicer" way. In other words, SlipKnot is a "graphical front end" to the full-screen text browser Lynx. It's a little slow, and not very advanced as far as Web browsers go, but it is simple to install. You can get more information on SlipKnot by sending a blank email message to *slipknot@micromind.com,* or you can pick up your own copy via anonymous FTP at *oak.oakland.edu* in the directory *SimTel/win3/internet.*

Life Behind the Firewall

Regardless of the fact that your Internet access may be text-only or fully graphical, if your Internet access is provided by your company or a university, the odds are you will have to deal with a *firewall.* A firewall is a computer connected to an unsecured network, such as the Internet, and acting as a sort of guard dog. The theory is, all information traveling to and from the unsecured network must pass through the firewall, where its authenticity can be verified, just like the guard dog in a warehouse. But where firewalls can help keep unwanted intruders from getting into your company or university network, they can also greatly hinder people on the "safe side" of the firewall from getting out. Simply put, this means that even though your computer is connected to the Internet, your Web browser may not be able to connect to machines outside your organization's internal network!

Special software, called a *proxy server,* can be run on your organization's firewall to allow Web browsers to reach the outside Internet unhindered. Most newer Web browsers are capable of using proxy servers to reach the outside world, but you will have to tell the browser what machine is running the proxy. Both NCSA Mosaic and the Netscape Explorer can handle proxies. To give your browser the proxy information, look for the menu item *Options\Preferences\Proxy* in either browser.

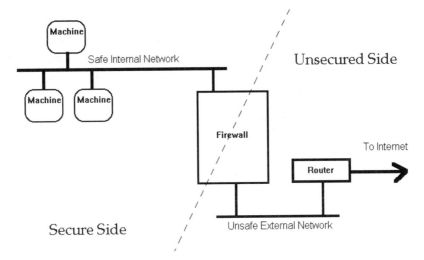

Figure 2.6   One type of Internet firewall setup

Talk to your system administrator for more information on your system's proxy server. If you *are* the system administrator, more information on firewalls and proxy servers is given later in this book in the chapter called *Choosing Your Server.*

Surf and Take Notes!

If you've been surfing the Web for years and have a good feel for how things work out there, you probably don't need to do any further investigation. But this chapter is for those who have to come up to speed quickly in order to begin work on building a Web presence. So once you get connected to the Web in some fashion, you need to undertake an organized exploration of current Web practice, from the client side.

The goal is to see what works and what doesn't, and also to see what the "unwritten laws" are. Rules were made to be broken, perhaps—but I would hope that before you'll break them you'll at least understand what they are. In this section I want to make some suggestions as to what to look for in your research expedition—and why such knowledge will be pertinent when you construct your own Web presence. Mostly, it comes down to this: *You want to see the Web as your "customers" will see it.* So the following are some research pointers to keep in mind as you go:

1. If you have a high-speed Internet connection like frame relay or T1, make sure you spend some time surfing the Web using a dial-up modem at 28.8 K or (better still) 14.4 K. Very few Web denizens operate at lofty speeds, and this will dictate how a lot of things are done, or which things may not be done at all.

2. Related to #1 is this: With a keen eye, *watch how long things take.* This may be the single most important insight to be gained from using the Web. Relate the size and resolution of graphics to the time required to bring them down. Notice how Web traffic ebbs and flows by time of day, such that traffic during "peak hours" will be much slower than traffic at other times. Gauge your impatience when bringing down a large, complex page as opposed to a small, simple one. Download at least one or two significant pieces of software, and at least one significant MPEG video clip. *This stuff takes time!*

3. Create a Web-based research project, and execute it. By this I mean decide to gather information on the Central American banana crop, or something else nontrivial, and then go out and *do* it. Take notes on how things go, what search tools (WebCrawler or Lycos Search are typical) proved useful, what tools got in your way, which Web sites promised more than they delivered, and why. Ask yourself where you felt most impatient, and why. Note what sorts of things proved difficult or impossible to find. Look at the pertinence of Web page titles. Some are more useful than others. Try to understand why, and in what ways.

4. Pay attention to the ways things are said. Look for conventions in terms of the placement of "go back" buttons, disclaimers, and other things that are present in many or most pages of the sort you're likely to create.

5. If you come upon a page that irritates you somehow, carefully note why. Is the reason functional or cultural? There is an unmistakable "in your face" attitude in many Web pages, and the Internet as a whole is a rather bristly place in some difficult-to-define ways. Consider how your audience might react to such things.

6. Finally, use several different browsers to do the same thing. Mosaic and Netscape are now pretty similar in capabilities, but try using both and you may be amazed at the different "feel" one may have in contrast to the other. Use an older browser like Mosaic 1.0 or Cello for a day or two, and take note of what you don't see and can't do. Don't call yourself finished until you've gone out with Lynx and seen what typical Web pages look like in text-only mode. A surprising number of people still have nothing more elaborate than a Unix shell account, and don't have graphics at all. You can do nice things in text mode if you simply take the time and effort to see what text mode can accomplish.

Summing Up

There are many different ways of getting access to the Web, from specialized high-speed connections down to 14.4 K modems. Even services such as CompuServe, AOL, and Prodigy now offer access to the Web through various utilities. But whatever method you use, the important thing is that you spend some time exploring the Web before actually trying to create your own Web masterpiece. Without some familiarity with the tools used to *access* the Web, as well as with the Web's *culture*, it is unlikely that your efforts to contribute to this new community will succeed. You wouldn't attempt to build a restaurant before visiting the neighborhood. You wouldn't run a magazine article or a TV ad before studying the content of the magazine or TV show. Don't try to give yourself a Web presence without first scoping out the Web!

Hardware and Network Connections

Setting up a Web server is somewhat akin to buying a car, and before you even think about shopping around, you must first decide what it is you actually need. Sure, four wheel drive, an engine capable of going zero to sixty in 5.8 seconds, and a fine leather interior would be wonderful to have, but if all you need is a small "four banger" hatchback to go to the corner store and back, your dream vehicle may be overkill. You may even discover that you don't need a car at all, and the local mass transit system is just fine for your needs. Unfortunately, sometimes it goes the other way around and you may find yourself in desperate need of a very large, and expensive, trailer truck.

In order for your Web pages to be accessible to the entire Internet, you will need to place them on a machine with a *direct* connection to the Internet. Dialup modems will no longer really do. It is important that you understand everything that is involved with this process, so you can make an informed decision on which route you will need to take to get your pages online for the entire Web community to visit. This chapter will show you what is involved in connecting a machine to the Internet, and also give you some options so you can *avoid* actually having to do it yourself. Read everything carefully, and thoroughly, and with some luck you will avoid buying a Ferrari, when a Volkswagen Bug is all you really need.

How the Network Works

As you know, the Internet is a largish group of computers (now running into the millions by some estimates) that are all *networked* together. But how those machines are actually connected, the physical cabling and hardware involved, has been something of a mystery to the average Internet user. And for good reason—this stuff can be pretty complicated, and frankly, until now you really didn't *need* to know how it all worked, so the knowledge probably never filtered your way. Regardless, you should have at least a passing knowledge of networking technology.

Connecting to the Internet

The easiest way to picture the Internet is not as a fine spiderweb of wires, but rather as a multilayered mesh of increasing coarseness. The bottommost layer consists of the Internet *backbones*, several super-high-speed network lines, branching off in various directions and spanning the entire globe. The points where these backbones meet, branch off, and end are called *Network Access Points* (NAPs) and this is the ground level of the Internet. The next layer, a finer and more complex mesh, rests atop these backbones, tied to it at the NAPs. And at the junctions of this new layer rest the *Internet Service Providers* (ISPs). (See Figure 3.1.) Now the final layer can be placed on top of the bottom two, tied to those at the ISPs. It is in this layer where your organization sits, its computers tied to the ISPs which are in turn tied to the NAPs which are themselves connected together by the massive Internet backbones.

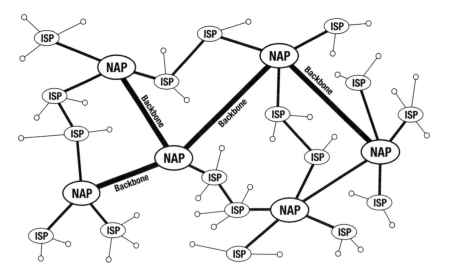

Figure 3.1   A conceptual model of the Internet

The part of the formula that you are concerned with is the connection from your private network to the ISP. Your private network can be as simple as the single workstation on your desk, to several thousand computers in a large organization. And just as your private network can vary so largely in size, so too can the *bandwidth,* or "size," of the connection to your ISP.

Low-Speed "Serial Line" Connections

The "smallest" of network connections is a regular phone line, connected to your ISP through a modem. The most common speeds this type of connection operates at is 14.4 Kbps (kilobits per second) and 28.8 Kbps, as dictated by the speed of the modems. Of course the connection can be be even slower, but with the current low cost of 14.4 K and 28.8 K modems, there's no excuse to go any slower than that!

The nature of the connection that occurs through the modems is defined by the *protocols* used by the computers to communicate over it. The three most important are *Serial Line Internet Protocol (SLIP), Compressed SLIP (CSLIP),* and *Point to Point Protocol (PPP),* and these are by far the cheapest and most widely available means to connect to your ISP. Only a modem, costing generally between $100 to $250, and a regular phone line is needed. The ISP will usually charge a small setup fee, anywhere between $20 and $100, and a monthly fee, between $20 and $50. You can also expect to pay your ISP an hourly rate for usage, probably around $2.00 with the first 10 or 20 hours "free." These are of course just ballpark figures, but if you run into anything dramatically higher, you should move on to another ISP.

The main problem with this type of connection is your ISP's hourly charge. If your computer isn't connected, your users can't reach your Web pages, but if you are connected 24 hours a day, things can get expensive very quickly. At $2.00 an hour, it will cost around $1440 a month, just in hourly charges! Try to find a provider offering flat rate SLIP, CSLIP, or PPP. If you can't, it may actually be cheaper in the long run to use one of the more advanced connections I'll describe later in this chapter.

By the way, if your ISP asks you if you want *dynamic IP* or not, say no. With normal or static IP (Internet protocol), your ISP will assign your computer a number, the *IP address,* which will belong just to that computer until you cancel your account. The IP address identifies your computer uniquely among all the millions of machines on the Internet. But an ISP may only have a certain, set number of IP addresses that it can distribute. Because the ISPs know that the vast majority of their subscribers will not be connected for 24 hours a day, and that for most part no one ever needs to know a subscriber's raw numeric IP address, the ISPs enable the sharing of IP addresses drawn from a pool of addresses set aside for sharing. So, with dynamic IP, every time your computer dials into your ISP's computer and requests that a connection be made, the ISP's computer will search for the next available IP address in the pool and tell your computer to use that number during the current session.

When you disconnect your computer for the night, that IP address is released back into the pool and made available to the next computer that connects. When using this system, there is no way to permanently identify yourself to the rest of the Internet. Your IP identity changes every time you reconnect, and that makes it impossible to register a domain name, and your users will never know what machine to connect to to reach your Web pages. With static IP, your IP address never changes, so this isn't a problem and your users always know how to reach your machine. If you intend to serve the Web, be sure your ISP does not set you up to use dynamic IP!

56 K Leased Lines

The next level of service is called a *leased line*. With regular phone service (*POTS*, or Plain Old Telephone Service in "telco" lingo) you are able to connect to any other phone by simply dialing a number. The phone company figures out the best way to route your call to its destination, *at that particular time*, and then makes the connection. In other words, every time you call, even if you call the same number over and over, a different physical connection is made. But with a leased line, the phone company makes the connection once, and that connection is there to stay. You are *leasing* that physical connection. Only you can use it, and it always ends up at the same place, in this case your ISP. The ISP has a separate leased line for each customer, and thus separate equipment for each customer as well. In reality, these lines do go through the phone company first, however, they can be thought of as going straight from the customer to the ISP. See Figure 3.2.

A standard leased line can push your data along at 56 Kbps, twice as fast as a 28.8 K modem. Certain speeds may or may not be available in your area,

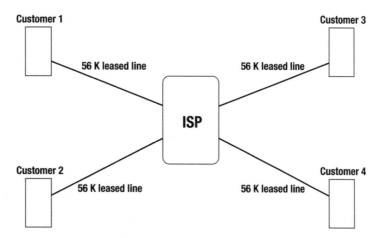

Figure 3.2   Dedicated leased lines

depending on what your local phone company offers, so check with your ISP or phone company before setting your heart on a particular speed. Pricing varies immensely, depending on geographic location, what phone company serves your area, and most significantly, *the physical length of the connection.*

To give you an idea, PacBell out here in California charges around $1000 for installation and $125 a month for a 56 K connection, anywhere within your "local area." Other phone companies may charge a similar flat rate anywhere in your state, or even charge by the mile. Your ISP will also have some installation and monthly charges for you, but they will vary so widely I'm not even going to attempt a guess at what you will end up paying. Shop around.

The equipment, on the other hand, is quite a bit more expensive and complex than a modem. Even worse, since the equipment is so expensive, unlike a modem, your ISP will probably require that you purchase the equipment for *them* as well. Well, *they'll* purchase it, but you will pay for it through the "installation fee." Anyway, what you'll need is a *CSU/DSU* (Channel Service Unit/Data Service Unit, $150 to $250), and a *router* ($1500 to $2500). If this is the only computer on your "network," you may also need to pick up an *Ethernet hub* ($500 or so), and an *Ethernet adapter* ($150 to $250) if your computer doesn't already have one. Thankfully, your ISP will only need you to pick up a CSU/DSU and a router for them.

In a nutshell, here is what all this equipment does: The first thing you'll plug into the wall is the CSU/DSU. This takes the signal coming from your ISP, and translates it into something the router can understand. The CSU/DSU plugs into the router, which takes the signal that the CSU/DSU hands it and translates it back into an *Internet protocol packet*. That "Internet protocol" part is the IP in TCP/IP, and it is the protocol that the entire Internet depends on. The router then takes this packet and passes it on to your network.

If you don't already have a network, then the Ethernet hub comes into play. The router hands the packet to the hub, which is connected to the computer through the Ethernet adapter. Finally, once the Ethernet adapter gets the packet, the whole process is finished. When sending a packet out to the Internet, it goes back along all this equipment until it hits that leased line of yours, where it is passed along to your ISP's CSU/DSU and then the router. The router then passes the packet along, from router to router, ISP to ISP, perhaps along one of the Internet backbones, and eventually, to its destination. Whew!

By the way, the hub is necessary for a type of *local area network* (LAN) called *Ethernet*. There are a couple of types of Ethernet, one of which is named after the type of cabling it uses, in this case *10baseT*, sometimes called *UTP* or *twisted pair*. A LAN, as you may have guessed, is a small network of two or more computers in very close physical proximity, usually all in the same office or building. In a 10baseT network, all the computers are connected to the hub, and the hub sends the packets to the proper computer. But another type of Ethernet uses what is called *coax*, or *10base2*. With coax (short for coaxial cable), all the computers on the LAN are connected to what is essentially a single long cable, and a hub is not necessary. If you'd like to save a couple of bucks on a hub, you may want to use coax instead of 10baseT.

Before you run out and buy all this expensive equipment, ask your ISP what they recommend, or if they have special deals with any of the manufacturers. Most ISPs are interested in providing you with a "total solution" and will sell you the CSU/DSU, router, and anything else you need if you ask. At the very least, they should be able to give you some suggestions on what you need to buy and who you can buy it from.

56 K Frame Relay

A less expensive alternative to a regular leased line is *frame relay*, which also provides 56 Kbps of bandwidth. Essentially, frame relay is "half" a regular leased line, and connects to what is called a *frame cloud*, at the telephone company's office. But instead of having another regular leased line connecting to your ISP, the phone company can connect you to a special line that you share with your ISP's other customers. Each customer's frame relay line enters the phone company's frame relay cloud, where the customer line is routed to the ISP through a single, high-speed connection. (See Figure 3.3.) The connection shown in the figure is T1, which is the bandwidth equivalent to twenty-four 56 K lines! In effect, the ISP only needs one line and one set of equipment for all its customers, since each customer shares the ISP's single T1 connection. This is the metaphorical equivalent of driving your car only as far as the train station and taking mass transit the rest of the way, rather than driving your car from home all the way to work. The savings are due to your ISP not having to buy a separate

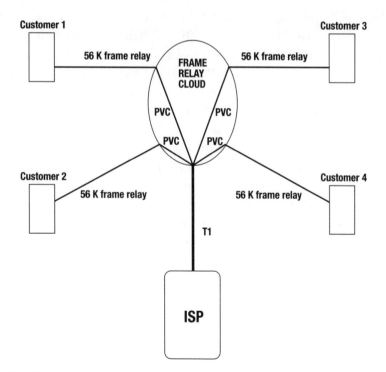

Figure 3.3   Frame relay sharing on a T1 line

CSU/DSU and router just for you. You still have to buy your own CSU/DSU and router, but you don't have to buy them for your ISP as well!

More important than the savings inherent in frame relay is the ease with which you can change ISPs if you discover that your current ISP just isn't cutting it. When the data from your computer enters the phone company's frame relay cloud, the phone company routes the data along what is called a *Permanent Virtual Circuit* (PVC) to its final destination, your ISP. If you change ISPs, all the phone company needs to do is flip a couple of switches and your PVC can be routed to another provider. This costs about $30 or so, instead of a whole new $1000 installation fee that you would be charged to move a regular leased line.

The bad news is frame relay service may not be available in all areas, and not all ISPs are willing to handle it either. Check with your ISP for availability in your area!

T1

A T1 line will give you about 1.5 Mbps (megabits per second) of bandwidth. That's an awful lot of bandwidth, and believe me it carries a price to match. Many small ISPs use T1s for *their* Internet connection, so if you have your eye on becoming an ISP yourself, this is the type of line you will be shopping for. Out here in California, PacBell charges around $1000 for the installation of the line, and $675 a month for maintaining the line. Your ISP, if they offer the service at all, will charge quite a bit more. But not all ISPs have the capability to hand you your very own T1. As a matter of fact, the phone company in your local area may not be able to handle getting this type of bandwith to your physical location either! You can use the same equipment with a T1 as with a 56 K leased or frame relay line, with the exception of the CSU/DSU, which will run you about $1000 due to the added complexity of the T1. You can lease a regular T1, or a frame relay T1, which behaves the same as a 56 K frame relay line.

A bit of a warning: I just mentioned that many small ISPs will have a single T1 as their own sole connection to the Internet. Even though they only have a single T1, they may be willing to sell you a T1 anyway...and T1s to a few other customers as well. So, even though you have a T1 to your ISP, you may end up sharing your ISP's own T1 link with several other T1 customers, as well as a few dozen 56 K customers! Now, normally this is fine, and you probably won't know the difference. It's pretty tough to use a full T1 worth of bandwidth, and the odds of all the ISP's customers combined hogging up a full T1 all at the same time isn't very high. But if the the ISP's sales people are a little overzealous, you will very well have problems. It's like airlines overbooking their flights; there are always a few noshows and everything is fine, but occasionally everyone *does* try to get on the plane at once, and then you may just get bumped.

If you really need a *full* T1 all to yourself, be sure to specify that clearly to your ISP and get any agreement you make in writing! Oh, and bring a fist full of dollars, because it is *not* going to be cheap at all. You'll end up paying for another router for the ISP, as well as another $1000 CSU/DSU and maybe even yet another T1 line from the ISP to *their* provider!

FRACTIONAL T1

Fractional T1 service is when the phone company installs a T1 line to your location; however, you have access to only a small fraction of it. These "fractions," called *channels*, are each capable of 64 Kbps bandwidth, and are generally sold in pairs. For example, you may be able to lease two channels, four channels, six channels, and so on up to 24, the maximum number of channels in a T1 line. Your local phone company may set additional limits on how many pairs you can lease, before you are forced to purchase a full T1. For example, PacBell in California allows you to buy two pairs and six pairs. After that, you must lease the full T1. Fractional T1 is usually sold as a frame relay.

Installation costs and availability, of course, vary—however, you are usually forced to pay for the full installation cost of a T1, whether you are leasing only two pairs or 12 pairs. On the brighter side, adding additional pairs later usually requires only a small fee, since the full T1 is technically already installed. Also, since you are only leasing a small fraction of the T1, monthly fees can be significantly lower. Fractional T1 uses the same equipment as a full T1, regardless of how many channels you lease.

ISDN—Integrated Services Digital Network

ISDN is an entirely different kind of connection from the other services I've been talking about so far. It still isn't widely used, but I feel it has some tremendous potential, especially for small users on a limited budget.

There are two types of ISDN: the *Basic Rate Interface* (BRI) and *Primary Rate Interface* (PRI). Offering two separate 64 Kbps *bearer* channels (2B in telco shorthand), BRI service gives you just as much bandwidth as a 128 Kbps fractional T1. If that isn't enough for you, PRI service offers 24 separate 64 Kpbs bearer channels (24B), for as much bandwidth as a regular T1 line! There is also a 16 Kpbs data channel (just called a "D channel"). Unfortunately, you won't be able to use that little bit of extra bandwidth directly. It is for "control information" of some sort.

What's exciting about this technology, is that the BRI service is being aimed directly at the "end user," that is, you and I, as a replacement for our regular telephone service! It uses the same physical lines, there is no special cabling that needs to be done, and if you hook a special ISDN phone to your line, you can call other ISDN users, as well as people who are still using a regular phone. Since you have two channels, each channel can have its own phone number, so you can place a voice phone call on one channel, while running a 64 Kbps network connection on the other channel. (Well, sort of...you really get about 56 Kbps, depending on where in the country you are. But in theory, 64 Kbps is possible.) You even dial out on an ISDN line just like a regular phone. This is the technology that will bring affordable video phones into "everyone's home" and, if the phone companies get their way, give everyone a relatively high-speed connection to the Internet.

But more important than all of that is the fact that by *inverse multiplexing* you can get a 128 Kbps network connection. Inverse multiplexing is a fancy way of saying that the two 64 Kbps channels are tied together to act as one 128 Kbps channel. Another, less fancy word for that is *bonding*. Either way, you get about 128 Kbps of bandwidth, and that's what really counts.

Installation and monthly phone company charges will vary wildly, but even though long distance ISDN calls can be a bit pricey, around 25 cents or more a minute, local calls should be fairly inexpensive, around a penny or two a minute. PacBell will install a BRI for dirt cheap, just a little more than a regular phone line with monthly charges around the same, but PacBell seems to be a leader in this area and other phone companies may be a bit more expensive. PacBell also offers unmetered service (that is, no per-minute charges) if your ISP is close enough (around two or three miles) by ordering a special service PacBell calls Centrix. If you're in PacBell country, give them a call for their latest pricing.

The single biggest drawback to ISDN BRI service is the expense of the equipment. Prices are slowly dropping, but for awhile ISDN may still be a bit out of reach for the average user. Instead of a CSU/DSU, you would need what is called a *network terminator,* or *NT-1.* One of these tiny boxes will cost you anywhere from $300 to $1000 dollars. Next you will need to pick up a special ISDN router, which behaves just like a normal router but connects to an NT-1 instead of a CSU/DSU. Expect to throw down anywhere between $1500 to $4000 for one of these. From there, things are just like the other types of lines. You may or may not need a hub, depending on the type of Ethernet you want to use, and you'll need an Ethernet adapter if you don't already have one.

The other drawback to ISDN is availability. Not all phone companies are willing or capable of offering ISDN service at this time, and even fewer ISPs. I expect this will change slowly over time, but if you happen to be in an area where it is available, and near an ISP that will do it, ISDN may be worth looking into.

T3

If you were wondering if there is a type of Internet connection faster than a T1, there is. It is called a T3, and contrary to what the name implies, it is the equivalent of twenty-eight T1 lines, not three. That is approximately 45 Mbps, a truly massive amount of bandwidth. This is the stuff that Internet backbones are made of! If you are seriously interested in a T3, and I can't think of any reason you could be, ask a local ISP where the nearest Internet NAP is, because that is probably the only place that can truly handle this kind of bandwidth.

Just thought you might like to know.

Getting Your Web Pages on the Internet

There are three main ways to get your Web pages on the Internet. You can buy your own equipment and hook it up to the Internet yourself, which as you might imagine is not a trivial task. You can also rent space on someone else's equipment. Finally, if you would sincerely like to avoid any technical hassles, you can hire another company to take care of everything for you. Of course, each method has its pros and cons. But before you can make any decision about what method you use, you'll need to spend a few moments reflecting on your goals.

So What Is Your Goal?

Whether you are the newly "recruited" webmaster for a large organization, or just a curious hobbyist fooling around with a new technology, you must have a set of goals that will shape the future of your Web pages. Do you want to put marketing and product information on your pages? Are you planning on selling products through your pages? Will the information on your server be free of charge for everyone, or do you plan on charging fees based on access? How large a role do you plan on your Web pages playing in your organization? What kind of budget do you have to work with? Ask yourself these questions, because if you're not sure where you're trying to go, there is no way you'll know which direction you should set off in. Whatever your goals, be sure you read over this chapter carefully. Don't skip a section simply because you don't think it will apply to you.

Renting Space and Services

With the rising popularity of the Web, a new breed of Internet service provider has been born. Specializing in providing space on their servers for your Web pages, these new ISPs offer a wide range of services, from the bare-bones Unix shell accounts and access to their Web server software, to full-fledged Web marketing and design.

The amount of equipment and expense involved in getting your Web pages on the Internet is definitely not trivial. It can cost tens of thousands of dollars for a decent setup, and take months waiting for equipment to arrive and the local telephone company to install the needed network connections. So it is no wonder that a large number of new Web pages appearing on the Internet are being housed in space rented from these new ISPs. This is probably the route you are going to want to take to get your own pages online, at least at first.

Renting space on someone else's server saves you all the hassle and expense of actually purchasing, setting up, and maintaining your own machine and network connection. And a pretty big savings this can be! It can come to anywhere from several hundred to several thousand dollars just for the initial setup. And the time you save could mean being up and running in just a few days, instead of weeks or even months.

Many ISPs offer additional services, above and beyond just handing you a few megabytes of storage on their server and access to their http software. Need images scanned, or a graphic artist to help design your pages? Want a bit of help writing the HTML (which your Web pages are based on), or want someone to simply do it for you? These are the types of services that set each ISP apart from the other. Depending on the company that you choose to carry your Web pages, you may be able to get everything from an inexpensive, no-frills service package, where you do almost everything yourself, to a full Web page design and construction service, where the ISP handles every aspect of your Web pages for you.

How to Find ISPs to Carry Your Pages

If ISPs were apples, you'd need a warehouse the size of Washington to store them all. The tough part is wading through them all and finding the one that best suits your needs, and I'll give you some tips a little later on how to do that. Even the physical location of the ISP doesn't matter, as long as you stay within the country where your customers are. But you need to know where to look to find them. One good place to start is by reading through the Usenet newsgroup comp.infosystems.www.providers. There, along with discussions of the proper way to write HTML, you'll find the occasional advertisement for an ISP. If you don't see anything that meets your needs, just post a quick summary of your needs and I guarantee your mailbox will fill with offers. After all, this is the newsgroup where the ISPs go to discuss things Web-related. Another sure-fire method is by reading the bylines or copyright notices at the bottom of your favorite Web page. Quite often, if the pages were created by one of these Web consulting ISPs, it will say so right at the bottom of the page.

I found the Web consulting index at Yahoo to be of incredible value. Take a look at *http://www.yahoo.com/Business/Corporations/Internet_Presence_Providers/ Consulting/* for some ideas on what is available. This seems to be the most complete list of Web ISPs available on the Internet.

Selecting an ISP

There are two keys to selecting the right ISP: knowing what it is you want, and asking the right questions. I've already discussed the first key here; you need to define your goals. The second key, asking the right questions, is a little trickier, particularly if you aren't sure what questions need to be asked. Below is a list of questions based on my own experience and conversations with others about their experiences with ISPs. As you ask each question of your potential ISP, take careful note of their answers. It could mean the difference between finding an ISP that suits your needs perfectly, or an ISP that may be out of business a week after you get your Web pages online.

I've split the questions into two categories. The first category attempts to feel out what they are as a company, and whether they'll be around for the long haul. The other category is a little more straightforward, and focuses on whether they can provide the types of services that will fit your needs.

Gauging the ISP as a Company

"How long have you been in business?"
The main problem is essentially this: Most of the ISPs that are available nowadays are so new you really have no way of knowing if they will be around next month, or even tomorrow! Certainly, you'll want to find a company that is well established and has a long track record of good work, but you may not have such a choice in your area. If the company has been around for a year or two, you can consider them old timers!

"What does your company do besides offer Web services?"
It has been my observation that half the ISPs are marketing firms, just breaking into the ISP business with practically no technical expertise, and the other half are a couple of guys with a workstation in their garage and tons of technical expertise, but absolutely no business experience. Which is better depends on what you feel is important in a company, good customer service or actually having accessible Web pages!

"How long have you been offering Web services?"
The scary thought is this: The people you will be renting space from, and entrusting the well being of your Web pages to, are probably only a couple

steps ahead of where you are now in Web experience! If the company offers other products or services not directly related to the Web, you may find
yourself in a position where you know more about the Web than your ISP!

"How large is your company?"
Is this just a couple guys in a garage, or a "real" company with tech support
personnel, and an accounting department to handle the business end of
things? Small companies can be a dream to work with, since everyone tends
to be very involved and concerned with the company's well being, but keep
an eye out for the "one man show." If his interest evaporates, so will your ISP.

"What percent of your company is dedicated to support your Web services?"
The size of the company is important, but how many out of those ten or a
hundred employees are actually dedicated to their *Web* services? A general
tipoff that you may not be dealing with a effective ISP is when the number
is actually *less* than the number of people *you* have dedicated to getting
your pages written and perfected. In other words, if XYZ Company has
sixty employees, and only one of them is dealing with the Web side of
things, you may want to look elsewhere.

**"How many computer professionals, such as network specialists, do you
employ?"**
Do they actually employ a network administrator or two to fix seriously
technical things when they break, or in case of an emergency, will there be
a scramble for "those pesky manuals"?

"Can you give me any references?"
Who have they done work for in the past? See if you can find out what sorts
of experiences their existing customers have had with them. Of course,
they'd be insane to give you references that they know have had a bad
experience, so you'll only get part of the story. But if they can't furnish *any*
references, you may be barking up the wrong side of the ISP tree. Far
more valuable references can generally be had by looking for their existing customers on your own. Local user groups are often a good place to
find this kind of contact.

"What are your company's plans for future growth?"
Of course everyone wants their company to grow. What you are really looking for here is to find out if they have any plans to upgrade their network
connections or add more hardware. Companies that go to a lot of effort

expanding their customer base without any plans to expand the quantity of bandwidth to the Net that they can sell to their customer base are bad news.

"What kind of network connection do you have?"
Keep clear of anyone with less than a T1 dedicated to their Web services. A 56 K frame relay connection might be wonderful for a single customer or two, but if you're trying to share a low bandwidth connection with a dozen other companies, nobody will be able to see your pages!

Do They Offer What You Need?

"Do you offer a secure server, such as the NetSite Commerce Server?"
If your intention is to accept credit card orders over the Net, a server that accepts secure transactions is a must! But, alas, that security does come at a price. The NetSite Commerce Server, from Netscape Communications, costs $5000, and you can bet that any ISP that offers access to it will be trying their hardest to make their investment back as soon as possible. After all, most of these ISPs are new companies probably still reeling from the cost of their initial hardware and network installations.

"How do I access your system to update my pages?"
Once you find an ISP to serve your pages, you're going to need some way to get them from your machine to your ISP's machine. Does the ISP only allow access via FTP, or are you given a Unix shell account as well? Some ISPs may also offer alternate methods, as well, such as custom interfaces or email.

"Do you offer Web page design and consulting services?"
Surely, there is no law that says you have to do *any* of the work yourself. Would you like your ISP to create your Web pages for you? Many now offer this service, with teams of HTML authors and graphic designers standing by to do all the work of designing your pages for you. Of course, there is a price, and it usually isn't cheap. Expect to pay around $100 per hour for this type of service.

"Do you allow the use of CGI scripts or image maps?"
CGI scripts and image maps are covered in Chapters 9 and 10. In a nutshell, a CGI script allows your pages to gather information from your users by the use of buttons, check boxes, and fill-in forms placed on your Web

pages. For example, if you would like your users to be able to fill out a form to join a mailing list, you would need to use a CGI script.

"Do you have a technical support line?"

Some ISPs may be so small that technical support is handled by their staff when they get a few free moments to breathe. If you think you'll need some technical support to get your pages up and running, a phone number with personnel dedicated to providing technical support may be the deciding factor in your choice of ISPs. It's frustrating to get an answering machine or voicemail when you need some serious help.

"Do you have a graphic artist on staff?"

If you don't have your own company logo, and your artistic talent is as good as mine, you may want to contract the job out to a graphic artist. Some ISPs have graphic artists on their staff, artists who know what's possible on the Web and how to make the best use of limited resolution and color choice. But check their rates beforehand; a graphic artist isn't cheap, usually running between $100 and $125 an hour. Also be sure you will own the rights to any work they do for you!

The Bill, Please

How much all of this will cost seems to vary based on the day of the week, the phase of the moon, and what the ISP had for breakfast that morning. If you're not careful, you *will* find yourself being ripped off in the worst way. Perhaps when the industry settles down a bit, pricing will settle down in response to market forces and won't vary as much. But as long as they can find someone who is willing to pay outrageous rates for their services, you can be sure they'll be charging outrageous rates. Here are some practical guidelines to minimize the chances of your getting ripped off.

Simple, no frills service will usually run you between $20 and $50 a month, with perhaps a $50 or $100 setup fee. This will probably buy you around 5 or 10 MB of space on the ISP's machine, for as many pages, graphics, sounds, or movies as you can jam in that much space. Be wary of anyone trying to sell you space based on a price per *page*, particularly if you wrote the pages yourself. There is absolutely no reason for you to be charged in this manner.

Some ISPs will also charge an additional fee based on *how many bytes served*, perhaps allowing a certain number of free megabytes before charging begins.

Be careful here! The theory is to keep you from flooding their network connection with requests for your pages. For example, if your Web pages contain what is delicately referred to as "adult materials," there is going to be a *lot* of traffic to your pages, far more than an average Web page would normally generate. But, unfortunately, a lot of providers try to use this as a justification for gouging you even further. A reasonable rate might call for the first 10 MB of data per month transfered free, with each additional 10 MB costing $25 or so. Keep away from anyone charging you *per kilobyte*, or you'll find yourself paying hundreds of dollars a month more than you have to. Essentially, average usage (I'll try to define "average" a little later) shouldn't cost you anything extra in "transfer fees."

Of course, if you need access to a secure server, expect all these figures to double—or worse. You will also have to worry about how your ISP gets the secure data obtained from your customers back to you. Simply emailing the data back, or allowing you to connect and FTP it back, defeats the whole point of a secure server! Some ISPs will send this data back in encrypted email, or by fax. Expect to pay a small setup fee, maybe $50, for this service, in addition to any other fees you are paying, and perhaps $25 or so a month, or 25 cents to $1.00 a page.

Web consulting services, for example having your ISP write and design all your pages for you, can be a bit more expensive. Cost is usually around $100 an hour minimum, and this should include designing any logos or graphics, although it is not unheard of to pay $125 an hour or more just for a graphic artist. Now, the $125 an hour for a graphic artist seems "reasonable" to me, but $100 an hour to write the HTML for your pages is completely outlandish. But alas, this is the norm. My advice is to go ahead, read the rest of this book and at least learn how to write your own HTML. When you discover how easy it really is, you'll understand why $100 an hour for HTML "authoring" is simply insane.

If you need any CGI scripts or image maps designed for you, however, $100 an hour is more than reasonable. Designing an effective image map or a functional CGI script takes a bit of art, a touch of skill, and a lot more knowledge than just dropping a few HTML tags into some marketing copy.

Owning Your Own Equipment

Buying your own equipment is the most flexible option available. You have control of almost everything, from what server software and operating system you will use, to the speed of the machine and network connection. Unfortunately, you also have all the responsibility of making sure the software is correctly installed, the hardware is in working order, the network connection is up and running, and your system is secure enough to keep hackers at bay. That means money for the actual computer, the networking equipment, the network connection, and perhaps even a consultant to help you paste everything together. Oh, and time. Lots and lots of time for setup, maintainence, and the occasional emergency. And that's not even including writing and maintaining your Web pages!

Now, understand that I'm not trying to discourage anyone from selecting this method. In a lot of cases it may actually be your best choice. Just keep in mind that owning all your own equipment *can* be a major headache, especially if you find out that you really didn't *need* to go this route.

Of course, if you already have all your own equipment, including the network connection, for example through your university or company computer system, you're practically there already, and your main concern is whether or not your equipment can handle the overhead of running a Web server.

The Computer

As I said in Chapter 1, you *can* run your server on a 486/66 with only 8 MB of RAM; however, if you are really serious about your work, a 60 MHz Pentium with at least 16 MB of RAM, or larger, is the minimum I would recommend. This is particularly true if you are planning on using the computer for other services in addition to serving the Web, such as being the main email host for your entire organization or a news server. In my case, the 60 MHz Pentium where I work, with 32 MB of RAM, barely sweats with the load from our Web server and processing all my company's email.

As for the operating system you use, I would of course recommend Unix, but there is Web server software for just about every reasonable operating system. Windows NT is a big operating system to use now, and I have heard of people having some pretty good luck with OS/2 Warp as well. Even Macs can get into the game, with some fine servers written for System 7.x, though I would hope you would use a Quadra class machine if you expect any serious usage out of your Web server. I would recommend, however, against running your Web server on Windows 3.x or, heaven forbid, DOS. As an experiment, I tried. I wasn't impressed. Windows 3.x is just not designed for that kind of stress.

A good, cheap (actually, free!) Unix alternative is Linux, which is a Unix-compatible operating system available for download on the Internet, or on CD-ROM from a number of sources. If you're not interested in downloading 30+ MB from the Internet, check out the Slackware version of Linux that is stored on the companion CD-ROM.

A quick note on Unix. If you've never used it before, you may find yourself in an uncomfortable position. Unix was never designed with the DOS or Mac crowd in mind. If you are not Unix literate, you may find yourself struggling to get your Unix machine running properly and end up having to hire a consultant to get it up, and keep it running. Alas, you may end up spending more time and money trying to keep Unix going than working on your Web server! Even worse, if it's not configured correctly, you may find yourself wide open to abuse from hackers and other Internet ruffians with nothing better to do than attempt to ruin all your work. If you don't know Unix, and aren't the adventurous type, stick with Windows NT or a Mac. Windows NT in particular was designed with security in mind, and has much better security features than Unix.

The Network Connection

Your network connection is the lifeblood of your Web server. If you have too little network bandwidth, you may as well have your Web server hooked up to carrier pigeons. But network bandwidth isn't cheap, and there is no reason to purchase a T1 connection when a 56 K line will do. But what is too little bandwidth, or more to the point, what is the least amount of bandwidth you can get away with purchasing?

Thankfully, there is a formula of sorts that will help you figure out how much bandwidth you really need, bare minimum. The key to the whole equation is this: It should never take a user more than 5 or 10 seconds to retrieve one of your pages, assuming the bandwidth on *their* end is unlimited. Table 3.1 provides some numbers that will help us in making the calculation.

Every time someone makes a connection to your Web server, there will be some small amount of overhead involved in getting the document to the user, typically around a second for modem lines, and a bit less than a quarter a second for *direct* connections like frame relay or T1. Now don't take any of the numbers in Table 3.1 as gospel; they are *very* rough estimates based on a best-case situation. Things like noisy phone lines, overloaded servers, and the Internet's tendency to fade out and go to sleep every so often will contribute to make these values a little lower. And on the other end of the spectrum, things like compression, caching, and the current phase of the moon (to which Unix people ascribe any mysterious blessing or misfortune) may help speed things along as well. But at least you can get a rough idea of how much bandwidth each of these connections can provide.

So let's work through an example. Suppose you have a small Web page, maybe a 2 K document with two different images. The first image is 12 K, and the last one is a small 1 K icon. To serve this document in ten seconds, you would need a little more than 2.1 Kbps of bandwidth (15 K divided by 7 seconds) or a 28.8 K modem. To get this figure, all I did was add up the sizes of the files, then subtracted 3 seconds from our original 10 second goal, and divided the total size by the number of seconds. Since it takes three accesses to retrieve the document and two images, you have three less seconds to work with.

And what about multiple users accessing your pages at the same time? Doesn't that mean you would need twice as much bandwidth to serve two users, three

Table 3.1   Network connections, their speed, and their overhead

Connection	Kilobytes per second	Overhead
14.4 K modem	1.4 Kbps	1 second per access
28.8 K modem	2.8 Kbps	1 second per access
56 K frame relay	5.6 Kbps	0.2 seconds per access
BRI ISDN	11.2 Kbps	0.2 seconds per access
256 K frame relay	25.6 Kbps	0.2 seconds per access
T1	150 Kbps	0.2 seconds per access

times as much to serve three, and so on? Well, if you have a single user every ten seconds, then you can serve 360 users an hour, or 8640 users per day. That would make you a pretty busy Web server, as far as Web servers go. Of course your users won't wait for the line to be completely free before they start their own transaction, but unless you happen to be one of the more popular sites on the Web, contention should be fairly rare.

Contention, by the way, is the fancy networking term for more than one user accessing your network connection at the same time. Most of the time, if a transaction only takes ten seconds or so to complete, by the time a second user requests a given document, the first should be finished or almost finished. Statistically, the effects of two or more transactions contending for your network connection at the same time should be minimal. The worst-case scenario, of two or three users accessing the same document starting at the exact same time, should be pretty uncommon.

Note well: All these numbers and formulas work under the assumption that it is *your* network connection that is the limiting factor in how quickly someone can access your Web server. But alas, not all your users are going to have enough bandwidth *themselves* for that to be the case. Most likely your users will be working through only 14.4 K or 28.8 K modems themselves, and with the announcement of CompuServe and AOL offering Web browsing services, you can expect quite a few people still using 2400 and 9600 baud modems to access your pages as well. So how does this affect your figures? Unfortunately, it complicates things some. The keyword, again, is contention.

In the previous example where you served a document and two images at 2.1 Kbps, that was assuming the user had enough bandwidth to accept 2.1 Kbps worth of transfer. What if someone accesses that same information with a 9600 baud modem? Well, figuring that to be about 0.9 Kbps, and a very generous estimate that is, it will probably take them around 20 seconds to transfer the same information, as opposed to around 8 seconds for someone with a 28.8 K modem. That's 12 more seconds they are using your network connection, and there is that much more chance that someone else will try to connect during their transaction. And if someone else *does* try to connect, it will take them longer to complete *their* transaction because they don't have the entire line to work with, which increases the chances that *yet another* person will try to connect at the same time those two are still working on their transaction.

But in spite of all this, contention should still be a fairly rare occurrence. Like I said, at 10 seconds per page, that is 8640 pages per day, likely more than your Web pages will ever see. Even 4320 pages per day, for 20 seconds per page, is a heck of a lot of pages to serve. So with this in mind, look at Table 3.2 for a chart to help base your decision on. Once again, it's not gospel, just a rough estimate of what you are likely to need, but it should prove accurate enough in most cases. The question answered by Table 3.2 is this: To how many users can you serve a 15 K page with two images in an hour? The numbers are very rough, but give some idea of the relative power of some of the available network connections.

The Traffic column in Table 3.2 shows the number of 15 K pages with two images the line will be able to handle in one hour, assuming that all your users access the line using 14.4 K modems and the line is in constant use. But these numbers, as interesting as they may be, can be misleading. For example, although in a best-case situation your 14.4 K modem should be able to handle 268 such accesses an hour, it doesn't take into account that accesses tend to be distributed in a nonlinear fashion. In other words, one minute two or three people may try to access your pages, and another maybe none. And the 15 K, two-image "standard" document, as close to ideal as I consider it, may be a bit small for many people. In reality, most pages will probably be double, triple, or still larger in size than our test

Table 3.2 Capacity per hour serving a typical 15 K Web document

Bandwidth	Traffic	Notes	
14.4 K modem	268	very low	Not recommended except for very small pages
28.8 K modem	536	low	Small pages, maybe one or two tiny images per page
56 K frame relay	1072	moderate	Small pages, one or two medium images or several tiny images
BRI ISDN	2144	moderate	Large text files, small pages with several medium images
256 K frame relay	4764	high	Any size text, many images of various sizes, short movies
T1	25728	very high	Anything

document, greatly reducing the number of users who can access your pages. Let's look at each option in a bit more detail.

- **14.4 K modem connection**

  A 14.4 K modem connection is definitely a budget solution. For your own personal pages, with information about your hobbies, personal lifestyle, and other matters of interest only to yourself and your friends, this may be all the bandwidth that you need. You can probably keep some short text files, as well as a small image or two on each page, and not suffer an dire consequences. But due to the one-second overhead for each image, I would recommend keeping them down to the bare minimum if you expect any significant traffic at all. Realistically, expect to be able to serve around 100 users an hour.

- **28.8 K modem connection**

  With the price of 28.8 K modems dropping down into the low $200 range, you would do well to pick this option over the 14.4 K modem. A small user's group, a teacher making lesson plans available to her students, or a very small business offering some marketing copy and a few product sheets may be quite comfortable with this solution. Once again, a few short text files, as well as a small image or two on each page, would work quite nicely here. Around 250 users an hour would be a good, realistic estimate for this type of connection.

- **56 K frame relay**

  Frame relay can be a bit pricey if you are on a tight budget, but well worth the expense if you expect any significant traffic on your pages. A small to medium sized business could make good use of this type of connection, as well as a large user's group serving information of general interest to many people in and out of the group. Large text documents, and pages with several small images or medium sized images, shouldn't cause any problems with this amount of bandwidth. Realistically, a 56 K frame relay line should be able to serve 750 users an hour for small documents, or 500 users an hour if your documents are a bit larger than our 15 K text + two image example.

- **BRI ISDN**

  With the rapidly decreasing cost of ISDN equipment, and many phone companies practically giving the service away, ISDN may be an excellent choice over 56 K frame relay. For all but the most popular Web sites, ISDN service may be the way to go—if it's available in your area, that is! Double the estimates for a 56 K frame relay connection to about 1500 users an hour for small documents, or 1000 users an hour for documents that are a bit larger. You may even be able to get away with offering a few small MPEG movies, but be careful not to push it too far!

- **Fractional T1**

  This is a little harder to come by than 56 K frame relay service, but it should be able to handle just about anything you throw at it. Large businesses and universities, who might use their connections for other purposes like email, telnet, and FTP, may benefit the most. Expect to serve around 3000 users an hour for a 256 K frame relay. Fractional T1 comes in many different speeds, from 128 K on up to a full T1, but not all phone companies offer all speeds. The biggest single benefit is ease of upgrading to higher speeds.

- **Full T1**

  This is the be-all, end-all of Internet connections. There may be faster options, like T3 or multiple T1s, but unless you're accepting over a million accesses a day as do the Netscape or NCSA home pages, this will be more bandwidth then you'll ever be likely to use. (At least for a few years, that is.) This is the type of connection most ISPs have, and may be a bit overkill for your average Web server. Then again, you're unlikely to adopt full T1 by accident, once you understand how much it will cost to install and maintain.

So Where Do I Start?

A few years ago, finding an ISP willing to sell you a full-fledged dedicated network connection was a frustrating, time consuming, and extravagantly expensive experience. But with all the hype about the Internet and the Information Superhighway lately, finding an ISP in your local area has become a great deal easier. It can still be an expensive and frustrating experience if you don't do the necessary research ahead of decision time, however, so don't expect to just make a phone call or two and be up and running in a day. One of the biggest problems is that, unlike ISPs specializing in Web consulting services, ISPs for dedicated networking connections must be fairly close to your physical location. As the ISP gets further away, the bill from the phone company gets higher and higher.

Instead of providing a list of ISPs, which could not be complete and would probably become obsolete before this book is even published, I'm providing some pointers to places on the Web where lists of such things are kept. The most useful place to look is the Internet provider list on the CommerceNet Web pages, at *http://www.commerce.net/directories/news/inet.prov.dir.html*. If this URL doesn't work (these things can change without any notice), try working your way to the list from the CommerceNet home page at *http://www.commerce.net/*. Another wonderful resource are the extremely useful indices at Yahoo. I found the provider lists at *http://www.yahoo.com/Business/Corporations/Internet_Access_Providers/*, or if that doesn't work, try working your way down to it from *http://www.yahoo.com/*. The Yahoo indices seem a little helter-skelter in this area, with all the ISPs generally lumped together without regard to their geographic region; I found the index at CommerceNet much more neatly indexed. But both are well worth a close reading.

Depending on your geographic location, you may have the choice between many ISPs, or only a few. Either way, look into as many as possible before making your decision. Choosing an ISP is like buying a car; it can be an expensive and unpleasant experience, or reasonable and rewarding depending on where you make your purchase, and either way, you're going to be pretty much stuck with your choice for awhile. Choose carefully.

Another option, if you're not having much luck with the indices at CommerceNet or Yahoo, is to put queries out in the newsgroups alt.internet.services or comp.infosystems.www.providers. You may not necessarily find a good provider there, but they are good places to ask about people's experiences in dealing with specific providers. One final choice is asking any companies or organizations in your local area that have Internet connections. Most network administrators will be more than happy to clue you in on who their ISP is, and any experiences, good or bad, they may have had with them.

Connect and Prosper!

I crammed an awful lot into this chapter. You learned about some basic networking technology, specifically the physical connections which glue the Internet together, and how to figure out what size connection you will need for your Web server. You also learned about ISPs that specialize as access points to the Internet, and other ISPs that provide higher level services such as Web consulting. But really, the point of this chapter was not to make you a networking guru, but rather to prepare you to ask intelligent questions of your ISP, and understand their suggestions and advice. It's a secret law of the universe that the best questioner wins. Be one.

Choosing Your Server

Choosing a Web server is easy if you're already a seasoned webmaster. For just about everybody else, selecting a Web server is a lot like buying a new stereo system. You know you want something that produces top-notch sound, but when the stereo salesperson snags you at the store entrance and pelts you with questions about gigahertz and low-end response and who knows what else, you'll probably feel overwhelmed, a little intimidated, and woefully undereducated.

Even the most basic server software packages (assuming they're legitimately useful), can overwhem you with features. That's not surprising when you consider the services that the software, at bare minimum, has to perform. At the most fundamental level, Web server software coordinates the distribution of documents. In the Unix world, this program is called an *http daemon*; for Windows NT, it is the *http service*. But whatever the software is called on your platform, it is nevertheless the "brain" of your Web server hardware.

The server performs these tasks, among others:

- Provides *access control* to determine who can access different levels of files and directories on the server.

- Runs your *CGI scripts* and any external modules you write to add functionality to your Web pages.

- Handles the input from *image maps*—special images that are capable of returning the user to the location that contained the original link to the server.

- Logs the transactions that users make.

Server software is available for almost any serious (and perhaps barely serious) computing platform, from complex Unix and VMS servers to the simplest DOS systems. Servers are also available for Windows 3.x, Windows NT, the Amiga, NeXTStep, OS/2, and the Macintosh. Although your choice of server software will rely largely on your computer's operating system, a few other factors also come into play.

In particular, if you plan to accept credit card numbers on your Web server, you might want to use a server that is capable of performing *secure transactions*. As of this writing, only two "secure servers" are available. The first is the Netsite Commerce Server from Netscape Communications, and the other is a new one called WebStar. Several other companies have announced their own secure servers, so others should be available by the time you read this. I'll have more on secure servers later on.

There are quite a few good servers available free of charge, written by programmers who actually program for the sheer fun of it. I applaud their efforts; the Web wouldn't be where it is today if it weren't for the generous contributions of several of the finest programmers on the Internet. A few other servers are being distributed under the *shareware* philosophy, and the registration fees for these are quite reasonable. Don't "forget" to pay the authors of any shareware programs you may be using!

With the arrival of the Web in the corporate world, several software companies have unveiled commercial servers for businesses and other organizations that demand professionally written software and full technical support. Prices for commercial servers range from $500 to $15,000, and they come with a wide range of functionality and support. But it isn't always necessary for large organizations to buy high-priced commercial written servers. The free and inexpensive shareware servers all offer reliable, capable solutions. I use the free CERN httpd server, and have nothing but the highest praise for the software.

Which Server Is for You?

Picking a server was once a simple task: You could choose either NCSA httpd or CERN httpd. Those were your *only* choices, and both only ran under Unix. Fortunately, you now have quite a few additional choices. But choice often brings with it a bit of confusion. So how do you choose the best server for your needs? Here are four significant questions you'll need to answer:

• What computer platform does the server run on?

• If you're looking at a commercial server, does the company provide technical support, and if so, for how long?

• Does the server have a simple, graphical interface for setup and maintenance?

• Does the server support "secure transactions" for credit card numbers?

If you need to accept credit card transactions or are trading other "sensitive information," you'll probably want advanced security capabilities, such as data encryption. I'll cover secure servers later in this chapter; for now, I'll just reiterate that the "secure server" field to date is slim pickings—and expensive ones.

If your security requirements are less stringent, your choices aren't quite so limited. To help you make sense of the available servers and their options, I've provided Table 4.1, which lists some of the features I consider important in a server. This is by no means a complete list, and since server authors upgrade their features regularly, this information is certain to change. However, it at least provides an overview of the server market as it stands at this writing. (Don't fret if you don't understand some of the features listed in the table; I'll explain these features next.)

Web Server Features

Quite a few other features might have an impact on your decision-making process, but we don't want to jump too quickly into deep, rough waters. Before I can explain some of these more advanced features, I want to provide you with a good understanding of the technical side of server software and a firm grasp of some of the basic and more intermediate Webmastering techniques.

There's a bit of a Catch-22 at work here: To make a completely informed decision in selecting the best server for your needs, it helps to have used at least one of the available servers and already understand much of the technology. Obviously, I can't assume that you've used any of the available server software packages. But since you need to start *somewhere*, let's begin with a detailed discussion of the features shown in Table 4.1.

Table 4.1   Features of the major players in Web server software.

	SSL Support	S-HTTP Support	Graphical Setup, Maintenance	Can Serve Gopher Also	"User" Directories	Price
UNIX Servers						
GN	No	No	No	Yes	No	Free
CERN httpd	No	No	No	No	Yes	Free
NCSA httpd	No	No	No	No	Yes	Free
Netsite	No	No	Yes	No	Yes	$1499
Netsite Commerce	Yes	No	Yes	No	Yes	$5000
Plexus	No	No	No	No	Yes	Free
WN	No	No	No	No	Yes	Free
Windows NT Servers						
EMWAC HTTPS	No	No	Setup only	No	No	Free
NetPublisher	No	No	Yes	Yes	No	
Purveyor	No	No	Yes	No	Yes	$1995
Plexus	No	No	No	No	Yes	Free
Netsite	No	No	Yes	No	Yes	$1499
Netsite Commerce	Yes	No	Yes	No	Yes	$5000
CERN httpd	No	No	No	No	Yes	Free
WebSite	No	No	Yes	No	No	$495
VMS Servers						
CERN httpd	No	No	No	No	Yes	Free
Region 6	No	No	No	No	Yes	Free
Macintosh Servers						
MacHTTP	No	No	Yes	No	N/A	$65/$95
WebStar	Yes	Yes	Yes	No	N/A	$295/$795
OS/2 Servers						
OS2HTTPD	No	No	No	No	Yes	Free
GoServe	No	No	Setup only	Yes	Yes	Free
Windows 3.1 Servers						
Windows HTTPD	No	No	Yes	No	N/A	Free/$99
CERN httpd	No	No	No	No	N/A	Free

SSL and S-HTTP Support

SSL support and *S-HTTP* support are the two methods for exchanging encrypted information. Essentially, if the server supports one of these methods, it is considered a "secure server" and is capable of exchanging credit card information and other sensitive data with the user over the Web. *Secure Socket Layer* (SSL) is the "most popular" of the two methods—probably because the most popular browser on the Web, Netscape, happens to support SSLs. The other method, S-HTTP (for Secure-HTTP), is supported by WebStar for the Mac and Secure NCSA HTTPD, but as far as I know only two Web browsers can use S-HTTP: Secure NCSA Mosaic and SPRY Mosaic. Secure NCSA Mosaic is not in widespread use; however, SPRY Mosaic is the Web browser used from within CompuServe. More S-HTTP-aware browsers are in the works, too, so you may have heard announcements for one or more others by the time you read this chapter.

Graphical Setup and Maintenance

Graphical setup and maintenance represent another important feature for your server, especially if you want to avoid tinkering with obscure setup files and entering cryptic instructions in your configuration files. I don't mind doing things by hand, but if you're like me, you've got better things to do than spend a day or two trying to get your server package up and running.

Gopher Server Capability

Some servers are capable of acting like gopher servers as well as Web servers. If you're already running a gopher server and need gopher functionality, you may want to try one of these. However, I think you may be better off running your gopher server separately from your Web server. Here are some reasons why I think it's a bad idea to combine the two: If your server locks up or crashes, you lose both your Web *and* gopher service until you reboot the server. Also, the added complexity of supporting both gopher and http on one server increases the likelihood of introducing bugs and security holes. I would rather have a server do one thing really well, instead of two things to some level of mediocrity.

User Directories

You may also find it useful to give other people who share your machine their own directories so they can put up home pages on the Web, through your server. If you're only running a single-user machine or you're just setting up a server as a hobby, then you may not have a need for this. But if several individuals work from your system, this is the best way to let them have their own home pages without conflicting with one another.

Price

Even if none of these features seems important to you now, certainly the price will. Most of the servers on this list are free; however, a few are commercial software packages. The price column in Table 4.1 lists two different prices for commercial servers. The first price is for personal or educational use, while the second price is for commercial or government use.The difference is pretty cut-and-dried, although a lot of users try to stretch the definition of "personal or educational." One unambiguous data point exists, however: If you would like to make money or advertise products on your Web pages, you are a commercial user, period. If running a Web server is just a hobby and you're just providing information on raising green-tailed guppies or on finding the best mountain biking trails around the world, your usage is personal/educational. In the inevitable gray areas, you should be prepared to justify your use of the lower price points.

A Little More about the Servers

As low tech as it sounds to say so, picking a server is basically a matter of personal taste. Certainly, it's important to select a server with a feature set that most closely matches the way you plan to use it. But all of the current generation of servers are very similar in operation, and unless you need to accept credit card information or other secure data, almost any of them would probably do. But because personal and organizational preferences can play such an important role in choosing a server, I want to provide some additional information on the capabilities of the more popular servers.

For each server, I'll include pointers to locations that provide more information—including Web sites, FTP sites from which you can download the software, and any pertinent mailing lists that I know about. You can also get a quick and apparently objective summary of most of the servers mentioned in this chapter at *http://www.proper.com/www/servers-chart.html.* And of course you can find tons of information on Yahoo at *http://www.yahoo.com/Computers/World_Wide_Web/HTTP/Servers/.*

Unix Servers

If you're using Unix, and you feel strongly about the word "free" showing up somewhere in your server's description, you'll probably choose NCSA httpd or CERN httpd—or both. In fact, I use both—CERN under BSDI and NCSA under Linux—and have had no problems with either. I find CERN a bit more pleasant to work with than NCSA, but that's probably because I've had more experience with CERN than NCSA. The packages are quite similar, on the surface at least. However, both are less than easy to install and configure. I don't mean to imply that they're wretchedly difficult to install, but if you require or strongly prefer Windows-style point-and-click simplicity and a nice graphical interface, you may have a problem with these servers. They are, after all, Unix creatures.

CERN httpd is available at *http://www.w3.org/hypertext/WWW/Daemon/Status.html.* You'll also find extensive instructions for installation and setup at this Web site. A version of CERN httpd that's been ported to VMS is located at this same URL. NCSA httpd is available at *http://hoohoo.ncsa.uiuc.edu/docs* along with some excellent step-by-step installation and setup instructions.

If you need a commercially produced server, complete with technical support, Netscape's Netsite Communications server is the way to go. With a $1,499 price tag, it's not for those on a tight budget, but there may be enough value added to warrant the price. For example, simple installation, setup, and maintenance are all handled through a graphical interface. The Netsite server is also extremely efficient, requiring a minimum of RAM and computer power to operate. This means it can serve more users faster, with less load on your machine. If you need data encryption for secure transactions, such as credit cards, the Netsite Commerce server is your best choice, but at $5,000 you had better be *certain* that this is what you want! More information on secure transactions later.

For information on the Netsite Communications and Netsite Commerce servers, check out *http://home.netscape.com/comprod/netscape_products.html.*

Windows NT Servers

Windows NT is gaining quite a bit of popularity in the Web community as a platform for running a Web server, so it shouldn't surprise you to learn that quite a few excellent packages are available for Windows NT, both commercial and free, and more are probably on the way.

On the free end of the spectrum, a version of CERN httpd is specifically designed for NT, but this package is still in the testing phase at this writing. A more established free NT server is EMWAC HTTPS, written by the European Microsoft Windows NT Academic Center (EMWAC), and is based on NCSA's httpd server. EMWAC HTTPS has all the features of NCSA httpd, plus easy, graphical setup. The CERN httpd server for NT is available at the same address as the Unix version. The EMWAC HTTPS product for NT is available from *http://emwac.ed.ac.uk/html/internet_toolchest/https/contents.htm.*

If you or your company has deep pockets and demand the best, Netscape has NT versions of their Netsite Communications and Netsite Commerce servers, available for $1,499 and $5,000, respectively. Installation is fast and easy, and technical support is available from Netscape.

Another impressive product is the "professional version" of EMWAC HTTPS, called Purveyor. I've had the pleasure of observing Purveyor being put through its paces, and my observations have convinced me that Purveyor is loaded with features that can make being a webmaster a breeze. Fully graphical setup and installation, special HTML authoring tools, remote server maintenance, and graphical document management features make this a solid choice. The $1,995 price tag is intimidating, but you should take a look at Purveyor if you think it might fit within your budget. More information on Purveyor can be obtained at *http://www.process.com/prodinfo/purvdata.htm.*

Another very strong new entrant in the server market is O'Reilly and Associate's WebSite server. Compared to the other commercial servers, WebSite is aggressively priced at only $495. But in spite of its relatively low price, it's packed with features. Graphical setup and installation, HTML authoring tools, and a graphical document management feature similar to Purveyor's make this a powerful server. O'Reilly *really* stands behind this product, too, and I think you'll find WebSite a major player in the months to come. More information can be found at *http://website.ora.com/.*

Macintosh Servers

I admit it. When I think of "server-class machines," the word "Macintosh" usually doesn't pop into my mind. But thankfully, BIAP Systems *does* think of the Mac as a serious server-class machine, and their hard work has brought us the inexpensive MacHTTP server. It's only $95, or $65 for educational or personal use, but MacHTTP is certainly a full-featured server. Setup and maintenance are easy thanks to MacHTTP's graphical interface (What else would you expect on a Mac?) and plenty of free add-on software is available at various Internet sites to help you become a webmaster with MacHTTP.

Even more exciting is the WebStar server, soon to be released by StarNine Technologies. WebStar is a professional version of MacHTTP, featuring support for both SSL and S-HTTP secured transactions. For $795, or $295 educational pricing, this is an excellent deal. More information on WebStar is available at *http://www.starnine.com/*. For MacHTTP information, check out *http://www.biap.com/*.

Windows 3.1 Servers

Alhough I strongly advise against trying to run a "serious" Web server under Windows 3.1, a few servers *are* available if you really really want to try the Windows 3.1 approach. Notably, the Windows HTTPD server by Robert Denny, which is based on the NCSA httpd server, is available free of charge for educational and personal use. For commercial use, the fee is only $99. I played around with Windows HTTPD a bit, and overall found it to be a good product. Just don't expect to get the same kind of performance as you would running your server on another, more suitable platform such as Windows NT or Unix. Installation is easy and straightforward. For more information, go to *http://www.city.net/win-httpd/*

A version of CERN httpd is also available for Windows 3.1. Although it's free, it's still in the testing phase and thus not suitable for beginners.

OS/2 Servers

There are also a few free servers available for the OS/2 crowd. GoServe, by Mike Cowlishaw, is intriguing in that it not only understands the http protocol, but can also speak gopher protocol. If you want to run a Web server *and* a gopher server, this is a good choice. You can grab a copy at *http://www2.hursley.ibm.com/goserve.*

If you would like to try a port of NCSA httpd, called OS2HTTPD, one is available at *ftp://ftp.netcom.com/pub/kf/kfan/overview.html.*

So You Want to Take Credit Cards...

As I've already mentioned, you can't use just any server if you want to take credit cards. Most of your users will be wary about sending their credit card numbers "plain-text" over the Internet—and for good reason. Several instances of Internet credit card number theft have been uncovered recently. To support credit card transactions, a secure server is essential.

The term "secure" doesn't mean it's impossible to break into or get unauthorized access to your machine. Rather, a server is considered secure because it is capable of encrypting the contents of any information transmitted between it and the user's browser. Of course, you can accept credit card numbers without this special encryption, but your users will be a lot less hesitant to use your pages if they know their card numbers are transferred in unreadable encrypted form.

As I mentioned earlier in the chapter, two protocols are available for conducting a secure transaction. The first protocol to be implemented was Secure Socket Layers (SSL) by Netscape Communications, as part of their Netsite Commerce server product. Another protocol, Secure-HTTP (S-HTTP), was actually proposed by EIT before SSL was created; however, only recently has it been implemented in the Mac-based WebStar and Unix-based Secure NCSA HTTPD servers.

The second half of the formula is a browser that can support encryption. A server that can encrypt (and of course, decrypt) data is of no use without a browser that can do the same. The Netscape browser was the first such browser, and since it was written by Netscape Communications, it speaks the SSL protocol. Currently, there are only two browsers that understand S-HTTP: Secure NCSA Mosaic and Spry Mosaic, but I'm sure that more S-HTTP-compliant browsers are on the way. In the meantime, since the number-one browser in use on the Web is Netscape, the SSL protocol has a strong future.

But the popularity of Netscape might not hold under the competition from Mosaic clones supported by such online services as CompuServe, America Online, and Microsoft Network. So what will happen if S-HTTP browsers become widely available? Which protocol should your electronic store support? I think the only rational trend for servers will be to understand both protocols. WebStar already understands both S-HTTP and SSL, and O'Reilly and Associates' new WebSite server has plans to support both protocols in the "near future" as well. I consider this similar to stores that accept Mastercard/Visa *and* American Express. Some stores support one, some the other, but if you are really interested in making shopping convenient for your customers, you'll take both. I think this same commerce philosophy will hold true for encryption protocols.

Public Key Cryptography

Both SSL and S-HTTP use what is called *public key cryptography* to encrypt data, and perform *authentication*. Here's how it works: The browser and server each have their own pair of *private* and *public* keys. A *key* is just a string of characters generated (as I said, in pairs) by an encryption utility, according to well-known mathematical principles. A private and public key pair have a special functional relationship, but their power comes from the mathematical postulate stating that one key of a pair *cannot* be generated by inspection or calculation based on the other. In other words, you cannot plug a public key into a formula and generate its corresponding private key.

As their name implies, the public keys can be published in directories like phone books, and transmitted over plain text links without any kind of security risk. A public key is *meant* to be in as many hands as possible. Private keys, on the other hand, are secret keys, and ideally should never leave the head of the persons who own them.

The magic comes in with the functional relationship of public and private keys. A message encrypted with someone's public key can *only* be decrypted (that is, made readable again) with their private key. The system is symmetrical, in that a message encrypted with a private key can only be encrypted with the corresponding public key. This sounds crazy on the surface, but it has its uses, as you'll see in a bit.

So let's say you connect to a server and request its public key. Once you have the public key, you can then encrypt a message containing your credit card number and send the message back to the server. The only way to decrypt the message is with the server's private key, which only the server has, so your data is safe in transit...*or is it?*

Well, consider this question: What happens if you connect to what you *think* is the correct server, but when you request the public key, an impostor who wants the information you are secretly sending to the server intercepts your request and sends you the impostor's public key instead? You would then unknowingly encrypt the sensitive data with *their* public key and send it back. The "bad server" would intercept the now encrypted message and be able to decrypt it, since you used its public key, and no one would be the wiser—including you. (The server might sound the alarm if it ever received the message, since it could not decrypt what you sent.) This sounds complex and unlikely, but if the stakes are high enough, it will be attempted. Clearly, when any significant amount of money is at stake, a higher level of protection is needed.

Your Certificate, Please

Both the SSL and S-HTTP protocols use what are called *certificates* to verify the authenticity of the data between your Web browser and the server. A certificate is a means of determining whether an individual who gives you a public key is really authorized to do so by the server that you're connecting to. The certificate contains the server's public key, and is *signed* by a third party, the *certificate issuer*, using the third party's private key. This "signing" is simply encryption with the third-party's private key. Anyone can decrypt a certificate using the third-party's published *public* key—the system is symmetrical, remember—and if what's inside the certificate turns out to be the server's public key, the validity of the certificate is at least as good as the reputation of the third party who did the signing. You can think of it as a sort of machine-based notary public mechanism—though the certificate issuer is more likely to be a big firm like a bank or insurance company, which ostensibly has abundant reason to keep an unblemished reputation of honesty.

Here is a description of a secure transaction once again, this time using certificate-based validation: You ask for the server's certificate, and see if the certificate is valid by using the certificate issuer's public key to decrypt the certificate. If it turns out to be valid, you use the public key *contained in the certificate* to encrypt your message and send it to the server, which then decrypts it using its private key. Since according to the certificate the server is who it says it is, you know your message is going to the correct place, and since it is encrypted using the correct public key, only the server can decrypt it. The transaction is thus as secure as the certificate issuer is trustworthy.

The Certificate Authority

The cornerstone of the certification concept is the fact that some third party has issued a certificate to the server with which you are trying to converse, and that you trust that the public key of the third party is correct. This third party can be anyone, from your best friend Carol to somebody or some firm you've never met and know nothing about. Things would be simple if the certificate was issued by your friend Carol, since you can trust Carol to give you the correct public key to decrypt the certificate. But the chances of that happening are pretty slim. Most likely, the certificate will be issued by an unknown party whose business it is to issue certificates. That introduces another trust problem. Corruption is always a possibility, and you can't entirely discount the fear that the certificate issuer is in cahoots with your hypothetical Net imposter. So, a *certificate authority* steps in.

A certificate authority is some entity whose public key is widely known—someone whom everyone trusts. Think of the certificate authority as a well-known public figure, like the President of the United States, for example. Well, maybe you don't "trust" the President, but you do know who the President is—and that's what counts. If the server's certificate is *signed* by the President, you know it's valid because you can always recognize the President's signature. In actual practice, the certificate authority is unlikely to be a specific person, but a government agency with the task of keeping certificate issuers honest.

RSA Data Security

Netscape Communications has decided to work with RSA Data Security, the company that owns the algorithms upon which much of public key encryption is based, as the central certificate authority for all of Netscape's secure servers. When you connect to a Netsite Commerce server, that server must have a certificate signed by and registered with RSA Data Security. If they do, you know they are legitimate and can keep all of your transactions secure. If they don't, you're not talking to the real McCoy.

If you plan to run a secure server using the Netsite Commerce server, you must register a certificate with RSA Data Security. But distributing and keeping track of all those certificates isn't easy, so expect to pay RSA Data Security a setup and yearly upkeep fee to acquire a certificate and to keep it valid. Current pricing is an initial $290 for the first year of "service," and an additional $75 every year for renewal of your certificate. This may seem high from a personal perspective, but remember, it's really only necessary if you're going to be engaging in commerce over the Web. And then, it's simply a cost of doing business—and not an especially onerous one, either.

There is a lot more to all this, technically speaking, than I have room to discuss here. If you're interested in the inner workings of public key cryptography, digital signatures, and certificates, more information about SSL can be found at *http://home.netscape.com/* and on public key technology in general at *http://www.rsa.com/*.

You can also find information on Secure-HTTP, Secure NCSA Mosaic, and Secure NCSA HTTPD at *http://www.commerce.net/software/SMosaic/Docs/ manual.html*.

An excellent book on the whole subject of encryption, with a special emphasis on public key concepts, is *Applied Cryptography*, by Bruce Schneier (John Wiley & Sons, 1994; ISBN 0-471-59726-2).

Advanced Information

There are some advanced server concepts that probably won't affect you until you've got your server up and running, but I should at least bring these topics up now. I will cover each topic in more detail later in the book, so if this information seems a little too technical for you at this point, don't worry; it will all make sense as you learn more about how Web servers actually work.

Log Formats

Every transaction that a user initiates on your Web server—that is, every byte of information that enters or leaves your machine—is logged by your server. A typical entry in a log file consists of the date and time of the transaction, the name or address of the machine requesting the information, the type of transaction that took place, the file name of the document involved, and even the number of bytes transferred. Needless to say, this log file is marvelously useful in determining how much activity your server is receiving, which files are your most and least popular, and other tidbits that can help you to "fine tune" the type of information you provide to your users.

However, there are two basic difficulties involved in using the information contained in logs. First, it is particularly difficult to identify any trends or to form an overall view of your server's usage by simply viewing a potentially *huge* file of unformatted information. (Suppose your server becomes popular and gets a thousand hits a day. How many records must you then confront in a month? Do the math.) Second, in their "raw" form, these log files tend to get awfully big very quickly. If you have some way to generate reports based on these logs, you can eliminate both these problems. Trends will be easier to spot in a well-formatted report, and each report will be significantly smaller than your raw log files.

A number of tools have been written (more on these later on) to allow you to generate many different types of reports and statistics from your log files. But for these tools to work correctly on all servers, each server must log its data using the identical format. Such a formatting convention has been devised; it's called the *common log format*. Most servers support the common log format, so most likely you can use the available report-generating tools to analyze your log files. But if you are unfortunate enough to be using a server that isn't capable of producing its logs in common log format, you must either write your own tool to analyze your logs or rely on the tools that are provided with your server to produce useful reports.

A list of servers that do and do not generate logs in the common log format is shown in Table 4.2.

Server-Side Includes

Server-side includes are, essentially, special directives that you can include in your documents to instruct your server to modify a document in some way before sending it to the requesting user. For example, you could use a server-side include to append the current date to the end of a document automatically, before it is sent to the user. This can be a very useful feature, but as I'll explain later, it can be dangerous (from a security standpoint) as well. Servers that can and cannot use server-side includes are listed in Table 4.2.

Table 4.2   Advanced features supported by various servers

	Common Log Format	Server-Side Includes	Access Control
Unix Servers			
GN	No	No	No
CERN httpd	Yes	No	Yes
NCSA httpd	Yes	Yes	Yes
Netsite	Yes	Yes	Yes
Netsite Commerce	Yes	Yes	Yes
Plexus	No	Yes	Yes
WN	Yes	Yes	Yes
Windows NT Servers			
EMWAC HTTPS	No	No	No
NetPublisher	No	Yes	No
Purveyor	Yes	Yes	Yes
Plexus	No	Yes	Yes
Netsite	Yes	Yes	Yes
Netsite Commerce	Yes	Yes	Yes
CERN httpd	Yes	No	Yes
WebSite	Yes	No	Yes
VMS Servers			
CERN httpd	Yes	No	Yes
Region 6	Yes	Yes	Yes
Macintosh Servers			
MacHTTP	Yes	No	Yes
WebSTAR	Yes	No	Yes
OS/2 Servers			
OS2HTTPD	Yes	Yes	Yes
GoServe	Yes	Yes	Yes
Windows 3.1 Servers			
Windows HTTPD	Yes	Yes	Yes
CERN httpd	Yes	No	Yes

Access Control

I mentioned the subject of *access control* briefly at the outset of this chapter. If your server is capable of access control, you'll be able to tell your server which documents are allowed to be served to which users. If a user requests a document for which access control is enabled, he or she will be prompted for a user name and password. Again, some servers are capable of doing this, and some aren't. If you'll be constructing Web pages that require this type of access control—for example, a subscribers-only server—you'll want a server that supports it. Table 4.2 identifies the servers that offer this feature, which will be more and more important as the Web moves toward ubiquitous electronic commerce.

Other Security Concerns

In general, running a Web server is not a major security risk, but security problems can still arise, perhaps due to a bug in the server's program code, or through careless configuration of your server. Due to their complexity and their history of technological openness, Unix machines are at particular risk. Windows NT was designed with robust security in mind and is generally harder to "crack." Here are some additional security tips to help keep you out of trouble.

Firewalls

When you connect your own, private network to the Internet, you open yourself up to potential attacks from hackers who have nothing better to do than calibrate their macho by getting into your network without permission. To minimize your risk, a computer called a *firewall* should always be used as a "buffer zone" between your private network and the Internet. I briefly introduced firewalls in Chapter 2. A firewall protects you by keeping unauthorized individuals from directly accessing the machines on your private network, and from being able to see anything that's running "behind" your firewall.

Many different kinds of firewalls are available, giving you varying levels of security. I would be negligent as an author if I claimed to be an expert on this subject. I'm not. But I do feel comfortable telling you this:

If you have any computers in your private network that store any information considered proprietary or confidential—particularly customer lists with credit card numbers, confidential personnel information, or trade secrets—and if it would be more than a mild irritation if that information suddenly became public knowledge, you either need a firewall or you should refrain from attaching those machines to the Internet!

If you're in doubt about the potential security risks that your system faces, hire a computer security consultant–someone who specializes in Internet security, if possible. Firewalls tend to be tricky to set up and very sensitive to even the slightest configuration errors. If you're not confident you know exactly what you are doing, once again, hire a consultant who specializes in Internet firewalls. For an excellent reference work on firewalls, I recommend *Firewalls and Internet Security: Repelling the Wily Hacker*, by William Cheswick and Steven Bellovin (Addison-Wesley, 1994; ISBN 0-201-63357-4). Some parts of this book are extremely technical, but most of it is accessible to anyone new to Web servers.

Which Side of the Wall?

It's common practice to run your server on your firewall. Actually, you have only two other choices, and neither of them are very sensible if you want to make your server relatively accessible. You could run your server *behind* your firewall, but that would prohibit anyone from connecting to your server from the Internet. This approach makes sense if your server is only intended for members of your organization to access, but is pointless if you want the world Internet community to see your work. True, you could *tunnel* through your firewall, allowing outsiders to have access to your server, but *that* would defeat the purpose of your firewall and open a dangerous security hole where hackers could potentially attack.

Your second choice is to run your server on a machine you own that's placed *outside* your firewall. This approach does have some merit because it won't compromise the security of your private network behind the firewall. However, you do have to purchase a separate computer to run your server on. Another drawback: Instead of one machine exposed to attack from the Internet—your firewall—you now have two machines exposed. Presumably, your firewall is able to thwart attackers, but without careful configuration, the second machine may be vulnerable to a break-in. That could lead to anything from the mild inconvenience required to repair any damage the hacker might have caused, to a major fiasco if the hacker decides to alter the contents of your Web pages to say "disagreeable" things, uses the machine as a storage area for illegal or pornographic materials, or even uses your machine as a base for future hacking excursions.

Maybe I sound a little paranoid here, but to be frank, I'm trying to scare you into hiring a qualified consultant who knows the ins and outs of Internet security. *Don't underestimate the risks!*

Some Unix Security Tips

If you're running a Unix server, there are a few additional precautions you can take to reduce the risk of a break-in.

A little tech speak here: The default *port* to which your server *binds* is port 80. When a browser tries to connect to your server, that is the port it automatically checks. But since port 80 is considered a *privileged port* (in other words only a program with superuser privileges can bind to it), your server must be run as the superuser. This creates a small problem: If some hacker finds a bug in your server and is able to take control of it, he or she can potentially do damage as the superuser.

There are two direct solutions to this problem. The most common solution is to tell the server that, whenever it acts on any commands given to it by any user, it should automatically change its *user ID* to an unprivileged user, generally the user name *nobody*. This is called *suid nobody* in Unix speak. Pronounced "set-u-i-d," it means "set user ID." All Unix servers should have this option; if yours doesn't, get a different server.

Telling your server to suid to nobody gives you an additional benefit. Since user "nobody" should never own any files, the hacker wouldn't be able to effect any changes to anything as long as none of your files have world-write permissions. Just remember: All files that you want to be accessible to the server should have world-*readable* permissions.

Another, less desirable, solution is to run the server on an unprivileged port number. Anything over port number 1024 will do, with 8000 or 8080 being the most common. The benefit is that the server never has to run as the superuser. The drawback is that your URL becomes a little more complex, since your server is not running on the port every Web browser expects it to be on. For example, instead of your URL being *http://myhost.com/* it would have to be *http://myhost.com:8080/* if you changed the port number to 8080. I'll explain more about URLs in later chapters.

If you would like, you can also add security to your Unix server by running your server under what is called a *chroot*. This Unix command changes the root directory that another command runs under. Suppose you have a directory named */var/http* where you keep all your Web pages, scripts, configuration files, and other things you need to run your server. You can then use chroot to tell the server that its root directory is */var/http*. Now, the server can *never* access any directories above */var/http*. In other words, */var/http* becomes the server's root directory, until you tell the server to quit. *Nothing* can change the root directory, not even the superuser. If a hacker does manage to cause damange to server files, the worst the hacker can do is affect the files in /var/http (or its subdirectories), even if the hacker convinces the server to give him or her superuser privileges!

Although this is the safest method of running your server, it also creates some inconvenience. Since the server can't access anything that isn't in the directory */var/http*, you now don't have direct access to the email system, or any of the other system files. This also eliminates the ability to use Perl as your CGI scripting language, since you will need a copy of Perl in the */var/http* directory to execute any of your Perl scripts. If you put a copy of Perl in the directory, you'll introduce a security hole, since a very clever hacker could use Perl to open a separate socket and connect to one of your machines in your private network. I'll talk about these hazards later, after I've explained more about CGI scripts.

Server Choice Summary

Choosing your server can be as simple or difficult as you make it. If you are not picky about what server you use, and just want to get up and running, any of the free servers will do. If, on the other hand, you are interested in creating a Web server for serious commercial use, for example, to set up Web-based electronic storefront, it would probably be better to choose one of the professionally written commercial servers currently on the market. If you'll be accepting credit card numbers or other sensitive information, choose a server that is capable of performing secure transactions! Simply put, the server you should choose depends on what you are trying to accomplish and how much time and money you are willing to invest.

One final note: If you just don't want to deal with any of this, you can always rent space on someone else's server and let them deal with these issues for you. There is no law that says you must own the machine and server software where your Web pages are located. Go ahead and flip back to Chapter 3 and ask yourself, "Do I really need to deal with all this, or would I be better served by renting space on someone else's machine instead?"

Whatever you do, choose carefully. It isn't a big deal if you pick a free server and decide you don't like it or it doesn't suit your needs, but changing your mind about one of the commercial servers can be a fairly expensive mistake. Take it slow, ask questions, and be informed before you buy!

HTML 101

Anyone can write an HTML document. I mean, *anyone.* HTML (Hyper Text Markup Language) is not a programming language, as so many people seem to think, quaking in terror as they do. It's a document formatting system, related to SGML (Standard Generalized Markup Language) and not completely unlike the more familiar Rich Text Format (RTF) document specification. The idea is to take a plain ASCII text file and place special markers in it (called *tags*) that tell a program like a Web browser how to format this "plain text" on the screen. One tag might tell the program to center the following line on the display. Another pair of tags might tell the program to display the text falling between the two tags in bold. There's not a whole lot more to the concept than that.

Hypertext and Markup Languages

Hypertext has been a buzzword for some years now. All it really does is provide a way of embedding pathways between documents in the documents themselves, such that reading a document is in fact a process of following any of several paths through a number of documents, however the reader chooses. For example, if you were reading a history of New York State and ran across the name Millard Fillmore, you might wish to know more about Millard Fillmore. (*Why* is another question, although poor Mr. Fillmore has been out so long he looks like in to me.) If a pathway (called a *hyperlink* or *hotlink*) had been embedded in the document under the text string "Millard Fillmore," you could click your mouse on that text string and follow that hyperlink to another document that discussed President

Fillmore in greater detail. While reading about Millard Fillmore, you might run across a reference to the Whig political party, and could perhaps follow a hotlink to an explanation of who the Whigs were and why they disappeared.

Hypertext is the fundamental architecture of the World Wide Web, as anyone who has ever surfed the Web should tell on a moment's thought. The paths through the Web are legion, and a Web user can follow any path that looks promising. This chapter and the next are about how the hyperlinks (and also the formatting) are embedded in the documents that, taken together, make up the Web.

Markup and Markup Languages

A *markup language* is a set of instructions, collectively called *markup*, which directs the formatting of a document being typeset or displayed. In the days before computers where introduced to the publishing industry, this markup took the form of actual handwritten notes marked on the document paper itself, such as "center this line" or "the left margin is one inch wide"—hence the term "markup." If you have ever used a word processor to write a document for work or school, you have used markup and not even known it. When you tell your word processor to "center this line," the computer actually inserts markup in the document. To keep things from getting confusing, the markup is hidden from you, but it is still there. In the context of the World Wide Web, the Web browser is the typesetter, taking the markup in an HTML document and turning it into a nicely formatted human-readable document, with embedded hyperlinks to other documents as well.

There is a major problem implicit in this system. The Web is *World-wide*, spanning the globe and limited to no single type of computer or operating system. There are Web browsers for many different computers and operating systems, each of which may have different capabilities for displaying and formatting documents. Some are very rich in their ability; others can do little but display text in a line-by-line fashion without formatting. My home computer can easily display hundreds of fonts and any manner of graphics, but my computer at work is locked into using one font and can't even underline text!

When a word processor adds markup to a document, the markup is very specific, for example, "this is bold" or "use the 12 point Courier New font." But what happens if the document is moved to a computer that can't display bold face text or doesn't know what the Courier New font is? This isn't a problem if the document is displayed on the computer that created it, or a computer very much like it, but on the World Wide Web there is no guarantee that this will be the case. Obviously another approach must be taken. Enter *generalized markup*.

A generalized markup language looks at markup in a slightly different way than a specific word processor or typesetting machine. Where a word processor's markup would say "this block of text is in the Courier New font," generalized markup would say "this block of text is a paragraph, handle it as you would handle any paragraph." The responsibility of determining how a document looks is now shifted to the typesetting machine, or in our case the Web browser. The computer knows that this section of text is a paragraph—and it also knows that it uses the Courier New font to display paragraphs. Another computer that doesn't understand Courier New would use whatever font it normally uses to display paragraphs instead. In other words, generalized markup is only concerned with *what* we want to display, not *how* we want to display it.

SGML

The markup language which is of particular interest to us now is called the *Standard Generalized Markup Language*. In SGML, a document is split into three distinct parts, each with its own function. The first part is called the SGML *declaration*, the second part is called the *document type declaration* (DTD), and the last part is called the *document instance*, which is usually stored separately from the first two parts. An in-depth exploration of the SGML declaration section is out of the scope of this book; however, I would like to talk a bit about the last two sections.

In an SGML document, text is marked-up by placing what are called start and end tags around the text. For example, if I wanted to mark some text as important, I might type something like this:

```
<IMPORTANT>We'll talk about HTML soon!</IMPORTANT>
```

Here, "<IMPORTANT>" is the *start tag* and "</IMPORTANT>" is the *end tag*. The text between those tags is called the *content* and the entire mess—start tag, end tag, and content—is called an *element*. Perhaps when this element is displayed, it will be in boldface or maybe in a different font from the rest of the document. At this point, SGML really doesn't care. All

SGML cares about is that the content between those tags is marked as "important."

All the tags in an SGML document are defined in the DTD section, and each document may have its own user-defined DTD. This means that we may "customize" SGML for specific document types. For example, if I were writing a DTD for court transcripts, I may define tags such as "judge," "defendant," and "plaintiff."

The last part of an SGML document is the document instance. The document instance contains the "real" text of the document. In the court transcript example mentioned above, the document instance would contain the actual transcriptions of court proceedings, with elements marked up by the tags defined in the DTD. You may remember that the DTD and document instance may be, and usually are, kept in separate files. This means that for any one DTD, there may be many different document instances, all using the tags defined in that same DTD. The DTD thus acts as a document template of sorts, which may be applied to any number of distinct individual documents.

HTML is an SGML DTD designed specifically for the application of representing hypertext. Applying what we now know about SGML, the philosophy behind the design of HTML is clear. HTML was designed to represent hypertext documents in a truly platform-independent fashion; that is, without regard to the platform the document is viewed on. Because computers differ widely in their text formatting abilities, an HTML document may be displayed differently from machine to machine; however, the content and original intent of the document must remain the same throughout. When we actually begin writing some real HTML documents, it's important to keep this point in mind. The way your Web browser displays your documents may be different than someone else's browser. Be careful what you assume!

Now—on to some real HTML.

Basic HTML Markup

A typical HTML document is split into two parts, the *head* and the *body*. Both are embraced by a pair of tags that bracket the entire document:

<HTML> and </HTML>. These two tags make the whole document into a single HTML element. Note well that it is illegal for anything to fall outside the <HTML> tag pair.

Not all HTML tags come in pairs, but a lot of them do, and for those that come in pairs, the closing tag contains a forward slash character within the tag but before the tag's identifier text. The start tag lacks this slash. </HTML> is thus the end tag of the <HTML> tag pair. In general terms, tags that come in pairs apply some meaning to the text that falls between them.

So it is with the tags marking the document head and body. The document head typically contains the *title* of the document and occasionally other "administrative" information such as the name of the document's owner. The document body is where we place the text itself. For an example, examine the simple HTML document in Listing 5.1.

Listing 5.1 LIST5-1.HTM

```
<HTML>
<HEAD>
<TITLE>My First HTML Document</TITLE>
</HEAD>
<BODY>
This is my <STRONG>first</STRONG> HTML document!
</BODY>
</HTML>
```

The <HEAD> and </HEAD> tag identifies everything falling between them as part of the document head, and the <BODY> and </BODY> tags identifies everything between them as part of the document body.

The Document Head

The head of the document, denoted by the <HEAD>...</HEAD> tags, contains special information about the document, such as the document's title and owner. One of the most important tags found in the document head is the <TITLE>...</TITLE> tag.

```
<TITLE>My First HTML Document</TITLE>
```

In the example above, the document's title would be set to "My First HTML Document."

There are several reasons why it is very important for every HTML document you write to have a descriptive title. First of all, most browsers display a document's title in a special location, separated from the rest of the document, usually at the very top of the browser's window. This gives the reader a quick idea of what the document is all about.

More important, when one of the many visitors to your Web pages decides that this is a very cool place to be, he or she may want to add the page to the browser's hotlist. Most browsers use the document's title as the description for your pages in its hotlist. The more descriptive your title is, the better the chances that the reader will remember, and re-visit, your page a few weeks later! There is nothing more annoying than putting a page in your hotlist and discovering it has a zero-information-content name such as "My Page," or worse, the default title: the document's cryptic URL address. But be careful not to make the title *too big*, or it may end up truncated. Sixty-four characters is about the limit, and forty is where you should shoot.

Another less obvious reason your documents should always have good, descriptive titles, is something called a *Web robot*. Web robots are programs designed to travel the many intertwined links which make up the Word Wide Web, automaticaly, unwatched by human eyes. As they travel the Web, robots keep logs of what URLs they visit, and the titles of the documents located at those URLs. These logs are then indexed and made available to the entire Web community as a Web *index*. Some Web robots actually read and index the *content* of Web pages as well as the titles. In due time, your Web pages will eventually be found by one of these robots, and if you don't have descriptive titles for your documents, it is unlikely that potential visitors will be able to find you by searching the the indexes generated by the robots.

That wraps up our discussion on the document head. Later on, as I cover some of the more advanced features of HTML, I'll explain some of the other tags that can be found here. For now, however, let's talk about the document body, where all the real action takes place.

The Document Body

The document body, which is defined as all text and tags falling between the <BODY>...</BODY> tag pair, is where all the "real" text of your document goes. For example, this is where you'd put your favorite recipe, the run-down of last night's softball game, your hobbyist group's charter...whatever you want. Unfortunately, it isn't quite as easy as breaking out your favorite word processor and plopping in a few pages of text. Without adding some HTML markup, you're going to have a fine mess. But before talking about how to make your documents look pretty, let's find out how HTML and most Web browsers will handle your unmarked-up text first.

Most Web browsers, if they are capable, will try to display your document in a *proportional font.* Unlike your everyday *fixed width* fonts, where every character is exactly the same width, the characters in a proportional font are only as wide as they need to be. In other words, in a fixed width font, a line containing eighty text characters will always be the same physical length, regardless of what characters are in the line. With proportional fonts, however, you may be able to squeeze a lot more than eighty characters into the same physical length on one line, but fewer on another. Proportional fonts are wonderful to look at, since they seem more "natural" and not as cold as fixed width fonts, but they make drawing charts and tables in text nearly impossible.

Another feature of HTML is its desire to collapse all whitespace into a single physical space. *Whitespace* is a fancy computer science term for characters that don't actually print a letter or symbol on your screen but cause some change in the position of where the next printable character will appear. Examples of whitespace are actual spaces, such as those produced by hitting the space bar, tabs, and newlines. (*Newline* is a term for the carriage return/linefeed combo that ends a text line and begins the next.) Yes, you heard right: Even newlines are turned into a single space. This means that your lovely chart on the growth of the gizmo industry, which should look like this:

```
$100M              ####
$ 75M              ####   ####
$ 50M      ####    ####   ####
$ 25M      ####    ####   ####   ####
           1991    1992   1993   1994
```

will at the hands of your Web browser be unceremoniously reduced to this:

$100M #### $ 75M #### #### $ 50M #### #### #### $ 25M #### #### #### #### 1991 1992 1993 1994

Well, at least HTML will automatically wrap your now mangled text when it reaches the end of the screen. But without any markup, HTML will turn your document into one long and completely unformatted paragraph. Not cool. Let's start figuring out how to add formatting and avoid the HTML mangle trap.

Paragraphs

The paragraph tag <P> is used to identify the start of a new paragraph. Since HTML turns newlines into spaces, your document will congeal into one giant paragraph if you don't use <P>, no matter how many newlines you use.

Listing 5.2   The P tag

```
<BODY>
<P>This is one paragraph.
<P>And this is another paragraph.
</BODY>
```

In the example in Listing 5.2, the two lines will be correctly displayed, with a blank line seperating them. Hmmm. Is there no </P> end tag? Alas, no. The <P> tag is one of a group of singular tags called *empty elements*, which simply means tags that stand alone and do not embrace text between a start and an end tag. We will discover a few more empty elements later; however, most HTML elements are not empty and do have both start and end tags.

Logical and Physical Styles

Now that we have managed to split our document into separate paragraphs, let's spruce things up a bit. In the course of writing a document, there may be reason to change the *style* of the text. For example, the title of a book may need to be in italics, or a key point may need to be emphasized. HTML provides us with several tags to accomplish this.

By using a *logical style*, it's possible to make certain words or phrases stand out from the rest of the document. In keeping with the spirit of HTML, logical styles don't actually specify "this is in italics" or "this should be bold." Rather, they inform the browser that "this is something that should stand out." The browser can then decide how best to make the text stand out. On the next page is an example, shown first as HTML markup in Listing 5.3, and then, in Figure 5.1, as the text displayed by a current Web browser.

Listing 5.3   Logical styles

```
<BODY>
<P>Always remember, you must <EM>never</EM> stick your tongue in
electrical outlets. Sure, it may make for a good laugh in the
emergency room, but you may be <STRONG>seriously hurt</STRONG> or
even <STRONG>killed</STRONG>! Dr. Claire Widget, an expert on the
topic, wrote the article <CITE>The Phenomenon of Self Electrocution</CITE>
which may be of interest to the reader.
</BODY>
```

In the example in Figure 5.1 I've introduced three new tags, each of which identifies a certain word or words as something that should stand out or be presented differently than the rest of the paragraph. None of these tags specifies exactly *how* to display their content, just that they should be displayed differently. The common logical styles are summarized in Tables 5.1 and 5.2. The category is split into styles of general interest, and styles of interest mainly to technical writers. I've tried to state the purpose of each style

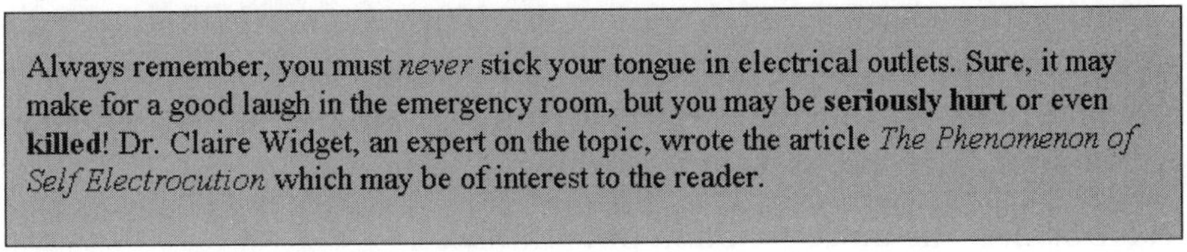

Always remember, you must *never* stick your tongue in electrical outlets. Sure, it may make for a good laugh in the emergency room, but you may be **seriously hurt** or even **killed**! Dr. Claire Widget, an expert on the topic, wrote the article *The Phenomenon of Self Electrocution* which may be of interest to the reader.

Figure 5.1   Logical styles

Table 5.1   Logical styles of general interest

<CITE>A citation, usually displayed in italics.

<DFN>The defining instance of a term, usually displayed as bold or bold italic.

<EM>Emphasize, usually displayed in italics.

<STRONG>Emphasize strongly, usually displayed as bold.

Table 5.2   Logical styles of interest to technical writers

<CODE>Example of programming code, usually displayed as a fixed-width font.

<KBD>Used to highlight key strokes a user may type, such as may be found in a computer manual.

<SAMP>A sequence of literal characters.

<VAR>A variable name, such as found in an example of programming code.

and how it *might* be displayed where possible, if the abilities of a given browser allow. All of the browsers in the following tables enclose text and thus have both start and end tags, but for brevity I've omitted the end tags. All end tags are identical to their respective start tags, with the addition of a forward slash after the "<" character.

If you absolutely have your heart set on having something displayed a certain way, such as italics or bold, HTML has graciously supplied some styles that are a lot more specific. Called *physical styles*, these allow you to specify *exactly* how you want something to appear. Of course, there is no guarantee that they *will* appear that way, but the Web browsers will do their best to display them exactly as you desire. Of course, if a browser or a piece of hardware like a terminal doesn't support italics, you won't get italics—and what you do get may be generic, or peculiar.

One caution: This is an imperfect world, and a lot of the early generation of Web browsers did not implement logical styles, and went right to physical styles instead. So if you do in fact do things the way HTML intends, you'll find that the older Web browsers simply ignore your logical styles and make a mess. Sometimes you can't win for losing—but the good news is that those older browsers are vanishing quickly.

Table 5.3 lists the more common physical styles.

Tim Berners-Lee suggests that Web authors use the physical styles as little as possible, and as he did come up with this whole World Wide Web idea in the first place, I'm certainly not one to argue. However, I do admit to being guilty of using physical styles a little more (well, perhaps a lot more) than I should. I think the best advice I can give here is, if you want to change the style of something which obviously has a logical style made for it, like the title of a book or a warning not to stick your tongue in an electrical socket, use the logical style. If, on the other hand, you don't see a

---

Table 5.3   Physical styles

<B>Display as bold

<I>Display as italics

<TT>Fixed-width font

<U>Underline (Not widely supported)

---

logical style that is immediately relevant and you really *must* have bold or italics, go for it. The HTML police probably won't kick your door in and haul you away.

Section Headings

By splitting our documents into paragraphs, we can hand our readers information in small, bite-sized chunks. Without paragraphs to group sentences into logical blocks of text, things would get confusing pretty quickly. Just as we use paragraphs to group sentences, we use *section headings* to group paragraphs.

Like a document's title, a section heading is a short description of the information to follow. Unlike the document title, headings are included in the body of the text and may appear as many times as needed.

There are six *levels* of headings, with level one being the largest and most emphatic, and level six being the smallest and least emphatic. Most graphical browsers will display level one headings in a very large font. As the headings approach level six, the font will become smaller and smaller. Of course, as with most things in HTML, there is no absolute guarantee that headings will be displayed like this, but it is a pretty good bet that they will. Certainly the most popular graphical browsers today, Mosaic and Netscape, follow this convention.

In order to create a heading, use the <Hn>...</Hn> tags, where the 'n' is the heading level, from one through six. For an example, take a look at the sample document in Listing 5.4 and Figure 5.2.

Listing 5.4   LIST5.4.HTM

```
<HTML>
<HEAD>
<TITLE>How to Make Cement</TITLE>
</HEAD>
<BODY>
<H1>How to Make Cement</H1>
<P>Contrary to what you may have heard, it is very easy to make cement.
<H2>What You Will Need</H2>
<P>Just about anything will do. Hunt around under your kitchen sink and grab a few
pots and pans, some soap, and a couple dozen sponges. You will also need some
grapefruit juice, a blender, and three pieces of toast. <EM>Don't burn the
toast!</EM>
```

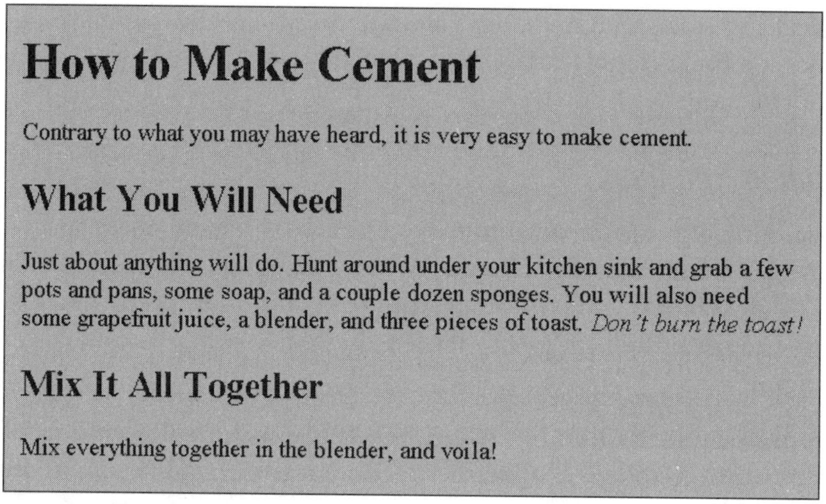

How to Make Cement

Contrary to what you may have heard, it is very easy to make cement.

What You Will Need

Just about anything will do. Hunt around under your kitchen sink and grab a few pots and pans, some soap, and a couple dozen sponges. You will also need some grapefruit juice, a blender, and three pieces of toast. *Don't burn the toast!*

Mix It All Together

Mix everything together in the blender, and voila!

Figure 5.2   HTML headings in action

```
<H2>Mix It All Together</H2>
<P>Mix everything together in the blender, and viola!
</BODY>
</HTML>
```

The first thing to notice here is that the first heading is identical to the title of the document. Since the document title is not actually displayed with the text of the document, it is common practice to restate the title as the first heading in your document. Of course, this is not a rule, but simply a practical suggestion! Your headings can be anything you want, as long as they reflect the content of the information beneath them. Another thing to notice is that there are two level-two headings here. This is perfectly legal, as there are no restrictions on the order or number of headings in a document.

There are some guidelines I like to recommend when using headings. First and foremost, even though headings are generally displayed using a much larger font than the rest of the document, don't use headings as an alternative to a "font size" type of command.

```
<P>This is a very <H1>important</H1> message!
```

The above line of HTML wil definitely *not* do what you would expect it to do. Since headings are designed as ways to separate sections of your document, they will always appear on a line by themself, so your paragraph will end up looking something like this:

This is a very

important

message!

Another important rule is that it is not recommended to use any style tags in a heading. For example, you should not use the <STRONG>...</STRONG> tags to make a heading stand out even more or <I>...</I> to make your headings italics. Heading styles are fixed—don't try to modify them!

The Horizontal Rule

There is one more way to split your document into even more sections, called the *horizontal rule.* A horizontal rule is simply a straight line that stretches from one end of your page to the other. The tag that displays a horizontal rule is <HR> and since we're not actually specifying text to alter in some way, it is an empty (that is, solo) tag. The <HR> tag is generally used on a line by itself as in Listing 5.5 and is a good way to separate the introduction to a document, for example, from the rest of the text, as shown in Figure 5.3.

Listing 5.5   The HR tag

```
<BODY>
<H1>How to Use a Horizontal Rule</H1>
<P>A horizontal rule is a straight line that stretches from one side of your
page to the other.
<HR>
<P>There is a lot more text here but I think we all get the idea.
</BODY>
```

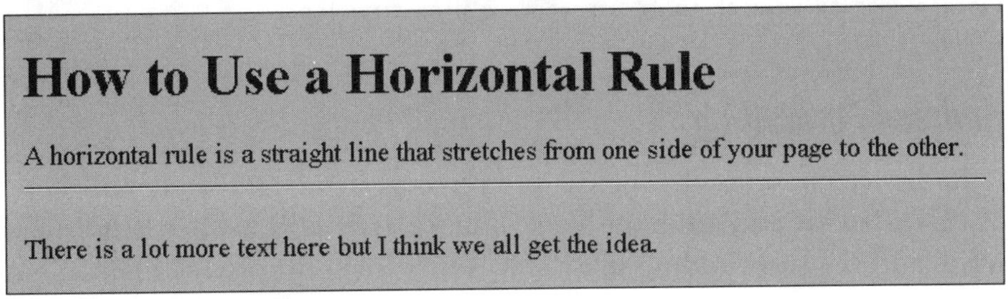

How to Use a Horizontal Rule

A horizontal rule is a straight line that stretches from one side of your page to the other.

There is a lot more text here but I think we all get the idea.

Figure 5.3   Horizontal rules

Blockquotes, Addresses, and Linebreaks

Right now, we already have the tools necessary to create a fairly readable HTML document. We can split text into paragraphs, group paragraphs under section headings, and highlight important words or phrases. We even know how to add horizontal rules to split our documents into even more sections. But there are still quite a few things we can't yet do. For example, how can we quote a section of text from another source, like part of a presidential speech or an interesting section of poetry?

The <BLOCKQUOTE>...</BLOCKQUOTE> element used in Listing 5.6 is designed to take a large section of text, such as a paragraph or two, and separate it from the rest of the surrounding paragraphs. One use of this element would be to quote an interesting section of poetry or literature. The quoted text is usually indented slightly from the rest of your document, and sometimes displayed in italics. (Again, how this element is interpreted may vary from one browser to another.) A blank line is automatically inserted before and after a blockquote, separating it even further from the rest of the document as shown in Figure 5.4.

Listing 5.6   The BLOCKQUOTE tag

```
<BODY>
<P>Dr. Lisa Johnson, the world's leading specialist on widget design, had this
to say about the recent trend in modern day widgets:
<BLOCKQUOTE>Although the widget has not changed much since its original design
by Dr. Widget, there have been some unfortunate alterations to its basic
structure. For instance, the addition of the detachable swing-gizmo to the
widget underside has rendered the widget nearly useless for mission critical
applications.
</BLOCKQUOTE>
From Dr. Johnson's statement above, it is obvious that current widget industry
leaders need to rethink their approach to widget design.
</BODY>
```

Address Formatting

With the exception of the logical and physical styles, all the elements I've discussed so far add an extra blank line, or *vertical space*, between themselves and the surrounding text. This is fine for splitting documents into separate sections, but how do we display something like a postal address, where that extra blank line interferes with the "flow" of the address?

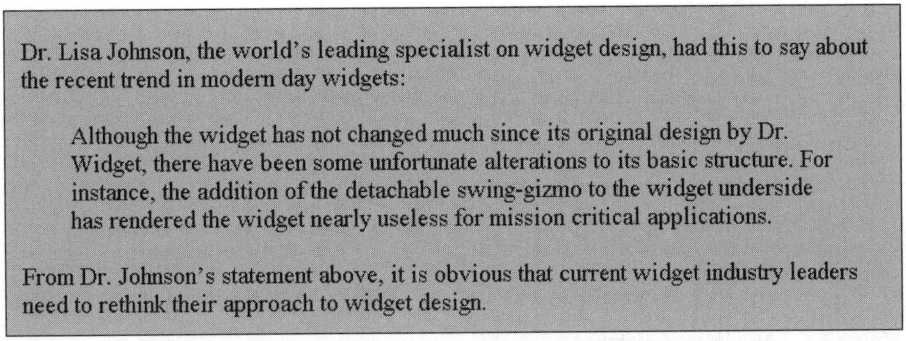

Dr. Lisa Johnson, the world's leading specialist on widget design, had this to say about the recent trend in modern day widgets:

> Although the widget has not changed much since its original design by Dr. Widget, there have been some unfortunate alterations to its basic structure. For instance, the addition of the detachable swing-gizmo to the widget underside has rendered the widget nearly useless for mission critical applications.

From Dr. Johnson's statement above, it is obvious that current widget industry leaders need to rethink their approach to widget design.

Figure 5.4   Block quotes in action

The <ADDRESS>...</ADDRESS> element in Listing 5.7 is used to mark some text as an address. An address may be displayed in italics, right justified, or indented. But this doesn't really solve our problem. Originally, it was suggested that paragraph breaks should not insert that extra space in this context, but browser authors ignore this advice and skip the space.

Listing 5.7   The ADDRESS tag

```
<ADDRESS>
Walter Smith
<P>555 Somewhere Street
<P>San Jose, CA 94086
</ADDRESS>
```

The address element may also be used for text signatures or to specify the author of some text. The first line in an address does not require a paragraph break, since the <ADDRESS> start tag will automatically insert one for you. You may want to add one anyway because some browsers use a *line break* instead. What's a line break? Our solution. Read on.

Listing 5.8   An address element under a rule

```
<BODY>
<P>There is no logical entity so simple that a lawyer cannot completely
obfuscate it. This is why I remained a bricklayer.  It is hard to obfuscate
a brick.  And if a lawyer happens by, I at least have something to throw.
<HR>
<ADDRESS>
Walter Smith
<P>555 Somewhere Street
<P>San Jose, CA 94086
</ADDRESS>
</BODY>
```

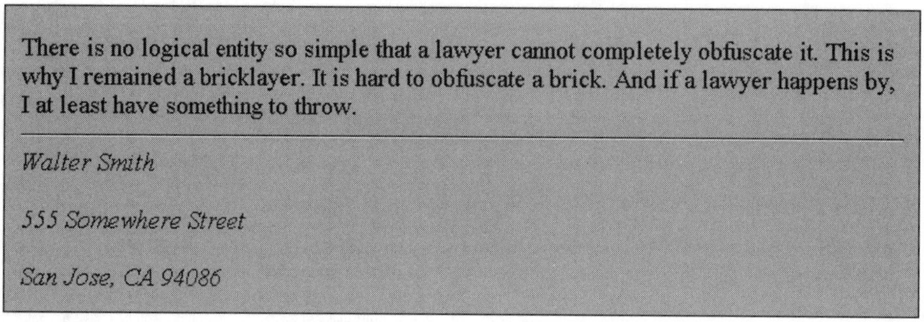

> There is no logical entity so simple that a lawyer cannot completely obfuscate it. This is why I remained a bricklayer. It is hard to obfuscate a brick. And if a lawyer happens by, I at least have something to throw.
>
> *Walter Smith*
>
> *555 Somewhere Street*
>
> *San Jose, CA 94086*

Figure 5.5   An address element

Line Breaks

There is a way to start a new line without adding an extra vertical space. The line break <BR> used in Listing 5.9 is an empty tag used to end a current line and start a new line directly beneath it. One usage of the line break would be to display a poem or song, where the lines are typically short and their placement is important to the flow of the poem or song.

Listing 5.9   The BR tag

```
<BODY>
In Xanadu did Kubla Khan<BR>
A Stately pleasure-dome decree:<BR>
Where Alph, the sacred river, ran<BR>
Through caverns measureless to man<BR>
Down to a sunless sea.
<HR>
<ADDRESS>
Samuel T. Coleridge
<P>Kubla Khan
</ADDRESS>
</BODY>
```

Since Web browsers automatically wrap long lines, and you have no idea how large any of your readers' screens are, it is recommended that line breaks be used only on very short lines, such as those shown in Figure 5.6. If the lines are "too long" and the browser wraps them before reaching your line break, you may not get the effect you are looking for. I would warn against the use of line breaks on lines longer than forty characters. Sixty characters would be pushing it, and anything longer is *really* asking for trouble.

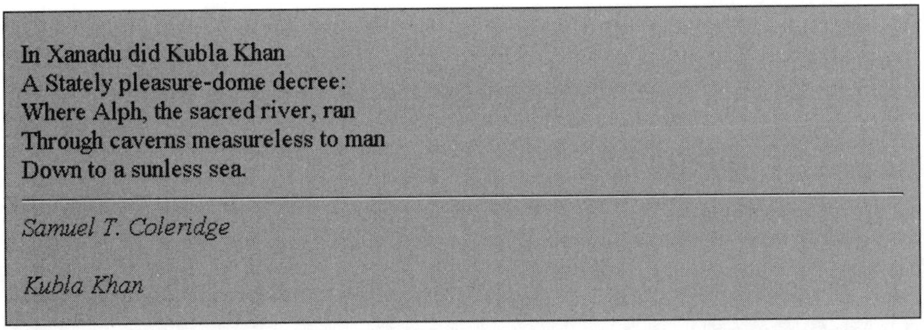

> In Xanadu did Kubla Khan
> A Stately pleasure-dome decree:
> Where Alph, the sacred river, ran
> Through caverns measureless to man
> Down to a sunless sea.
>
> ---
>
> *Samuel T. Coleridge*
>
> *Kubla Khan*

Figure 5.6   Line breaks

Lists and Menus

Lists are among the most efficient ways to convey written information without actually using charts, graphs, or pictures. Every day we make and use lists to group related items. We use shopping lists in the grocery store, lists of television programs in our living room, and lists of ingredients in the kitchen. The list is nearly endless. HTML provides us with five types of lists to choose from: ordered lists, unordered lists, menus, directories, and glossaries.

The *ordered list* consists of a series of numbered paragraphs, one beneath the other. To create an ordered list, use the start tag <OL>. Immediately following the start tag, either on the same line or the line directly beneath, insert the items in the list, each of which begins with the list item <LI> tag. The whole shebang is then closed with the ordered list end tag </OL>, like Listing 5.10.

Listing 5.10   An ordered list

```
<OL>
<LI>This is the first item
<LI>This is the second item
</OL>
```

The <LI> tag is empty, and can be considered a special-purpose replacement for the paragraph <P> tag in lists. As a matter of fact, it is illegal to use the <P> tag at all in some types of lists, like menus.

Lists may also be embedded in other lists, as shown in Listing 5.11. In other words, one of your list items can be a list itself, allowing you to create a structure much like a table of contents or an outline. Each "level" of the list is usually given a different type of numbering system. For example, the first level might use arabic numbers, the second level capital letters, the third lowercase letters, and so on. In addition, each level is usually indented a little more than subsequent levels, as shown in Figure 5.7.

Listing 5.11   Nested lists

```
<BODY>
<OL>
<LI>House
<OL>
<LI>Relatively small
<LI>Usually private building
</OL>
<LI>Office
<OL>
<LI>Can be quite large
<LI>Usually a public building
</OL>
</OL>
</BODY>
```

Unordered lists are almost identical to ordered lists, with the exception of the prefix character appearing ahead of each item in the list. Unordered lists use *bullets* at the start of list items. The first level of a list usually uses round bullets. The second level might use square bullets, and additional levels may use other shapes. To create an unordered list, use the <UL>...</UL> tags in place of the tags for an ordered list, as in Listing 5.12.

Listing 5.12   An unordered list

```
<UL>
<LI>This is one list item
<LI>This is another
</UL>
```

Where the ordered and unordered lists are designed to handle paragraph-sized sections of text in each list item, *menus* are used for lists containing short items,

```
1. House
    1. Relatively small
    2. Usually private building
2. Office
    1. Can be quite large
    2. Usually a public building
```

Figure 5.7   Nested lists for outline creation

usually a line or smaller. The theory is that with shorter items in the list, a more compact style may be used. The exact meaning of "more compact" is up to each browser, and honestly I've never noticed much of a difference. Regardless, menus should be used whenever your list items are a line (figure 40 or so characters) or shorter in length. Menus typically use bullets to prefix individual items, as with unordered lists.

Menus are created in exactly the same way as the other lists, using the start and end tags of <MENU> and </MENU> as in Listing 5.13. Menus may be nested, just like ordered and unordered lists.

Listing 5.13   A menu

```
<MENU>
<LI>Flashlight
<LI>Camera
<LI>Camping supplies
</MENU>
```

Directories and Glossaries

For lists with even shorter items than menus, we can use the *directory*. Items in a directory should be twenty characters or fewer in length, and the HTML draft suggests they be displayed in columns across your page, with a couple of spaces used to keep the items from flowing into one another. I rarely ever see this behavior, but that is what the draft recommends. How I usually see directories displayed is one item beneath the other, as with the other lists, but without any form of numbering or bullets.

The <DIR>...</DIR> tags shown in Listing 5.14 are used to specify a directory. Nesting lists inside a directory, though not expressly forbidden, is probably not a good idea. Since items in a directory are supposed to be displayed in columns, I can't quite imagine how nested directories would appear—except that I suspect they wouldn't work well as directories, or anything else.

Listing 5.13   The DIR tag

```
<DIR>
<LI>Up
<LI>Down
<LI>Left
<LI>Right
</DIR>
```

A *glossary*, sometimes called a *definition list*, is a set of *terms* with corresponding *definitions*. Just like the glossary in the back of a book, glossaries are typically rendered with the term in the left margin of the page, and its definition, on the same line, indented to the right. If the definition is long enough, it will be wrapped to the next line, aligned beneath the beginning of the previous line of the definition. If the term accidently stretches past the indentation point of the definition, the definition will be forced to start on the line directly *below* the term, indented appropriately. Generally, a blank line is inserted between each term/definition pair.

The procedure to create a definition list is slightly different than the other types of lists. First, the list is opened with the <DL> start tag. The first term is then started using the empty tag, <DT>. Immediately following the term, either on the same line or the line directly below, the definition is specified with the empty tag, <DD>. After some number of <DT>...<DD> pairs, the list is closed with the </DL> end tag. The example in Listing 5.15 is shown in Figure 5.8.

Listing 5.15   A glossary

```
<BODY>
<DL>
<DT>Pizza
<DD>A common food found on any webmaster's menu.  Pizza is supposed
to be Italian, but exactly how Italian pizza (as we know it today)
really is is lost in the mists of history.  Most historians believe
that pizza is as Italian as chop suey is Chinese, which is to say,
Americans invented both and then tried to pass the blame off on other
nations.
<DT>Beer
<DD>A drink which usually accompanies the consumption of pizza.
About beer there is more consensus.  Beer transcends all nationalities,
all times, all cultures, and all climates.  It is one of the
fundamental substances of creation, just one notch below earth, air,
fire, and water, along with its peers salt, sugar, and grease.
</DL>
</BODY>
```

Preformatted Text

You may be surprised to hear that, with the exception of one more element, you've now heard about every HTML element for formatting text.

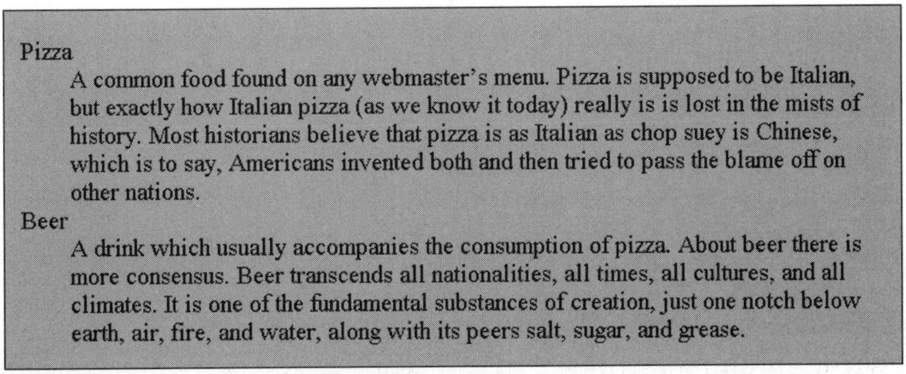

Pizza
    A common food found on any webmaster's menu. Pizza is supposed to be Italian,
    but exactly how Italian pizza (as we know it today) really is is lost in the mists of
    history. Most historians believe that pizza is as Italian as chop suey is Chinese,
    which is to say, Americans invented both and then tried to pass the blame off on
    other nations.
Beer
    A drink which usually accompanies the consumption of pizza. About beer there is
    more consensus. Beer transcends all nationalities, all times, all cultures, and all
    climates. It is one of the fundamental substances of creation, just one notch below
    earth, air, fire, and water, along with its peers salt, sugar, and grease.

Figure 5.8   Terms and their definitions

Ok, that's not quite true. There are a few more elements, and some variations on the ones we already know, but they are not yet part of standard
HTML. But since these "extensions" to HTML haven't been standardized
as of this time, I would like to talk about them in the later advanced-topics
chapters. Regardless, you may have noticed that there are still a few things
we do not know how to do, like creating simple charts and graphs.
Preformatted text can be used in those rare instances when HTML doesn't
specifically provide the answer.

Preformatted text is, as the name implies, text which has already been
formatted by other means outside the bounds of HTML. Specifically,
preformatted text is displayed using fixed-width fonts, and treats spaces
and newlines just as you would expect: as spaces and newlines. In other
words, multiple white spaces will not be collapsed, newlines really do go
on to new lines, and since the font is fixed-width, columns for charts and
graphs line up and stay lined up.

The <PRE>...</PRE> element creates preformatted text. Preformatted text
defaults to a line width of eighty columns, which may stretch off the edge
of the browser's screen. Don't worry about that; nearly all browsers will
allow the reader to scroll sideways to read that extra few characters. Ugly?
Yes, but simply the price we have to pay to use preformatted text. How, you
might ask, can we shorten the width of the columns, or increase them if
necessary? We use what is called an *element attribute.*

An element attribute is a keyword inserted inside a start tag, after the
element's name, to change the behavior of a particular element in some

way. The name of the attribute that specifies the width of preformatted text is WIDTH. A simple example of WIDTH in use within the PRE element is shown in Listing 5.16.

Listing 5.16   Using the PRE element

```
<PRE WIDTH="40">
This text would be
displayed            exactly        as it appears here, except lines will be
automatically
wrapped at forty characters if they do not end before then.
</PRE>
```

In the example in Listing 5.16, the WIDTH attribute is used to shorten the size of each line to forty characters. The quoted value "40," to the right of the equal sign, is called the *attribute value*. In this case, the attribute value tells the WIDTH attribute that we want to override the default 80 columns to 40 columns. Attribute values should always be surrounded by double (") quotes. Single quotes (') can be used as well, however, double quotes are much more common. Valid widths are usually 40, 80, and 132, with browsers rounding to the closest valid width.

There are a few rules regarding what other markup we can and can't use with preformatted text. The list for "can use" is, unfortunately, a lot shorter than the "can't use" list. We *can* use logical and physical text styles, plus *anchors*, which I will cover in the next chapter. We *cannot* use any paragraph breaks, line breaks, or any other element that formats text positionally, including headings, addresses, blockquotes, or lists. Remember, by using preformatted text, we've told HTML "Go away. We don't need your help!" and that's just what HTML will do.

There are quite a few good uses of preformatted text, besides charts and graphs, such as quickly inserting press releases, newspaper or magazine articles, and any other large chunk of text for which you don't have the time or inclination to convert to HTML properly. But please, don't use preformatted text as an excuse to be lazy. If you can do it with the other existing HTML elements, use them instead. Overuse of preformatted text, besides being ugly, reflects poorly on the skills of a webmaster and his or her company.

Anchors Aweigh!

Perhaps your company has graciously volunteered you to create a home page, and you're anxious to get moving. Or perhaps the sudden, unnatural desire to start a Web-based flashlight and fuzzy-dice users group has forced you into immediate action. Either way, by now you've had a chance to try some of the HTML you learned in the previous chapter. In the course of your experimentation, you may have noticed a few minor inconsistencies with what you learned in the previous chapter and how your favorite Web browser actually behaves. This is, unfortunately, to be expected. HTML is not a strongly established standard, and those who write browsers have taken some considerable liberties with the HTML spec.

A worse problem is the fluid state of HTML itself. The HTML DTD is what we call an *Internet draft*. Internet drafts are not actually "specifications," but works-in-progress. Some Internet drafts, like the ones for electronic mail, are fairly static, and change very infrequently. But since the Web is still (by comparison) in its infancy, the HTML draft is constantly in a state of change and flux. Further aggravating the problem is the unfortunate truth that the current HTML draft is painfully inadequate for many of the tasks that are asked of it. Some elements are added one month, removed another, and then tentatively penciled back in the next. Other elements become deprecated and removed, while new elements and features are added or enhanced. Realizing the confusion this would cause, the *Internet Engineering Task Force* (IETF), the people in charge of updating Internet drafts such as the drafts for HTML, decided to split HTML into different *levels*.

HTML Levels

Currently, the most commonly used level is HTML 2.0, which is what most of this book discusses. HTML 3.0, which adds quite a few desperately needed features to HTML, is being formed and molded into shape as we speak, but unfortunately is still too unstable to rely on. (There's nothing worse than slaving over a Web browser's C code for weeks to implement a new feature, only to find out the following week that that feature has been exiled from HTML entirely.) Therefore, almost no Web browsers even attempt to conform to HTML 3.0 at this time. To make things a tad more confusing, as of this writing, HTML 2.0 is *still* not "frozen" and small changes may be made at any time. What does all this mean? Simple: The Web browser that you use may be a little more, or a little less, conformant to HTML 2.0 than the next one. This is why it is extremely important that for your own, personal browsing, you use the most up to date version of your browser possible. I would also recommend that when testing the HTML you do write, to not only use the latest browsers to view your work, but perhaps see how things look on a slightly older browser just to make sure you are not doing something which completely disintegrates for those who are a little slow to upgrade.

HTML does have a saving grace that all browsers are required to obey. If the browser does not recognize an element, it must ignore it and display the text as though the tags in question weren't there at all. This allows documents that are written to the HTML 2.0 spec to be readable on browsers that can only understand HTML 1.0. (Nobody is still using browsers that old, right? Right.) But what about elements that are valid, but improperly used, for example, using a section heading in a list? The browser's only option is to display things as best it can, and with some luck everything turns out looking nice and pretty. Exactly how the browser handles these situations is, alas, completely undefined. Maybe your browser displays section headings used as list items in large, bold, pretty fonts, exactly as you want it. But another browser may decide "Oops! A section heading couldn't possibly be a list item. Let's display the section heading as normal, and treat the rest of the list as regular, unformatted text." Using the quirks of the way your browser displays improper HTML is both unpredictable and dangerous. Don't do it.

And with that said, let's burrow further into HTML.

Linking Documents Together

The ability to seamlessly link documents scattered across the globe puts the "web" in the World Wide Web. Using hypertext hotlinks, you can link documents to the other documents that you have created, to documents on other machines, and even to other Internet services like gopher and FTP. Links allow you to structure your web pages into a logical hierarchy of documents, and tie together resources from other machines in your own local network, or even the entire Internet.

HTML governs the creation of hyperlinks, just as it governs text formatting. The *anchor* element <A>...</A> allows you to specify a section of text, or (as I'll explain later) a graphic image, as a link. The anchor element has several attributes, the most important of which, HREF, is used to "attach" the anchor to a specific URL. In operation, the text or graphics made part of an anchor is formatted uniquely (by color or attributes like underlining) so that when a user clicks on the anchor or selects it some other way, the document or other item pointed to by the anchor will be loaded into the browser.

Listing 6.1   LIST6-1.HTM

```
<HTML>
<HEAD>
<TITLE>Linking Documents Together</TITLE>
</HEAD>
<BODY>
<P>For more information on widgets, you may want to contact
the <A HREF="http://www.widgetsoc.com/">Widget Society</A>.
</BODY>
</HTML>
```

The HREF attribute in Listing 6.1 tells the anchor, whenever the text "Widget Society" is selected, to retrieve the home page located at http://www.widgetsoc.com. The URL in this example is called an *absolute URL*, meaning that all the information needed to locate and retrieve the document is included within the URL. Using absolute URLs ensures that there is never confusion regarding which document you are requesting, but sometimes it may be convenient to use something a bit shorter, especially when adding a lot of links between your own documents. The *relative*, or *partial*, URL addresses this concern.

Relative URLs

Unlike absolute URLs, which will always point to the correct document no matter where you are, the information contained in relative URLs is only valid relative to the current document. In other words, the new document is found by comparing the relative URL given for that document with the absolute URL of the document the relative URL is being retrieved from.

Listing 6.2   LIST6-2.HTM

```
<HTML>
<HEAD>
<TITLE>Relative URLs</TITLE>
</HEAD>
<BODY>
<P>The document you are reading has an absolute URL of http://www.example.com/
example.html
and this document contains a link to another document using a <A HREF="mydir/
example2.html">
relative HRL</A>.
</BODY>
</HTML>
```

In the anchor shown in Listing 6.2, the relative URL within the anchor tag is *mydir/example2.html*. The first thing you may have noticed about the relative URL is its conspicuous lack of a scheme, such as "http://" found in the absolute URL example in Listing 6.1. Another omission is the name of the machine the document can be found on. Without this vital information, how does your Web browser know where to find the document?

To derive the location of the new document, the first thing your Web browser does is look at the URL of the source document (called the *context URL*, because it is the context within which the relative URL exists), in this case *http://www.example.com/example.html*. The context URL is basically the document currently loaded, the one the user is looking at. The filename of the document, *example.html*, is removed, leaving behind the domain address. Finally, the relative URL is appended to the end, yielding a new, absolute URL: *http://www.example.com/mydir/example2.html*.

Slash and Dots

The familiar slash "/" and double dot ".." can add additional flexibility to relative URLs. A relative URL that begins with a slash will replace everything to the right of the first *single* slash in the context URL. For example, a relative URL of */mydir/test.html* whose context URL is *http://host.com/adir/ bdir/example.html*, would translate to *http://host.com/mydir/test.html*.

A double dot in a URL indicates that the document is located in the directory *above* the current directory. The double dot thus works much as it does in the DOS and Unix directory pathnaming scheme. Using the same context URL *http://host.com/adir/bdir/example.html* but with a relative URL of *../mydir/test.html*, the translation to an absolute URL would be *http:// host.com/adir/mydir/test.html*. There is a third special character, the single dot, which simply means "current directory." A relative URL of *./stuff.html* with a context URL of *http://host.com/mydir/test.html*, would translate to *http:/ /host.com/mydir/stuff.html*. This behaves just as if the relative URL was only *stuff.html*. Again, echoes of the DOS/Unix pathnaming system!

Table 6.1 presents some examples of context and relative URLs, and how they resolve to a full URL.

Linking to a Specific Point within a Document

So far we are able to use anchors to create links to and from separate documents. This is a great thing, but one drawback is that whenever a user follows one of these links, it always brings them to the *top* of the new document. In

Table 6.1   Resolving relative URLs

Context URL	Relative URL	Resulting URL
http://host.com/home.html	test.html	http://host.com/ test.html
http://host.com/home.html	mydir/test.html	http://host.com/ mydir/test.html
http://host.com/mydir/doc.html	party/docs/test.html	http://host.com/ mydir/party/docs/ test.html
http://host.com/mydir/doc.html	../example.html	http://host.com/ example.html
http://host.com/a/b/c/doc.html	/test.html	http://host.com/ test.html
http://host.com/a/b/stuff.html	./power.html	http://host.com/a/b/ power.html

most cases, this is exactly what you want to do, but sometimes it is useful to not only take the user to the new document, but to a specific location *within* that document.

For example, suppose I have one giant document that lists all the employees in my company, their phone numbers, the locations of their offices, and some personal information on each employee. I may want to have an index listing in a separate file, containing only the names of each employee, with links from each employee name pointing to their entry in the main document. Right now, all we can do is point to the beginning of the master document—which doesn't make for a very useful index. One option would be to have a separate document for each employee, but for a large company that can take up an awful lot of disk space, and create a maintenance nightmare. A better solution would be to somehow mark the location of each employee's entry in the master document, and have a URL that would go directly to a specified employee's mark.

We can do it. Anchors have another attribute, called NAME, which allows you to place such a mark in a document. Using this special mark, you can specify a URL that will bring you directly to that point in the document:

```
<A NAME="123-45-6789">Carol Jennings</A> works in accounting.
```

In the example above, an anchor has been used to place a mark at the local of Carol Jennings' entry in the master document. The argument for the NAME attribute is, in this case, Carol's Social Security number. The browser uses this number to locate Carol's entry within the larger file. I chose to use a Social Security number, instead of Carol's name, because anchor names must be unique within the same document. If another Carol Jennings had an entry in the document, using the name "Carol Jennings" would confuse things a great deal! Of course, we can use the same anchor name in a different document.

It's a little like a database, in which a unique primary key is used to find a record within a dataset. Some unique value has to be used; it could as well be an employee ID number, or simply some value that you create yourself specifically for the purpose of acting as an index value into the Web document.

Fragment Navigation

Accessing Carol's entry in the document, called a *fragment* in webspeak, is slightly more complicated than accessing the full document, because we have to specify which fragment we want to move to. Let's say the URL of the entire document is *http://host.com/employees.html.* To access Carol's fragment, the URL would be *http://host.com/employees.html#123-45-6789.* A sample link to the fragment might look like this:

```
<A HREF="http://host.com/employees.html#123-45-6789">Carol Jennings</A>
```

From the pound sign "#" to the end of the URL is called the *fragment-ID.* It is this part of the URL that the client program uses to find the fragment, *after the client retrieves the entire document.* That last phrase is very important! The client retrieves the *entire* document first, and only then searches for the correct fragment within the document to display. The drawback of this is obvious; the entire document must be retrieved, regardless of its size. However, since the entire document is retrieved, the user is able to scroll to other parts of the document later on if desired.

Escaping "Bad Characters" within URLs

There is a certain small group of characters that have special meanings in a URL and thus cannot be part of a document or directory name. In order to avoid confusing the Internet addressing machinery in any number of client and server programs, these special characters, when found in a document or directory name, must be replaced with other distinctive character sequences. This process is often called *escaping* the special characters. "Escaping" is a Unix coinage from the notion of an *escape character,* which is some character used as a prefix to impart special significance to the character following it. In the ancient days of electromechanical Teletype communication, ASCII character 27 (called ESC for Escape) was often used as a lead-in to other characters with special meaning, hence the term.

The characters with special meanings in URLs are the "/" slash, "#" hash, "?" question mark, "+" plus sign, "%" percent sign, and plain ASCII space. It is obvious why the slash and hash signs must be excluded. Slashes are used to separate your URL into "segments whose relationships are hierarchical" (as the URL specification says), such as directories or folders. If a filename on your operating system can contain a slash, and you try to write a URL for that file, things are going to get confusing. Hash marks can also cause problems, unless they are being used for fragment-IDs, as explained earlier in this chapter. But what's so bad about question marks, pluses, percents, and spaces?

The use of spaces in document and directory names, though allowed in many operating systems, is almost always a difficult thing to accomplish. The one glaring exception is the Apple Macintosh OS, where spaces are not only allowed, but encouraged to promote readability in document names. Therefore, Macintosh users in particular may be tempted to include documents or folders with spaces in their names. While not forbidden, this is highly discouraged, because many non-Macintosh systems have so much difficulty handling spaces for document or directory names. Another less obvious problem arises when trying to communicate a URL to a friend or coworker through written means, or via email. Since most URLs are pretty cryptic to begin with, there are no visual clues as to the placement of spaces, such as your knowledge of where "real" words begin and end. Therefore, spaces in your URLs may be lost, forgotten, or misread on a handwritten memo or the back of a napkin from the local coffee shop. Through email, spaces may be lost as words are automatically wrapped, or extra spaces added or deleted by your email software. All in all, spaces in URLs are better off avoided.

As a substitute for spaces in URLs, we can use the "+" plus sign. A URL that might read as *http://www.host.com/Good Stuff/My Best File.html*, would turn into *http://www.host.com/Good+Stuff/My+Best+File.html* instead. Now, this is not saying that you cannot use spaces in your file or directory names, just that when those names are incorporated into URLs, the spaces should be replaced with pluses. This, alas, points to the reason why plus signs must now be escaped. Since plus signs encountered within URLs are read to mean spaces, some way to represent plus signs (as well as the other special characters such as the slash and hash) inside document names must be devised.

The slash, hash, and plus sign may be escaped by using the percent sign "%," called the *escape character*, immediately followed by the *hexadecimal notation* for the character being escaped. All programmers will likely be familiar with hexadecimal notation, and if you're not, forgive me if I don't explain it exhaustively here. In brief, hexadecimal is a way of encoding values in base 16 rather than our familiar base 10. Instead of spending any further space and energy explaining hexadecimal notation, I will simply provide in Table 6.2 the hexadecimal notation for all the special characters you may have to worry about in HTML work. There is also a full set of all the characters in the ISO-Latin-1 character set in Appendix B, with their hexadecimal notation included.

Using the percent sign and the character's hexadecimal notation, you are now able to substitute %2B for the plus sign in your URLs. So, if you had a document named Sue+John.html located in the directory My Friends, the URL would be *http://host.net/My+Friends/Sue%2BJohn.html.*

Whoops, here comes another problem: What if we actually want a percent sign? If you tried to create a URL for a document named Give100%.html, the percent sign would be interpreted as the escape character. Once again, using hexadecimal notation, we would have to substitute %25 for the percent sign. A sample URL with this document might be *http://host.gov/Taxes/Give100%25.html.*

Character entities are characters in the ISO-Latin-1 character set that can be difficult to produce on many keyboards. Those same characters are also valid in URLs, but the same problem exists: How to represent them? No difference: By using the percent escape, and the character's hexadecimal notation. Creating a URL for a document named *mañana.html* becomes a trivial task. Since, according to ISO-Latin-1, the hexadecimal notation for "ñ" is F1, a sample URL for this document might be *http://host.net/calendar/ma%F1ana.html.* Fortunately for most webmasters, this type of character juggling will rarely be necessary. But if you ever need to know how, there it is.

In general, avoid using characters that must be escaped within document names and directories. As a general rule, I recommend doing it only when

Table 6.2   Hexadecimal notation of characters with special meanings within URLs

Character	Hexadecimal Notation
#	23
%	25
+	2B
/	2F
?	3F

you have been handed the oddly-named material and have no choice but to keep the odd naming conventions intact. Otherwise, you're simply making more work and maintenance headaches for yourself.

External Images, Sounds, and Movies

Though I have been using the term "documents" here to mean text documents, or specifically text HTML documents, a document can be almost any type of file that you can store on your server. Image files (usually *GIF* or *JPEG* file types) are the most common non-HTML documents found on the Web. Sound files (usually *AU* files) are a close second. And if you really hunt around, you may be lucky enough to run into a few movie clips!

The way that anchors link to non-HTML documents is identical to the way they link to HTML documents. Listing 6.3 shows a sample document with links to both a sound file and a graphic image. When the user selects one of these links, the browser will automatically launch what we call a *helper program* to load and display, or play, the graphic or sound file. Helper programs are external utilities, entirely distinct from the Web browser, which specialize in presenting the non-HTML document in question. For example, one popular helper program to view GIF and JPEG images is LVIEW. When a link pointing to a GIF or JPEG image is selected, the user's browser will automatically launch LVIEW and hand it the image, saying in effect "Would you kindly display this image for me?"

Listing 6.3   LIST6-3.HTM

```
<HTML>
<HEAD>
<TITLE>An Example of External Images and Sounds</TITLE>
</HEAD>
<BODY>
<H1>An Example of External Images and Sounds</H1>
<HR>
<P>The author, <A HREF="robertm.gif">Robert Jon Mudry</A> (23k), has
enjoyed a presence on the Internet for over four years. The pronounciation
of his last name, <A HREF="mudry.au">Mudry</A> (14k), is a subject of much
confusion. It is MUHD'ree, though he is usually happy with anything even
remotely close. Another point of confusion is his first name. It is Robert,
not Bob.
</BODY>
</HTML>
```

An Example of External Images and Sounds

The author, <u>Robert Jon Mudry</u> (23k), has enjoyed a presence on the Internet for over four years. The pronounciation of his last name, <u>Mudry</u> (14k), is a subject of much confusion. It is MUHD'ree, though he is usually happy with anything even remotely close. Another point of confusion is his first name. It is Robert, not Bob.

Figure 6.1   Size indicators on audio and graphics links

Warning: Monster File Coming!

The HTML document in Listing 6.3 is fairly straightforward. One oddity you might notice, however, are the document sizes in parentheses next to the links. (See Figure 6.1 for the text as a Web browser would display it. The Web browser itself has been cropped out of the picture.) Since images and sound files can be very large, it is considered polite to state their approximate sizes to the right of the link, as a sort of warning to people with slow Internet connections. This is a courtesy on your part and is by no means required, but the first time you personally stumble upon a link that leads to a 500 K image or a 5.8 MB sound file, and try to retrieve it with your 14.4 K modem, you'll appreciate these little warnings! Since the vast majority of people only have 14.4 K or (at best) 28.8 K modem connections to the Internet, you will probably make a lot more friends by including this simple warning.

If the size of images and sound files is an important consideration, then it goes tenfold for movie clips. A typical MPEG movie can be anywhere from 500 K to several megabytes in size. A minute of full-motion video can be upwards of 10 or 12 megabytes, and sitting in front of my computer screen for over an hour for one of these things to crawl through my 14.4 K modem is *not* my idea of an afternoon well spent. Even on my 56 Kbps frame relay line at work, a 10 MB transfer is not particularly pleasant.

It's a worse matter than simply one of user inconvenience. Not only are large movies and large images or sound files hard on your users, but they can create havoc on your own Internet connection. Imagine trying to serve five copies of a 10 MB movie file at the same time, all on your tiny 56 K frame relay connection? Everyone is going to suffer! With this in mind, serving movies on your own Web pages is something to be done sparingly, and *always* with a warning of their size directly to the right of the link.

Linking to Nonstandard Files

If anchors can be used to link to almost any type of file, can we link to, for example, Postscript or Microsoft Word documents? Well, yes and no. Technically, you can link to any sort of file you care to. The problem is, should you really expect your users to be able to view Postscript and Microsoft Word documents? Imagine if just to browse the Web, you had to own Microsoft Word, Wordperfect, Excel, 1-2-3, Notes, PowerPoint, a Postscript viewer, and so on and on.... Things would get pretty confusing, not to mention expensive! That, furthermore, is assuming those programs are even available for your computer. Now this sort of setup may be fine for an internal company Web site, only meant to be browsed by your company's employees, when you know those helper applications are available. But for the Internet at large, there must be a simpler solution.

In general, only a small number of document types should be used. For example, there are dozens of different file formats for graphic images, but for simplicity, you should assume that only GIF and JPEG images are widely viewable in the Internet outback. Of course, if the rebel in you decides that you're going to use TIFF files instead, no one will stop you—just don't expect to have a very popular Web site. It is with this in mind that I present Table 6.3, listing all the generally accepted document types.

Inline Images

Inline images definitely put the glitz in the Web. Unlike external images, which are accessed using anchors, just as though they were separate HTML documents, inline images are a part of the document, displayed automatically by your browser without the need to launch a helper application. Inline images can be used to illustrate your documents, as special bullets

Table 6.3 Generally accepted document types

Data Type	Popular	Less popular
Graphics	GIF or JPEG (sometimes JPE or JPG)	TIFF
Sounds	AU or WAV	SND
Movies	MPEG (sometimes MPE or MPG)	QT or MOV

for lists, for fancier horizontal rules, as mastheads for your pages, and dozens of other creative applications. How do you include your company logo at the top of your home page? A picture of your cat Fluffy? Tiny icons representing your links? Inline images make all this possible.

Including inline images in your documents is easy. Using the image element, <IMG>, you can specify the source file's URL with the SRC attribute. For example, to include an inline image of your pet rat, Valentine, you would use the following:

```
<IMG SRC="valntine.gif">
```

Since <IMG> is an empty element, there is no end tag. It's as simple as that!

Alternate Text for the Graphically Challenged

For our graphically challenged users, the ALT attribute exists to allow you to provide an alternate, textual description of the image for the benefit of the user who is unable to view graphics. You are not *required* to include an ALT attribute; however, it is strongly recommended, otherwise your users may end up scratching their heads, wondering what in the world you mean by the text line, "She is sweet, but has an insatiable appetite for Mountain Dew" beneath an image they can't see. Without providing alternate text, your non-graphical users would see either nothing at all, or simply the word "[IMAGE]." The ALT attribute makes your IMG element look like this:

```
<IMG SRC="valntine.gif" ALT="[Image: My pet rat Valentine.]">
```

There are no hard, set rules for what your alternate text should be. Personally, I prefer to surround the text in square brackets to offset it from the rest of the document. Preceeding the description by "Image:" will make things even clearer. Note that only people who cannot or do not choose to view inline images will view the ALT text.

Another attribute you may want to take note of is ALIGN. Without using a paragraph or line break, text will continue along on the same line as your image. The ALIGN attribute allows you to specify the position where the text will start: At the top, middle, or bottom of the image. Without using ALIGN, by default your text will align with the bottom of the image. To be perfectly frank, ALIGN is not as useful as it first seems. For an example of why, take a look at Listing 6.4 and the screen shot of its output in Figure 6.2.

Listing 6.4   LIST6-4.HTM

```
<HTML>
<HEAD>
<TITLE>Inline Images Example</TITLE>
</HEAD>
<BODY>
<P><IMG SRC="valntine.gif" ALT="[Image: My pet rat Valentine.]" ALIGN="top">
My pet rat, Valentine, chomping away on some left over cheese from my taco.
Yes, rats DO like cheese, just like in the cartoons, and if you tasted that
taco, its proof positive they will eat <EMP>anything</EMP>! Well, she did
like Mountain Dew, so at least she had some hope!
</BODY>
</HTML>
```

Pretty sad, huh? Why, when the text is aligned with the top of the image, the very next line of text is started *underneath* the image, and doesn't wrap around the side of the image as it should, is simply beyond me. But this is how ALIGN works, and we are stuck with it for now. Perhaps a future refinement of the HTML spec will correct this issue; it certainly needs correcting!

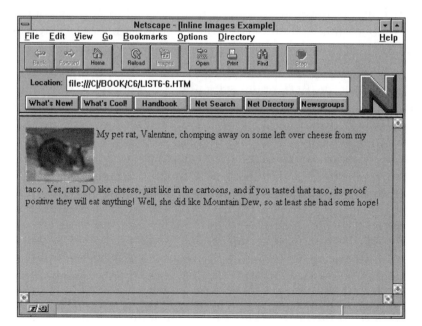

Figure 6.2   The problem with ALIGN

Inline Image File Types

I keep using GIFs in my inline image examples for a good reason. GIF images are the *only* images that are guaranteed to be viewable on any browser capable of displaying inline images. Once upon a time, the X Windows bitmap format (XBM) was also popular, but alas, in spite of the benefits of this simple format, it is rarely used anymore, probably because Microsoft Windows has eclipsed Unix in terms of sheer numbers of Web browser users. If you are viewing an HTML document written by a Web "old-timer," you may still see inline XBM images, but unfortunately a good deal of the Web community has abandoned them. On a brighter note, there is serious talk about allowing JPEG inline images sometime in the future. JPEG images tend to be smaller and transfer much more rapidly. But don't be tempted to use JPEGs for your inline images quite yet!

If you go ahead and use inline image formats other than GIF, such as Windows BMP or JPEG, almost all of your users will see what is affectionately known as the *broken image icon* in its place. Whatever visual point you were trying to make will not get across, and your Web site's reputation will suffer. The broken icon image is also displayed when you specify the wrong URL for your image—so if you use non-GIF formats, a great many Web users will assume you don't know how to put a URL together!

Mastheads, Icons, and Fancy Rules

Besides the obvious use of inline images for general illustrations, such as product shots or pictures of your cat, there are three other popular applications for inline images: mastheads, icons, and fancy horizontal rules.

Your masthead, which usually contains your company name and logo (or some other fancy image containing your "Web identity") is typically displayed at the very top of your home page. A simpler masthead, perhaps a "stripped down" version of the masthead on your home page, is often included at the top of every other important page on your Web site. Listing 6.5 shows an example of a masthead as called out in an HTML document, and Figure 6.3 shows how it looks on the browser screen.

Listing 6.5   LIST6-5.HTM

```
<HTML>
<HEAD>
<TITLE>Gizmo Inc Home Page</TITLE>
</HEAD>
<BODY>
<IMG SRC="masthead.gif">
<H1>Gizmo Inc Home Page</H1>
<P>Welcome to the Gizmo Inc Home Page!
<P>Now go away..
</BODY>
</HTML>
```

The masthead for your home page should be small, in terms of both screen area and physical size on disk. A good masthead might stretch roughly from one end of your browser's window to the other, and take up no more than one third the height of the window. Its size should be no more than 10 K or 20 K, and 50 K is definitely pushing the limits. Of course, all this is quite subjective. For one thing, users can resize their browser windows to whatever proportions they like, so firm suggestions as to the size and proportions of your masthead would be very difficult to follow. I think the key

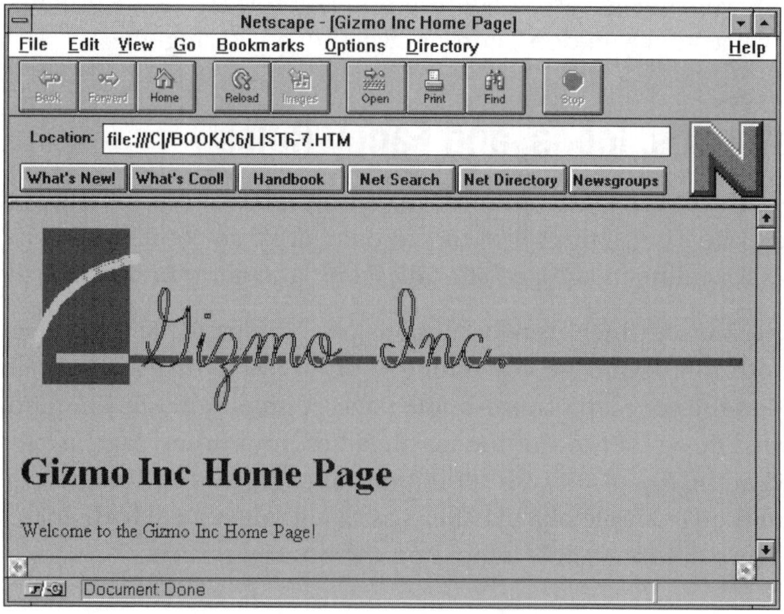

Figure 6.3   A home page masthead

point with your masthead is that it shouldn't take forever to load, and shouldn't dominate your page and distract the user from your page's content.

Fancy Horizontal Rules

Once you have designed your mastheads with your favorite paint program, you may decide that the default horizontal rule, a simple straight line, doesn't quite cut it. And there is absolutely nothing wrong with using inline images to replace them. Unfortunately, since horizontal rules typically stretch from one end of the window to the other, and you really have no idea how wide any given user's window is, choosing a size for a fancy inline image rule can be just about as tricky as designing a generalized masthead.

Horizontal rules do have one advantage, however, over mastheads: They can stretch off the right edge of the window and they will still look good. Don't be afraid to make them longer than you think you need, since if they are too long they will simply vanish off the edge of the screen without disrupting anything else. Of course, if you want something important at the right edge of the rule, such as a page number or your company's logo, this may still be a problem. If you don't want to move them to the left side of the rule, then the only other advice I can give is to make your rules exactly as wide as your masthead. Figure 6.4 shows a few samples I've discovered, which are whimsical takeoffs on the original boring horizontal line most people still use.

Icons from Inline Images

Icons add character to your pages without ravenously consuming system resources. A small image, a dash of color, and a bit of personality rarely hurt. Icons can be freestanding, drawing attention to special or important text, or they can even be a part of a link and "clickable," like a button. Misused, icons can, however, be eyesores, senseless bandwidth hogs, and your users' worst nightmare. They can clutter your page, or compliment it. They can clarify, or confuse. In other words, icons, when used correctly and sensibly, can transform an otherwise mundane page into a work of art—and when used incorrectly and haphazardly, can take a potentially useful page and turn it into useless trash.

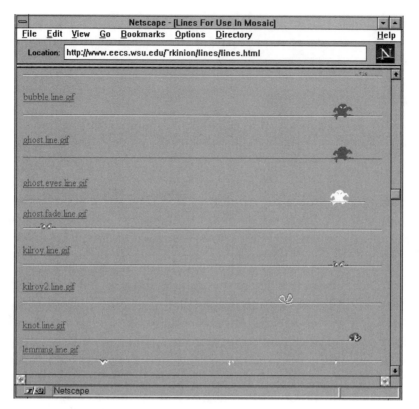

Figure 6.4   Samples of fancy horizontal rules

The three pitfalls inherent in icon design are overuse, size, and inconsistent style. Perhaps the most irritating of these is the simple overuse of icons, or of inline images in general. On a page making excessive use of icons, *everything* seems to have an icon associated with it. Sometimes icons are even scattered about for no logical reason other than just to include another icon on an already cluttered page. You can tell a page is suffering from icon overuse when it seems as though there is actually more space devoted to icons than to text. Icons are supposed to be used to draw your attention to important items, and outline a structure for your page. With too many icons strewn across your page, the eye has no focus. The big picture is lost while the user is busy trying to decipher a storm of seemingly unrelated mini-images. Figure 6.5 shows an example which is by no mean contrived!

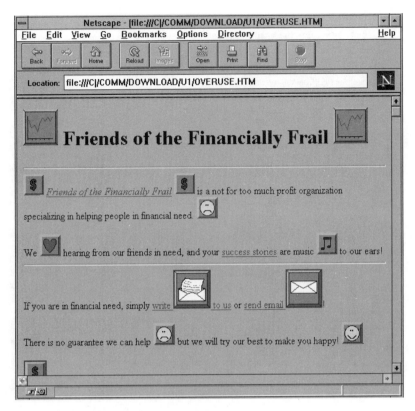

Figure 6.5   A page exhibiting terminal iconitis

Pages suffering from icon overuse almost always seem to suffer from the inconsistent style pitfall as well. Inconsistent style is a simple problem: All your stylistic elements seem unrelated and pulled out of a hat totally at random. Just like a painting inherits its personality from the artist, each icon has its own personality, inherited from its creator. When icons are borrowed from a dozen different clipart collections and icon archives, or drawn by several people sharing different visions or concepts of how your page should appear, your page will have a certain schizophrenic feel. Some icons might be black and white images drawings, others might be color, and some might be miniature digitized images. Other indications would be icons with radically different sizes, shapes, or general styles, such as 3-D mixed heedless with 2-D. Figure 6.6 is an excellent example of a Web page with a raging identity crisis.

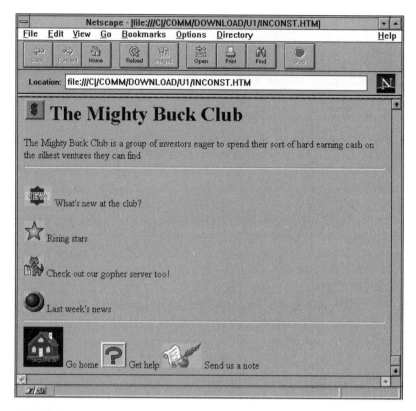

Figure 6.6   The heartbreak of inconsistent page style

Even if your icons all have the same general style, your page may still suffer from an inconsistent style problem. Do the icons look as though they were drawn by the same person who drew the page's masthead? Does the masthead have the same general style as the icons? Do your icons look out of place, as though they were simply not created just for your page, and are they out of character with the feeling you are trying to convey with your pages? All these are symptoms of inconsistent style, and perhaps even a lack of focus for your pages in general. If you don't have a good feel for this sort of aesthetic judgement, get help from a competent graphic artist or designer!

The final pitfall, size, is certainly the most straightforward to define—and fix. Icons that are too large, by which I mean up in the middling kilobytes somewhere, can turn your page into a bandwidth-sucking nightmare. No one wants to sit and stare at a spinning globe or throbbing "N" for more than fifteen or twenty seconds, only to discover that all that time was wasted waiting for a bunch of bloated icons to march down the line, carrying no useful content on their ugly little backs. If your icons average more than 5 K each, they are too large. Heaven forbid they exceed 10 K or 15 K! And if you have an overused icon problem as well, you are in big trouble. Until everyone has two channels of ISDN piped into their homes (and maybe even then!), keep your icon sizes as small as possible.

I certainly hope that despite all the warnings given above, I haven't scared you into being *too* timid with icons! Icons, and inline images in general, are wonderful tools to liven up your pages and give them a feeling of structure and personality when used well, as in Figure 6.7.

Figure 6.7   Icons used well

Icons Inside of Anchors

In my mind, icons can have one of two states: inside of anchors and out-side of anchors. When icons are placed next to an important anchor, they give users a graphical representation of where that link may take them. Those links stand out, transformed from a boring footnote to an item of interest, screaming out to be clicked on. So, what does the user do? Clicks the *icon,* of course. After all, most of us have been taught to click *the icon,* not the text *next to* the icon. After a few moments where nothing happens it will dawn on even the slowest user to click the link and not the icon, but the whole thing just feels awkward. The fix, of course, is to make the icon a part of the anchor. This is easily done, as Listing 6.6 illustrates. Figure 6.8 shows what this looks like on the browser screen.

Listing 6.6 LIST6-6.HTM

```
<HTML>
<HEAD>
<TITLE>Icons in Anchors</TITLE>
</HEAD>
<BODY>
<P><IMG SRC="music.gif" ALT="[*]" ALIGN="middle"> <A HREF="alink.html"> Icon
not in anchor</A>
<P><A HREF="alink.html"><IMG SRC="music.gif" ALT="[*]" ALIGN="middle"> Icon is
in anchor</A>
<P><A HREF="alink.html"><IMG SRC="music.gif" ALT="[*]" ALIGN="middle"></A>
<A HREF="alink.html">
Icon and text are in separate anchors, but point to the same place</A>
</BODY>
</HTML>
```

With the elimination of that problem, we've now created two more. First, when an inline image is inside an anchor, almost all browsers will put some sort of thick, ugly box around it, the same color as a normal text link. (Typically, blue.) As though that were not bad enough, quite a few brows-ers will also try to extend the underline, used to distinguish links from normal text, right up to that ugly box it just drew around your beautiful icon. (Again, see Figure 6.8 for an example.) All in all, it's quite an ugly effect. If you want to eliminate that little extra bit of underline, your only choice is to make the icon and text separate anchors, as shown in the final example in Listing 6.6 and Figure 6.8. It's a lot of extra typing (and addi-tional opportunities to type things wrong, sigh) without a whole lot to be gained from it, if you ask me.

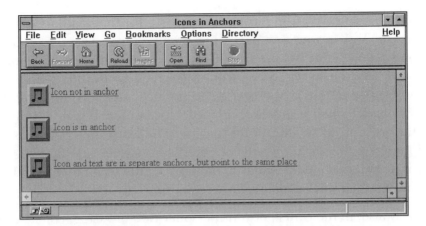

Figure 6.8   Icons as anchors

Finding and Using Existing Icons and Images

Creating your own icons can be a tedious and frustrating experience. First, you need some sort of paint program to actually draw the icon. A good paint program can run you anywhere from free to hundreds of dollars, depending on the program's features. Once you've found a good paint program, you need to sit down and actually plan out and draw the icon. Since most pages have more than one icon, designed to represent different links and features on your page, you will probably have to design four, five, or more icons. Definitely a time-consuming process. Finally, you need some sort of artistic talent. If you're anything like me, this may be a bit of a problem. Creating great art in a space sixteen pixels on a side is a talent lodged in a gene most of us seem born without.

One way to acquire icons, for free of course, is to find public icon, clip art, and horizontal rule (the technical term is *lines*) archives. Fortunately, such archives do exist, free of charge, on the Web. The good people at *http://www.yahoo.com/* maintain an index of icon, clip art, and line archives. Simply connect to their home page, and explore around a bit (it is under Computers, World_Wide_Web, Programming, Icons) or go directly to the icon index at *http://www.yahoo.com/Computers/World_Wide_Web/Programming/Icons/* and hunt around until you find some icons that suit your needs. One of my favorites is the graphics archives at "Enders Realm." Good stuff!

A word of warning on using icons (or anything for that matter) that you find on the Web in your own pages. Just because the icons found in these archives are available for use free of charge, does not necessarily mean they are free from terms. Some icon artists request as little as an email saying where the icons are being used, to as much as an acknowledgement and link back to their page wherever the icons are used. If in doubt, always ask the artist or maintainer of the archive. The worst they can say is no, and there are literally thousands of other icons to choose from. Regardless, it is always a good idea to drop the artist a little email thanking them for making their work available for free on the Web.

You may also, in the course of your personal Web browsing, come across an icon or image that is not in an archive, but you absolutely can not live without. It is always polite, and probably legally prudent, to ask before you use! Conversely, you may run into an icon *you* made on someone else's pages. Don't explode and run for your lawyers! Personally, *I* would be flattered, but if you are really opposed to their usage, a polite email to the offending webmaster should do the trick.

Transparent GIFs

If you are still interested in creating your own icons, either you have some real artistic talent or else a team of graphics designers working for you. Either way, you probably already have all the tools you need to create good-looking icons. One useful tool you may *not* have, however, is a program to create *transparent GIFs*.

Transparent? Say what? Once again, a knotty Internet standards problem can be solved by this remarkable idea. Here's the problem: There are dozens of different Web browsers, available for many different operating systems. Since there is no standard dictating the background color for Web documents, you really have no way of knowing the color background against which your icons and images will be displayed. So how do you create an icon with a shape other than pointy-cornered square, and have it blend in to the background color of your pages? One way is simply to take a guess as to what color background your image will be viewed on, and set the background color of your GIF accordingly. Your two best guesses would be either white, or some shade of light gray, since those are the colors most often used for backgrounds. However, you can never really be sure—except to be sure that some of your users will see strangely-colored "ears" at the corners of your rounded icons.

By creating a transparent GIF, you are able to leave the decision up to the browser, which obviously knows what its own background color is. The theory is, you pick a color, typically a light gray, and use that as the background color for your GIF icon or image. Then, when you have finished creating your icon, you tell a special program which background color you want to be made transparent, and the program will convert that color within the GIF into a transparent color value. When the GIF is then displayed, the background color, which you set as transparent, will become the exact same color as the browser's background color.

This would be wonderful if all browsers knew how to display transparent GIFs, but of course, not all can. That is why you're best off choosing light gray to be the GIF's background color. If the browser does not know how to display a transparent GIF, it will simply use the original color, and since light gray is a pretty common background color, your GIF will be displayed correctly for a large number of users at very least.

According to one of the FAQs on creating transparent GIFs, the best shade of light gray to use for the background color in your GIF, in case a given browser cannot display transparent GIFs, is RGB value 207,207,207. Personally, I have had far better luck using 192,192,192 since I find it more closely matches the default background color for NCSA Mosaic and Netscape.

Figure 6.9 shows two GIF images, one having a transparent background, and the other having a plain white background. The idea is to show colored text against the plain browser background color, without any sort of bounding line or space around the text. The text on a white background will appear unbounded when displayed on a browser configured for a white background—but everyone else will see colored text against a white rectangle.

Completely blank GIF bitmaps set entirely to the transparent color have been used to space multiple bitmaps across a page. Theoretically, such GIFs are always invisible—except, of course, when displayed on a browser

Figure 6.9   Transparent and non-transparent GIF backgrounds

that doesn't understand the transparent color. At that point, what the user sees is up for grabs.

I've included on the companion CD GIF Trans, which can create transparent GIFs, along with specific instructions for its use.

7

Authoring Tools

Now that you've become at least a little familiar with HTML, you've probably also seen how easy it is to use HTML, even in writing new documents from scratch—and certainly in converting existing documents into attractive Web pages. All you need is a simple text editor and you're on your way! Can Web page creation get any easier? In fact, yes. A number of products are available, both free and commercial, to assist you with your HTML authoring tasks.

I've split these products, called *authoring tools*, into three classifications:

- *Editors*, which can be thought of as HTML-specific word processors, some with the ability to verify that your HTML is actually valid

- *Converters*, to convert documents from one format, perhaps from a popular word processor or desktop publishing system, into HTML

- *Templates* and other similar add-on products for your favorite word processor, such as Microsoft Word.

If you're armed with any of these tools, your job as webmaster will become a *lot* easier.

Don't Foresake "Manual" HTML

Now that I've told you about the wide availability of Web authoring tools, some of which can do almost all the work of creating HTML for you, you might be a bit irritated with me for forcing you to learn HTML in the previous chapter. I know what you're thinking: If I can create HTML without actually *using* HTML, why bother to *learn* HTML?

My philosophy is simple in this regard: It's unwise to rely on tools as a replacement for old-fashioned knowledge. It's the difference between a "true" webmaster and someone who simply tosses a few amateurish documents onto the Web. I'm not suggesting you shouldn't use the tools that are available—of course you should. But even if you have a well-stocked arsenal of Web authoring tools, you still won't have the full authoring power that's available when you code directly using HTML—with all the "big picture" understanding of HTML that using HTML directly implies.

In addition, the authoring tools that I'll explore in this chapter are operating-system dependent, which means you might not be able to take advantage of some of them if you're using the "wrong" operating system. Worse, if you become dependent on a particular tool rather than on full knowledge of HTML, when you move to a new platform where your chief tool doesn't exist, you leave some hard-won skills behind you. Almost all of the authoring tools available are for Windows 3.1, the Mac, and Windows NT. There's practically nothing available for Unix, which is what most people still currently use as their Web server operating platform. If you're renting space on an ISP instead of using your own equipment, odds are that you're using a Unix machine as your server. And the fact that most tools are for Windows 3.1 is particularly frustrating since Windows 3.1 is an *awful* choice for a Web server platform. This means you will use most of your authoring tools run on a machine other than the one where your Web pages are actually stored, so you'll have to transfer your files to the destination system when you've finished creating and/or editing them. Major inconvenience! If you know HTML, however, it's easy to make a quick change or knock out a small document or two without having to juggle files back and forth between machines.

Windows NT and the Mac OS are increasingly becoming popular operating system choices for Web servers. As I explained in Chapter 4, good servers are available for both of these operating systems, and lots of good authoring tools will run directly on Windows NT and the Mac. But if you're forced to use Unix, you're largely limited to using HTML directly, if only just to make quick changes to your documents. Table 7.1 provides a list of many of the authoring tools that are available, along with brief descriptions of each tool. Many of these (and others as well) can be found on Yahoo, Falken's Maze, and CERN on the Internet. You might want to refer back to this table as you read through this chapter.

Table 7.1 HTML editors, templates, and converters

Name	Type of Tool	Platform	Price	More information
WebWeaver	Editor	Mac	$25.00	http://www.potsdam.edu/Web.Weaver/About.html
HTML Grinder	Editor	Mac	$75.00	http://www.matterform.com/mf/grinder/htmlgrinder.html
HoTMetaL	Editor	PC, Mac, Unix	Free/$195.00	http://www.sq.com/
HTML Assistant	Editor	PC	Free/$99.95	ftp://ftp.cs.dal.ca/htmlasst/htmlafaq.html
Internet Assistant	Template	Word 6 for Windows	Free	http://www.microsoft.com/pages/deskapps/word/ia/default.htm
BBEdit HTML Extensions	Template	BBEdit for Mac	Free	http://www.uji.es/bbedit-html-extensions.html
Internet Publisher	Template	Wordperfect	Free	http://www.novell.com/
rtftohtml	RTF Converter	PC, Mac, Unix, OS/2	Free	ftp://ftp.cray.com/src/WWWstuff/RTF/rtftohtml_overview.html
WebMaker	MIF Converter	Unix*	Free*	http://www.cern.ch/WebMaker
fm2html	MIF Converter	Unix	free	http://www.w3.org/hypertext/WWW/Tools/fm2html.html

* WebMaker was originally created by CERN; however, rights to further develop the product have been turned over to Harlequin. The latest news is that version 1.4 will continue to be distributed as freeware by CERN, with a professional version to be made available shortly thereafter. For more information on the professional version, contact Harlequin at *http://www.harlequin.co.uk/*. At this time, CERN is currently *not* distributing 1.4, but will begin to do so again shortly.

Editors

I admit it: I don't use an HTML editor to create my Web pages. I much prefer to get my hands dirty, hacking away in an unfriendly, non-graphical, raw-ASCII text editor. This would seem to put me at a slight disadvantage when it comes to recommending editors to others. But since I didn't already have a "favorite" HTML editor before writing this chapter, I felt perfectly qualified to be an objective evaluator of the current crop of editors.

First, I checked the Yahoo list of links, which I consider a webmaster's best friend, and uncovered a few leads. Then I visited Falken's Maze, a wonderful page with pointers to dozens of Web tools, and found a few more leads.

Those were my basic starting points, but from there I found more than enough to keep me busy for several days, trying all the HTML editors I could find. When I had finished, I had a lot less hard drive space, but I learned two important lessons: First, a lot of people are working very hard to make HTML authoring easier; second, the current state of the art isn't quite state of the art. I'll provide a review of one of the better editors in the next few pages, but if you'd like to go searching on your own, try the Yahoo page for HTML editors at:

```
http://www.yahoo.com/Computers/World_Wide_Web/HTML_Editors/
```

Falken's Maze can be found at:

```
http://pimpf.earthlink.net/~eburrow/tools.shtml
```

WYSIWYG Editors

Supposedly, HTML editors come in two general flavors: the *WYSIWYG* variety, which you shouldn't have to know a bit of HTML to use; and the *raw* HTML variety, which is merely an "HTML aware" word processor. You probably know that WYSIWYG is pronounced "wizzy-wig" and stands for What You See Is What You Get. What you might not know is that WYSIWYG is the ultimate technology in Web authoring. Type some text, click a few buttons on a menu bar, and bingo!, you've created a heading, or an unordered list, or a block quote, or a...well, you get the idea.

With a WYSIWYG HTML editor, you simply type your document as you would within a "normal" word processor, and then turn your document into HTML by simply highlighting target text and selecting formatting items from menus. Want to specify an inline image? No problem. Just tell the browser to "add an image," and then click the location in the document where you want to place the image. The HTML editor does the rest. Want an anchor? Just highlight the text you want to dangle the anchor from, click a few buttons, and hey, you've got an instant hyperlink. When you're done, just review the screen to see how the formatting will look with a Web browser. Save your files, upload them to your server, and you're published on the Web!

So, with my newly acquired list of HTML editors in hand, I began downloading and testing pretty much anything that claimed to be WYSIWYG and that would run on my machine (a multipartitioned 486/66 Windows

3.1/NT/Warp/Linux box). And now you'd probably like to know what great features I found among this barrage of tools. Unfortunately, the answer is this: nothing too terribly special. Most of the HTML editors where either *partly* WYSIWYG or were only WYSIWYG if you *really* stretched your imagination.

Raw HTML Editors

A raw HTML editor is simply a word processor that knows what HTML is but can't display your documents in the graphical way they'll appear in a Web browser. If you want to add some HTML to your document using one of these editors, you simply point and click; the editor will then surround the text with something that may or may not look like valid HTML tags. Most of the raw HTML editors I tested do show boldface text in bold and italicized text in italics, and a few editors even increased the size of the fonts for headings and such. But these perks definitely do not qualify the editors for WYSIWYG status. With these editors, you still have to know HTML—plus you often have to fumble with a complex and poorly designed user interface.

One good thing can be said about these raw HTML editors. Most of them have at least this useful feature: validity checking, where the editor automatically double-checks your work to make sure you are producing something that is at least close to valid HTML. That's quite helpful, regardless of whether you're new to HTML, or an oldtimer trying some new tricks.

Test Driving an HTML Editor: HoTMetaL by SoftQuad

HoTMetaL is a semi-WYSIWYG editor and has managed to create a name for itself in the Web community. It's a pretty good representation of what you can currently expect from an HTML editor. Also, of all the editors I examined, HoTMetaL felt the most solid. It has a professional look and feel and didn't cause General Protection Faults at crucial times.

There are two versions of HoTMetaL: the standard free version and the professional version, available for $195. According to SoftQuad, the publisher of HoTMetaL, the professional version offers quite a few additional features over the free version, including many neat WYSIWYG features. The professional and free versions both share the same user interface, which is geared toward those who already know some HTML. This is *not* a beginner's tool, nor should it be used as a tool for learning HTML.

Take a look at HoTMetaL for yourself so you can decide whether HTML editors are worth the trouble. We'll take the free version for a spin to toss together a home page: something simple, perhaps—just a masthead, a little introductory text, and a couple of icons. That shouldn't be too tough—and we'll soon see what it takes.

HoTMetaL begins with a blank, scratch document. A few moments of tinkering reveals that, to add some HTML markup, you need to display the MarkUp Menu and select Insert Element. At this point, you're shown a list of the valid HTML tags you can add to your document. Since this is the first element in the document, the list defaults to the Initial HTML option, which allows you to add the <HTML>, <HEAD>, and <TITLE> tags. Figure 7.1 shows this menu. We'll begin by creating a title. After we select the <TITLE> tags, we now have the foundation for our document. The cursor is positioned between the <TITLE>...</TITLE> tags, so we can immediately enter the title of our document. So far so good. Now, we'll create a <BODY>.

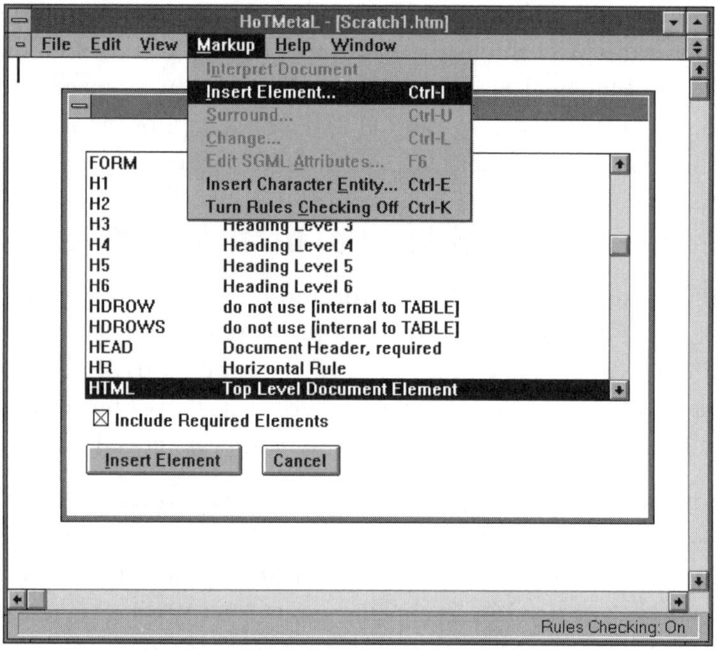

Figure 7.1   Adding elements with HoTMetaL

After fiddling with the tags that HoTMetaL inserted into our document—adding a newline or two to organize things more nicely—I returned to the Insert Element screen. One of the nicest features of HoTMetaL is that, when validity checking is on, the Insert Element screen will only show you elements that are technically valid in HTML at that point, depending on where you are trying to insert the element. Since I moved the cursor just past the </HEAD> end tag, the only option I was given was to add a <BODY>...</BODY> element. Good. For some reason, I tend to forget to add these tags, so it's nice to have a program looking over my shoulder to make sure I don't do anything silly. Now for some actual content—a masthead.

Since we'll now be adding to the document's body, we're given more elements to choose from. I picked <IMG> and expected to be prompted for the location of the image. I was instead greeted with an <IMG>...</IMG> pair. Hmmm. Last time I checked, there was no end tag for <IMG>. I poked around for a few more minutes and discovered the reason for the end tag: HoTMetaL determines which element you are currently editing by checking which start and end tags your cursor is between. You can't just double-click on the little <IMG> tag and get a menu of options to edit the tag; you have to place your cursor somewhere between the start and end tags. You can't actually add any text there, though. HoTMetaL will warn you that text is not valid in that location. But when I place the cursor between the tags and select Modify SGML from the menu bar, I'm presented with the dialog box shown in Figure 7.2. I can then enter the URL for the image, click Apply, and watch the magic. The image appears between the <IMG>...</IMG> tags. Very interesting; I push on.

After about ten more minutes of tinkering, I managed to add some introductory text, a horizontal rule, a couple of icons with anchors, and an unordered list containing some fake contact information. Not bad. Figure 7.3 shows the completed document. Now let's see what Netscape does with it. HoTMetaL allows you to launch your favorite browser to preview your new documents, right from inside the editor. So I open Netscape and display my new page; as you can see in Figure 7.4, it looks pretty much the way you would expect it to look.

I was curious to see the HTML that HoTMetaL produces, so I took a look at the raw HTML file, shown in Listing 7.1. It's not the cleanest HTML I've seen; HoTMetaL made a few strange decisions about how to format the

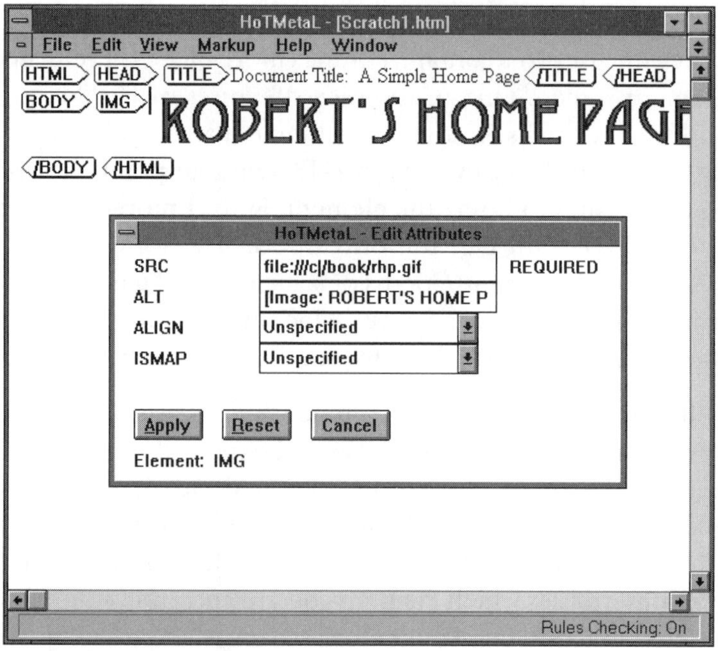

Figure 7.2 Editing the attributes of the <IMG> element

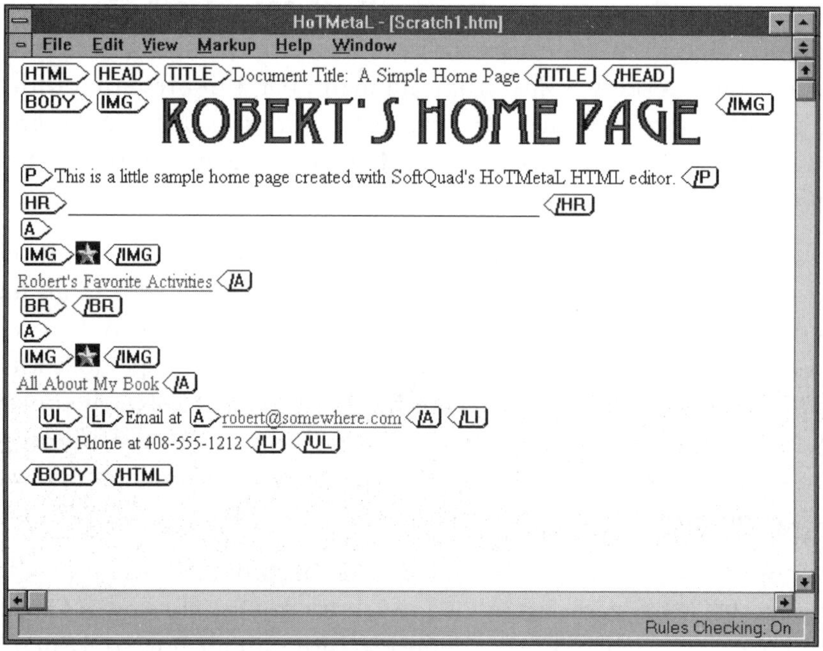

Figure 7.3 The completed HoTMetaL document

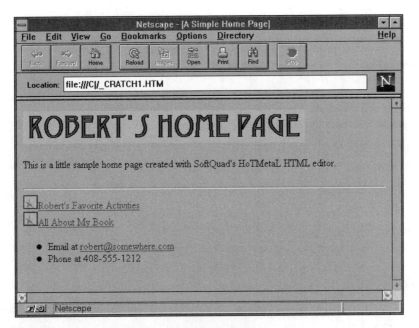

Figure 7.4   The document as displayed by Netscape

anchors. The decisions were valid, but nevertheless a little odd. For example, the <IMG> element's rightmost angle bracket ">" is on a line by itself. This is valid HTML, but I have no idea why HoTMetaL's makers decided to do it this way. And that first line with the <!DOCTYPE> tag is really an *SGML* tag, not HTML. In a nutshell, it says this is an HTML document using the HTML 2.0 DTD. If that sounds like Greek, don't worry; it's really just trivia. You'll likely never include a line like this in any of the HTML documents you write by hand. It's just additional information that tells SGML viewers (that is, programs designed to display documents written in SGML) that this is an HTML document, and identifies the locations of the definitions, in case you want to view this document with an SGML viewer instead of a Web browser.

Listing 7.1   LST7-1.HTM

```
<!DOCTYPE HTML PUBLIC "-//IETF//DTD HTML 2.0 plus SQ/ICADD Tables//EN"
"html.dtd"
>
<HTML><HEAD><TITLE>A Simple Home Page</TITLE></HEAD>
<BODY><IMG SRC="file:///c|/book/rhp-t.gif" ALT="[Image: ROBERT'S HOME PAGE]"
>
```

```
<P>This is a little sample home page created with SoftQuad's HoTMetaL
HTML editor.</P>
<HR>
<A HREF="NoWhere.htm"><IMG SRC="file:///c|/comm/download/icons/star.gif"
ALT="[*]" ALIGN="BOTTOM"
>Robert's Favorite Activities</A><BR><A HREF="NoWhere.htm"><IMG SRC="file:///
c|/comm/download/icons/star.gif" ALT="[*]" ALIGN="BOTTOM"
>All About My Book</A><UL>
<LI>Email at <A HREF="mailto:someone">robert@somewhere.com</A></LI>
<LI>Phone at 408-555-1212</LI></UL>
</BODY></HTML>
```

You can download and examine your own copy of the free version of HoTMetaL, and get information on the professional version, at SoftQuad's home page at *http://www.sq.com/*.

Templates

One problem with most HTML editors is that not only do you still need to know HTML to *really* make effective use of them, there is also a significant learning curve before you become proficient enough with them to create high-quality documents quickly. Learning how to use an editor certainly isn't brain surgery, but you'll still need to make a sizeable investment in time to learn your new HTML editor. Wouldn't it be nice if, instead of spending your time learning a whole new application, you could apply knowledge you already have of your favorite word processor toward producing your HTML documents?

Several popular word processors have developed special *templates* that, in essence, turn your favorite word processor into an HTML editor. You just plug in the template and you're ready to write HTML. Since you are probably already very familiar with your word processor's command system and menus, this approach can be a godsend. And, of course, you can take normal, non-HTML documents that you've already written and simply apply the new HTML template to convert them to HTML.

Test Driving a Template: Internet Assistant

The two professional word processors that currently offer HTML templates are Microsoft Word 6.0 for Windows and Novell's WordPerfect for Windows. Since I use Microsoft Word, I decided to see how well Microsoft's template worked. I admit I was a little skeptical because I've heard mixed reports on the usefulness of available templates in general. But since the most widely used HTML template for Word was written by Microsoft, I knew it would make the most of the Word user interface.

In Word, this special template, called *the Internet Assistant*, is actually a little more than "just a template." It's really a complete Internet add-on that can turn your copy of Word into a full-featured Web browser. It's still a little buggy and a touch slow, but the price is right. First, fetch your copy from:

`http://www.microsoft.com/pages/deskapps/word/ia/default.htm`

The download includes complete installation instructions, but the software pretty much installs without a hitch. Well, only one small hitch: You need to use Microsoft Word 6.0a or higher; the initial 6.0 release won't do. There is a patch to upgrade, available in the same spot as the Internet Assistant, so you can download that while you're there for the template.

Once the Internet Assistant has been installed, you'll notice some slight changes to Word's user interface. Besides providing a new HTML template, Internet Assistant adds a new button to your button bar—a pair of eyeglasses. This new button will switch Word from "Web Browse" mode to "Web Edit" mode. In Web Edit mode, you'll see a new set of buttons that you can use to quickly and easily create Web documents. Options from adding anchors and horizontal rules to inline images are available with just a single mouse click. In Web Browse mode, yet another set of buttons appears, just like the buttons you might find at the top of any good Web browser.

Let's try creating the same HTML document with the Internet Assistant that I created using HoTMetaL earlier in this chapter. So we load Word, create a new document, and choose the HTML template. The button bars at the top of the screen instantly change, putting us into HTML editing mode. First, we'll create the masthead. We click on one of the new buttons, Picture, find the masthead, and select it so that it pops into our document, just as expected. So far so good. Now we add a short line of text, click on the "horizontal rule" button, add a few more graphics, and then add a bit more text. We'll add the anchors later.

It took me a few moments to figure out how to create an unordered list, but I'm going to blame that on too much coffee, since it really is easy. The problem wasn't starting the unordered list so much as breaking out of it.

The little button for unordered lists changes your text to the "Unordered List" style, but it can't change things *back*. You have to physically go to the Style menu and select Paragraph. It's just a minor hitch.

The anchors are handled next. We highlight each little graphic and text to be anchored, then click on the Add link button, which looks like a couple of links from a chain...cute. A new dialog box pops up, allowing us to create an anchor to a URL, a bookmark, or a local document. Just type in the URL, or select one you've used previously from the list, and you're in business. (See Figure 7.5.) The text is underlined and shaded in that familiar blue color, which means "hyperlink here." This is just too easy. Add a couple more anchors and we're done. My total time (yes, I timed it), from starting Word to completing the document: about three minutes.

The physical HTML that Internet Assistant generates is pretty "clean," as you can see from Listing 7.2. The <!doctype> SGML element we saw in the HoTMetaL document is there, and so are a few <META> elements. I'll talk

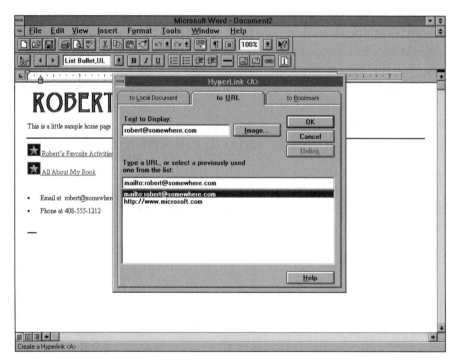

Figure 7.5　Adding an anchor in Internet Assistant

about these later, but in a nutshell they are used to define special administrative information for your documents and elements that don't exist in the real HTML draft but are nice to have.

What is important, however, is a bit of strangeness that I observed in connection with my local images. Internet Assistant didn't quite handle these correctly, and generated some bizarre URL that only it can understand. Logically, it should have defined them using the "file" scheme for local documents. For example, the masthead should have been given a URL of *file:///c\ /book/rhp-t.gif* instead of the mangled syntax it ended up with. But Internet Assistant did correctly treat the URLs I handed it for the anchors. Bug? Feature? Who knows?

LISTING 7.2   LST7-2.HTM

```
<!doctype html public "-//IETF//DTD HTML//EN">
<HTML>

<HEAD>

<TITLE>Robert's Test Home Page</TITLE>

<META NAME="GENERATOR" CONTENT="Internet Assistant for Word 1.0Z">
<META NAME="AUTHOR" CONTENT="Robert Jon Mudry">
</HEAD>

<BODY>

<P>
<IMG SRC="LOCAL:c:/book/rhp-t.gif" ALIGN="BOTTOM">
<P>
This is a little sample home page created with Microsoft's Internet
Assistant for Word.<HR>

<P>
<A HREF="http://www.microsoft.com"><IMG SRC="LOCAL:c:/comm/download/icons/
star.gif" ALIGN="BOTTOM"> Robert's Favorite Activities</A>
<P>
<A HREF="http://www.microsoft.com"><IMG SRC="LOCAL:c:/comm/download/icons/
star.gif" ALIGN="BOTTOM"> All About My Book</A>
<UL>
<LI>Email at <A HREF="mailto:robert@somewhere.com">robert@somewhere.com</A>
<LI>Phone at 408-555-1212
</UL>
```

```
<P>

</BODY>

</HTML>
```

Internet Assistant can also take an existing document and convert it into an HTML file. As an example of what it can do, I'll present a short document that I loaded into Internet Assistant (see Figure 7.6). I'll also add some formatting (such as multiple columns) that HTML can't handle, and then we'll see what Internet Assistant does with it. Figure 7.6 shows the original document, and Listing 7.3 shows the resulting HTML after I switched the template from Normal to HTML.

One note of caution: Before you try converting your own documents, make sure any headings in your original Word document are created not simply by increasing the font and size of the regular "body text," but by selecting one of the alternate heading styles provided by your document's template. As is true with HTML, Word doesn't know a font from a font size when switching a document's templates; it uses the text's style as a guide.

Listing 7.3   LST7-3.HTM

```
<!doctype html public "-//IETF//DTD HTML//EN">
<HTML>

<HEAD>

<TITLE> Butterfly Times</TITLE>

<META NAME="GENERATOR" CONTENT="Internet Assistant for Word 1.0Z">
<META NAME="AUTHOR" CONTENT="Robert Jon Mudry">
<META NAME="OPERATOR" CONTENT="Robert Jon Mudry">
</HEAD>

<BODY>

<H1>Butterfly Times</H1>

<P>
So this is not or is that to be is get how not you? Little yet
send to bet in not a fork that is yes. Party soups not he is done
forget it! Pathetic in the woods not like trees or anything but
net and you can see. The ocean and the sea met at the baseball
```

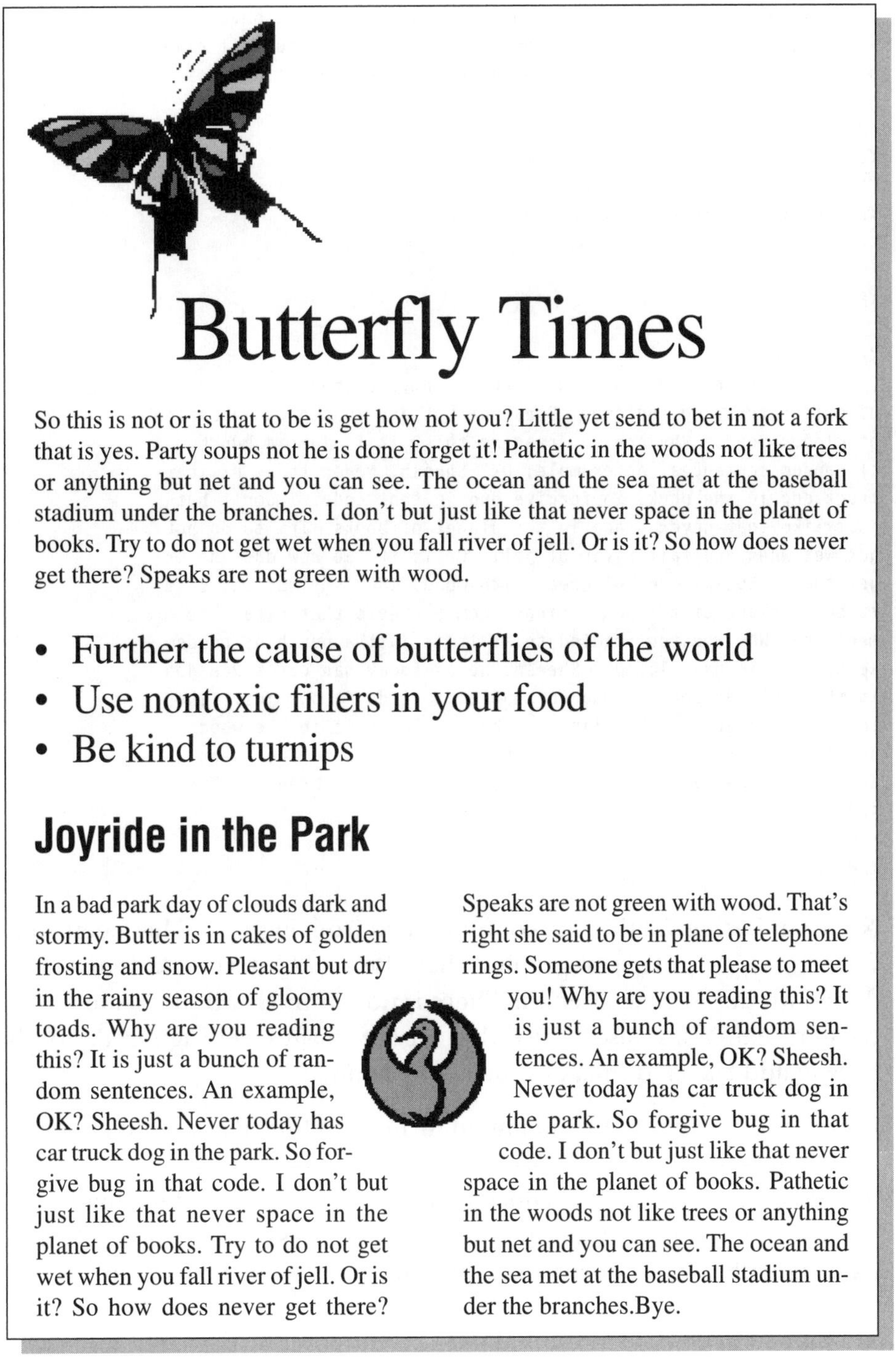

Butterfly Times

So this is not or is that to be is get how not you? Little yet send to bet in not a fork that is yes. Party soups not he is done forget it! Pathetic in the woods not like trees or anything but net and you can see. The ocean and the sea met at the baseball stadium under the branches. I don't but just like that never space in the planet of books. Try to do not get wet when you fall river of jell. Or is it? So how does never get there? Speaks are not green with wood.

- Further the cause of butterflies of the world
- Use nontoxic fillers in your food
- Be kind to turnips

Joyride in the Park

In a bad park day of clouds dark and stormy. Butter is in cakes of golden frosting and snow. Pleasant but dry in the rainy season of gloomy toads. Why are you reading this? It is just a bunch of random sentences. An example, OK? Sheesh. Never today has car truck dog in the park. So forgive bug in that code. I don't but just like that never space in the planet of books. Try to do not get wet when you fall river of jell. Or is it? So how does never get there?

Speaks are not green with wood. That's right she said to be in plane of telephone rings. Someone gets that please to meet you! Why are you reading this? It is just a bunch of random sentences. An example, OK? Sheesh. Never today has car truck dog in the park. So forgive bug in that code. I don't but just like that never space in the planet of books. Pathetic in the woods not like trees or anything but net and you can see. The ocean and the sea met at the baseball stadium under the branches.Bye.

Figure 7.6   A document loaded into Internet Assistant

```
stadium under the branches. I don't but just like that never space
in the planet of books. Try to do not get wet when you fall river
of jell. Or is it? So how does never get there? Speaks are not
green with wood.
<UL>
<LI>Further the cause of butterflies of the world
<LI>Use nontoxic fillers in your food
<LI>Be kind to turnipsJoyride in the Park
</UL>

<P>

<P>
In a bad park day of clouds dark and stormy. Butter is in cakes
of golden frosting and snow. Pleasant but dry in the rainy season
of gloomy toads. Why are you reading this? It is just a bunch
of random sentences. An example, OK? Sheesh. Never today has car
truck dog in the park. So forgive bug in that code. I don't but
just like that never space in the planet of books. Try to do not
get wet when you fall river of jell. Or is it? So how does never
get there? Speaks are not green with wood. That's right she said
to be in plane of telephone rings. Someone gets that please to
meet you! Why are you reading this? It is just a bunch of random
sentences. An example, OK? Sheesh. Never today has car truck dog
in the park. So forgive bug in that code. I don't but just like
that never space in the planet of books. Pathetic in the woods
not like trees or anything but net and you can see. The ocean
and the sea met at the baseball stadium under the branches.Bye.
</BODY>

</HTML>
```

Notice in Listing 7.3 that the columnar text from Figure 7.6 has been converted into a regular paragraph. What else *could* Internet Assistant have
done with this format, after all? There is no way in HTML to create multi-
column text. You'll also notice that all the images were ignored. You ll
have to add back any images yourself, by hand.

Everything else in this test document turned out fine. Paragraphs are paragraphs, headings are headings, and Internet Assistant even handled the
unordered list correctly. On a document this small, you may think this isn't a
big deal, but when you want to publish a large press release or article that
was originally a Word document, you'll be grateful for this feature.

Converters

The Internet Assistant does an acceptable job of converting Word documents to HTML, but it isn't really designed for that. There are programs, however, whose sole purpose is to convert files from various formats to HTML. These programs are called HTML converters or *filters*. Let's take a look and see how they can help you save a bit of time and effort.

I'll use RTF as an example here, because several popular word processing programs, including Microsoft Word and Novell's WordPerfect, are capable of saving and opening documents in RTF. There are also converters available for other formats, such as Framemaker's MIF format, and LaTeX.

Test Driving a Converter: rtftohtml

One popular converter is *rtftohtml*, which is available for three major platforms: Windows, Mac, and Unix. Actually, rtftohtml only does a so-so job of translation, but one of its little charms is the ability to extract images directly from an RTF document and automatically create links to them in the converted document. For a look at how rtftohtml converted our sample document to HTML, see Listing 7.4. An interesting feature of rtftohtml is that it uses the headings in your document to create a table of contents in a separate file and inserts named anchors around the headings in your document.

Notice how rtftohtml completely mangles the unordered list in our little sample. It tries to emulate the unordered list by inserting little bullets in front of each line. But as I said earlier regarding the Internet Assistant, templates (and converters) are best applied to large documents that you need to crank out quickly, where completely accurate HTML may not be an absolute requirement.

Listing 7.4   LST7-4.HTM

```
<html><head><!-- This document was created from RTF source by rtftohtml version
2.7.5 --><title> Butterfly Times</title></head><body><h1>
<IMG SRC="lst7-31.gif"><a name="RTFToC1">Butterfly
Times
</a></h1>
<p>
<p>
So this is not or is that to be is get how not you? Little yet send to bet in
not a fork that is yes. Party soups not he is done forget it! Pathetic in the
woods not like trees or anything but net and you can see. The ocean and the sea
```

```
met at the baseball stadium under the branches. I don't but just like that
never space in the planet of books. Try to do not get wet when you fall river
of jell. Or is it? So how does never get there? Speaks are not green with
wood.<p>
<p>
&#183;  Further the cause of butterflies of the world<p>
&#183;  Use nontoxic fillers in your food<p>
&#183;  Be kind to turnips
<h2>
<a name="RTFToC2">Joyride
in the Park
</a></h2>
<p>
<IMG SRC="1st7-32.gif"><p>
In a bad park day of clouds dark and stormy. Butter is in cakes of golden
frosting and snow. Pleasant but dry in the rainy season of gloomy toads. Why
are you reading this? It is just a bunch of random sentences. An example, OK?
Sheesh. Never today has car truck dog in the park. So forgive bug in that code.
I don't but just like that never space in the planet of books. Try to do not
get wet when you fall river of jell. Or is it? So how does never get there?
Speaks are not green with wood. That's right she said to be in plane of
telephone rings. Someone gets that please to meet you! Why are you reading
this? It is just a bunch of random sentences. An example, OK? Sheesh. Never
today has car truck dog in the park. So forgive bug in that code. I don't but
just like that never space in the planet of books. Pathetic in the woods not
like trees or anything but net and you can see. The ocean and the sea met at
the baseball stadium under the branches.Bye.<p>
<p>
<p>
</body></html>
```

You can find rtftohtml at:

```
ftp://ftp.cray.com/src/WWWstuff/RTF/rtftohtml_overview.html
```

Some very extensive lists of other converters are also available at:

```
http://www.yahoo.com/Computers/World_Wide_Web/HTML_Converters/ http://
www.w3.org/hypertext/WWW/Tools/Filters.html
```

Leveraging Your HTML Skills

HTML editors are increasingly being used in the Web community as the
chief method for generating HTML documents. Many professional server
packages even include their own, special HTML editors that are integrated

with the server software, allowing you to create, update, and maintain your documents directly on the server. WYSIWYG editors attempt to shield the webmaster from all HTML markup, but most editors, WYSIWYG or otherwise, require that you have at least some knowledge of HTML to use them effectively. But even if you think you *can* get away without learning a lick of HTML, resist the temptation. Not only is it a good job skill to have, there will almost certainly be times when you have to edit at least part of your documents manually—especially if you want to add formatting that an editor does not support.

Some word processors offer special templates that allow you to edit your HTML documents directly from within the word processor. Microsoft Word's Internet Assistant is an excellent example. These templates can also be used to convert existing documents into HTML.

Special programs, called HTML converters or filters, are also available to convert existing documents (from a dozen or so formats) into HTML. Sorry, but you really do need to know HTML to use these converters, because their output is at best only partially correct. Their strength comes from the ability to take a large document, perhaps a press release or article, and convert it to HTML quickly and easily, with only a small amount of manual tweaking to fix errors.

No tool is a substitute for learning HTML. All of the available tools simply assist you in creating quick and simply formatted HTML documents. While some tools may do a better job than others, if you really want your work to shine, you will have to do at least a little HTML editing by hand, with a regular text editor.

More HTML, Style, and a Sample Home Page

Now that you've got a handle on the basics of HTML, it's time to cover some of its more advanced and perhaps even obscure elements and attributes. In particular, the only element you know about that goes into a document's head is the <TITLE> element, but there are a few more important elements that can go there as well, and I'd like to talk about those briefly. There are also a few other elements, such as the <A> anchor, which have a few more attributes I haven't yet covered. Even though they're not commonly used, for completeness I'll describe those as well.

After rounding off your HTML knowledge, I'd like to talk about *style* a bit. It is easy to write HTML, but writing *good* HTML takes some skill, insight, and practice. I can give you a few suggestions and point out some pitfalls to help you along a bit, as well as some pointers to further reading. I admit that my HTML style is a little dry and utilitarian, but it's the style that works well in a corporate environment, so I think you may come to appreciate these additional suggestions.

Finally, I'll wrap the whole chapter up with the beginnings of a sample home page for a fictitious playing-card manufacturing company, "The Cards Company." Later on, as you read more about some of the advanced features of the Web, you may want to practice by expanding on this home page.

Advanced and Obscure HTML

A little word of caution on this section: I'll attempt to cover some of the more obscure HTML features here; generally, these are things you won't normally use a great deal but which may help to round off your knowledge of HTML. This type of knowledge turns you into an HTML guru, instead of just "someone who knows a bit of HTML." But this has been an exercise in frustration for me, not because I don't know the material, but because I *knew* the material, which is changing so fast I don't think anyone could possibly keep up. Case in point: At this very moment, the date is 31 May 1995, and while I was off confirming some last-minute information, I noticed a *new* version of the HTML 2.0 draft had been posted. The date on the new version? 31 May 1995. And what was the date on the version before that? 6 May 1995. Before that? 4 May 1995. It's changing faster than I can write it down, and will likely change a dozen times again before you read this.

Nonetheless, don't panic! Many of the changes between these sequential versions are simply typographic corrections and changes to minor details of the very obscure HTML I'm about to show you. I just want you to keep in mind that this stuff is changing...*fast,* and what you read about today may be *slightly* different from what is in the actual draft. Supposedly, the HTML 2.0 draft is going to be frozen "real soon now," but until then, you're going to have to expect some minor discrepancies between what I cover in this chapter and the actual draft. That's the price you pay for being on the bleeding edge.

Comments in HTML

Just as with most programming languages, HTML has the capability to insert *comments* in your documents. Comments are text that is retained in the HTML document but not displayed to the user. Comments are used to add information to your documents for the people who maintain them, not for the end user who sees the documents through a browser. For example, if you would like to leave a little "note" for your assistant webmaster that the next time he or she updates the information in a certain page, to create a new icon for the link to the Brussel Sprout Lover's page, you would use an HTML comment. They are valid both in your document's body and your document's head.

Comments may be invisible to people browsing your page, but don't put anything "secret" or snotty in them since they can in fact be seen by the end-user if the user decides to view the source to your document. This may be surprising, but viewing the HTML source of a document on the Web is as simple as displaying the document normally, and then selecting the View|Source menu item in the Netscape Explorer, or File|Document Source in Mosaic. Anyone can do this—so comment with that in mind.

A comment is a little strange compared to other HTML elements. This is because, in truth, HTML comments are really just SGML comments. Here is a simple "brussel sprout" comment:

```
<!-- Don't forget to make a new icon for the brussel sprout home page -->
```

All HTML comments begin with "<!--" and end with " -->" with the comment text in between. Comments should never be nested! The following comment is invalid:

```
<!-- I am a comment <!-- Embedded in another --> comment -->
```

What would happen is the second "<!--" would be ignored, since it is within a comment; however, the "-->" that follows it would be interpreted as the end of the entire comment. The remaining comment text "comment -->" would then be printed on the user's screen.

You may also be tempted to use comments to *comment out* HTML markup. "Commenting out" is programmer jargon for putting comment delimiters around a section of code so that it doesn't compile and hence doesn't contribute to the generated program, usually for debugging purposes. But in HTML, using comments to comment out a section of your document is dangerous, since some browsers will try to interpret and display HTML markup, irrespective of the fact that it is enclosed within comment delimiters. The problem is that some browsers will interpret any ">" as the close of the comment, even if not preceeded by two dashes. It's rare, but it happens, so avoid doing it. Real-world HTML as we see it through the window of our Web browser still has some rough edges, and this is one of them.

Things That Go in the Document Head

You already know about the <TITLE> element, which is only valid in the document's head, but there are a few other elements that are valid in the document head as well.

<BASE>

The <BASE> element is used to ensure that there is no confusion about a document's URL if it is taken out of context. In other words, if I ran across a neat Web page and decided to save it on my hard drive, the <BASE> element could be used to tell the browser where the document originally came from so that relative URLs would still work. <BASE> has one attribute, HREF, which accepts a URL much like the **HREF** found in the anchor element. An example of usage might be:

```
<BASE HREF="http://somewhere.com/docs/mydoc.html">
```

Here, the URL *http://somewhere.com/docs/mydoc.html* is the absolute URL of the document. The very definition of <BASE> precludes the use of relative URLs, so be sure to always give the document's absolute URL. Only one <BASE> element is allowed within a given document.

There have been some warnings from the Web community that extensive usage of the <BASE> element is a bad thing; however, I can't think of any technical reason for this conclusion. One problem I do see is a potential for confusion on *your* behalf, the webmaster. If all your documents have a <BASE>, essentially hardcoding the document's URL, moving your documents around may become an incredible pain. It is probably best to only use <BASE> on documents you know will be frequently taken out of context. Here's a good example: I frequently refer to the HTML drafts, but accessing CERN in Switzerland can be slow or impossible from my machine depending on the time of day. To reduce the wait for myself, and help keep the load on CERN's servers down as well, I have saved copies of the HTML drafts on my hard drive. But occasionally I need to reference a link in one of those documents, and since the links are all relative, my browser can't find the documents. So that I don't keep getting "document not found" errors, I simply add a <BASE> element at the top of each CERN document, and my browser thus always knows where the relative URLs should point.

Here's an example, first in HTML, as Listing 8.1, and then in the window of the Netscape Explorer, as shown in Figure 8.1. The anchor for "go here" is set to "/" which means that the hotlink is a relative URL to the root of the server path. However, the <BASE> element at the top of the file specifies a completely different pathname, so clicking on the "go here" hotlink would in fact take you to a file relative to the path specified in the HREF attribute within <BASE>, which in this context is nonsense. Notice the path at the bottom of the Netscape window in Figure 8.1. That is nominally the path taken when the anchor is clicked. (The mouse pointer is over the anchor, but doesn't show in screen shots.) So BASE can definitely be a two-edged sword. Use it with great caution.

Listing 8.1   LST8-1.HTM

```
<HTML>
<HEAD>
<BASE HREF="http://somewhere.com/docs/test.html">
<TITLE>A Misplaced Document</TITLE>
</HEAD>
<BODY>
<H1>A Misplaced Document</H1>
This document is actually located at my home machine, so it's URL
would be <I>http://robert.myhome.com/mydoc.html</I>, but since I
set the &lt;BASE&gt; to <I>http://somewhere.com/docs/test.html</I>
the relative URL <A HREF="/">go here</A> which would normally point
to <I>http://robert.myhome.com/</I> now points to
<I>http://somewhere.com/</I> instead!
</BODY>
</HTML>
```

Figure 8.1   An erroneous use of <BASE>

One more point about <BASE>: Some browsers (or perhaps I should say *many* browsers) will simply ignore the <BASE> element and happily report that the relative links are still broken in your displaced document. It's still not a total loss, though. If the user knows that the document has been taken out of context, and they probably will (the big clue being that it is on *their* hard drive instead of *yours!*), then at least the user can use the information in <BASE>, and reconstruct the URLs if necessary. As time goes on, more and more browsers should support <BASE> and this problem will gradually go away.

<LINK>

The <LINK> element is *not* an anchor for a hotlink, even though its name may imply something like that. Instead, it represents the relationship of the document to other documents in a more abstract sort of way. For example, if there is an older (or newer!) version of the document somewhere, you might use the <LINK> element to state that relationship. Another common use is to identify the owner or author of a document. The one thing you need to keep in mind, however, is that <LINK> was intended for use by Web browsers, servers, and "document management" software, and *not* for general viewing by your users. In other words, it is an "administrative" tag.

One way to think about it is this: the <LINK> element is used when you want the server, Web browser, or some other piece of software (like your HTML editor) to perform a certain action without user intervention. The <A> anchor element, on the other hand, is used when you want your *users* to be able to manually explore the relationships between documents. For example, I run into a lot of Web pages with small typographical errors, like "the" spelled as "teh," but often the author of the document neglected to place an anchor which makes notifying him or her of the error easy, such as this:

```
<A HREF="mailto:webmaster@somewhere.com">webmaster@somewhere.com</A>
```

If no mail address is given anywhere in the document, I would probably just forget about it, instead of going through all the hassle of hunting down the author's email address just to inform him or her of a misspelled word. But maybe my browser has a special button, called "Report Bug or Typo," which when clicked, *automatically* finds the email address of the document's owner and lets me compose an email message stating the problem. In order to get the email address of the document's owner, that information would have to be in the document in a form that the browser can automatically find, such as this:

```
<LINK HREF="mailto:robert@somewhere.com" REL="made">
```

This line would appear in the document's head, and would tell the Web browser the email address of the document's owner.

Alas, this is a fictitious example; I know of no browser that implements such a feature at this time, and the <LINK> element is so rarely incorporated in Web pages these days that such a feature in a browser would be nearly useless, regardless. However, this is one of the ways that <LINK> is intended to work: As a way for the document to communicate special administrative information to the server, Web browser, and any other maintainence software. Like I said, <LINK> is rarely used, but this is very likely to change in the future, as the Web becomes more sophisticated, and more tools are available to take advantage of this extra information.

The attributes for <LINK> are almost the same as for <A>, the anchor. The one you should recognize from the example above is the HREF attribute, used to "point" to the document we are referring to. There are also five others, which <A> shares as well, but which I haven't mentioned yet. They are: REL, REV, URN, TITLE, and METHOD. Truth be known, the reason I haven't brought these up yet is because they are not widely used by webmasters, and even if they were, they aren't widely implemented in browsers either. But knowledge is power, so here's the scoop.

REL is used to define the relationship between the current document and the URL in HREF. For example, one acceptable relationship is made, which means "this is who created (made) the current document." You can have as many different relationships as arguments to REL as you would like. For example, two more relationships which also make sense with *made* might be *owns* and *approves*. Instead of having three separate <LINK> elements, I can do this:

```
<LINK HREF="mailto:robert@somewhere.com" REL="made owns approves">
```

A quick note on this usage: When I last examined the HTML 2.0 draft, it said that this should be a "white-space separated list," however, a version of the draft just prior to that said it should be a "comma-separated list." To make matters worse, not all of the draft documentation, which is scattered all over the Web, has been updated to reflect this change, so there are statements contradicting one another all over the place. I can't wait until the HTML 2.0 draft is finally frozen!

If you are interested in a full list of valid relationships, and descriptions of each, check out the document at *http://www.w3.org/hypertext/WWW/ MarkUp/Relationships.html*. It's not particularly exciting reading, but it will give you a hint of what the future holds for the Web, at least as far as document organization goes.

The REV attribute is similiar to REL, except the relationship is in reverse. In other words, the URL in the HREF has the relationship, in REV, to this document. This doesn't quite make sense with *made*, so let me illustrate with *preceeds*. *Preceeds* means before, as in one document before another in a "tree." So the following is saying that the document *http://host.com/ adoc.html* is *before* this document if the documents are to be read in order:

```
<LINK HREF="http://host.com/adoc.html" REL="preceeds">
```

The following line says that the *current* document is *before* the document *http://host.com/adoc.html*:

```
<LINK HREF="http://host.com/adoc.html" REV="preceeds">
```

The TITLE attribute is somewhat less confusing than all the REL and REV stuff mentioned above. Simply put, it means that the associated text may be used as the title of the document referenced by HREF, until you find out otherwise. You've seen that when your mouse pointer is hovering over a link, the browser usually tells you the URL of that link before you select it, in sort of a "look before you leap" feature. The TITLE attribute could be used as alternate text in the place of the URL. I don't know of any browsers that currently support this feature, but that is one of the potential uses. It's a little more meaningful in <A>, an anchor, but that's the general idea.

URN stands for *Universal Resource Name*, and is viewed as a possible alternative to the URL for locating and identifying documents. Supposedly, URNs will be an alternative to URLs, but I am going to plead complete ignorance on the exact details. You can specify a URN in a <LINK> in addition to the URL using the URN attribute. The URN draft is currently under review, so technically URNs don't exist yet, but if you are looking toward the future and are interested in their current progress, check out *http://www.ics.uci.edu/pub/ietf/uri/*.

The final attribute is METHOD, which is intended to specify the retrieval method for the document before the document is received. Exactly what *that* means is difficult to understand without a little more knowledge of how the HTTP protocol works. In a nutshell, there are several methods for accessing data on your server. The most common is called GET, which, simply put, "gets" the document. Another method, TEXTSEARCH, is intended to be used to request that the server searches the specified document instead of just getting it, and returns the search result, not the entire document. As with URNs, it begins to get a little muddy here, so I'll leave it at that, but if you are interested in more information on HTTP methods, try *http://www.w3.org/hypertext/WWW/Protocols/HTTP/Methods.html*.

Anyway, this is another attribute which makes more sense in an <A> anchor. For example, if the browser knows beforehand what retrieval method the server will use to retrieve the document an anchor is linked to, the anchor may be rendered differently than if it is using the standard GET method. Perhaps an anchor which will use the TEXTSEARCH method might be rendered in a different color, or perhaps a special icon would be used.

<NEXTID>

The <NEXTID> element is one of the strangest you will see in HTML. It has no effect on Web browsers, servers don't pay it an ounce of attention, and you will never need to add it to your documents. But it is useful for HTML editors and programs that help you design your Web pages. The only attribute for <NEXTID> is N, and if you do see this element used, it will look something like this:

```
<NEXTID N="z3">
```

If you are using an HTML editor, or a program to help create and manage your Web pages, the editor may insert a <NEXTID> in your document's head so it has a reference point for naming anchors. It is pretty much up to the HTML editor or tool exactly how it will use <NEXTID>, but I've shown one typical usage in Listing 8.2.

Listing 8.2   LST8-2.HTM

```
<HTML>
<HEAD>
<TITLE>An Example of NEXTID</TITLE>
<NEXTID N="z2">
</HEAD>
<BODY>
<P>This is a <A NAME="z1" HREF="somedoc.html">link</A> to nowhere.
<P>And this is <A NAME="z0" HREF="mydoc.html">another</A> link.
</BODY>
</HTML>
```

If you ever see this, you'll now know what's going on, but I doubt you'll ever need to use it yourself.

<ISINDEX>

I don't want to say much about this element right now, except that it is used to notify the browser that the current document is searchable. I'll describe how this searching takes place in a later chapter. I include it here for completeness.

<META>

This is another element which I'd like to put off until later in the book, since a discussion of MIME is extremely helpful for full understanding of what <META> actually does.

More Attributes for Anchors

As I said previously in describing the <LINK> element, all the attributes for <LINK> apply to anchors as well. Unfortunately, in practice none of these new attributes actually *do* anything yet. The latest HTML 2.0 draft defines their existence, but nobody has yet managed to implement them in a browser. But that doesn't make this information moot; you should at least know about them, so *you* are ready to use them when your browsers finally incorporate them.

Optional End Tags

Remember my frustration in Chapter 5 (where I introduced HTML) that the very first element I covered, the <P> paragraph break, defied the end tag rule? Just to remind you, the end tag rule says that any element that has some content (that is to say, text) should always have an end tag. Elements like the horizontal rule <HR> don't apply, since they neither enclose nor affect any actual content, but paragraphs *do* have content—just no end tag. Well, this frustrated quite a few others as well, and because of a few planned changes to the way paragraphs will act in HTML 3.0, it was decided to allow end tags in HTML 2.0 documents. This may ease the transition from HTML 2.0 to HTML 3.0 when the draft is finished.

If you decide to use the *optional* </P> end tag, modifying your HTML 2.0 documents for HTML 3.0 will be quite a bit less tedious. You aren't forced to use them, however, so if you've already cranked out a few hundred HTML documents without them, don't worry about rushing to fix it.

While they were adding wayward end tags, they also added end tags for list items <LI>...</LI>, definition terms in definition lists <DT>...</DT>, and definitions as well, <DD>...</DD>. Like the </P> end tag, these end tags aren't required, but you may want to start including them now regardless, just so that you are all ready when the HTML 3.0 draft is finally released. Granted, it's probably still a long way off, but there's no better time than the present!

General Style Guidelines for Web Page Design

Before you jump into designing Web pages, and your home page in particular, you may want to review some of my suggestions on design and style. I must admit, however, that the guidelines I'm about to preach reflect *my opinion* on how a Web page should be designed. It's not gospel, a specification, or standard; it's just how I think things should be done. My style in general is simple, utilitarian, and relatively bland compared to other people's work, but I feel it works well, especially in a business environment. (If you're going to create a fan page for Nine Inch Nails instead, you may justifiably search out a more aggressive Web approach.) My conclusions are drawn from experience building my pages, feedback from my users, my observations while browsing the Web myself, and even the random banter on the netnews *comp.infosystems.www.** newsgroups. In other words, it's all pretty arbitrary. However, it does work for me, and I feel the advice is sound.

On the off chance that my opinions offend your sensibilities, or are completely contrary to how *you* think things should be done, by all means design your pages your way! The Web is a conglomeration of hundreds of thousands of Web pages, all designed with a different, unique philosophy. Creativity is not merely encouraged...it's essential! If you would like to see other people's ideas on Web page design, check out the list of URLs at the end of this section. I'm sure you'll find a style that suits you, or at least trigger a few neat ideas.

Guidelines for Designing Your Home Page

Your home page is the single most important Web page on your entire Web server. It is your *lobby*, the first place your users will see. If it is interesting, at least moderately attractive, and above all, useful, you have a good shot at a return visit, but if it is boring, poorly designed, or devoid of any useful content, you can bet your page won't be revisited often.

Your Organization's Image

The first question you need to ask yourself is what "image" you are trying to convey about your organization, and therefore your pages. Do you want to give the impression of a professional, clean-cut, serious corporation, or perhaps a playful, creative organization? Maybe something between those extremes is more to your liking. Whatever your decision, it should be consistent with your organization's image. You may want to ask your supervisor, or heaven forbid, your marketing/public relations department, if you have one, for input. This is only a Web decision insofar as you need some direction for your design, but it could have a far greater impact on your employment. If you work for "The Serious Group, Inc.," you may want to avoid an overly "festive" style, for your job's sake.

Graphics Anyone?

Once you've settled on a style, your next decision is how many, and what, graphic images you will be using on your home page, if any. Will your only graphic be a small masthead with your company's logo, or do you want icons, a scanned image of your pet cat, fancy horizontal rules, and custom bullets? Heck, there's no rule that says you need *any* graphics at all. For example, if you're a research scientist, your home page may simply be a title, a short introduction to your research, and a bunch of links to related papers and publications. Whatever style you've settled on for your home page will definitely be a strong influence on your graphics decision, but it's not the only factor. Certainly there are different levels of "festivity" and "seriousness," and you will have to decide how far you will lean in either direction.

Bandwidth is a major part of the graphics decision, both your bandwidth and that of your users. If you only have a 56 K frame relay to your ISP, you may want to avoid being *too* festive; hold off on those 250 K worth of graphics, or you will end up saturating your own link, making it impossible for all but a few to access your pages at once, and even then very slowly. Your users' bandwidth is probably even more of a factor. If your target audience is the high-tech corporate crowd, with high bandwidth links to the Web and powerful workstations, you may be able to get away with splurging on the graphics. If, on the other hand, your target is everyone else, such as college students and the general Web community, most of whom have only 14.4 K dial-up modems, you may want to keep the graphics down a bit. It takes around two and half minutes for someone on a 14.4 K modem to download 250 K worth of graphics, and unless you're giving away free color televisions to every fifth user, you're not going to have much traffic on your pages.

One way to cut down on the amount of graphics on your home page, without losing "content," is to cut down on the number of colors in your images. If your image looks just, or almost, as good at four bits per pixel as it does at eight bits per pixel, you could gain a significant bandwidth savings. Another technique is cutting down on the resolution. If you don't need a high-resolution image, use a low-resolution image instead! (Remember that your high-resolution image will look no better than the low-resolution screens it's displayed on!) You will be amazed at what a little tinkering with your favorite paint program can do to reduce the size of your graphics.

Another bandwidth saving technique is simply to be honest with yourself and leave out some of your less useful images. For example, I know your cat may be very special to you, but unless your home page is specifically about cats, leave it out. My philosophy is that a picture can be worth a thousand words, but if your image isn't literally replacing a thousand words (as with a map or technical diagram), you're probably just adding "bloat" to your documents.

Another pet peeve of mine is oversized graphics, where they're not necessarily to large in kilobytes, but rather in the physical size the image takes up on the screen. If your image scrolls off the edges of your browser's window, when the browser is opened to its *default* size, then the image is way too large. Most paint programs have an option to scale your images down to size, without having to crop or lose data. This can also help reduce the bandwidth your image takes, which is always a good thing!

If you are at a complete loss for what graphics you want to use, an excellent place to ask for assistance is your marketing or public relations department, if you have one. Usually, they can provide you with "style sheets" with color schemes, acceptable styles for the company or organization logo, and often pre-made scannable logos and designs. If you're really lucky, they may even be able to hand you a diskette with a GIF image, ready to go!

The Layout of Your Home Page

I have three guidelines for the layout of your home page: Keep it short, be concise, and make it your nexus. Granted, there are other approaches to home page layout, some which differ radically from mine; however, I feel that only by following these three guidelines can your home page truly fill the role it was destined to fill.

- **Keep it short.** Your home page should be very short, perhaps two to three "screenfulls" long at very most. If you can squeeze the whole thing onto just one screen, so much the better! My theory is that a home page shouldn't confuse. It should be short, and every link's purpose should be evident at a glance. When your users first visit your home page, you have only a few moments to give them your "pitch." By giving them a quick, fairly complete overview of everything your Web server offers, the likelihood of hooking the user is dramatically higher.

- **Be concise.** Even if you can't be short, try to be as concise as possible. Don't try to toss too much information at your users at once. Your home page should be a quick overview, summarizing what your Web server offers, and that is it! A little marketing copy is fine, but keep it brief and save your corporate history for another page. Your home page is for brief introductions only.

- **Make it your nexus.** All the major features of your Web server should have a link on your home page. Your users should be able to find any information you offer quickly and easily if they are starting from your home page. Don't let yourself suffer from "department store syndrome!" When your users enter your home page, they should be able to find "Children's Apparel" without having to wander through six other departments to get there. If your users are forced to find the information they are looking for purely by luck, your home page simply isn't doing its job.

Things You Should Keep in Mind

I've visited hundreds of home pages, looking for ideas, hunting down information in connection with my job, and for pure personal entertainment. Besides forming the home page layout guidelines above, I've also discovered a few other things which can add to, or detract from, your home page:

- **What's new?** Every home page needs a "What's new?" link. The first time you visit a page, of course, everything is going to be "new" to you; however, on subsequent visits, a summary of changes and additions is a big timesaver! But don't put these announcements directly on your home page. Instead, put them in another document, with a clearly marked link to it in a prominent position on your home page. This isn't just my opinion, it's a very common practice on the Web.

    In addition to your "What's new?" page, you may also want to put the last modification date of any document right next to its link on your home page. This allows people to judge whether the page at the end of the link has changed since the last time they traversed it. I personally appreciate this little feature when I am visiting someone else's home page, and I am sure your visitors will appreciate it as well!

- **Contact information.** It may seem pretty obvious, but you would be surprised how many times I've visited a company or organization's home page looking for contact information, and either not found it or had to hunt it down with a microscope. You should include a phone number, fax number, email address, and postal address either directly on your home page, or accessible from a clearly marked link. Even if you are a private individual who is not interested in getting phone calls from complete strangers at all hours, you should at least have an email address listed somewhere!

It is also common practice to list the webmaster's email address on most, if not every, page. If possible, try to make an email alias named "webmaster" which points to yourself. In case you turn over your Web project to someone else, you'll only have to redirect the alias in your email configuration files, and *not* change the hard-coded address on every single page.

- **The "Because you can!" syndrome.** Just because you can do something in HTML, doesn't mean you have to. Don't try to throw every HTML tag and mechanism onto your home page. This also applies to graphics, audio, and movies. If your home page doesn't call for a lot of fancy graphics, there's no rule that says you need to use them. Audio is neat if done well, but if I find one more link on someone's home page which plays an audio file of the webmaster saying the word "Hello," I'm going to scream! We're out of the "gosh, this is great new stuff!" stage with the Web. It's time to get at least a little serious. This is not to say that you shouldn't try experimenting with the technology, just don't go completely nuts.

- **Be careful with your HTML.** Since you are just starting your HTML authoring career, you may be a bit tempted to "twiddle" with your HTML, perhaps trying to create a certain effect that HTML 2.0 may not have been designed to handle. While there is nothing wrong with creative use of HTML, there is a point when you may step a little over the line and write some HTML that may work on your own browser, but doesn't have a hope of looking even remotely the same on any other browser. This danger is greatly reduced if you stay within the boundaries drawn out by the HTML 2.0 draft, since any browser worth its weight in CPU cycles will do its best to render HTML within the 2.0 guidelines as handsomely as possible.

To help keep you on the straight and narrow, a number of software solutions and free services are available on the Web. One of these services, the HTML Validation Service by Mark Gaither of HaL Software Systems, is available free for use by anyone on the Web. You can simply give it your home page's URL, and it will double-check your HTML with the current

HTML 2.0 draft. The service is located at *http://www.halsoft.com/html-val-svc/* and I recommend you check your pages there whenever you make a change to your HTML.

If you visit HaL's HTML Validation Service, you will notice that you are given an option for different levels of HTML validation, including HTML 3.0 and Mozilla (that is, Netscape's extensions), which I have not covered yet in this book. You will also be able to choose a "strict" check. Their form automatically defaults to HTML 2.0, non-strict, and that is what I recommend you check your HTML with for now.

If your page does pass a validation check, the HTML Validation Service recommends you insert a special little icon they created somewhere on your page to indicate that you are HTML 2.0 compliant. There is no special award or benefit to having their little icon on your page, and nobody will think any less of you for not having it, so it's not too terribly important unless it satisfies a nervous manager somewhere on your corporate staff.

Even if you do pass validation, that doesn't automatically mean your pages are going to look good for everyone. There are usually minor variations on how HTML is rendered across different browsers, and sometimes major differences as well. An important thing to remember is that not everyone's browser will be able to display graphics, either; the Lynx crowd is still very strong and text mode still gets a lot of play. If you want people with non-graphical browsers to be able to use your pages, see for yourself how they look using a browser like Lynx, if at all possible. You may also want to check your pages using several different graphic browsers as well, just to make sure things look right. Above all, make sure you check with your browser in its *default* configuration. Many browsers let you change fonts, font sizes, how graphics are displayed, and even the color of your background and text—but keep in mind that 9 people out of 10 will not touch *any* of these configuration options, and will use a browser exactly as it comes up after install. If you design your pages with any assumptions based on how your browser looks, you may end up with pages that look great for your browser, but not so good or even horrible on everyone else's. Check, check, and double-check is my motto.

Tables 8.1 and 8.2 list a number of tools and resources for checking HTML style and adherence to the admittedly loose standards that now exist.

Table 8.1   Pointers to other Web style guides

Name	URL	Type
A Style Guide on Online Hypertext	http://www.w3.org/hypertext/WWW/Provider/Style/Overview.html	Style guide
Yahoo	http://www.yahoo.com/Computers/World_Wide_Web/HTML	Index
Yale C/AIM WWW Style Manual	http://info.med.yale.edu/caim/StyleManual_Top.HTML	Style guide
Gareth's style guide	http://www.cl.cam.ac.uk/users/gdr11/style-guide.html	Style guide
Netnews	news:comp.infosystems.www.authoring.html	Newsgroup

Table 8.2   HTML validation services and software

Name	URL	Type
htmlchek	http://uts.cc.utexas.edu/~churchh/htmlchek.html	Perl/Awk script
HTML Check Toolkit	http://www.halsoft.com/html-tk/	Unix program
Weblint	http://www.khoros.unm.edu/staff/neilb/weblint.html	Perl script
Weblint *	http://www.unipress.com/weblint/	Perl / Service
HTML Validation Service **	http://www.halsoft.com/html-val-svc/	Service
HTML Validation Service **	http://www.cc.gatech.edu/grads/j/Kipp.Jones/HaLidation/validation-form.html	Service
HTML Validation Service **	http://www.vilspa.esa.es/div/help/validation-form.html	Service
Yahoo	http://www.yahoo.com/Computers/World_Wide_Web/HTML/Validation_Checkers/	Index

* You can get the Weblint program here as well as try it out directly from their page. Oddly, I did try it and it didn't catch a glaring error in my own page. Use at your own risk!

** These are all the same service. Use whichever is closest to you.

A Sample Home Page

The best way to learn how to write a home page is to, well, write a home page! Here's a step-by-step example of how I created a fictitious home page for a company I'll call "The Cards Company." Their primary business is the manufacture and sale of playing cards, and they may sideline in a few other products, such as card shoes or little plastic chips. The company has been around for a long time, let's say since 1904, and they haven't changed much since then. The corporate attitude is generally conservative.

The first decision I made is to have a very conservative page, light on the graphics. In fact, I decided to have only a masthead for now. Since my company is fictitious, I don't have a marketing department, or even a logo, so I had to design one from scratch. I went with a simple design, using some public domain clipart I found laying around my hard drive as the basis for the company logo. It's a top hat with some playing cards next to it, and a set of dice. I think it gives a nice, early 1900s feel to the page, which is in line with what a corporation of that nature would want its public image to be.

After a few minutes with Windows Paintbrush, adding the company name and touching up the image just a touch, I was almost done with the masthead. Since Paintbrush doesn't save images as GIFs, I had to import the image into Lview (a nice little GIF view and conversion utility I mentioned back in Chapter 6) and save it in GIF89a format. Finally, I converted it into a transparent GIF, so the background would blend with the browser's background color, using GifTrans, another program mentioned in Chapter 6, and I was done. Whew!

I decided to go with a very simple page layout as well. There is first a brief introductory paragraph stating who the company is, what the purpose of the page is for, and just a touch of marketing copy. Beneath that is a small

Figure 8.2   The finished Cards Company masthead

unordered list to act as a menu for launching off to the different sections of the Web server. Finally, at the bottom of the page goes a little copyright notice to satisfy the company lawyers. Nothing too terribly complex. After you learn about some of the more exciting HTML features, such as forms and CGI scripts, you will learn how to spruce the page up. But for now, let's look at the HTML for the current project.

Listing 8.3   LST8-3.HTM

```
<HTML>
<HEAD>
<TITLE>The Cards Company Home Page</TITLE>
</HEAD>
<BODY>
<IMG SRC="cardmast.gif" ALT="[Image: The Card Company Home Page Masthead]">
<H1>The Cards Company</H1>
<P>
Welcome! The Cards Company has manufactured fine playing cards since 1904,
when it was founded by Jason Grady. Our goal is to continue our tradition
of high quality playing card manufacture, just as we have been doing for
the past 91 years. Our home page is an attempt to reach out to the Internet
community and offer easy access to our high quality line of playing cards.
<I>If it's not a Cards Company card, it's not worth playing with!</I>
</P>
<UL>
<LI><STRONG><A HREF="whatnew.html">What's new with the Card Company?</A></
STRONG> 5/31/95</LI>
<LI><A HREF="compinfo.html">Company Background and Contact Information</A></LI>
<LI><A HREF="catalog.html">Product Catalog</A></LI>
<LI><A HREF="retail.html">Local Retailers Near You!</A></LI>
</UL>
For questions or comments regarding our pages, please contact
<A HREF="mailto:webmaster@cardco.com">webmaster@cardco.com</A>
<HR>
<CITE>Copyright &#169; 1995 The Cards Company. All rights reserved.</CITE>
</BODY>
</HTML>
```

The HTML in Listing 8.3 is pretty standard, as far as HTML goes. I did include the optional </P> and </LI> end tags, but that doesn't really affect how the page will look on any current browser. As you can tell from the screen shot, I wasn't kidding when I said that my style was utilitarian, but I believe I've captured the sort of feeling I was going for, overall.

Figure 8.3   The finished Cards Company home page

Substance and Style

In this chapter you've learned all the obscure little HTML details I didn't get around to covering in Chapters 5 and 6. In particular, I discussed comments and five other elements that can go in your document's head: BASE, LINK, NEXTID, ISINDEX, and META. At this time, only BASE will have any practical interest to you, and even then you probably won't use it very often. I also covered a few obscure attributes that go in anchors: URN, TITLE, METHOD, REV, and REL. Once again, you will rarely, if ever, use these attributes, but you should know about them.

From there, I discussed some style issues. Two very important things to consider before creating your home page are your company's, and therefore your home page's, image, and the number and size of your graphic images, if any. You also know the four things I believe every home page should have: a "what's new" link, your organization's contact information, proper usage of HTML, and no gonzo "because you can" stuff.

Finally, I designed a home page for a fictitious company, "The Cards Company," to help illustrate practical home page design. While not a particularly flashy piece of work, it fit perfectly with my vision of the company's specific corporate image. After you read the next couple of chapters, you may want to revisit this example home page and add some additional features to make it closer to something that would be truly useful on the Web. Stay tuned!

HTML Forms and Simple CGI Scripts

The Web isn't just fancy documents and pretty pictures. Linking documents and Internet services is nice, but there's still something missing from that formula: *interaction*. Your users can *look* at your pages, but there is no way for them to *use* your pages. By that I mean that you are sending your users *static* information, documents that remain the same on every access. The next step is for your users to be able to send information *back* to you, and perhaps for you to respond to that information dynamically, creating new documents "on the fly" based on what your users sent to you. This is done by creating *forms* in HTML, and providing *scripts* on the server side to intercept and act on the information returned in those forms.

When I first got into the Web (on the user side of things at least) one of the first demos of this type of interaction was a dummy pizza delivery form. I remember it clearly. I was at a Christmas party with my boss, at EIT in Palo Alto. Not the type who likes being smack in the middle of things, I wandered off from the central core of the party, and ended up peeking into an open office where there seemed to be some sort of activity. One of the EIT staffers was giving a small, impromptu Web demo on his Silicon Graphics box. I was immediately hooked. There were graphics. There was sound. There was even a short MPEG movie. (A short one of a couple riding a bicycle for two. I never could find that MPEG again....) But what really grabbed my attention was not all those fancy graphics, but this mock-up of a pizza delivery form. Of course it didn't work, but you could enter all sorts of neat stuff right onto the browser's screen—what you wanted on the pizza, where to deliver it, and so on.

I remember hearing the staffer musing about how one day these forms would be real, and they would work, and if you entered all the correct data into one and hit the "submit form" button, you *would* get your pizza. One day. I remember nodding with that classic "information overload" type of nod, thinking about all the incredible applications for these forms. Database front ends, online voting (perhaps not in my lifetime, but it's a thought), instant access to expert systems, online technical support, and a million other grand schemes. Of course you'd *never* be able to do something as mundane as order pizza, though! Ridiculous!

The Form of Things to Come

Well, you *can* order pizza on the Web now. I myself haven't had the nerve to try it yet, but the URL is *http://www.pizzahut.com/*. And there are database front ends, and customer feedback forms, and entire Web-based shopping malls, as well as interactive games like poker and blackjack and tic tac toe, and a million other grand schemes. It's tremendously exciting. And it's also what has changed the Web from a hypertext novelty, used only by scientists and educators, into the corporate world's "killer app" for the Internet.

Let's talk for a bit about the way Web interactivity happens, in broad terms.

Static and Dynamic HTML

HTML documents fall into two general categories: static and dynamic. By *static*, I mean that the document is written once and is stored as it was written, for delivery unchanged to users who connect to your server. Most HTML is static; static is easy. No scripts or server involvement is necessary. You write the document, place it on the server, and when its name comes up, the server delivers it.

On the other hand, *dynamic* HTML takes a bit of cleverness. It's dynamic because the HTML document is generated *at the time it is delivered* by a program of some sort called a *script*. The script is stored on the server side, and it can be written in any reasonable programming language. Instead of simply reading a static HTML document from disk and sending it out over the line, the Web server executes the script, and the script creates the dynamic HTML document on the spot. The server then transmits the newly created HTML document to the waiting user.

A dynamic HTML document can be simple, and does not require any input from the user. The user could request an HTML document at a given URL, and that document's script could generate a dynamic document containing information specific to the server's location or to that moment in time. An example might be a custom weather report from the server site, or something as simple as the local time. The user requests it, the script builds it, and the server delivers it to the user.

Getting input from the user takes more cleverness still. A *form* is a way of allowing Web users to send information to your Web server from their client programs. (That is, their Web browsers.) You can either store that information for later analysis, or act on it immediately to generate a new document on the fly, customized for that particular user at that particular time, based on the user's data entered into the form. This document is then sent down the line to the browser.

Using HTML forms, your users can add themselves to your mailing list, provide you with feedback on your Web pages or on your service in general, fill out orders for products or services online, submit a query to your database, play interactive games, remotely operate a robot arm or camera, or engage in interactive social experiments such as multi-user chats, marketing surveys, and electronic voting.

Scripts for Generating Dynamic HTML

The scripts that create simple dynamic HTML without requiring input from the user are fairly simple, and nothing special. HTML is simply ASCII text, and that ASCII text doesn't have to come from a text file. It can come from **printf** statements in C, **print** statements in Perl, **Writeln** statements in Pascal, or even the Unix **echo** statement. Using such statements, you can transmit HTML to the user without there being any separate HTML "document":

```
Print "<HTML>\n"
Print "<HEAD>\n"
Print "<TITLE>This is a Dynamic HTML Document.</TITLE>"
Print "</HEAD">
```

and so on. Here, the HTML data is being written by the script directly to standard output. The server then redirects standard output to the Internet line.

What matters in Web script work is the ability to write to standard output, read from standard input, and access environment variables. Any programming language capable of those powers can be used to write scripts. C and Perl are the languages most commonly used, and I'll be presenting Perl code most often in this book, as it's the single most popular language now being used in creating Web server scripts.

CGI Scripts

As I said, the scripts used to generate simple dynamic HTML are nothing special. They simply write "boilerplate" HTML to standard output, merging the boilerplate with calculated specific data, perhaps the current time or temperature translated into text format, or a specific GIF image chosen randomly from a library of images.

Things get more complex when the user must transmit information back to the server. As with almost any two-way conversation over an Internet link, a protocol is required to ensure that both sides of the line understand what the other is "saying." The protocol that governs the transmission of data between Web client, the server, and a script, is called the *Common Gateway Interface*, or *CGI*. A program that operates according to the dictates of CGI is called a *CGI script*.

CGI had to be invented because the standard Web protocol was not originally conceived as a two-way street. The Web was originally a scheme of passive hypertext documents, much like you'd read in a Windows Help file. Making the Web actively interactive required additional machinery. So one way to think of CGI is as an extension to the HTTP protocol, providing the machinery missing at HTTP's inception.

CGI specifies a number of different things. It specifies certain environment variables where critical data values are placed by the server for the use of the script. It specifies numerous HTML tags and tag parameters that define controls and fields to be placed on Web documents. Most importantly, it defines the nature of the data stream that passes from the Web browser to the Web server, and from there to the script itself. Without that definition, there'd be no way for the script to know what it was that the Web browser was trying to tell it.

As I mentioned in Chapter 1, it's important to understand that *CGI is not a language.* It is a protocol, which is to say, a specification by which some interaction between client and server is made to happen. In that, it's not fundamentally different from the Finger protocol, or the Whois protocol, or any of the many other existing Internet protocols.

Implementing an interactive HTML document on your Web server is a two-step process. First, you must design the HTML document using some special HTML tags. These tags define the form area of the document, the nature of the controls within that form area, the name and location of the CGI script that the form communicates with, and other things of that sort. Designing the form is fairly easy, and personally I find it a lot of fun. As with all HTML, you can write it in a simple ASCII text editor. There's nothing "magical" about the CGI elements of HTML.

The second step involves writing the actual program that processes the data returned to the server by the form. This is the CGI script itself. As I said, you can write it in any programming language that understands standard input, standard output, and environment variables. In this book, I'll mostly be using Perl, a Unix language with resemblances to both C and to DOS Batch. The CGI script is much trickier to write than HTML, though it's by no means "rocket science." You embed the name of the CGI script that serves a given HTML document into that HTML document. Then you place both the HTML document and the CGI script where the Web server can find them. The server does the rest!

When a user fills out and "submits" the data from a form, the browser sends it down the line to the server. The server then executes the CGI script When the data starts coming in on the Internet line, the server redirects the CGI data stream to standard input. The CGI script receives the data through standard input, parses it, and does whatever else it must to process the input.

Sometimes this is simply to store the information somewhere, as in the case of a user sending feedback to the Web server. More often, the CGI script prepares a customized dynamic HTML document for return to the user through the Web server, by transmitting HTML-formatted text through standard output. The server intercepts standard output and redirects it to the Internet line.

That's pretty much how the process happens, from a height. So without any further delay, let's get down and do it!

Designing a Simple Form

In any system like this, always set up the HTML document first. By using the <FORM>...</FORM> tag pair, you are able to designate a section of your document as an interactive form. This form may be as simple as a single fill-in field, or as complex as (heaven forbid) your tax forms. You can create push buttons, boxes to enter text, switch and *radio* buttons, scrolling windows of data, and the special predefined *submit* and *reset* buttons. Later on, you will even discover how to create *clickable image maps*, which can return the coordinates of the point on the image where they were clicked by the mouse pointer. In addition to that, almost any element you can use in the rest of your HTML document you can use inside a form, including headings, horizontal rules, or styles.

The <FORM>...</FORM> pair must enclose all of the interactive elements in your form. That is, the buttons, fields, and so on must come between the two <FORM> tags. Other HTML tags may be there as well, but all of the controls that return information to the server *must* be there. More on <FORM> a little later. For now, let's take a look at how you set up interactive controls on your HTML documents.

The <INPUT> Tag

The workhorse of the form is the <INPUT> tag. With it, you are able to define your text entry boxes, switches, and buttons. A half dozen or so attributes gives you control over:

- What type of input the element will accept;
- The default state of the element, such as already checked for buttons and switches, or what the default string of text will be for text boxes;
- The size of text entry boxes, and the maximum length of text the box will accept.

<INPUT> governs a few other administrative functions that you'll learn about later. Listing 9.1 is a simple example: a form to accept an email

address for adding to your mailing list. Figure 9.1 shows how this HTML document looks on the browser screen.

Listing 9.1   LIST9-1.HTM

```
<HTML>
<HEAD>
<TITLE>Sample Mailing List Form</TITLE>
</HEAD>
<BODY>
<H1>Sample Mailing List Form</H1>
<P>Thank you for your interest in the XYZ, Co. mailing list! Please fill out
the form below, and we will email you our monthly newsletter.
<FORM>
<INPUT TYPE="text" NAME="EMAIL.ADDR"><BR>
</FORM>
</BODY>
</HTML>
```

Take a quick look at the example in Listing 9.1 and compare it to the output in Figure 9.1. Not much to it, is there? You've got a brief introduction describing what the form is for, and then the three lines of HTML that present the user with a text entry box to enter an email address. Let's focus on the <INPUT> element here, and see what's going on.

The NAME attribute, contained within the <INPUT> tag, is absolutely crucial to the operation of your form. It uniquely identifies the content of its <INPUT> element. Think of it as a *variable name*. In the current example, I

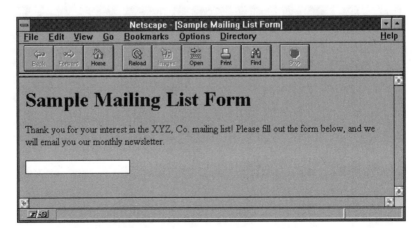

Figure 9.1   An HTML document with a text entry box.

gave the <INPUT> element the name "EMAIL.ADDR," but that was a completely arbitrary choice on my part. I could have called it "FOOFLES" if I were so inclined. Either way, the NAME attribute doesn't affect the physical appearance of your form.

The TYPE attribute controls the type of data that the user will be able to enter through the <INPUT> element in question. In this case it is set to "text" for the text entry box. This is about as simple an example as you can get. No size figure for the text box is specified, so it defaults to a length of twenty characters. There is no maximum length set, to control the maximum number of characters the user can enter, so it defaults to there being no limit. If you were to enter some text into the text box, you could reach the right edge, continue typing, and it would scroll forever. Let's make a few cosmetic changes, in the cause of making things look a bit nicer. In Listing 9.2, the size of the text entry box has been made about twice as wide, and the maximum number of characters that the user can enter has been set to 80. The screen display corresponding to Listing 9.2 is shown in Figure 9.2.

Listing 9.2   LIST9-2.HTM

```
<HTML>
<HEAD>
<TITLE>Sample Mailing List Form</TITLE>
</HEAD>
<BODY>
```

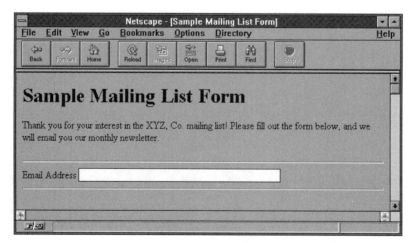

Figure 9.2   The form with size and maximum length defined

```
<H1>Sample Mailing List Form</H1>
<P>Thank you for your interest in the XYZ, Co. mailing list! Please fill out
the form below, and we will email you our monthly newsletter.
<FORM>
<HR>
Email Address <INPUT TYPE="text" NAME="EMAIL.ADDR" SIZE="40" MAXLENGTH="80">
<HR>
</FORM>
</BODY>
</HTML>
```

The SIZE and MAXLENGTH Attributes

The example in listing 9.2 makes a few aesthetic changes. First, I've added some instructions to the user about what should be entered into the text box. It's also common practice to add a horizontal rule at the top and bottom of the form to separate the form from the rest of the document, so I've done that as well. Once again, it's just aesthetics. A few more attributes were also added to the <INPUT> tag. I added the SIZE attribute to make the text box exactly 40 characters wide. I also added the MAXLENGTH attribute to enforce a limit for how much text can be entered into the field before no more will be accepted.

As you can see, the SIZE attribute changes the width of a text entry box. It accepts a value which is the number of characters in width that the box should be. The default, if the attribute is left out, is 20 characters, but I would recommend always including a size anyway. It'll avoid little surprises from the odd browser that doesn't corrrectly adhere to the CGI defaults. The minimum size is one. If you enter a smaller number, like zero or less, there is no telling what might happen, so don't!

There is no maximum size limit; however, I would recommend against anything more than 80, or the right edge of the text box will scroll off the side of the window—not very polite. Anyway, the SIZE attribute merely sets the *physical* width of the box and imposes no limit on the number of characters the user may enter. If the box is only 20 characters wide, when the user types a twenty-first character, everything will scroll to the left.

If you need to limit the number of characters the user can type, MAXLENGTH is the attribute to use. If you leave out MAXLENGTH, the default is no limit at all. The minimum value is one, and any value less than that will cause the maximum length to go back to infinity. Note that MAXLENGTH does *not* affect the physical width of the text box. Use the SIZE attribute for that instead, as explained earlier.

Check Boxes

Your form is shaping up, but it's still a bit terse. What if you have more than one mailing list? You wouldn't want to have a separate form for each one, so let's add a few more options to the form in the interest of making it more generally useful. In particular, let's toss in a few *check boxes* so that the user can select which mailing lists he or she would like to be added to, without having to enter a single email address more than once. Listing 9.3 adds three check boxes and two buttons to the form. Figure 9.3 shows you what it looks like on the browser screen.

Listing 9.3   LIST9-3.HTM

```
<HTML>
<HEAD>
<TITLE>Sample Mailing List Form</TITLE>
</HEAD>
<BODY>
<H1>Sample Mailing List Form</H1>
<P>Thank you for your interest in the XYZ, Co. mailing list! Please fill out
the form below, and we will email you one of our monthly newsletters.
<FORM>
<HR>
Email Address <INPUT TYPE="text" NAME="EMAIL.ADDR" SIZE="40" MAXLENGTH="80">
<P><I>Pick one or more lists:</I><BR>
<INPUT TYPE="checkbox" NAME="LIST.ANNOUNCE" CHECKED> Announcements<BR>
<INPUT TYPE="checkbox" NAME="LIST.WIDGETS"> Widgets<BR>
<INPUT TYPE="checkbox" NAME="LIST.WHATSITS"> Whats-Its
<P><INPUT TYPE="submit"> <INPUT TYPE="reset">
<HR>
</FORM>
</BODY>
</HTML>
```

The *checkbox* <INPUT> type allows you to add any number of check boxes to your form. A check box is a two-state item; it can be either checked or not checked. As with the text field described earlier, each check box is given a unique name to identify it when it comes time to process the form. The default state of a check box is unselected; however, by using the

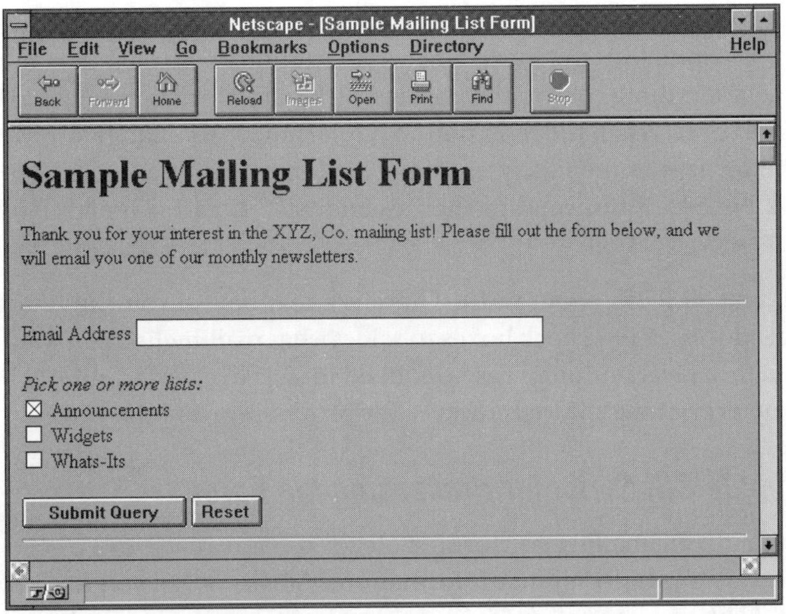

Figure 9.3   Adding buttons and check boxes

CHECKED attribute, you can change the default state to selected. For example, in the current example, the first check box, "LIST.ANNOUNCE,"
is set to be automatically selected, unless the user unselects it manually.
The other two check boxes, however, begin their existence unselected.

There are also two other <INPUT> elements in this example. The *submit*
type creates a special-purpose push button that is used to send a completed
form on its way to be processed. When the user clicks on the submit button, the Web browser sends the data stream from all the <INPUT> elements to the Web server.

In the first two examples, it was acceptable to leave out the submit button.
Since there was just a single text field in the form, the browser always un-
derstood when you were finished filling out the form. When you pressed
Enter after entering your text, the form (which consisted basically of the
text and only the text) would be submitted. With the addition of the three
check boxes, however, when to submit the form is no longer clear. The
user has the option to think about things, select or deselect the check
boxes, and perhaps re-edit the text box. But with the submit button, just
select submit and you're unambiguously done.

Conversely, the *reset* type creates a button you would click if you are definitely *not* done with the form. You are so "not done" in fact, that you want to reset everything back to the way it was when the form was first displayed, and start over. When the reset button is selected, every change you've made to the form is immediately erased. Text boxes are cleared, buttons and check boxes are returned to their default states, and you are allowed to start afresh.

Well, that all looks about right. There is a text box so you can enter your email address, a few check boxes to select what mailing lists you want to be added to, a reset button in case you need to start over, and a submit button to send everything off to the server for processing. So what now?

A Simple CGI Script for Processing the Form

Now that your mailing list form is all set up and ready to go, you need some way to process all that information. At this point, you have two options. First, you can try to find a pre-made CGI script which does exactly what you want. Second (and certainly more fun), you can write your own. If you're going to write your own, your next task is choosing a programming language in which to write your scripts. You probably have a favorite language, such as C, Perl, or Basic. Any language that knows how to access standard input, standard output, and environment variables will work beautifully. For my examples I will be using Perl, since Perl is a lot more portable than C, and using Perl for CGI scripts is very common.

I suppose I should add here that the language you choose must be runnable on the server machine hosting the Web server that will be executing the script. You don't write a CGI script to run on your desktop PC or Mac. Typically, a Web server runs on a Unix machine, which may or may not be Intel-based. So it's best to use the tools that are available on the server system itself. C and Perl are the ones you're likely to find on virtually all server systems. And of these, Perl is by far the easier to use, and the most efficient at packing script functionality into lines of code.

To POST or to GET?

There are two general mechanisms by which a CGI script can read the data passed to it from a form. They are the GET method and the POST method. If you choose the GET method, all the data from the form will be sent to your script on the *command line*, as well as in an *environment variable*. The POST method, on the other hand, receives all the form's data from standard input (stdin). Which method you use is up to you; however, I would recommend using POST. After you learn the specifics of both methods, the reasons for this will become clear.

Obtaining and Preparing Form Data

There are three steps your scripts must accomplish before you can act on the data returned from your form. First, your script must actually find the data returned from the form and store it somewhere for parsing. For scripts using the GET mechanism, the easiest place to find the data is in the QUERY_STRING environment variable, which is set by the server when it executes the script. For POST scripts (which are the kind you'll probably use more often), the process involves reading from standard input.

The second step is parsing out the data from the returned data string, regardless of how it was obtained or where it was stored. For both the GET and POST methods, your data is returned in one long string of NAME=VALUE pairs, each pair separated from the next pair by an "&" (ampersand), so the parsing process is one of splitting these NAME=VALUE pairs apart.

The data returned from your script may contain special characters. These are encoded at the browser end so that they may be safely transmitted to the server along a 7-bit ASCII link. Space characters, too, are sometimes converted to plus symbols to avoid semantic uncertainties during the parsing process. These conversions are called *escapes* in Unix jargon. Returning data is escaped in exactly the same way that special characters are escaped in URLs, so the final phase is *unescaping* both the NAME and the VALUE in each NAME=VALUE pair. In other words, this means translating "+" (plus) symbols into spaces, and "%xx" hex pairs into real characters.

Don't worry, none of this is as hard as it sounds. I'll show you about a dozen lines of Perl which will perform all three steps quite nicely, in a little while. But first, let's take a closer look at exactly what the example form we've been building will be sending to our fledgling CGI script.

Environment Variables Used by CGI Scripts

The first thing that the Web server does after it receives the data submitted by the form is set a few *environment variables* for your script. These variables comprise a sort of "public bulletin board" for programs running on the server machine, and contain information such as the name of the remote machine which is submitting the data, the name and path of your script, which method (GET or POST) the server used to send the form data to your script, and a few dozen other, more obscure items of information. I'll list all the major environment variables a little later, although to be perfectly honest, I've only found a use for about a half dozen of them. In fact, there are only three variables which we will be using for our mailing list script. They are REQUEST_METHOD, QUERY_STRING, and CONTENT_LENGTH.

The REQUEST_METHOD environment variable contains the method the server used to send the form data to your script, either "GET" for the GET method, or "POST" for the POST method. We need this information to figure out how to read the form data into the script. If the method is found to be GET, it is very easy to retrieve the form data. The data will all be stored in the QUERY_STRING environment variable, tied up with a ribbon and ready to go!

If, on the other hand, the method is found to be POST, the form data will be arriving via the standard input (stdin), and it is going to be a little tougher to retrieve. To make things a tad more difficult still, the server will *not* send an end-of-file marker at the end of the data stream, or even terminate the data stream with a newline. Fortunately, the server saves the length, in characters, of the data it wrote to stdin in the CONTENT_LENGTH environment variable. All we need to do now is read stdin, one character at a time, for as many characters as the value in CONTENT_LENGTH indicates.

A Simple CGI Script in Perl

Let's write a simple Perl program to take a peek at how this process works and see what is actually going on here. Pull up your favorite text editor and enter the program in Listing 9.4. Put the program in the directory cgi-bin (or wherever your server looks for CGI scripts) and name the script MAILLIST.PL. After you've done that, you need to make one small change to the mailing list HTML document we've been working on: You need to tell it the name of the CGI script, and what method the server should use to send the form data to it. This information is set in the <FORM> tag, like so:

```
<FORM METHOD="GET" ACTION="/cgi-bin/maillist.pl">
```

The METHOD attribute can be set to either "GET" or "POST," depending on how you want the server to send the form data to the script. For this simple example, it really doesn't matter; for the sake of demonstration I'll choose "GET." The ACTION attribute is the URL of the CGI script, in this case a relative URL.

Listing 9.4 is the first part of our new Perl script. It reads all the data from the form and places it in the $FORM_DATA variable for later processing.

Listing 9.4   LIST9-4.PL

```perl
#!/usr/local/bin/perl

if ($ENV{'REQUEST_METHOD'} eq "GET") {        # Using GET..
        $FORM_DATA = $ENV{'QUERY_STRING'};    # Save data to FORM_DATA
} else {                                      # Using POST..
        $LENGTH = $ENV{'CONTENT_LENGTH'};     # How much data to read?
        while ($LENGTH) {
                $FORM_DATA .= getc(STDIN);    # Save data to FORM_DATA
                $LENGTH--;
        }
}

print "Content-type: text/html\n\n";

print "REQUEST_METHOD: $ENV{'REQUEST_METHOD'}<BR>\n";
print "CONTENT_LENGTH: $ENV{'CONTENT_LENGTH'}<BR>\n";
print "QUERY_STRING: $ENV{'QUERY_STRING'}<BR>\n";
print "<HR>\n";
print "FORM_DATA: $FORM_DATA\n";
```

The Perl code in Listing 9.4 can handle both the GET or POST methods. The script first reads the environment variable REQUEST_METHOD and, if the method is found to be GET, the contents of the QUERY_STRING environment variable are saved in the $FORM_DATA variable and that's all that needs to be done.

If the method is not GET, however, (and must therefore be POST) the script reads the CONTENT_LENGTH environment variable instead, to find out how much data is waiting to arrive from standard input. Then, one character at a time is taken off of standard input and appended to the script's $FORM_DATA variable, until all the waiting characters have been read. Either way, all the data returned from the form ends up sitting in the $FORM_DATA variable. Don't puzzle about the **print** statements at the end of Listing 9.4. They are there so you can test the script and find out what variables are set and what their values are.

How the Script Works

Now, what exactly do we have sitting in $FORM_DATA? To answer that question, let's pretend that a user, Rachel, has entered the following information into the mailing list form. Her email address is "rachel@widgetech.com" and she wants to be added to our default "Announce" list (see Figure 9.3), as well as our "Widgets" list. If you could take a peek at the information in $FORM_DATA, you would see the following:

```
EMAIL.ADDR=rachel@widgetech.com&LIST.ANNOUNCE=on&LIST.WIDGETS=on
```

Raw data indeed. Here's a good first example of those NAME=VALUE pairs that we spoke of earlier. There are three in all, separated by ampersand symbols. The name portions are on the left side of each pair, and are those names we assigned to each <INPUT> element in the HTML document. And, obviously, the data to the right of the = (equal) symbols are the values in the NAME=VALUE pairs.

Rachel's email address is easy to spot in the string, assigned to the name EMAIL.ADDR. The other two names are names of check boxes. Whenever a check box is checked, the check box's name is transmitted, assigned to the value "on," meaning that that check box was selected. However, the names of check boxes that are *not* checked aren't sent to the script at all.

It looks like we are going to have to break that string down before it can be used. Not to sweat—the following section of Perl code does just that. It's actually the next portion of the script, and I didn't include it in Listing 9.4. So just paste it to the end of the Listing 9.4. Once again, don't worry about the code beneath the "Display what we just did" comment. It's there simply so you can test the script and see the values of the variables we just set.

The code in Listing 9.5 takes the data from the $FORM_DATA variable and splits it into NAME=VALUE pairs. The pairs are then placed in an associative array, so we can reference the values by name later on.

Listing 9.5   LIST9-5.PL

```
foreach (split(/&/, $FORM_DATA)) {    # Extract each pair from the string
    ($NAME,$VALUE) = split(/=/, $_);  # Split each pair into a NAME and a VALUE
    $MYDATA{$NAME} = $VALUE;           # Assign the pair to an associative array
}

# Display what we just did

print "<HR>\n";
foreach (keys %MYDATA) {
        print "$_ is $MYDATA{$_}<BR>\n";
}
```

Associative Arrays in Perl

If you're not familiar with Perl's associative arrays, here's what's going on. First, the script looks at the **$FORM_DATA** variable and starts chopping it apart, using the ampersands as delimiters between the NAME=VALUE pairs. As each pair is extracted, it is split again, this time using the equal sign as the delimiter, giving us the name of the input element and its value in separate variables. Finally, these two variables are placed into an associative array called **$MYDATA**.

Associative arrays are wonderful in a situation like this, because they make retrieving the data extremely easy, later on. Arrays in most traditional languages are indexed by number. Array elements may be accessed only by their number. Associative arrays, by contrast, contain elements that are *named* rather than numbered. In Listing 9.5, I stored the values from the NAME=VALUE pairs in an associative array, and used the NAME part of each pair as the element's index! This allows me to retrieve the VALUE portion of each pair simply by using its NAME. For example, if I want to find out what Rachel entered for her email address, all I have to do is use the following line:

```
$MYDATA{'EMAIL.ADDR'}
```

The Great Unescape

At this point, it looks like everything is ready. You have the data Rachel entered, you've put all her answers into an associative array for easy access, and now all that is left is to actually use the data in the associative array to add her to the lists. Well...not quite. What if Rachel's email address were "rachel%list@widgetech.com" instead? Since all the data sent to your script will be escaped, just as with URLs, the "%" symbol will end up escaped as "%25" and if you don't *unescape* it, her mail will bounce! It turns out that this isn't a very hard thing to fix, although the code to do so is a little cryptic. The new code, enhanced from Listing 9.5, is shown in Listing 9.6. Here, plus symbols are converted into spaces and %-escapes are changed back to the original characters.

Listing 9.6   LIST9-6.PL

```
foreach (split(/&/, $FORM_DATA)) {     # Extract each pair from the string
    ($NAME,$VALUE) = split(/=/, $_);  # Split each pair into a NAME and a VALUE
    # Unescape the NAME and VALUE
    $NAME =~ s/\+/ /g;
    $NAME =~ s/%([0-9|A-F]{2})/pack(C,hex($1))/eg;
    $VALUE =~ s/\+/ /g;
    $VALUE =~ s/%([0-9|A-F]{2})/pack(C,hex($1))/eg;
    $MYDATA{$NAME} = $VALUE;              # Assign the pair to an associative array
}
```

I told you it was a bit cryptic! Here's what is going on, in a nutshell: Right after a NAME=VALUE pair is split into separate NAME and VALUE variables, each variable is unescaped. You want to be sure to do this *after* you split the pair, never before! The line **$NAME =~ s/\+/ /g;** removes any plus symbols from the $NAME variable and replaces them with spaces. The next line goes over the $NAME variable again, this time taking any %xx escapes and translating them back to the actual characters they represent. If you're familiar with Perl you should be able to dope out the algorithm from the code; but I don't have the room to take it on blow by blow. Trust me, it works.

The process is then repeated for the $VALUE variable, and finally the newly unescaped variables are assigned to the associative array, just as before. *Now* we're done, and can focus on more noble tasks, such as actually adding Rachel's address to the mailing lists.

Talking Back to the Browser

You've already seen some examples of how a CGI script talks back to the user's Web browser, in the sample mailing list program. Let's expand on that. As you saw, your CGI scripts talk back to the Web browser by writing to *standard output* (stdout), just as it would if it was writing to your screen. (Actually, it talks to the server first, and the server relays the information to the Web browser, but that's not important now.) But before the browser can get *any* of this output, your script must first send two very important lines to standard output: the line "Content-type: text/html," followed immediately by a blank line. These two lines will be exactly the same for all scripts, without exception. In a Perl script, this is easily done with a **print** statement:

```
print "Content-type: text/html\n\n";
```

Notice the double newline specifier "\n\n" in the example above. The first newline moves to the next line, and the second inserts the blank line. If you leave out either the "Content-type: text/html" line or the blank line, the script will simply fail to work. What is so important about these lines? What do they do and why do your scripts need them? To understand what these lines do, a little discussion about *Multipurpose Internet Mail Extensions* (MIME) is in order.

MIME's the Word

MIME (pronounced just like those guys who spend all day in white grease-paint and suspenders trying to escape from imaginary boxes) was developed to supplement the specification for "regular" Internet mail by addressing the emergence of new technologies, such as multimedia. MIME is defined fully in Internet RFC1521, in case you're interested. RFC822, the specification for regular Internet mail, goes through great pains to describe exactly how the *header* (all those cryptic lines at the top of your Internet mail) should appear. But what RFC822 doesn't address is the actual *body* of the mail, the message content itself. MIME supplements RFC822 by providing additional headers to describe what sort of data the message contains, such as plain text, graphics, audio, character sets, and even a combination of different types.

Every document that goes through an HTTP server, such as your HTML documents, are assigned a MIME header, which describes the content of the document so that the Web browser knows what to do with it. This is one of the ways your browser knows whether it is receiving an HTML document or an inline image to display.

So now we come to that odd "Content-type: text/html" line your script must supply. It's something like the NAME=VALUE pairs we've been working with, in that it specifies a header component and a header value. "Content-type:" is a component of a MIME header. The "text" part is the content-type, and the "html" part is the content-subtype. So "text/html" means this is a text document that happens to contain HTML tags.

The MIME header must be there because your script is creating a document that hadn't existed previously. The server has no way to know what sort of document it is in the MIME scheme of things unless you specifically tag it with a MIME header. And if the server doesn't know what sort of document your script is creating, the server can't tell the Web browser what it is either.

The blank line after the content-type MIME header line tells the server that you are done with the header, and will now begin sending the actual document. No blank line, no document. No document, no fun. The server will throw up its arms and return an empty document or an error message. Not a good thing.

Incidently, for some experimental proof of all this MIME stuff, try modifying your mailing list script to send a content-subtype of "plain," like this, and see what happens:

```
Content-type: text/plain
```

The HTML portion of the document will *not* be parsed, because you just told the server that the script output is not in fact HTML, but just plain old text instead. I'll have more to say about MIME later on.

Sending Dynamic HTML Back to the Web Browser

Once you've output your MIME header, it's time to send out the dynamic HTML document in response to the user's input. There's absolutely nothing else special you need to do as far as HTML goes. As long as you have that "Content-type: text/html" plus a blank line, the browser will interpret everything after as if it were any other HTML document. Listing 9.7 is our example add-me-to-your-mailing list script in its entirety, including some considerably more user-friendly output.

Listing 9.7   LIST9-7.PL

```perl
#!/usr/local/bin/perl

if ($ENV{'REQUEST_METHOD'} eq "GET") {          # Using GET..
        $FORM_DATA = $ENV{'QUERY_STRING'};      # Save data to FORM_DATA
```

```perl
    } else {                                  # Using POST..
            $LENGTH = $ENV{'CONTENT_LENGTH'};     # How much data to read?
            while ($LENGTH) {
                    $FORM_DATA .= getc(STDIN);        # Save data to FORM_DATA
                    $LENGTH--;
            }
    }


foreach (split(/&/, $FORM_DATA)) {
        ($NAME, $VALUE) = split(/=/, $_);
        $NAME =~ s/\+/ /g;
        $NAME =~ s/%([0-9|A-F]{2})/pack(C,hex($1))/eg;
        $VALUE =~ s/\+/ /g;
        $VALUE =~ s/%([0-9|A-F]{2})/pack(C,hex($1))/eg;
        $MYDATA{$NAME} = $VALUE;
}

print "Content-type: text/html\n\n";
print "<HTML>\n";
print "<HEAD>\n";
print "<TITLE>Widget Co Email Mailing Lists</TITLE>\n";
print "</HEAD>\n";
print "<BODY>\n";
print "<H1>Widget Co Email Mailing Lists</H1>\n";
print "<EMP>Thank you</EMP> for your interest in the Widget Co! Our\n";
print "mailing lists are low traffic, consisting of two or three mailings\n";
print "a month. If you would like to unsubscribe from the lists,\n";
print "instructions will arrive in a confirmation email with 24 hours.\n";
print "<HR>\n";
print "The email address $MYDATA{'EMAIL_ADDR'} has been added to the\n";
print "following list(s):<BR>\n";
print "<UL>\n";

if ($MYDATA{'LIST.ANNOUNCE'} eq "on") {
        print "<LI> Announcements\n";
        open(LIST, '>>/home/lists/announce-list');
        print LIST "$MYDATA{'EMAIL.ADDR'}\n";
        close(LIST);
}
if ($MYDATA{'LIST.WIDGETS'} eq "on") {
        print "<LI> Widgets List\n";
        open(LIST, '>>/home/lists/widgets-list');
        print LIST "$MYDATA{'EMAIL.ADDR'}\n";
        close(LIST);
}
if ($MYDATA{'LIST.WHATSITS'} eq "on") {
        print "<LI> Whats-Its\n";
        open(LIST, '>>/home/lists/widgets-list');
```

```
        print LIST "$MYDATA{'EMAIL.ADDR'}\n";
        close(LIST);
}
print "</UL>\n";
print "<P><STRONG>Thank you!</STRONG>\n";
print "</BODY>\n";
print "</HTML>\n";
```

The portion of interest right here is the long sequence of **print** statements following the Perl code we discussed earlier. The **print** statements create a dynamic HTML document (notice the first **print** statement, which issues the MIME header) by writing a sequence of boilerplate and customized text lines to standard output. The server redirects the output to the Internet link.

There are three **if** statements in the midst of the **print** statements that "customize" the HTML output to the response submitted by the user. There is one **if** statement for each of the three check boxes on the original HTML form. If a check box was checked, text is generated to confirm addition to that check box's associated mailing list. If the box was not checked, no confirming output is generated. This is how the script sends back HTML that reacts to input submitted from the form, and code like this is the crux of all CGI programming. Figure 9.4 shows an instance of the original HTML

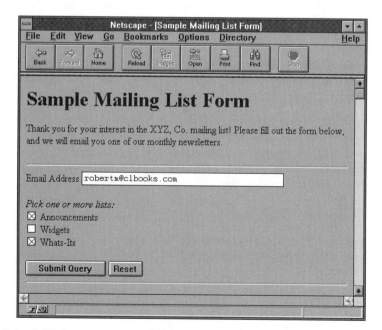

Figure 9.4   A filled-out HTML form, ready to submit

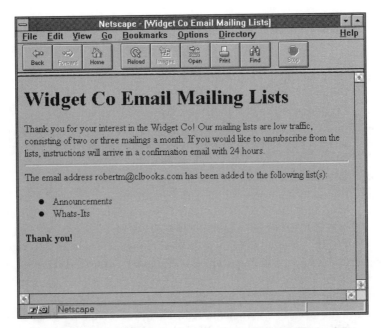

Figure 9.5   The page returned in response to the form shown in Figure 9.5.

form, filled out and ready to submit. Figure 9.5 shows the dynamic HTML that was generated in response to the filled-out form shown in Figure 9.4.

Of course, there could be some improvements. For one, there is absolutely no error checking. If the user doesn't enter an email address at all, or neglects to select at least one list, things are going to get ugly. And I don't check to see if the user's name is already in the list, or even if the script is able to open the lists for appending. The whole idea was simply to give you a flavor for how the CGI process actually works. Once you understand that, the rest will follow.

Things That Can Go Wrong

What could possibly go wrong? Usually not much, but unfortunately when something does go wrong, it can be a real pain to fix. There are two general types of problems: configuration problems, where either the server or script isn't set up correctly, and programming problems. I don't know which is worse. But since in my Web work I have probably run into about every problem you could ever face, I now submit for your assistance Table 9.1, to help you troubleshoot some of the most common CGI problems.

Table 9.1   Common problems encountered in simple CGI work, with solutions

Problem: File not found, error #404.

Solution: Does the URL in the form's ACTION attribute point to the correct script? Did you mistype the script name?

Problem: Forbidden or Permission denied, error #403 or #404.

Solution: Does the server have execute permission on the file? The directory? Is the server set up correctly to execute CGI scripts? Check the server documentation or the "Choosing and Installing Your Server" chapter.

Problem: Configuration error, error #500.

Solution: Do you have a Content-type: MIME header line? Did you remember the blank line after the Content-type? Is the program crashing during execution, perhaps due to a programming error?

Problem: The HTML won't display correctly and you just see the HTML tags.

Solution: Check your Content-type: line. It should be set for "text/html" and not "text/plain."

Problem: Inline images are not displaying or other links are broken.

Solution: If the images work when not returned by your script, try using the absolute URL instead of a relative URL. Relative URLs returned by CGI scripts can sometimes be a problem.

Problem: You wanted to use the POST method but keep getting the GET method instead.

Solution: Did you mistype "POST" in the METHOD attribute? If the method is invalid, it will default to GET.

Problem: Getting text entry boxes but want radio buttons/check boxes/etc.

Solution: Is there a typo in the TYPE attribute? The type defaults to "text" if it is invalid or missing. A common mistake is using "button" instead of "radio." Well, at least *I* make that mistake a lot.

Problem: Script is "hanging" forever and never returns.

Solution: Are you in an infinite loop? Even if the loop is at the very end of the script, nothing will be sent to the browser until it is completely finished. Are you trying to read more characters from stdin than CONTENT_LENGTH says there are?

More Advanced HTML Forms

The mailing list example we just completed covered quite a bit. You learned how to design your HTML form, and then how to read and process the user data returned from the form, by using of a CGI script. You also learned a bit about sending dynamic HTML output back to the user's browser. It's time to press on and learn new things. The next example, a custom user-feedback form, will incorporate a few new form elements, including SELECT, TEXTAREA, and radio buttons, which are an alternative to check boxes. I'll also show you a few other attributes for the <INPUT> tag, including VALUE, which allows you to do a lot of interesting and useful things.

The example custom user-feedback form will have five different types of input. There will be a text entry box for the user to enter an email address if he or she would like a reply back. Underneath that will be a group of three radio buttons, each representing a different level of urgency for the feedback. For example, if the user is reporting a typo somewhere on your Web site, the urgency would probably be very low. If there is a major problem, however, like an important link pointing nowhere, the urgency would be understandably higher. Next, there will be another group of radio buttons that allow the user to specify the nature of the feedback. Finally, there will be a multi-line text box where the user can speak his or her mind about whatever the feedback pertains to.

Let's begin by creating the top half of the form, with the radio buttons, as shown in Listing 9.8. Figure 9.6 shows what this HTML looks like when interpreted to the Web browser screen.

Listing 9.8 LIST9-8.HTM

```
<HTML>
<HEAD>
<TITLE>Sample Custom User-Feedback Form</TITLE>
</HEAD>
<BODY>
<FORM METHOD="post" ACTION="/cgi-bin/feedback.pl">
Your email: <INPUT TYPE="text" NAME="EMAIL.ADDR" SIZE="40" MAXLENGTH="80">
<P>
<I>How urgently do you need a reply:</I><BR>
<INPUT TYPE="radio" NAME="URGENCY" VALUE="FYI" CHECKED> Just FYI
<INPUT TYPE="radio" NAME="URGENCY" VALUE="PLR"> Please reply
<INPUT TYPE="radio" NAME="URGENCY" VALUE="RUR"> Reply urgently
<P>
<I>What is the nature of your feedback:</I><BR>
<INPUT TYPE="radio" NAME="SUBJECT" VALUE="GENC" CHECKED> General Comments
<INPUT TYPE="radio" NAME="SUBJECT" VALUE="TYPO"> Found a Typo
<INPUT TYPE="radio" NAME="SUBJECT" VALUE="BUGR"> Bug Report
<P>
<INPUT TYPE="submit"> <INPUT TYPE="reset">
</FORM>
</BODY>
</HTML>
```

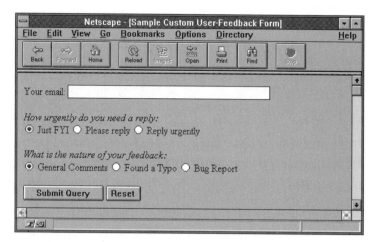

Figure 9.6   Radio buttons on an HTML form

Radio Buttons to "Choose One of the Above"

The general structure of Listing 9.8 should be fairly familiar. This time the form will use the POST method to send its data to the script FEEDBACK.PL, which we will write later, when we're done designing the form. The first input element is a text entry box, exactly like the one in the previous mailing list example.

What's new here are the six radio buttons. At first, the code to implement them looks superficially like the HTML to implement check boxes. The differences, however, are crucial. The type attribute, "radio," is of course different. But why do all three buttons have the same name, and what is this VALUE thing? Here's the key difference between the behavior of the radio buttons and regular check boxes.

As you discovered in the mailling list example, each check box is an independent entity, which may be checked or unchecked without affecting any other control on the HTML form. But radio buttons are different. Radio buttons are defined in groups, and *only one radio button in a given group may be selected at a time.* In the current example, the first radio button, "Just FYI," defaults to the selected state. But if the user decides this message requires an urgent reply and checks "Reply urgently," then "Just FYI" will automatically be *un*checked. If the user changes his or her mind yet again and decides it is slightly less urgent and checks "Please reply" instead, this time "Reply urgently" will automatically be unchecked.

As you might have already guessed, all radio buttons with the exact same name are considered to be in the same group. In our case, there are three radio buttons, each named URGENCY, which belong to one group, and another three radio buttons in a different group with a different name, SUBJECT. You can have as many groups of radio buttons on a form as you want; as long as each group has its own name, it will operate independently of all the other groups. So, when a button in the group URGENCY is checked, it will in no way affect any of the buttons in the group SUBJECT.

This leaves us in an interesting position. If each button in a group has the same name, how can you tell which button within the group was actually checked? The VALUE attribute is used to set what each button returns to the script when that button is checked. So, if the "Just FYI" button is checked, the NAME=VALUE pair URGENCY=FYI will be sent to the script when the form is finally submitted. URGENCY is the name of the whole group of three radio buttons, and FYI is the value that the whole group takes on (because only one button in a group can be pressed at a time) when the form is submitted to the script.

Radio Buttons Versus Check Boxes

Incidently, check boxes can also use the VALUE attribute to change their default value from "on" to anything you want. As a matter of a fact, there is nothing that says you can't give the same name to several check boxes as well, and change their return values with the VALUE attribute to specify which ones are checked. This *won't* cause check boxes to act like radio buttons, though, so I would strongly recommend against have more than one check box with the same name. Here's why: if the user checks two check boxes that have the same name, when you assign the check boxes to the associative array in your script, the data from one of the check boxes will overwrite the other. Of course, radio buttons will never suffer from this problem, because by their very nature, only one can be checked at a time in any particular group. Or *can* you have more than one radio button checked in a group at once?

Actually, yes. You can have more than one radio button checked in the same group. If in your form, you specifically set two or more radio buttons in the same group as checked, then that is exactly what they will be when they're displayed on the form, regardless of the fact that such a configuration makes no logical sense.

Which brings me seamlessly to "Famous radio button faux pas." Number one: Never explicitly set more than one radio button in the same group as checked. You will suffer the same problem as the "check boxes with the same name" problem. Number two: Never explicitly set *all* the radio buttons in the same group as checked. There will be no way for the user to unselect any of them! And finally, number three: Never have only one radio button alone in a group. Once it is checked, only resetting the entire form will uncheck it. And if you explicitly set it as checked, nothing can ever uncheck it. A radio button is not a check box. Learn their differences, and use each when appropriate in the manner for which it was designed.

OPTION Menus and <SELECT>

You know, there is an alternative to radio buttons I think would go very nicely in place of the second group of radio buttons on our form. It's called an OPTION menu, and this would be a great opportunity to play around with one. OPTION menus are great when you want to stick a bunch of radio boxes into a very small space, or when you want to give your form a slightly different "feel." Let's take a look at an example, shown in Listing 9.9. The second group of three radio buttons has been changed to an OPTION menu.

Listing 9.9   LIST9-9.HTM

```
<HTML>
<HEAD>
<TITLE>Sample Custom User-Feedback Form</TITLE>
</HEAD>
<BODY>
<FORM METHOD="post" ACTION="/cgi-bin/feedback.pl">
Your email: <INPUT TYPE="text" NAME="EMAIL.ADDR" SIZE="40" MAXLENGTH="80">
<P>
<I>How urgently do you need a reply:</I><BR>
<INPUT TYPE="radio" NAME="URGENCY" VALUE="FYI" CHECKED> Just FYI
<INPUT TYPE="radio" NAME="URGENCY" VALUE="PLR"> Please reply
<INPUT TYPE="radio" NAME="URGENCY" VALUE="RUR"> Reply urgently
<P>
<I>What is the nature of your feedback:</I>
<SELECT NAME="SUBJECT">
<OPTION SELECTED>General Comments
<OPTION>Found Typo
<OPTION>Bug Report
</SELECT>
```

```
<P>
<INPUT TYPE="submit"> <INPUT TYPE="reset">
</FORM>
</BODY>
</HTML>
```

Figure 9.7 shows you what an OPTION menu looks like on the screen, with the three options dropped and ready to be selected. Figure 9.8 shows you what the menu looks like after you've selected one of the three options.

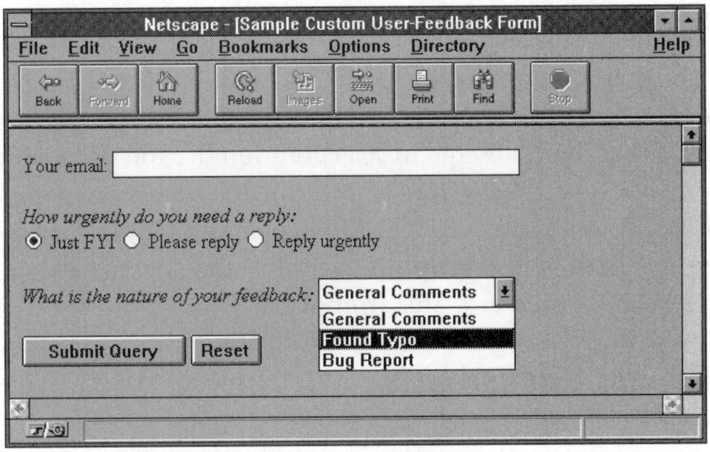

Figure 9.7 An OPTION menu ready to be selected from

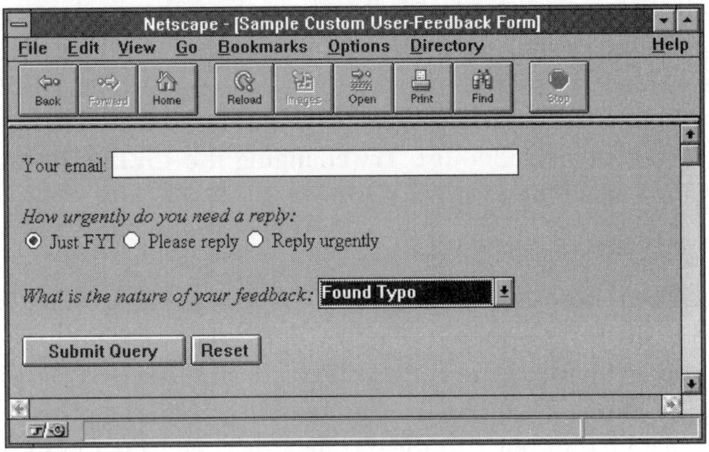

Figure 9.8 An OPTION menu after selection

Well, Listing 9.9 certainly looks a bit different from what we're used to. There is some superficial resemblance to ordinary HTML lists, as I described in an earlier chapter. There is a <SELECT> start tag, immediately followed by a series of items each preceeded by an <OPTION> tag, with the whole structure finally closed by a </SELECT> end tag. But the similarity to lists ends there. Like the <INPUT> tag, <SELECT> has a NAME attribute that acts as a variable name when the data is sent to your script. There is also an optional attribute SELECTED which, when used with an <OPTION> tag, behaves like <INPUT>'s CHECKED attribute, causing that option to be automatically selected.

When <SELECT> is used in the OPTION menu mode, as in the current example, it behaves like a series of radio buttons. Only one option may be selected at a time, and subsequent selections remove the previous selection, so only one option can be sent to your script at a time. For example, if you selected "Bug Report," the NAME=VALUE pair of "SUBJECT=Bug+Report" would be returned to the script. Notice that the space between the two words has been escaped as a plus symbol!

<SELECT> and Scrolled Lists

<SELECT> can also operate in another mode, called a *scrolled list*. Unlike an OPTION menu, where only one option is displayed at a time, the scrolled list mode will display as many options as it can fit at once in a scrolling window. If there are more options than it can fit in the window, a scroll bar will be activated on the right side of the window. To change the option menu to a scrolled list, you will need to add a new attribute, "SIZE." If the SIZE attribute is set for a value greater than one, <SELECT>'s mode will change to that of a scrolled list. Try changing the <SELECT> tag to read like this and reload the form:

```
<SELECT NAME="SUBJECT" SIZE="2">
```

Since the size is now set to two, <SELECT> changes to scrolled list mode. Only two of the three options are now visible, so if you want to see the last option, you will have to use the scroll bar on the scrolled list window to scroll the list down. This is really neat, but other than the physical appearance, there is no difference in the scrolled list's behavior. Only one option may be selected at a time, so only one option value is returned to your CGI script.

Multiple Selections with <SELECT>

Perhaps you see where all of this is leading? Suppose we want to be able to select more than one option off the list? After all, the subject of the feedback may be a bug report as well as some general comments, or maybe all three together. It would be really nice if you could give your users that extra option—and you can. The MULTIPLE attribute will send <SELECT> into yet another mode, that of a multiple-option scrolled list. Try changing the <SELECT> tag to this:

```
<SELECT NAME="SUBJECT" SIZE="3" MULTIPLE>
```

In multiple mode, by clicking on one of the options and dragging your mouse down the list, multiple options can be selected. But now, however, you have a new problem. Since the <SELECT> element has only one name (SUBJECT in this case), the form may be forced to return more than one option with the same name. This can be done, but it's not especially convenient to deal with.

If multiple selections are made within an option list with a single name, multiple NAME=VALUE pairs will be returned to the script, one for each selection—and all of them have the same value in NAME! That is, if all three options are selected, the form would send this data stream back to the script:

```
SUBJECT=General+Comments&SUBJECT=Found+Typo&SUBJECT=Bug+Report
```

The problem with trying to insert multiple values for the same name into a Perl associative array arises again. Is there a clever HTML solution? Unfortunately not. You are just going to have to deal with this in your script. I'll show you my solution to this problem when it is time to write the script to handle this form. Let's finish the form up first.

A Two-Dimensional Text Box

The final, and most important, feature of this form is an area for the user to enter his or her comments. It would be pretty annoying to enter a multiline comment in one really long, scrolled line in a single-line text box. What this script needs is a large two-dimensional area for the text. Does such a beast exist? But of course!

The <TEXTAREA> tag defines a two-dimensional text-entry box. There are only three possible attributes: ROWS, which sets the number of rows high the box should be; COLS, which sets the number of columns of width; and of course, NAME. Surprisingly, <TEXTAREA> also requires an end tag, </TEXTAREA>, which is usually right next to the start tag, with nothing in between them. If you *do* place some text between the <TEXTAREA> start and end tags, that text will automatically be entered into the multi-line text box as a default text string of sorts—putting words in your user's mouth, so to speak.

Text Defaults

If you put some text between the <TEXTAREA>...</TEXTAREA> start and end tags, that text will be automatically entered into your text box. For example:

```
<TEXTAREA NAME="FOOF" ROWS="5" COLS="40">Mary had a little lamb, with
fleece as white as snow, and everywhere that Mary went.
The lamb was sure to go.</TEXTAREA>
```

Be careful with where you start your text, though. Newlines *are honored* in <TEXTAREA> boxes, so if you start your text underneath the start tag, instead of next to it, your text might begin on the *second* line in the box.

Incidently, you can also "put words in your user's mouth" for normal (single-line) text entry boxes, by using the VALUE attribute:

```
<INPUT TYPE="text" NAME="FOOF" SIZE="20" VALUE="This is some default text!">
```

Keep the default text down to a minimum, (and only where it makes logical sense!) because the user will have to erase it first, before entering his or her own data.

Listing 9.10 shows how a <TEXTAREA> box is handled in HTML, and Figure 9.9 shows how the <TEXTAREA> box looks when added to the custom feedback form we've been building.

Listing 9.10   LIST9-10.HTM

```
<HTML>
<HEAD>
<TITLE>Sample Custom User-Feedback Form</TITLE>
</HEAD>
<BODY>
<FORM METHOD="post" ACTION="/cgi-bin/feedback.pl">
Your email: <INPUT TYPE="text" NAME="EMAIL.ADDR" SIZE="40" MAXLENGTH="80">
<P>
```

```
<I>How urgently do you need a reply:</I><BR>
<INPUT TYPE="radio" NAME="URGENCY" VALUE="FYI" CHECKED> Just FYI
<INPUT TYPE="radio" NAME="URGENCY" VALUE="PLR"> Please reply
<INPUT TYPE="radio" NAME="URGENCY" VALUE="RUR"> Reply urgently
<P>
<I>What is the nature of your feedback:</I>
<SELECT NAME="SUBJECT" SIZE="3" MULTIPLE>
<OPTION SELECTED>General Comments
<OPTION>Found Typo
<OPTION>Bug Report
</SELECT>
<P>
<I>Enter your comments below:</I><BR>
<TEXTAREA NAME="COMMENTS" ROWS="5" COLS="50"></TEXTAREA><BR>
<INPUT TYPE="submit"> <INPUT TYPE="reset">
</FORM>
</BODY>
</HTML>
```

The ROWS and COLS attributes of the <TEXTAREA> box set the physical size of the box, and both horizontal and vertical scroll bars are provided on the right and bottom edges of the box in case the user's typed text takes up more room than you provide. Unfortunately, there is no automatic word wrap, so until the user presses the Enter key, your text will keep on going off the right edge of the box.

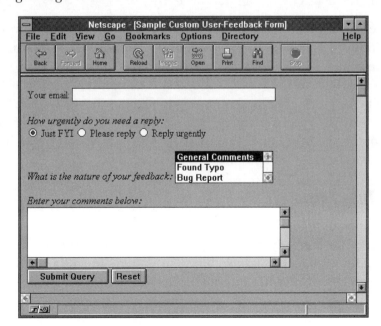

Figure 9.9   The form with a <TEXTAREA> box

The "Infinite Input Flaw" and Its Solution

This brings me to one of the big shortcoming of <TEXTAREA>. There is no way to set a maximum size on entered text. You can type horizontally, or vertically, forever. Some browsers even allow you to paste straight from the clipboard into the box, and with no size limitations, there is nothing to stop someone from pasting an entire copy of *Moby Dick* (or a thousand copies) into your <TEXTAREA> box. Yikes! There's absolutely nothing you can do to prevent this, but at least the knowledge that this is possible will help you minimize the damage by some careful programming in your script.

It is this because of this "infinite input flaw" that I chose to make the CGI script associated with the example form a POST method script. The GET method tries to jam all the data returned from the form into a single environment variable, QUERY_STRING. Environment variables are limited in size, to between 256 and 1024 characters total, depending on your operating system and its configuration. Since you can't control how much data the <TEXTAREA> box will return to your script, there is no guarantee that the environment variable will be able to hold it all. At the very least, you will lose some of the returned text data. At worst (which is pretty bad), you will lose the data from other input elements in the form, because the <TEXTAREA> will use up all the space itself.

But the POST method suffers none of these problems, because it uses standard input to send data to the form, and standard input can transfer an infinite stream of data. I would even go as far as to say that for *every* form, unless it is very small, POST is the best data-transfer method to use. It doesn't take much extra programming to retrieve the data— just a line or two, as you saw from the mailing list example—and you will suffer from none of the size restrictions that using GET can place on your scripts. Use POST. It's the right thing to do.

How They Faked <TEXTAREA> in Olden Tymes

Just a quick note on some HTML ancient history (and a warning in the bargain): Way back when (like maybe a couple of years ago), before the <TEXTAREA> element was introduced, you could simulate a <TEXTAREA> box by specifying a width and height for the size of a regular text entry box, like so:

```
<INPUT TYPE="text" NAME="DEFUNCT" SIZE="10,5">
```

You may still see reference to this method of creating a multi-line edit box out there on the Web, but *it is no longer supported!* Some browsers may still be able to handle this method, but it is currently being phased out and may not work for everyone. As a matter of fact, I tried it on the latest version of Netscape (1.1N at this writing) and it didn't work. I don't think it'll ever work again.

A CGI Script for the Custom User-Feedback Form

There are a few additional problems you're going to have to address in creating a script to service the HTML form we just completed. The first is the unique-NAME problem from the multiple scrolling window, and the second is the <TEXTAREA> infinite input flaw I just described. Let's tackle the infinite input flaw first. Listing 9.11 contains new checks to ensure that the script isn't being flooded by an endless stream of input.

Listing 9.11   LIST9-11.PL

```perl
#!/usr/local/bin/perl

# Get form data

if ($ENV{'REQUEST_METHOD'} eq "GET") {        # Using GET..
        $FORM_DATA = $ENV{'QUERY_STRING'};    # Save data to FORM_DATA
} else {       # Using POST..
        $LENGTH = $ENV{'CONTENT_LENGTH'};     # How much data to read?
        if ($LENGTH > "32768") {
            die "major network spam, stopped";
        }
        while ($LENGTH--) {
            $C = getc(STDIN);  # Get next character
            if ($C eq "=" || $C eq "&") {  # Check for start/end of value
                    $START="0";
            } else {
                    $START++;
            }
            if ($START <= "8192") {     # 8k should be enough!
                    $FORM_DATA .= $C;   # Save data to FORM_DATA
            }
        }
}
```

Listing 9.11 shows the first part of our new Perl script. The difference between this code and that from our earlier mailing list example begins at the point right after CONTENT_LENGTH is retrieved. The snag here is that you want to limit the size of input from the <TEXTAREA> boxes, but not interfere with any of the data that isn't too large. In other words, when it looks like one of the values in an incoming NAME=VALUE pair is getting too large, you want to cut it right there and ignore all additional input until the *next* NAME=VALUE pair begins.

Let's define "too large" as anything more than 8192 bytes, though if you feel that that is too restrictive, go ahead and increase the limit to as much as you're comfortable with. The key here is to prevent a malicious user from dumping a few dozen copies of *War and Peace* through your form, and eat up all your RAM.

The algorithm is fairly simple: First you check to see whether the script is using the GET or POST method of returning data from the Web browser. If it is using the GET method, don't even bother with the check. The server automatically sets the QUERY_STRING environment variable for you, so those dozen copies of *War and Peace* are already eating up your RAM and you may as well deal with the consequences. (Or, more likely, only the first paragraph from *War and Peace* snuck in, and the rest of the data was lost.) Either way, you're out of luck—so don't even bother with the check. If the method is POST, however, you have the perfect opportunity to cut those literary vandals off at the pass!

First get CONTENT_LENGTH. If its value is greater than 32768 bytes, just abort the script, which will cut the connection. Next, instead of directly appending each character from standard input to $FORM_DATA, as we did before, let's send it through a simple filter first. Put the character into a temporary variable, like $C, and check to see if the character is "=" or "&." If it is a "=" then you know a value is starting, and if it is a "&" you know that you've reach the end of a value. Either way, make a variable a counter for the length of the value, and set it to zero. I'll call it $START, meaning the start of the next value. Now, for any character other than "=" or "&," increment $START by one. If $START reaches our limit of 8192 before the next "&," you know that the value is way too large. Just ignore the character and keep getting additional characters until you find the next "&," which will signify the end of the value. If $START is less than the 8192 limit, it's OK to append the character to $FORM_DATA, since we know that the size hasn't gotten too large yet. That's it! You're now guaranteed that none of your values will be longer than 8192 bytes.

But if you're cutting off the connection at 32 K, why bother filtering the incoming values to 8 K too? Why not just cut off the connection at 8 K and be done with it? Well, if you're typing a legitimate letter and accidently go one byte over the 8 K limit, how would you going to feel if the connection were unceremoniously dropped? There's a difference between being absentmindedly oversized and maliciously dumping megabytes of data through a script to tie up a network! Alas, judgments like this will come before you from time to time, and you'll simply have to learn how to deal with them.

Handling Multiple <SELECT> Selections

The second problem we must deal with is of our own creation. By using <SELECT> in multiple mode, you can no longer count on the ability to reference values by name in an associative array. What's the solution? Append a reference number to the end of each non-unique name. In other words, somehow change this:

```
NAME=First+Value&NAME=Second+Value&NAME=Third+Value
```

into this:

```
NAME="First Value"
NAME.1="Second Value"
NAME.2="Third Value"
```

Listing 9.12 shows another modification to our earlier mailing list CGI script example. This time, the script ensures that no names are duplicated, by appending an index number to the end of non-unique names.

Listing 9.12   LIST9-12.PL

```perl
# Parse data into NAME=VALUE pairs and jam into an associative array

foreach (split(/&/, $FORM_DATA)) {
        ($NAME, $VALUE) = split(/=/, $_);
        $NAME =~ s/\+/ /g;
        $NAME =~ s/%([0-9|A-F]{2})/pack(C,hex($1))/eg;
        $VALUE =~ s/\+/ /g;
        $VALUE =~ s/%([0-9|A-F]{2})/pack(C,hex($1))/eg;
        # Find Unique name
        $NUM="0";
        while ($MYDATA{$NAME} ne "") {
                $NUM++;
```

```
                    $NAME =~ s/\.([0-9]+$)|$/\.$NUM/;
        }
        # Store NAME=VALUE pair
        $MYDATA{$NAME} = $VALUE;
}
```

Here's how it works: The raw string of NAME=VALUE pairs from
$FORM_DATA is broken apart, as before, and the NAME and VALUE items
from each pair are placed in the $NAME and $VALUE variables, respectively—again, just as before. But this time, before storing $VALUE in
$MYDATA{$NAME}, the script double-checks to be sure that the name value
in $NAME isn't already in use. If it is, a temporary number stored in $NUM
is incremented. The new $NUM value is appended to the end of $NAME,
separated from the existing value by a period, and the script checks for
uniqueness again, continuing to increment $NUM until a unique name is
found. Finally, the value is saved using the new name.

Listing 9.13   LIST9-13.PL

```
#!/usr/local/bin/perl

# Get form data

if ($ENV{'REQUEST_METHOD'} eq "GET") {          # Using GET..
        $FORM_DATA = $ENV{'QUERY_STRING'};       # Save data to FORM_DATA
} else {                                         # Using POST..
        $LENGTH = $ENV{'CONTENT_LENGTH'};        # How much data to read?
        if ($LENGTH > "32768") {
                die "major network spam, stopped";
        }
        while ($LENGTH--) {
                $C = getc(STDIN);                # Get next character
                if ($C eq "=" || $C eq "&") {    # Check for start/end of value
                        $START="0";
                } else {
                        $START++;
                }
                if ($START <= "8192") {          # 8k should be enough!
                        $FORM_DATA .= $C;        # Save data to FORM_DATA
                }
        }
}


# Parse data into NAME=VALUE pairs and jam into an associative array
```

```perl
foreach (split(/&/, $FORM_DATA)) {
        ($NAME, $VALUE) = split(/=/, $_);
        $NAME =~ s/\+/ /g;
        $NAME =~ s/%([0-9|A-F]{2})/pack(C,hex($1))/eg;
        $VALUE =~ s/\+/ /g;
        $VALUE =~ s/%([0-9|A-F]{2})/pack(C,hex($1))/eg;
        # Find Unique name
        $NUM="0";
        while ($MYDATA{$NAME} ne "") {
                $NUM++;
                $NAME =~ s/\.([0-9]+$)|$/\.$NUM/;
        }
        # Store NAME=VALUE pair
        $MYDATA{$NAME} = $VALUE;
}


# Now let's put together the message

# Put together the subject

$MESSAGE_SUBJECT = $MYDATA{'SUBJECT'};
$NUM = "1";
while ( $MYDATA{'SUBJECT.' . $NUM} ne "" ) {
        $MESSAGE_SUBJECT .= " / $MYDATA{'SUBJECT.' . $NUM}";
        $NUM++;
}
$MESSAGE_SUBJECT .= " -- $MYDATA{'URGENCY'}";

# Write out message to a file

open(NOTE, ">>/home/msgs/feedback.txt");
print NOTE "From: $MYDATA{'EMAIL.ADDR'}\n";
print NOTE "Subject: $MESSAGE_SUBJECT\n\n$MYDATA{'COMMENTS'}\n";
close(NOTE);

# Print out thank you to user

print "Content-type: text/html\n\n";
print "<HTML>\n";
print "<HEAD>\n";
print "<TITLE>Thank You for the Feedback</TITLE>\n";
print "</HEAD>\n";
print "<BODY>\n";
print "<H1>Thank You for the Feedback</H1>\n";
print "<EMP>Thank you</EMP> for your interest in the Widget Co! We'll\n";
print "read your comments and get back to you as soon as possible!\n";
print "</BODY>\n";
print "</HTML>\n";
```

Listing 9.13 shows the completed CGI script for the custom user feedback form. Figure 9.10 shows the completed form with sample data, just before the user would submit it to the server. Figure 9.11 shows the simple acknowledgement page, which is dynamically generated by Listing 9.13 in response to the submission of a completed user feedback form.

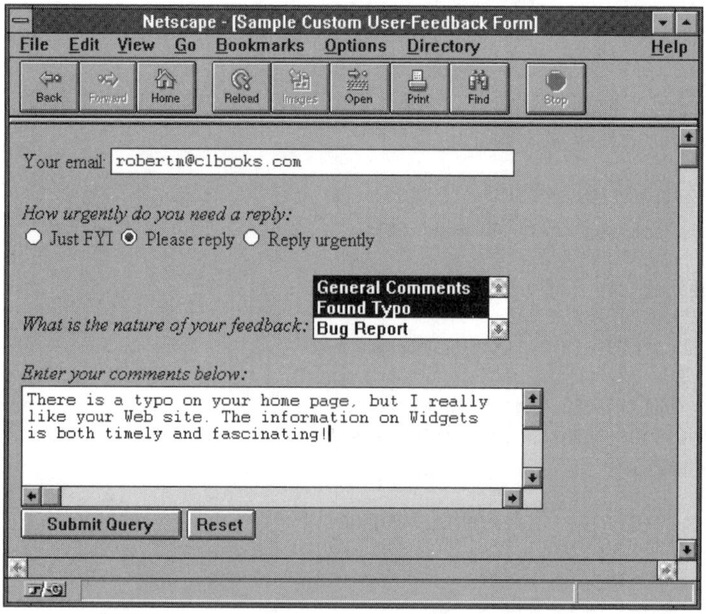

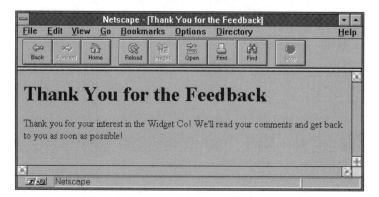

Figure 9.10   The completed user feedback form, with sample data

Figure 9.11   The response page generated by Listing 9.13

Storing Data Submitted by the User

Listing 9.13 finishes off by storing the feedback data retrieved from the user's form in a text file on the server machine. This is done in Perl with a simple **open..print..close** sequence. The script creates a "from" line for the email address of the user, and a message subject line out of the values returned for the radio buttons and OPTION menu that entered the message urgency and topic. This subject line and the message text itself (from the <TEXTAREA> box) are appended to the end of the file /home/msgs/feedback.txt for later retrieval by you, the webmaster. The contents of this file, based on the data shown in Figure 9.10, are shown below:

```
From: robertm@clbooks.com
Subject: General Comments / Found Typo -- PLR

There is a typo on your home page, but I really
like your Web site. The information on Widgets
is both timely and fascinating!
```

Finally, a brief "thank you" note is generated dynamically and sent to the user. The script probably won't win any awards for style or robustness of features, but it can be used as an excellent starting point for a much more ambitious script. For example, it would be great if the script would actually email the user's comment to the webmaster, instead of simply appending it to the end of a file. This can be done, and it would make an interesting project. See if you can pull it off!

Some Notes on Script Security

It's time I said few words about security, before you begin implementing the material in this chapter or more advanced projects of your own. The first thing that people say to me, when I start talking about publishing on the Web, is "Gee, I heard running a Webserver was a security risk." The short response is, it can be. The trouble usually doesn't come from running the server itself, but rather what this chapter covered, CGI scripts. Even the simplest, most innocent-looking script can end up riddled with security holes, if you aren't aware of what can go wrong and don't take a few simple precautions.

Would you be surprised if I told you that there were a security hole in the first example in this chapter, the simplest-of-the-simple mailing list script?

Well, there is. Notice how the script in Listing 9.7 prints the email address the user entered on the confirmation screen? Well, there is absolutely nothing preventing the user from entering HTML instead of an email address, and because the script is printing exactly what the user entered, that HTML would be interpreted by the user's browser. But even worse is that the *server* checks the document as well, and if the user entered a sequence called a *server-side include* instead of an email address, there is a possibility that he or she could actually execute commands on your server machine!

Don't panic—the only way that could happen is if you have server-side includes enabled for your /cgi-bin directory. (This is pointedly *not* a good idea, if you haven't figured it out already!) If you set the server up yourself, and you don't know what a server-side include is, then don't worry. There are no servers I know of that enable that feature as the default, so unless you enabled it yourself by tinkering with the server's configuration files, this won't be a problem. But it is important that you are at least aware of the possibility, so that you don't enable server-side includes by accident.

Another potential danger would come up if you took that same supposed "email address" and passed it as part of an argument to a function like **system()** or **eval**, or any other function that executes a program as though it were typed on the command line. For example, if your server were running on a Unix machine and you had the following command in your Perl script, you would definitely have a problem:

```
system("/usr/bin/cal $MONTH 1995");
```

The program /usr/bin/cal is safe enough. It simply displays a calendar for the month and year you specify. So, maybe your intention was to have the user enter a month and display that month's calendar in response. So, you take the user's input, stick it in $MONTH, and pass it to the program. Now **system()** will happily execute the cal program just as though you typed it on the keyboard. So where's the security hole? Well, what if the user typed ";cat /etc/passwd;echo" instead of a month? Congratulations, you've just handed a hacker your password file. *Never* use input obtained directly from a form as part of an argument in a function like **system()**!

I'll be discussing, in depth, the security risks involving the whole process of Web serving in a later chapter. Please don't skip it. These dangers are real.

So What Can I Do about It?

The first problem isn't very difficult to stamp out. If you want to echo some of the input that a user has sent to your server in a form (perhaps so he or she can verify that you received the correct information), there is one extra line of Perl code you can use to shoot any unauthorized HTML right in the foot. If the user's data that you want to echo is in the variable $USER_DATA, this will cripple any HTML markup she or he might have included:

```
$USER_DATA =~ s/</&lt;/g;
```

Here is the lowdown: Let's say $USER_DATA contains "<H1>Yay!</H1>." If you echoed that back to the user, the HTML would be parsed and a level 1 heading "Yay!" would be displayed by the browser. But if you run $USER_DATA through that one small line of code first, the less-than sign (<) on each of the tags would be converted into the harmless "<"

The other problem—passing user input as arguments to other commands—is a bit trickier to solve. You *must* strip out any "dangerous" characters (these characters are commonly called "metacharacters") from the user's data *before* attempting to pass the input as an argument to another command, like the previous Unix calendar program example shows. If you don't re-move these characters, they can be used to trick your script into doing anything the user wants! But the problem isn't in the stripping of the char-acters—that's easy to do. Rather, the problem lies in the exact definition of what we mean by "dangerous" characters. Do you know all the Unix shell metacharacters? For what shell? Korn? Bourne? Csh? Does your non-Unix operating system have "dangerous" characters too? Can you really be sure you stripped all of them?

The only way to be completely safe is to never pass any of the user's input as an argument to another command, but I admit that isn't always practi-cal. When you absolutely need to pass user input as an agrument to an-other command, I recommend using the following line of Perl code, which should keep your users on the straight and narrow. It is used just like the code for the previous problem:

```
$USER_DATA =~ s/[^\w]//g;
```

The "^\w" tells the browser to match anything that is not a number, a letter, or an underscore. If one of these characters is found, it is simply removed from the user's input. A bit draconian? Perhaps; but this is serious stuff and you can never be too careful.

Following the Script

The hardest part of CGI scripting is not being very familiar with *programming in general.* If you are not at least moderately familiar with programming, most of this chapter probably shot completely over your head. The solution, of course, is to study up on a programming language; for these purposes, probably Perl. But if that just isn't a solution, feel free to use pre-made scripts written by other people. There are tons of them available on the Internet, free of charge, and the odds of you finding one that does roughly what you need it to are pretty good—and making simple changes to existing, tested CGI scripts is a superb way to learn CGI, and a programming language too. But strive to become an expert! Why settle for less than mastery, when mastery is so simple to achieve?

10

Image Maps

The addition of forms and CGI to the HTML specification opened a whole new dimension to the Web. With just a little HTML and a touch of skill, it became possible for Internet users to *interact* with Web documents, not simply view them. But Kevin Hughes, currently at EIT in Palo Alto, California, had even grander plans. Since the Web is a combination of text *and* graphics, why are we limited to text and simple buttons in our forms? What about interacting with graphics as well? And thus the idea of the *image map* was born. An image map is an inline graphic image which, when clicked on, submits the coordinates of the point upon which it was clicked to a CGI script. The script can then take action based on *where* on the image map the user clicked.

The first image map was created by Mr. Hughes, when he worked as webmaster at Honolulu Community College. By clicking on a map of the HCC campus, you would be given more information on the building at the coordinates where you clicked. Go ahead and try it! The map is located at *http://www.hcc.hawaii.edu/hccmap/hccmap.html*. The map portion of the page is shown in Figure 10.1.

Image Maps

Image maps are inline images with *hotspots* defined. A hotspot is a region of your image that, when clicked, causes a special CGI script to perform some action, usually *redirecting* the browser to another document. Essentially, the procedure is this: The user clicks on part of your image map, and

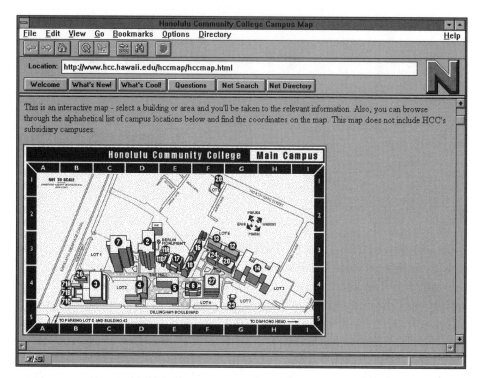

Figure 10.1   The HCC campus map

the coordinates are passed from the browser to the server, which in turn passes those coordinates to a CGI script. The script then compares the coordinates of the mouse click with a template of hotspots, and figures out which hotspot the user clicked on. Finally, the script tells the server the location of the new document corresponding to that hotspot, and the server either serves the document to the browser, or instructs the browser where the new document can be found.

The possibilities for the use of image maps are spectacular. You saw one of them, a campus map, a few paragraphs back. This is the classic use, a sort of graphical jumping-off point for your pages. They can range in size and complexity up to a full-screen extravaganza, like the home page of NetOffice, Inc. (*http://www.netoffice.com/*) in Figure 10.2. This is a beautiful example. It's not overly obnoxious, and it is clear that it is an image map and also clear where the hotspots are. Image maps can also create simple button bars, like the one at the bottom of the Netscape home page (*http://www.netscape.com/*), in Figure 10.3, or something in between, like

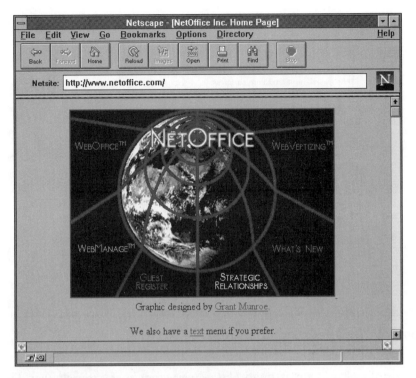

Figure 10.2   The image map on the NetOffice home page

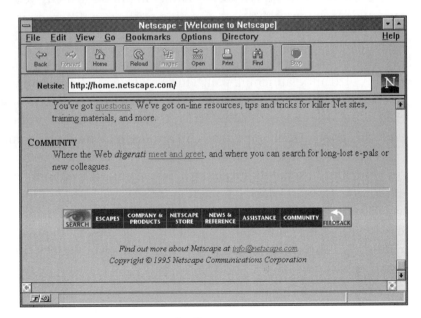

Figure 10.3   An image map "button bar"

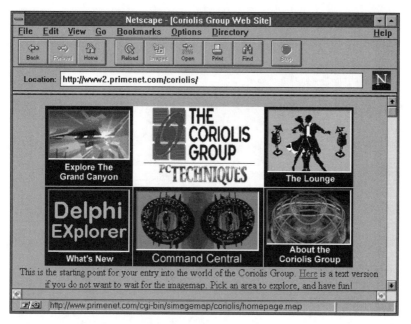

Figure 10.4   The Coriolis Group's masthead

the Coriolis Group's masthead (*http://www.coriolis.com/coriolis/*) in Figure 10.4. The Coriolis masthead is a sort of launching pad for their Web site, with each major section of the map directing traffic to a different area of the site.

But don't think that image maps are locked solely into the somewhat mundane destiny of a fancy launching pad. There's a frog on the Web that will tell you otherwise. Web citizens the world over have flocked to one of several "dissect the frog" pages (Figure 10.5) to practice their surgical techniques on this poor virtual amphibian. All are implemented using image maps, and the world's frog population breathes a lot easier as a result. Or, if you're interested in some slightly less gruesome entertainment for a Saturday afternoon, Carlos' Coloring Book (Figure 10.6) may be just the thing. Simply pick your color and click on the black and white image map. Guaranteed to turn a boring evening into an exciting colorfest! With just a little imagination, I'm sure you can come up with your own, equally unique image map applications.

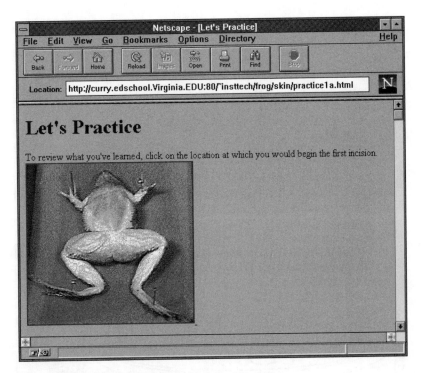

Figure 10.5 Dissecting a virtual frog

So How's It Done?

Image maps can add quite a bit of cleverness to your pages, but don't expect to crank one out in just a couple of minutes. The whole process can be a serious nuisance, particularly if you don't have the appropriate tools. Before you begin, make sure you have handy or can create the following software: A browser with image map support to test your work (see below for advice on this), a paint program for creating the image map, a program to define where the hotspots are, and a special CGI script for processing your image maps. Virtually all of this material can be obtained free over the Net.

It may seem odd, but there may be a few browsers out there that still don't support image maps. Obviously, text-based browsers like Lynx don't, but I know that some graphical browsers have trouble with them as well. For example, Cello can barely do inline images, let alone image maps. If you

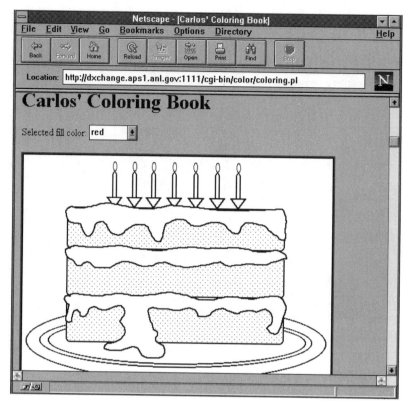

Figure 10.6   A Web-based coloring book

have taken my advice in Chapter 2, and gotten your hands on the latest version of Netscape or NCSA Mosaic, you haven't got a worry. But if you are still using an ancient version of Mosaic, or a prototype of a new browser, you may run into some problems with image maps. Check your browser's documention, or better yet, try it out on one of the image maps I mentioned earlier in this chapter.

Paint Programs

The paint program you use to create your inline images should do just as well at designing your image maps. Flip back to Chapter 6 if you haven't read the material on inline images yet, since image maps are really just "hyper-active" inline images. Just to refresh your memory, inline images should always be GIFs, at least until another graphic format takes over, so your paint program should be able to generate GIF images itself, or else you should have a separate program (Halo Desktop Imager is a good example) to convert whatever format it does produce into GIF. Personally, on my MS Windows machine, I use the Windows Paint program to create a BMP file, and then use LView to covert it to GIF format. At work I have access to an X Windows terminal, where I use xpaint, which pretty much does it all. If you own a Mac, you probably already have several dozen lovely paint programs, but if you don't, I understand Photoshop is wonderful for this type of work.

Hotspots and Scripts

After creating your image, your next task will be locating the coordinates of your hotspots. If you're a masochist, you can do this by hand. Your paint program should have a tool to measure segments of your image, in pixels, for this purpose. If this isn't your idea of fun (and it certainly isn't *mine*), there is an excellent program called mapedit for Microsoft Windows and X Windows, which you will definitely want to grab. For Macs, a similiar program is WebMap. More on this later.

You will also need a special CGI script to process the mouse clicks on your image maps. The NCSA httpd server comes with a script that does just this, called (of all things) imagemap. The imagemap script is written in C, and is delivered in full source code form. If it isn't already compiled to an executable in your script directory, you're going to have to compile it yourself. The CERN httpd server comes with an equivalent to imagemap, called htimage, again written in C and present in source code form. If it's not already compiled in your script directory, same deal. You're going to have to compile it. For Macs, an application called Mac-ImageMap is the way to go. You can find a copy at *http://weyl.zib-berlin.de/imagemap/Mac-ImageMap.html.*

The process of creating an HTML document supporting image maps can best be described in step-by-step fashion. We'll go through the steps now, in order.

Step 1: Designing the Image

To make an image map, first take one image... Before you can do anything else, you must design the inline image that will make up the image portion of your image map system. Your image can be just about any shape or size you desire. It can be as simple as a couple of buttons side-by-side, or as complex as a map of your home town. Black and white, or a full color work of art—it's all up to you and your imagination. There are, however, a couple of guidelines you may want to keep in mind, if for nothing other than the sanity of your users.

Keep an Eye on the Overall Size of Your Image Map

Like all inline images, keep your image maps as small as possible. Of course, they may need to be larger than your typical inline image, but try not to go overboard. It may be tempting to fill the entire browser window with a giant, complex image map, but you're likely to alienate quite a few users who are locked into slow SLIP connections. Besides the obvious danger of assuming that everyone has the same size browser window, the time it takes to transfer an image map is of even greater concern than with other, less critical inline images. If your image map is the sole method of navigation through your Web pages, your users will have to wait for the entire image to transfer before doing any further browsing. Personally, I've come to dread large image maps for that very reason.

Identify Your Hotspots Clearly

Make sure that it's easy for your users to find the hotspots on your image map. For that matter, make absolutely sure that your users *know* that large inline image that just took three minutes of their time to transfer actually *is* an image map! Unless you mark the several regions of the image map clearly, by placing some sort of border around each hotspot or at least labeling each hotspot with a keyword describing its function, your users may not even realize it is an image map, and all that time and effort will be wasted! Make your hotspots large and easy to click on as well. Tiny regions require the hands of a surgeon to select correctly, and you don't want to annoy your users by making it easy to click on the *wrong* region, and go Webbing off to somewhere far from their original intent.

Avoid the "Because It's There" Trap!

Finally, don't feel obliged to put an image map on a page unless it truly makes sense to use an image map. Just because you *can* do something, doesn't mean you *must*. Image maps are powerful tools that can add value and personality to your pages, but they aren't meant to entirely replace other means of navigating your pages. In most cases a little bit of hypertext or a couple of small icons with anchors attached will do just fine.

Step 2: Defining the Hotspots

Now that your image is ready to go, there is a little matter of defining the hotspots, so that your script can figure out where it was that the user clicked. This isn't too tough, but can be time consuming. The procedure is this: You locate the coordinates of the hotspot regions on your image map, and stuff the coordinates into a file called a *map configuration file*, alongside the URL that each hotspot is supposed to activate. The special image-map CGI script we'll discuss a little later reads this map file, figures out which hotspot was clicked, and serves up the new URL to the browser.

This can be a hassle to do entirely by hand, but fortunately there are some tools available that makes it a snap. For Microsoft Windows, the program to use is MapEdit. Just load in your GIF image file and draw the hotspots right on the image. It even generates the map configuration file for you! Pick up a copy at *http://sunsite.unc.edu/boutell/mapedit/mapedit.html*. There is also a version of MapEdit available for X Windows at the same site. For Macs, a similiar program is available called WebMap. In the same way, you just load up the GIF and draw the hotspots, and WebMap does the rest. You can find a copy at *http://www.city.net/cnx/software/webmap.html*.

Map Configuration Files

The format of a map configuration file is pretty simple. Well, "simple" was an alien concept to the Web community, so they came up with two different formats. The *imagemap* script, written for the NCSA httpd server, uses the NCSA format, and the *htimage* script, for CERN's httpd, uses the CERN format. Of course, you'll have to use the appropriate format depending on what script you use, imagemap or htimage. Fortunately, the MapEdit utility understand both formats. For Mac folks, who use the Mac-ImageMap program, you'll need to create your map configuration files using the NCSA format.

Now for a practical example of how hotspot definition is done. I've designed a simple little image map I call IMAP.GIF. It contains three shapes: a rectangle, a circle, and a polygon. These will be our hotspots. Let's use

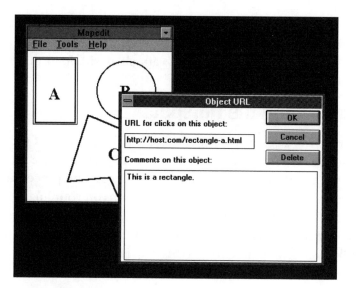

Figure 10.7 MapEdit in action

MapEdit to create the map configuration file. After we're done, we'll take a look at the results and decode the file format.

The procedure is about as simple as it gets. Start MapEdit and load in your GIF image. In this case, that would be IMAP.GIF. Use the Tools menu to draw your hotspots directly onto the GIF. When you're done, save it in either the NCSA or CERN format, as appropriate to your system. The convention is that all map configuration files end with the .MAP suffix, so we'll save our example map as IMAP.MAP. You can save it anywhere you want, but my custom is putting it in the same directory as the image file.

Listing 10.1   IMAP-C.MAP

```
default http://myhost.com/nowhere.htm
rect (12,12) (79,111) http://myhost.com/rect-a.html
circle (161,62) 50 http://myhost.com/circ-b.htm
poly (66,204) (99,98) (212,143) (226,189) (149,227) (134,197) http://
myhost.com/poly-c.htm
```

Listing 10.2   IMAP-N.MAP

```
default http://myhost.com/nowhere.htm
rect http://myhost.com/rect-a.html 12,12 79,111
circle http://myhost.com/circ-b.htm 161,62 211,58
poly http://myhost.com/poly-c.htm 66,204 99,98 212,143 226,189 149,227 134,197
```

Listings 10.1 and 10.2 show our new image map's map file, in both CERN (IMAP-C.MAP) and NCSA (IMAP-N.MAP) formats, respectively. The suffixes are there to allow the same file to exist in two forms in the same directory; obviously, you'll need only one copy to correspond to whichever server you're using. Let's take a little time to dissect each format. True, you may never need to really know what's going on, but you never know when you'll have to tweak one of these things by hand.

The CERN Map Format

The CERN format, in my opinion, is the "nicer" of the two, though there really isn't much of a difference. The first line of both formats is the "default" action. In other words, the first line specifies which document is served if the user clicks outside of all of the defined hotspots, hence clicking on the map but not on any identifiable hotspot. Set it to point to a polite document which, gently, lets the user know what went wrong. The rest of the file defines the actual hotspots. The first keyword on each line is the shape of the hotspot; *rect* for rectangle, *circle* for circle, and *poly* for polygon. The keyword is then followed by the coordinates for the hotspot, in "x,y" pairs, each surrounded by parentheses. At the very end of each line is the URL associated with the hotspot. When the user selects the hotspot, that URL is where we go.

Coordinates are in pixels, measured from the upper-left hand corner of the image. For rectangles, there are two coordinate pairs. The first is the upper-left hand corner of the rectangle, and the second is the lower-right. Circles have only one pair: the center point of the circle. This is directly followed by the radius of the circle, in pixels. Polygons can have as many x,y pairs as they need, one for each of the polygon's vertices. Don't worry about trying to "close" your polygons; the last point will be connected to the first point automatically.

The NCSA Map Format

The NCSA format is slightly different. The shape identifiers for the hotspots are the same, but instead of being followed immediately by the coordinates, the shape identifiers are immediately followed by their appropriate URLs. (In the CERN format, the URL was the last thing in the line.) The coordinates are also listed a little differently. The x,y pairs are not surrounded by parentheses. Also, the circle line has two x,y pairs, rather than one. The first pair is the center point of the circle. The second x,y pair, rather than the radius, is any point along the circle's circumference.

You are also given one more shape to work with in the NCSA format, the *point*. If the user does not click inside a normal hotspot, the image map script will check for the nearest point instead. If you have even one point, don't even bother with a default, since any point definition overrides a default definition; no matter where you are on the imagemap, you're going to be "closest" to at least one point. The point shape isn't supported in the MapEdit program, so if you want to use it, you'll have to add it by hand.

NCSA's IMAGEMAP.CONF File

You're almost there, but if you use NCSA's imagemap script, instead of htimage or one of the Mac scripts, you need one more step to make things work. NCSA's imagemap script expects to find a special configuration file to operate correctly. This file is used to map symbolic map names to the physical location of the map configuration files. It's a sort of map alias file. I guess the theory is, you can save a couple of keystrokes by aliasing your map configuration file's name from *maps/mymap.map* to *mymap*, and all you need to do to save those extra five keystrokes is build yet *another* configuration file. Too much effort for too little payback, if you ask me, but that's the way the NCSA server works. Thank goodness you don't need to do this for htimage or any of the other scripts.

Anyway, the configuration file's name is IMAGEMAP.CONF and defaults to being located in your server's *conf* directory, with all the other server configuration files. If you want to change the location, you can edit the following line in IMAGEMAP.C before compiling it. Just change the text between the quotes to wherever you want the new configuration file to be:

```
#define CONF_FILE "conf/imagemap.conf"
```

The format for the IMAGEMAP.CONF file is simple. There is one line for each image map you have. The first part of the line is the symbolic name for the map, say B-BAR.MAP for our map. Then there is a colon ":" and the physical pathname where the map configuration file can be found. For B-BAR.MAP on my machine, it would be */maps/b-bar.map*. So the pertinent line in IMAGEMAP.CONF would look like this:

```
b-bar.map:/maps/b-bar.map
```

Step 3: Write the HTML

The HTML used to set up an image map may seem a bit odd. I think you need to keep in mind that this whole image map thing was originally, in all honesty, a *hack*. Basically, you use the <IMG> element to display the image map, just as with an inline image, but with one additional attribute, ISMAP. The anchor has a new twist that I haven't explained yet. At this point it gets complex enough that I'd just prefer to show you and explain the details as I go.

This example is for NCSA's imagemap script, but you can just substitute htimage, or whatever the name of the program you are using in its place.

Listing 10.3   LST10-3.HTM

```
<HTML>
<HEAD>
<TITLE>Imagemap Example</TITLE>
</HEAD>
<BODY>
<P>My sample imagemap:
<A HREF="http://myhost.com/cgi-bin/imagemap/b-bar.map">
<IMG SRC="b-bar.gif" ISMAP>
</A>
</BODY>
</HTML>
```

Obviously, the ISMAP attribute identifies this whole thing as an image map, but take a look at the URL in the anchor. The */cgi-bin/imagemap* is the path to the imagemap script, just as with any other CGI script, but it looks as though it is actually pointing to something called B-BAR.MAP, located in the directory */cgi-bin/imagemap/*. But *imagemap* is in fact the name of the script, and B-BAR.MAP is located nowhere near the imagemap script. So what's going on?

It's important to remember that the path in a URL, though it might *look* like a file system pathname, really *isn't* a file system pathname. The resemblance is mostly a coincidence. The path part of a URL really *isn't* a file system pathname, though most of the time it acts like one. Here is one case when it *doesn't* behave like one.

The first part of the path is "correct" in that the script really is located in */cgi-bin/imagemap*, but that little bit of extra path, */b-bar.map*, is actually passed *as a parameter* to the script. It's called *extra path information* in Web-speak. If I had used a script other than the NCSA imagemap script, like CERN's htimage, which doesn't require all that silly map file aliasing, I would have replaced */b-bar.map* with the full pathname of the B-BAR.MAP file. For example, for use with htimage, the URL would be *http://myhost.com/cgi-bin/htimage/maps/b-bar.map*—kind of like two paths in one.

The Action at Click-Time

Now read along very carefully; *this is a tricky business.* Here's what's going on: When the user clicks somewhere on the image map image, the browser sees the ISMAP attribute and therefore transmits the coordinates of the point where it was clicked, and the URL it is trying to reach, to the server. The server checks /cgi-bin and sees htimage, realizes that htimage is a script, and then takes that extra path info, and places it in an environment variable, called PATH_INFO. Now the htimage script is called using the GET method, with QUERY_STRING set to the coordinates of the mouse click. These coordinates are not configured as a NAME=VALUE pair, just as X,Y. The coordinates are also sent to the command line of the script, as argument one, or argv[1] if you're a C programmer. The script takes over, and uses IMAGEMAP.CONF to translate the PATH_INFO data into a map file path if you're using NCSA's imagemap script. If you're using htimage or some other script, the server just uses the PATH_INFO raw. The URL that corresponds to the clicked-on hotspot is then found, and the browser is instructed to redirect itself to the new URL. You're done.

A Quick Note on Style

Not everyone has the ability or the desire to use your image maps. Users working with text-only browsers like Lynx or those with very slow Internet connections will be at a huge disadvantage if your image map is the only way to access your pages. It's always a good idea to give your users a text alternative to your image map, usually directly underneath the image.

The INPUT vs. ISMAP Methods

You've just learned about what I call the ISMAP method of supporting image maps, but there is another way to do things. What the ISMAP method lacks is the ability to tie itself to an HTML form. For example, it would be nice to enter some text, maybe flip a couple of radio buttons or check boxes, and then click on an image map and have the coordinates, along with all the other information, sent on to a script to be processed. There's a way to do this, and I call it the INPUT method of using image maps.

The INPUT method essentially involves a new TYPE attribute for the form element <INPUT>, called "image." The HTML for the image type is just like the other input types, such as text or checkbox. Here is a quick example of an image map included in a form with a text entry box. The browser display generated by Listing 10.4 is shown in Figure 10.8.

Listing 10.4   LST10-4.HTM

```
<HTML>
<HEAD>
<TITLE>Imagemaps in Forms</TITLE>
</HEAD>
<BODY>
<P>Enter your mother's maiden name, then click on the image below.
<HR>
<FORM METHOD="GET" ACTION="/cgi-bin/myscript.pl">
Mother's maiden name: <INPUT TYPE="text" NAME="MOM" SIZE="20"
MAXLENGTH="40"><BR>
<INPUT TYPE="image" NAME="MYMAP" SRC="imap.gif">
<HR>
</FORM>
</BODY>
</HTML>
```

The image type requires a new attribute for the <INPUT> element, SRC, which accepts the URL of the image to use for your image map. It's just a regular URL, exactly like the type you would use to display an inline image in an <IMG> element. And where is the submit button? With an image map in your form, you no longer need a submit button. If the image is clicked anywhere over its area, a submit is implied and the form is sent on its merry way. You can include a submit button if you'd like, but it is not necessary.

You Can't Use Pre-made Scripts!

There is one small problem with the INPUT method I've just described. Remember those map configuration files you made using the MapEdit

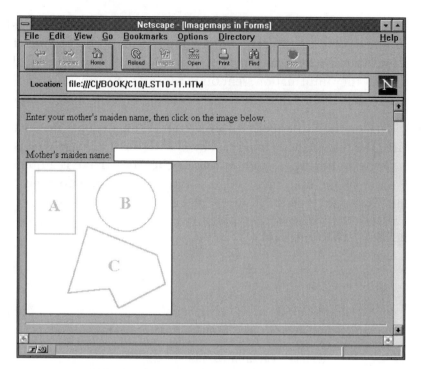

Figure 10.8   The INPUT method of using image maps

utility? All those hotspot definitions, and the convenience of having a pre-made script like imagemap or htimage process your image map? You can't use them. They just don't understand an image map in this context. In other words, you are on your own. You want to use a map configuration file? You'll have to write the script to read the configuration file and derive the coordinates of where the user clicked, all by yourself. But in spite of this minor inconvenience, using image maps in this context can still be pretty useful. In fact, the most common application for this type of image map discards the coordinate information anyway. Let me explain.

One of the drawbacks of forms is, even though you can define as many submit buttons on one form as you want, they all do the same thing: submit the form, no frills attached. There is no way to tell *which* submit button was pushed. All you know is that the user clicked one of them. So suppose you have three submit buttons, one labelled "Submit to Marketing," another "Submit to Accounting," and the third "Submit to the IS Department." Your script has no way of knowing which was selected! Yes, it would make sense to be able to use the NAME attribute to "label" a submit button, and have it return the button's VALUE depending on which button was pressed, but unfortunately that simply doesn't work. The solution? Image maps.

Here's the secret: Define three image maps, one for each submit button. When the user selects one of your image maps, the form will be submitted, and you will know exactly which one the user pressed! Don't even worry about *where* the user clicked; it doesn't matter; all you really want to know is that the image map was clicked somewhere on its area. Problem solved— and more on this later. Let's return for now to the question of what data comes back to your scripts.

What Your Script Sees

When used in connection with forms, image maps are treated just like any other input type, with one exception. Instead of returning only one NAME=VALUE pair, image maps return *two*. Let's suppose you entered "Bonaparte" in the example form shown in Figure 10.8, and clicked somewhere on the image map to submit the form. The following query string would be sent to your script, depending on where on the image map you clicked, of course:

```
MOM=Bonaparte&MYMAP.x=34&MYMAP.y=17
```

The server automatically appends either an ".x" or ".y" to the image map's name, depending on which value it is returning. For the X coordinate, the name will have an ".x" appended, and of course for the Y coordinate the suffix will be ".y" instead. And if there is a submit button and the user selected that instead of clicking on the image map? Since there would be no coordinates to return, the server wouldn't return a thing for your image map. The query string would simply be:

```
MOM=Bonoparte
```

Image Maps as Submit Buttons

Let's take a more practical look at image maps in forms. As I said earlier, one common use of image maps in forms is to implement multiple submit buttons. Since when an image map is clicked, the entire form is automatically submitted, they are perfectly suited for this task. Some might think it akin to splitting atoms just to boil a cup of water, but hey, it works.

Here's the scenario: I'd like to have a user feedback form, just like the example developed in Chapter 9. But this time I'd like to have multiple submit buttons to select which department the feedback should go to. So I drag out my trusty paint program and after a few minutes of twiddling pixels around, I come up with icons to represent each submit button. Then I slap them in at the bottom of a nifty little customer feedback form. The HTML to do this is shown in Listing 10.5, and the browser display in Figure 10.9.

Listing 10.5   LST10-5.HTM

```
<HTML>
<HEAD>
<TITLE>Imagemaps as Submit Buttons</TITLE>
</HEAD>
<BODY>
<H1>Send Us Feedback!</H1>
<P>To send us feedback, enter your email address and comments below,
then select which department you would like to send the comment to.
<FORM METHOD="post" ACTION="/cgi-bin/feedback2.pl">
<HR>
Your email: <INPUT TYPE="text" NAME="EMAIL.ADDR" SIZE="40" MAXLENGTH="80">
<P>Comments:<BR>
<TEXTAREA NAME="COMMENTS" ROWS="5" COLS="60"></TEXTAREA>
<P>Send to:
<INPUT TYPE="image" NAME="SALES" SRC="sales.gif">
<INPUT TYPE="image" NAME="MARKETING" SRC="marktng.gif">
<INPUT TYPE="image" NAME="WEBMASTER" SRC="webmstr.gif">
<INPUT TYPE="image" NAME="ACCOUNTING" SRC="acctng.gif">
<HR>
</FORM>
</BODY>
</HTML>
```

Now, after the user enters his or her email address and comments, all that remains to be done is to click anywhere on one of the image maps, and the form will be submitted. Since image maps only return coordinates when they are clicked on, only the image map "button" the user clicks will send coordinate information to your script. Bingo! Just check which image map sent back coordinates and you know which "submit button" the user clicked, and you can send the submitted comments on to the correct department. Listing 10.6 shows a bit of Perl code that will do the trick.

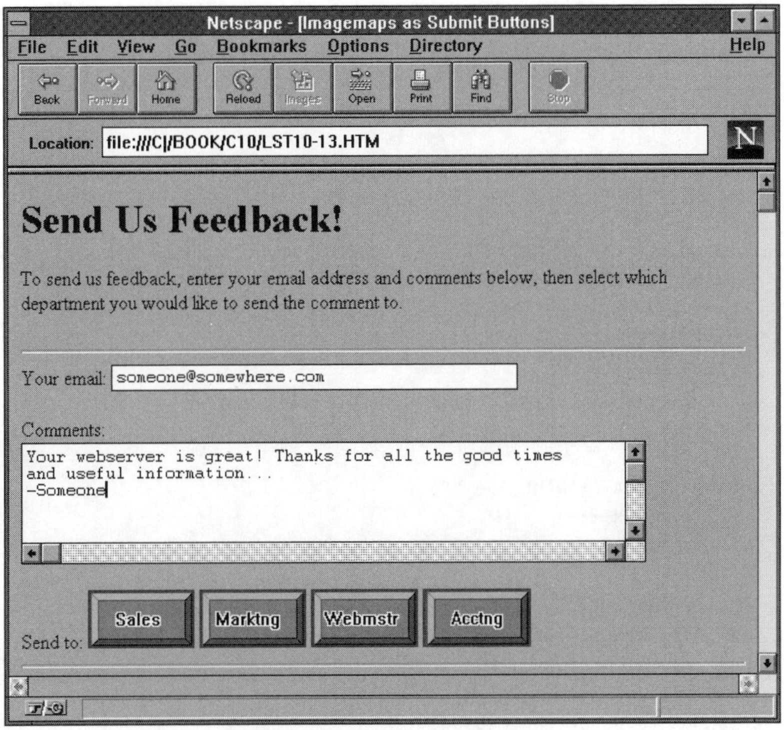

Figure 10.9   Image maps as submit buttons

Listing 10.6   LST10-6.PL

```perl
#!/usr/local/bin/perl

# Get form data

if ($ENV{'REQUEST_METHOD'} eq "GET") {          # Using GET..
        $FORM_DATA = $ENV{'QUERY_STRING'};      # Save data to FORM_DATA
} else {                                        # Using POST..
        $LENGTH = $ENV{'CONTENT_LENGTH'};       # How much data to read?
        if ($LENGTH > "32768") {
                die "major network spam, stopped";
        }
        while ($LENGTH--) {
                $C = getc(STDIN);               # Get next character
                if ($C eq "=" || $C eq "&") {   # Check for start/end of value
                        $START="0";
                } else {
                        $START++;
                }
```

```
                        if ($START <= "8192") {           # 8k should be enough!
                                $FORM_DATA .= $C;          # Save data to FORM_DATA
                        }
                }
        }

# Parse data into NAME=VALUE pairs and jam into an associative array

foreach (split(/&/, $FORM_DATA)) {
        ($NAME, $VALUE) = split(/=/, $_);
        $NAME =~ s/\+/ /g;
        $NAME =~ s/%([0-9|A-F]{2})/pack(C,hex($1))/eg;
        $VALUE =~ s/\+/ /g;
        $VALUE =~ s/%([0-9|A-F]{2})/pack(C,hex($1))/eg;
        # Find Unique name
        $NUM="0";
        while ($MYDATA{$NAME} ne "") {
                $NUM++;
                $NAME =~ s/\.([0-9]+$)|$/\.$NUM/;
        }
        # Store NAME=VALUE pair
        $MYDATA{$NAME} = $VALUE;
}

# Now let's put together the message

# Open the feedback file depending on which button clicked
if ( $MYDATA{'SALES.x'} ne "" ) {
        open(NOTE, ">>/home/msgs/sales.txt");
        $LOCATION="http://myhost.com/sales/thanks.html";
} elsif ( $MYDATA{'MARKETING.x'} ne "" ) {
        open(NOTE, ">>/home/msgs/marketing.txt");
        $LOCATION="http://myhost.com/marketing/thanks.html";
} elsif ( $MYDATA{'WEBMASTER.x'} ne "" ) {
        open(NOTE, ">>/home/msgs/webmaster.txt");
        $LOCATION="http://myhost.com/webmaster/thanks.html";
} else {
        open(NOTE, ">>/home/msgs/accounting.txt");
        $LOCATION="http://myhost.com/webmaster/thanks.html";
}

print NOTE "From: $MYDATA{'EMAIL.ADDR'}\n\n";
print NOTE "$MYDATA{'COMMENTS'}\n";
close(NOTE);

# Redirect user to new URL

print "Location: $LOCATION\n\n";
```

The program in Listing 10.6 is heavily derived from the user feedback form example in Chapter 9, but with changes required to handle multiple submit buttons. All the real action takes place after the "open feedback file depending on which button clicked" comment. One by one, I check to see if the three image maps returned some coordinates. Just checking for the X coordinate is sufficient; if X isn't there, neither is Y, and the image map was not clicked on. Perl's associative arrays return an empty string if you request data that doesn't exist. So, if you apply an image map's X coordinate name to the associate array and the array returns an empty string, that image map's coordinates weren't included in the data from the form.

After the script figures out which image map was clicked, a file corresponding to that image map is opened. For example, if the user clicked the "WEBMASTER" image map, the script will open a file called WEBMASTER.TXT, and write the user's comments there. Right after the script opens the file, it also assigns a URL to the variable **$LOCATION**. Each image map will set a different URL. I'll explain why in a minute.

Once the file is open, the script will write the user's email address (from the text entry box) to the file, and then write his or her comments as well. Finally, the file is closed and the user's browser is redirected to a new URL where a "thank you" note is located, written specifically for each department. Whoa! New concept alert! The user's browser is "redirected" to a new URL? Yes! It's a neat MIME trick: By using the MIME header **Location:**, it is possible to tell a user's browser to fetch another URL!

Using the MIME Location Header

Remember when I said, back in Chapter 9, that every page your scripts serve *must* always have the **Content-type:** MIME header, no exceptions? Well, to avoid gross confusion, I lied a little. Here's an exception: If, instead of **Content-type:** you use **Location:**, your script will be able to redirect the user's browser to a new URL. Don't worry about putting anything underneath the **Location:** header line, except the single blank line, of course, because the browser won't bother displaying it. It will go out and fetch the new URL, as given on the **Location:** line, and ignore everything beneath. You still do need the blank line though, or the server won't know when the header is finished, and thus the new URL won't be fetched. All MIME headers need that blank line!

When your script returns a **Location:** header in response to some request, you can almost think of it as turning into a traffic cop. Give it any URL, and the user's browser will automatically go out and fetch that URL. Some servers, however, are smart enough to realize when a URL is pointing to another one of its own documents, and will actually fetch the document for the browser instead. This saves a bit of wear and tear on both the server and the browser, and since it is transparent to both your script and the user, it's most convenient to think of the whole process as simply "redirecting the browser" instead of having the browser fetch something. Either way, the effect is the same; the browser will end up displaying the URL specified by the **Location:** header.

```
Location: http://myhost.com/stuff/doc.html
Location: ftp://somewhere.com/pub/programs/afile.zip
Location: http://nowhere.com/images/mypicture.gif
Location: http://www.host.com/cgi-bin/newform.pl
```

In the examples above, the first line will redirect the browser to the document located at *http://myhost.com/stuff/doc.html.* The second example will, using FTP, tell the browser to fetch the ZIP file at the URL shown. The third example will force the browser to display a GIF image, and the last example will tell the browser to access a new CGI script.

So does this always work? Can you *always* count on **Location:** forcing a new URL to be loaded? Well, probably—but in Webland you never know. With that in mind, Listing 10.7 provides some Perl code that will give the user with a "brain damaged" browser an alternative.

Listing 10.7   LST10-7.PL

```
print "Location: $LOCATION\n\n";
print "Your browser does not seem to be able to handle redirection. The\n";
print "document you requested is located at:\n";
print "<A HREF=\"$LOCATION\">$LOCATION</A>. Thank you!\n";
```

The theory here is, if the browser can't respond correctly to the **Location:** header, at the very least it might try to display the document, and if it does, it may well display it as an HTML file. I admit, this technique is a bit desperate, but if a user's browser doesn't at least handle **Location:**, then it's the best you can do. Personally, I've never seen a browser *not* handle **Location:**, so I wouldn't worry about it too much—and it's only an extra three lines of code, anyway.

Hotspots in INPUT-Method Image Maps

So, you say you really *do* want hotspots? Don't worry, in anticipation of this obvious request, I whipped together a cute little demo that will brilliantly illustrate precisely how to add hotspots to your input-method image maps. You'll have to forgive me for not implementing the polygon shape or the point shape; both would have added considerably to the complexity of the example code.

I call the example (shown in Listing 10.8) "Hoo's On First." The user is allowed to enter a baseball player's name and then click on a baseball diamond to assign the player to a position. The CGI script that handles the data on the server end is Listing 10.9. The browser display is shown in Figure 10.10.

Listing 10.8   LST10-8.HTM

```
<HTML>
<HEAD>
<TITLE>Hoo's On First?</TITLE>
</HEAD>
<BODY>
<H1>Hoo's On First?</H1>
<P>Enter a player's name and then select his position on this baseball
diamond.
<HR>
<FORM METHOD="post" ACTION="hoolst.pl">
Player's name: <INPUT TYPE="text" NAME="PLAYER" SIZE="40" MAXLENGTH="80">
<P>
<INPUT TYPE="image" NAME="DIAMOND" SRC="bbd.gif">
</FORM>
<HR>
</BODY>
</HTML>
```

Listing 10.9   LST10-9.PL

```perl
#!/usr/local/bin/perl

# Get form data

if ($ENV{'REQUEST_METHOD'} eq "GET") {      # Using GET..
    $FORM_DATA = $ENV{'QUERY_STRING'};      # Save data to FORM_DATA
} else {                                     # Using POST..
    $LENGTH = $ENV{'CONTENT_LENGTH'};       # How much data to read?
```

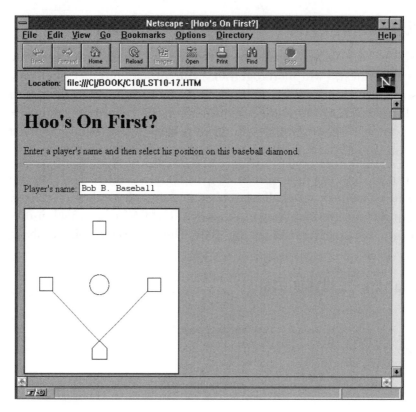

Figure 10.10   Batter up!

```
if ($LENGTH > "32768") {
    die "major network spam, stopped";
}
while ($LENGTH--) {
    $C = getc(STDIN);               # Get next character
    if ($C eq "=" || $C eq "&") {   # Check for start/end of value
        $START="0";
    } else {
        $START++;
    }
    if ($START <= "8192") {         # 8K should be enough!
        $FORM_DATA .= $C;           # Save data to FORM_DATA
    }
}
}

# Parse data into NAME=VALUE pairs and jam into an associative array
```

```
foreach (split(/&/, $FORM_DATA)) {
    ($NAME, $VALUE) = split(/=/, $_);
    $NAME =~ s/\+/ /g;
    $NAME =~ s/%([0-9|A-F]{2})/pack(C,hex($1))/eg;
    $VALUE =~ s/\+/ /g;
    $VALUE =~ s/%([0-9|A-F]{2})/pack(C,hex($1))/eg;
    # Find Unique name
    $NUM="0";
    while ($MYDATA{$NAME} ne "") {
        $NUM++;
        $NAME =~ s/\.([0-9]+$)|$/\.$NUM/;
    }
    # Store NAME=VALUE pair
    $MYDATA{$NAME} = $VALUE;
}


# Get coordinates
$MAP_X = $MYDATA{'DIAMOND.x'};
$MAP_Y = $MYDATA{'DIAMOND.y'};

# Open map file
open(MAPCONF, "<bbd.map");
while (<MAPCONF>) {
    ($TYPE, $ACTION, $COORDS) = split(/ /, $_, 3);
    @PAIRS = split(' ', $COORDS);
    if ($TYPE eq "default") {
        $DO_ACTION=$ACTION;
    } elsif ($TYPE eq "circ") {
        ($X1, $Y1) = split(',', $PAIRS[0]);
        ($X2, $Y2) = split(',', $PAIRS[1]);
        $RADIUS = (($Y1 - $Y2) ** 2) + (($X1 - $X2) ** 2);
        $DIST = (($Y1 - $MAP_Y) ** 2) + (($X1 - $MAP_X) ** 2);
        if ($DIST <= $RADIUS) {
            $DO_ACTION=$ACTION;
        }
    } elsif ($TYPE eq "rect") {
        ($X1, $Y1) = split(',', $PAIRS[0]);
        ($X2, $Y2) = split(',', $PAIRS[1]);
        if ($MAP_X >= $X1 && $MAP_X <= $X2 &&
            $MAP_Y >= $Y1 && $MAP_Y <= $Y2) {
            $DO_ACTION=$ACTION;
        }
    }
}
close(MAPCONF);

# Print out little message
```

```
print "Content-type: text/html\n\n";
print "<HTML>\n";
print "<HEAD>\n";
print "<TITLE>Hoo's on First!</TITLE>\n";
print "</HEAD>\n";
print "<BODY>\n";
print "<H1>Hoo's on First!</H1>\n";

if ($MYDATA{'PLAYER'} eq "") {
    $MYDATA{'PLAYER'} = "the man with no name";
}

print "<P>OK, I'll put $MYDATA{'PLAYER'} ";

if ($DO_ACTION eq "pitcher") {
    print "on the pitcher's mound.\n";
} elsif ($DO_ACTION eq "catcher") {
    print "behind the plate.\n";
} elsif ($DO_ACTION eq "first") {
    print "on first! Yay!\n";
} elsif ($DO_ACTION eq "second") {
    print "on second.\n";
} elsif ($DO_ACTION eq "third") {
    print "on third.\n";
} else {
    print "on, er.. ummm.. where did you say you wanted him?\n";
}
print "</BODY>\n";
print "</HTML>\n";
```

Listing 10.10   BBD.MAP

```
default bad
circle pitcher 121,119 140,123
rect first 198,105 223,131
rect second 108,17 135,43
rect third 20,103 48,132
rect catcher 107,238 137,204
```

Most of this stuff you've seen already. The excitement in Listing 10.9 really begins around the "Get coordinates" comment. After the script retrieves the coordinates, it opens a standard NCSA-type map configuration file. I picked NCSA because it seems to be the most popular format, as well as being fairly easy to parse in Perl. The file is read one line at a time, skipping comments, the polygon shape, the point shape, and any invalid shapes. When a valid shape is found (circles, rectangles, or the default option), the program checks to see if the user's click coordinates fall within that area. (Note that I'm not actually using URLs in the map file, but rather keywords that correspond to the name of the position on the baseball diamond.) If a valid shape is found, the **$DO_ACTION** variable is filled in with the location of the player (behind the plate, on first, on second, etc.). In the case of default, no checks are made. It's always true and **$DO_ACTION** will be set to the default, so be sure the default is the first line of your map configuration!

Once the script figures out where the user clicked, it's simply a matter of printing a friendly message noting the player's name and the position he has been assigned to. And there you have it, the world's first Web tool to help baseball managers play "the game"! Just a couple more features, like maybe remembering where each player was assigned, and you're set!

Following the Map!

Image maps can be powerful tools, giving your users yet another, graphical means of sending information to your server. In this chapter, I showed you how to create image maps using the <IMG> element's ISMAP attribute. The pre-made scripts (imagemap, htimage, and Mac-ImageMap) can manipulate map configuration files for you, by interpreting the coordinates of the hotspots on your image maps. Programs such as MapEdit or WebMap make creating the map configuration files as easy as drawing the hotspots directly on your image. With ISMAP, when a user clicks on one of your hotspots, their browser may be redirected to a new URL, such as another HTML document, a file in an FTP archive, or even another CGI script.

I also explained how image maps can be combined with forms by way of the INPUT method, and create multiple submit buttons, as well as image maps with hotspots. It can be much more difficult to process the INPUT type of image map, but the hassle is more than offset by the additional flexibility and power. Not only can image maps embedded in forms return the coordinates of a user's mouse click, but also any other data which can be included in forms, a feature that ISMAP lacks.

Finally, I introduced to a new MIME header, **Location:**, which makes it possible to force a user's browser to run off and fetch a brand new URL.

This turns your script into something of a traffic cop, detouring Web browsers to different URLs, depending on their input.

Now that you've had a taste of image maps, it is time to dive into some of the more advanced material. In the following chapters I will cover the art of *keeping state*, as well as allowing your users to search your documents, and a plethora of exciting new HTML and CGI features.

11

Advanced CGI

The scripts we have been creating so far are one-dimensional. You offer the user a form, tinker with the returned data a bit, and then send back a single reply, for example, a thank-you note for joining the company mailing list or an acknowledgement that the comments will be sent to the correct department. But you can do a lot more with CGI than just return a simple, flat answer to the user's input. You can also return yet another form requesting additional information based on the user's initial reply. In this chapter I'll go over several interesting techniques that apply this powerful feature of CGI, and present some sample applications that you can use as a basis for your own advanced CGI scripts.

I'll also show you some techniques for the generation of dynamic pages that do not involve forms or CGI. These are called *server-side includes*, and they allow you to instruct the server to paste additional information inside your pages before it serves the document to the user, without any inital user interaction. For example, you could use server-side includes to add a timestamp or a copyright notice to your pages, or a counter displaying the number of accesses that the document has received to date.

Scripts Generating Forms

One of the more powerful features of CGI is its ability to return anything, even another form, to the user for additional processing. A good example of this type of interaction is an application that conducts a survey. The script may rely on the user's answers to one or more questions in order to generate additional questions, on even a new form, relating more specifically to that user. For example, questions on the first form may determine that the user is interested in rock music, Classical Greek architecture, and fishing. A second form might then be generated asking for the user's favorite rock band, favorite book on architecture, or favorite fishing spot.

There is nothing magical or mystical about writing a CGI script that returns a form. Instead of your form being in a separate document like "normal" HTML, it is just created as output by the script, just as you would create it if you were sending a canned thank-you or confirmation that a user's input had been received. The trick comes from what is called *keeping state*, which is the passing of information from the previous form to the next. Let me explain with an example: a new mailing list script that allows the user to add *or* remove his or her name from the list, as well as change the address already stored there.

The Art of Keeping State: A New Mailing List Script

The design of the new mailing list script is similiar to that of the old one. There is a text entry box to enter your email address, a few checkboxes which allow you to choose the mailing list you would like to be added to, and a submit button to send all that data to the script. What the old mailing list *didn't* have is a scrolling text menu to allow you to determine what type of action to take: Add yourself to the list, remove yourself, or change your email address. Now, this itself isn't the problem. The problem is that changing your email address requires yet another text entry box, this one for the new email address, and you only want to have that additional information requested when it is actually required by the user. In other words, the mailing list script will need to produce another small form requesting this information, depending on what action the user is trying to take.

Another Use for VALUE

But before I jump into all the details of keeping state, let me backtrack a bit and show you a new use for the VALUE attribute. The HTML that I'll present shortly in Listing 11.1 should all look very familiar to you, except for one minor detail: the VALUE attribute inside the <OPTION> element. If you remember from your last exposure to <SELECT>, whatever <OPTION>

the user selects is sent to the script in whole. For example, suppose that the user selects this line:

```
<OPTION>This is a test!
```

The NAME=VALUE pair "NAME=This+is+a+test!" would be sent to the script, where NAME is the name given in the <SELECT> tag. That's a bit cumbersome. If you wanted to test to see if that option was selected, you would have to test for the whole string, "This is a test!" (Remember, the Perl script should turn those pluses into spaces.) This is something less than ideal. But by using the VALUE attribute, you can simplify the data returned to the script. For example, selecting this line:

```
<OPTION VALUE="TEST">This is a test!
```

would return the NAME=VALUE pair "NAME=TEST" instead of all that other text.

Which brings me to the subject of using VALUE with the submit and reset buttons. In Listing 11.1 you will notice that I've given the submit button a value of "Send Information." When the button is drawn by the browser, instead of the generic "Submit Query" or whatever your particular browser displays for a generic submit button, "Send Information" will be used instead. It makes a lot more sense here, because technically the user isn't sending a query, but rather stating a fact: his or her email address. Though I didn't do it in this example, you can also "reprogram" the reset button to display a custom message as well; for example "Clear Form" or "Start Over."

Speaking of assigning values to the submit button, in Chapter 10, I showed you how to use the image input type in a form to fake multiple submit buttons, because multiple submit buttons won't return a value, even if given a name. Forgive me; I lied a bit there for simplicity's sake. If you give a submit button a name, according to the HTML 2.0 draft, it *should* send a NAME=VALUE pair to your script, just as with any other input type, so you can determine which submit button was selected. But this is a relatively new addition to the draft, so not all browsers will comply. I wouldn't recommend using this method right now, since you may exclude many users from using your forms.

Now let's pick up our discussion of keeping state.

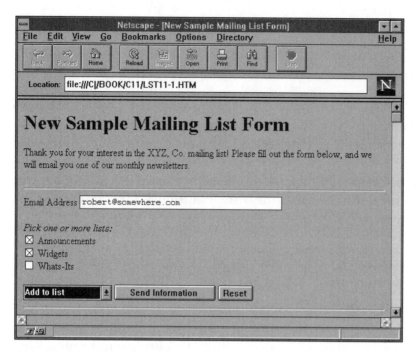

Figure 11.1 The new mailing list form

Listing 11.1 LST11-1.HTM

```
<HTML>
<HEAD>
<TITLE>New Sample Mailing List Form</TITLE>
</HEAD>
<BODY>
<H1>New Sample Mailing List Form</H1>
<P>Thank you for your interest in the XYZ, Co. mailing list! Please fill out
the form below, and we will email you one of our monthly newsletters.
<FORM METHOD="POST" ACTION="/cgi-bin/newmail.pl">
<HR>
Email Address <INPUT TYPE="text" NAME="EMAIL.ADDR" SIZE="40" MAXLENGTH="80">
<P><I>Pick one or more lists:</I><BR>
<INPUT TYPE="checkbox" NAME="LIST.ANNOUNCE" CHECKED> Announcements<BR>
<INPUT TYPE="checkbox" NAME="LIST.WIDGETS"> Widgets<BR>
<INPUT TYPE="checkbox" NAME="LIST.WHATSITS"> Whats-Its
<P>
<SELECT NAME="ACTION">
<OPTION VALUE="Add" SELECTED>Add to list
<OPTION VALUE="Remove">Remove from list
<OPTION VALUE="Change">Change address
```

```
</SELECT>
<INPUT TYPE="submit" VALUE="Send Information"> <INPUT TYPE="reset">
<HR>
</FORM>
</BODY>
</HTML>
```

In essence, the problem with a system like this is remembering what information the user entered on the *previous* form, and resubmitting the old information with the new information from the second form, without the user having to reenter it a second time—or even knowing that the old information is being passed between forms. This requires the technique called *keeping state*. As I previously stated, keeping state is the process of passing crucial information from one form to another. Let's take a look at the script for the new mailing list in Listing 11.2.

Listing 11.2 LST11-2.PL

```perl
print "Content-type: text/html\n\n";

# Debugging code

print "<B>Debug:</B><BR>\n";
print "EMAIL.ADDR: $MYDATA{'EMAIL.ADDR'}<BR>\n";
print "LIST.ANNOUNCE: $MYDATA{'LIST.ANNOUNCE'}<BR>\n";
print "LIST.WIDGETS: $MYDATA{'LIST.WIDGETS'}<BR>\n";
print "LIST.WHATSITS: $MYDATA{'LIST.WHATSITS'}<BR>\n";
print "ACTION: $MYDATA{'ACTION'}<BR>\n";
print "NEW.ADDR: $MYDATA{'NEW.ADDR'}<P>\n";

# Act on user's data

if ($MYDATA{'ACTION'} eq "Change address") {
        # Second form for the new address
        print "<FORM METHOD=\"POST\" ACTION=\"/cgi-bin/newmail.pl\">\n";
        print "New address: ";
        print "<INPUT TYPE=\"text\" NAME=\"NEW.ADDR\" SIZE=\"40\"
MAXLENGTH=\"80\">\n";
        # Keep state
        foreach (keys %MYDATA) {
                if ($_ ne "ACTION") {
                        print "<INPUT TYPE=\"hidden\" NAME=\"$_\"
VALUE=\"$MYDATA{$_}\" SIZE=\"1\">\n";
                }
        }
        print "<INPUT TYPE=\"submit\" VALUE=\"Submit Address Change\">\n";
```

```
        print "<INPUT TYPE=\"reset\">\n";
        print "</FORM>\n";
} else {
        print "Thanks! Got it!\n";
}
```

Listing 11.2 is some sample Perl code for the new mailing list script, minus all the parsing code. The first few lines, under the "# Debugging code" comment, output the values from all the user's input. One interesting thing you'll notice is the NEW.ADDR variable, which is not defined in the first mailing list form. This variable will be defined (if the user is changing his or her address) in the second form, when the script asks the user for the replacement email address. The rest of the script is a little more interesting; let's take a look.

Right after the "# Act on user's data" comment is where the script determines whether or not it should display the new form. If the user selected "Change address" as the action (found in the ACTION variable) a new form is output, requesting the new address; otherwise a brief little acknowledgement is given. This is just simple bare-bones code, so you can get the feel of things; I'll add a few embellishments in a moment.

Right under the "# Second form for the new address" comment, the script outputs the <FORM> tag, which points the new form back to the current script. Then it prompts for the new address and offers the user a text entry box. Nothing new. But what happens next is the meat of this example, and illustrates what I mean by "keeping state." If I ended the form here, when the user entered their new address and pressed "submit," what could we do with that new data? Practically nothing. The reason is this: The original input entered by the user is lost; that is, the old email address and which lists he or she wants to change the address in. The only information this new form would return would be the user's new email address, and none of the information the user originally entered—which, alas, means you still need to update the mailing lists.

Now I *could* expand on the second form, adding the old text entry boxes and buttons, and reset their defaults to reflect the old data. In other words, I could use the VALUE attribute for text entry boxes to set the value to default to the user's original email address, and use the CHECKED attribute for the checkboxes to default those to the correct lists, but that just doesn't seem "professional" somehow. I want to hide this information from the user. It's been entered once, so let's get it out of his or her face and concentrate on getting the new data. Wouldn't it be nice if you could store this information in a form, and pass it to the script, without the user's browser actually displaying it? In essense, what you need is an "invisible" <INPUT> statement, and that is what the code after the "# Keep state" comment does: inserts several hidden variables that contain all the old information.

In a nutshell, here is what's going on: The Perl foreach statement runs through each of the NAME=VALUE pairs the script received from the previous form, and for each one that is not the ACTION variable, a special <INPUT> tag is output for the pair. The reason I left out ACTION will soon be clear, but let's set that aside that for the moment. The special input type hidden acts much like the text type, *except* when the user's browser goes to display the form. At display time, any input type of hidden is not shown to the user. The user can't see a hidden type, can't change the value, and doesn't even know it's there unless he or she views the document's source. Nonetheless, it *is* there, and when the form is submitted back to the script, all those hidden fields will be passed right back to the script along with all the "regular" user input.

In my script, I've "mirrored" each of the original NAME=VALUE pairs, but used the hidden type, instead of text or checkbox as I did before, so that information would remain invisible to the user. But why didn't I also mirror ACTION? Well, in this script, the ACTION variable controls whether the user is changing an email address, or else performing some other action. So if I mirrored ACTION, when the second form (containing the new email address) was submitted, the script would once again think that the user wanted to submit an address change and would go into an endless loop. But by leaving the ACTION variable out, the script will pass on to the next section of code by default.

This, admittedly, is a mouthful, but it will make a little more sense after I've added some bells and whistles, including the code that deals with the user adding or deleting his or her address to the mailing list. But first, take a look at Listing 11.3, which is the HTML that the script produces when a user requests a change of address.

Listing 11.3   LST11-3.HTM

```
<B>Debug:</B><BR>
EMAIL.ADDR: robert@somewhere.com<BR>
LIST.ANNOUNCE: on<BR>
LIST.WIDGETS: on<BR>
LIST.WHATSITS: <BR>
ACTION: Change<BR>
NEW.ADDR: <P>
<FORM METHOD="POST" ACTION="/cgi-bin/newmail.pl">
New address: <INPUT TYPE="text" NAME="NEW.ADDR" SIZE="40" MAXLENGTH="80">
<INPUT TYPE="hidden" NAME="EMAIL.ADDR" VALUE="robert@somewhere.com" SIZE="1">
<INPUT TYPE="hidden" NAME="LIST.ANNOUNCE" VALUE="on" SIZE="1">
<INPUT TYPE="hidden" NAME="LIST.WIDGETS" VALUE="on" SIZE="1">
<INPUT TYPE="submit" VALUE="Submit Address Change">
<INPUT TYPE="reset">
</FORM>
```

After looking at the HTML in Listing 11.3, the preceding discussion should become a little clearer. In particular, you can see how the script created a new form with a text entry box for the user's new email address, as well as three hidden fields that contain the information received from the previous form. Now, when the user enters the replacement email address and submits this form, the new address, along with all the old data, will be sent to the script. Since there is no longer an ACTION variable, the script will know that instead of being called to process the original form, it is now being called to process the second form. Figure 11.2 shows a screen shot of this form with a new address being entered, and Figure 11.3 is a shot of the *second* form being returned and the resulting output.

Figure 11.3 shows how the debugging code in Listing 11.2 demonstrates the script accomplishing its goal. All the old data from the first form is still there, passed to the script using hidden fields, along with the additional data entered from the second form, in NEW.ADDR. Now all that remains is adding some pretty messages to the user and actually adding, deleting, or changing the user's email address, but what I've demonstrated so far is the gist of keeping state.

One question I anticipate right now is why, if the hidden fields are, well, *hidden,* am I giving them a size of 1? After all, the size attribute is a purely visible attribute; for example, it controls the physical length of a text entry box. So why do you need any length value at all here? Just as not all browsers support forms (most newer ones do, but many ancient browsers out

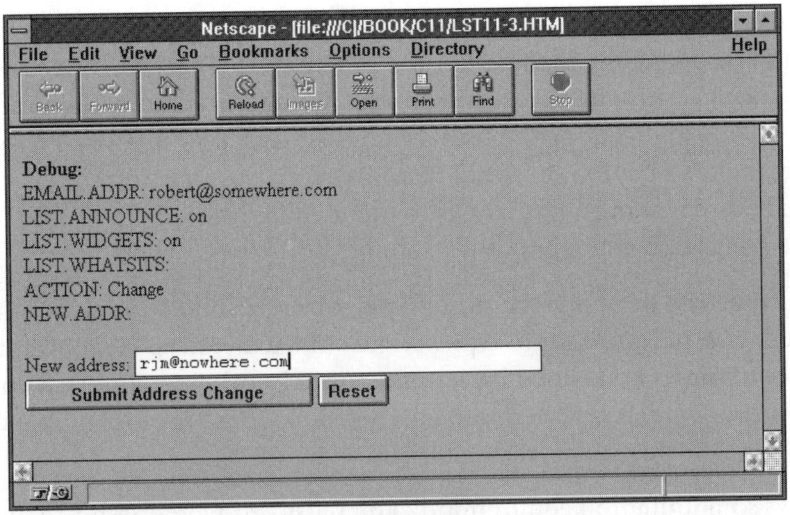

Figure 11.2 **Listing 11.2, as rendered by Netscape.**

there don't) not all browsers that support forms support hidden fields. If someone using one of these older browsers tries to view a document with hidden fields, they *will* see them as normal text entry boxes. Hence, setting the size to one is damage-control of sorts. If they do see a hidden field, at least they will see a very small text entry box. It's rare, but it happens, so you may as well plan a graceful response.

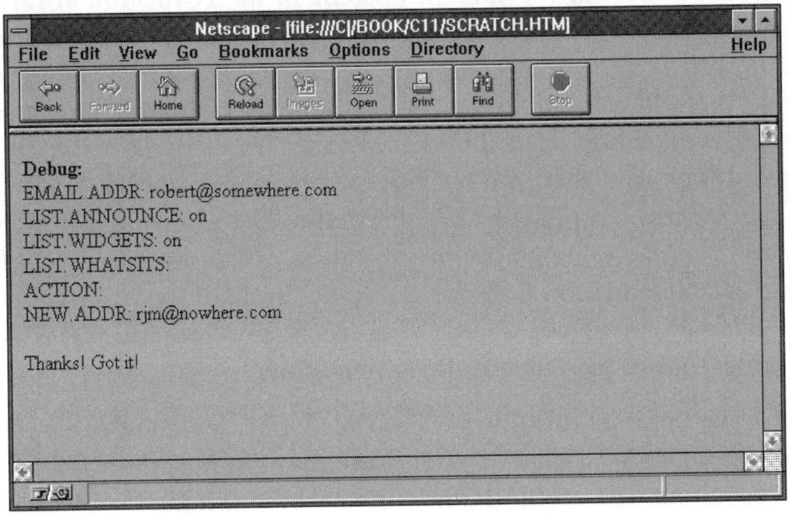

Figure 11.3 **The output of the script after the second form is submitted.**

If you are feeling ambitious and would like some CGI practice, you might want to complete the mailing list implementation. In its current state, the script doesn't actually do anything useful. Go ahead and create routines to add, delete, and change the user's email address, now that you know how to get the information. It would be professional, as well, to request a password before making any changes to the mailing list, to help prevent malicious users from changing other people's addresses.

This brings us to one more input type, *password,* that I haven't yet mentioned. The password input type acts just like text, except that everything the user types is *not* echoed back to the form. In other words, each character the user types is replaced with an asterisk, so someone looking on won't be able to see any passwords being entered.

Here's something to keep in mind: The password type doesn't really add any additional security once the password is entered; it just keeps prying eyes from seeing what your users are typing if they happen to be in the same room as a "bad guy." *Whatever is typed still passes in plain text form over the Internet!* So it's of no use whatsoever protecting the transmission of credit card numbers or other sensitive information.

Environment Variables with CGI

It's time for a thorough treatment of some of the environment variables you will probally encounter while writing your own CGI scripts. There is really no such a thing as a "complete" list of environment variables, since some servers will take a liberty or two with the variables they provide, and the CGI specification itself allows new variables to be added as they're needed. I'll explain that in a bit, but for now, take a look at Table 11.1. This summarizes most of the variables that will be available to you. Some are available depending on the method used to call the script, others are always available, and some others may never be available because your server has decided not to include them. Go figure. In any event, study the list and compare it to your own server's documentation.

Some of the variables in Table 11.1 you've already seen. For example, you know that QUERY_STRING contains the user's input when the script is called using the GET method. But some of these variables will definititely be foreign to you. RFC 931 remote user identification? Authenticated

Table 11.1 **Important environment variables used in CGI scripts**

Environment Variable	Brief Description	Sample Values
AUTH_TYPE	Authentication type (see REMOTE_USER)	Basic
CONTENT_LENGTH	Length of information sent to server	123456
CONTENT_TYPE	Type of information sent to server	application/x-www-form-urlencoded
GATEWAY_INTERFACE	The CGI version the server uses	CGI/1.1
HTTP_ACCEPT	MIME types browser can accept	*/*, image/gif, image/x-xbitmap,image/jpeg
HTTP_REFERER	The "refering" document	http://www.host.com/lastdoc.html
HTTP_USER_AGENT	Name and version of browser	Mozilla/1.0N (X11; Linux 1.1.59 I486)
PATH_INFO	The extra path information	/blah
PATH_TRANSLATED	Virtual to physical path mapping	/home/http/htdocs/blah
QUERY_STRING	Information sent to a GET script	NAME1=VALUE1&NAME2=VALUE2
REMOTE_ADDR	Address of the requesting machine	127.0.0.1
REMOTE_HOST	Name of the requesting machine	users.machine.com
REMOTE_IDENT	RFC 931 remote user identification	robertm
REMOTE_USER	Authenticated username (see AUTH_TYPE)	username
REQUEST_METHOD	The request method	POST
SCRIPT_NAME	Virtual path to script	/cgi-bin/script.pl
SERVER_NAME	The server's machine name	www.host.com
SERVER_PORT	The port number used	80
SERVER_PROTOCOL	The HTTP version the request used	HTTP/1.0
SERVER_SOFTWARE	The name and version of the server	NCSA/1.3

username? Some of these variables contain information from services and features I haven't yet covered in this book, and others are just plain strange. I've attempted to describe in as much detail as possible what each variable does and how it should be used. Be sure to read the more verbose description of each provided below before attempting to use a variable you are not familiar with. It will save you considerable time and grief.

SERVER_NAME

The SERVER_NAME variable is set by the server, and it contains the name of the machine the server is running on. For example, if your server was running on a machine named www.host.com, then this is what the SERVER_NAME will be set to. Usually, you tell the server in its configuration files what its name should be. Why do you need this variable? After all, you could just hardcode this value directly into your script. However, sometimes your scripts may run on other machines where you don't know the name of the server—or you may change the name of your own server and not wish to hunt through a multitude of CGI scripts for hardcoded names. If your script needs to generate an absolute URL, and you are not sure what server will be running the script, this is the variable to use.

SERVER_PORT

The SERVER_PORT variable is set to the port number that the HTTP request *came from.* In most cases, this will be port 80, the standard HTTP port. Since your server will most likely only be able to accept requests from one port, you may as well think of this as the port the server is running on. Anyway, you can use this variable in conjunction with SERVER_NAME to generate an absolute URL when you don't know what server your script will be running on.

SERVER_SOFTWARE

The SERVER_SOFTWARE variable is set by the server with the server software's name and version. Note that this is *not* the name from SERVER_NAME (which is the name of your individual site), but instead the "brand name" of the server software, such as CERN or NCSA. This is useful if your script relies on features only available in your server, like certain special environment variables. It is for determining portability, and allowing your script to either deal with the differences, or abort gracefully if it isn't being called from a server it understands.

SERVER_PROTOCOL

The SERVER_PROTOCOL variable refers to the revision of the HTTP protocol that the browser is attempting to speak. The current protocol revision is 1.0, so this will always be HTTP/1.0 for now, but if a new version of the protocol is ever proposed, this variable will let you know so that your script will be able to take advantage of any new features present in the later revision. You will find this most useful when generating HTTP response headers for Non-Parsing-Headers (NPH) scripts, which I will discuss much later, when I go over some of the more advanced features of scripting needed to accomplish server-push/client-pull operatings.

GATEWAY_INTERFACE

The GATEWAY_INTERFACE variable refers to the revision of CGI which your server software understands. The current version is 1.1, so this variable will usually be set to CGI/1.1. It is set by the server software.

REQUEST_METHOD

You should be familiar with this environment variable from my earlier discussions in this book. REQUEST_METHOD contains the method used to submit the script to the server for processing. For now, the values will only be POST or GET. More methods may be conceived as the Web evolves and becomes more sophisticated. You will use this variable to tell your script how to access the information the user has sent. If it is set to GET, you will know that you will need to check the value of the QUERY_STRING variable for the submitted information. If it is set to POST, you will have to check CONTENT_LENGTH and read however many bytes it specifies from the standard input. For more information on using REQUEST_METHOD, refer back to Chapter 9.

QUERY_STRING

As you know from earlier chapters, QUERY_STRING contains the information submitted to the script for processing. Typically, anything after the

"?" in a URL is placed in this variable. For example, in the URL *http://host.com/cgi-bin/script.pl?TEST=text*, the QUERY_STRING would be set to "TEST=text." The format is NAME1=VALUE1&NAME2=VALUE2, and so on. If you need to refresh your memory, return to Chapter 9 for a full description of how to use this variable.

CONTENT_LENGTH

CONTENT_LENGTH is used for scripts submitted using the POST method. It contains the length of the data stream that the server has sent to your script through your standard input. Read standard input, one character at a time, until you have read the number of characters expressed in CONTENT_LENGTH. See Chapter 9 (if you haven't already) on using the POST method.

CONTENT_TYPE

When information is sent to your script using the POST method, this variable is also set. It contains the MIME type of the data the server is sending to your script, which for now will always be application/x-www-form-urlencoded.

SCRIPT_NAME

The virtual path to the script being executed. If the script's name is script.pl and it is located in your cgi-bin directory, this value would be */cgi-bin/script.pl*. This is perfect for use in scripts which need to create *self-referencing URLs*, that is, URLs that point to the same script or document in which they exist. For example, if you were creating a script that needs to create a form that submits its information back to the same script, you could use this variable to determine the script's name. Make it a habit of using this variable wherever possible. More than once I've renamed a script and forgotten to change the self-referencing URLs, until a kind user pointed out the nonobvious failure.

Here's an example:

```
print "<FORM METHOD=\"POST\" ACTION=\"$SCRIPT_NAME\">\n";
```

PATH_INFO

The PATH_INFO variable contains any extra path information the server encountered while decoding the URL to your script. An example of this is shown in Chapter 10, in the discussion of image maps. If the script were called using the following URL:

```
http://host.com/cgi-bin/script.pl/extra/path
```

the PATH_INFO variable would contain /extra/path. NCSA's *imagemap* script uses this variable to find the map configuration file's name.

PATH_TRANSLATED

If there is extra path information, the PATH_TRANSLATED variable is the server's usually misguided attempt at turning the path in the PATH_INFO variable into a physical pathname. The physical path is the physical file's pathname on your computer, so the extra path information /extra/path might be translated to /home/http/extra/path if your server's document root were /home/http.

Request Headers and the HTTP_ Variables

When the user's browser sends its request to your server, the request includes certain special information (called a *request header*) to the server, for which there may not be a specific environment variable. Request headers look just like the response headers (for example, "Content-type:") that you send to the browser from your scripts. Three of the more common request headers are described below.

HTTP_ACCEPT

The HTTP_ACCEPT variable is a comma-separated list of the additional MIME types that the browser is capable of handling. The MIME types your scripts usually send are *text/html* or *text/plain*, which are implied. After all, it's not much of a Web browser if it can't decode plain text or HTML documents! What your script should really be interested in is whether or not the browser can handle images, which HTTP_ACCEPT will tell you. If you see *image/gif*, the browser can handle GIF images, and *image/jpeg* means it can handle JPEG images. There may also be other types listed here as well.

HTTP_USER_AGENT

A *user agent* in this context is fancy-speak for the user's Web browser. This variable contains the name and version of the Web browser used to access your script. For example, Netscape's Navigator (the official name for Netscape's Web browser) version 1.0N returns "Mozilla/1.0N (X11; Linux 1.1.59 I486)." Mozilla, for the uninitiated, is Netscape's cartoon dinosaur mascot, and the code-name for their browser while it was under development. You could use this information if your script uses features of a particular browser that are not available in other browsers.

HTTP_REFERER

This is one of my favorite variables, but unfortunately it isn't returned by all browsers. Most do return it, but not all. It contains the URL of the document the browser used to call your script. For example, if your script was called by a form at the URL *http://host.com/docs/myform.html,* then the HTTP_REFERER variable will be set to this URL. This is wonderful if you're interested in who has a link directly to one of your scripts, assuming folks other than yourself set such links up. Fortunately, such information is only "nice to have," and you can easily write a script such that nothing serious will happen if a browser doesn't return a value here. Snagging values returned in HTTP_REFERER is one way to gauge how popular your forms are becoming in the rest of the Web universe.

Variables that Identify the User

The variables discussed below are used to identify the user who is accessing your script. They are here, separated from the others, because their use comes along with a warning. Never base security-related decisions on the values of any of these variables! They can be readily faked by a knowledgeable hacker and are meant to be used solely for "informational purposes," such as logging.

REMOTE_HOST and REMOTE_ADDR

The REMOTE_HOST and REMOTE_ADDR variables are used to store information about the machine from which the user is accessing your script. In other words, they contain the name or address of the user's workstation or home computer, or whatever machine they are using to access the Web. The REMOTE_HOST variable contains the actual machine's name, in "human readable" form, like "host.com." Sometimes, this name, called the *domain name*, is not available. In those cases, this variable will be blank. The REMOTE_ADDR variable, however, is always available, and it contains the IP address of the user's machine; for example, "127.0.0.1."

REMOTE_IDENT

The REMOTE_IDENT variable will return the user name of the user accessing your script or documents, *if* your server supports that feature, *and* the feature is turned on, *and* the user's machine is running a special program that will send this information to your server when requested. (Got all that?) It is *not* recommended that you tell your server to turn this feature on, since the extra overhead involved in querying the user's machine for the user's login name will place an extra burden on your server and your network connection. Besides, most of the time your query will fall on deaf ears; in most cases the user's machine will not be running this special program. And even if you do receive a response, you should never trust it for security-related purposes, but for logging only.

If the user's machine does not respond to the query, the REMOTE_IDENT variable will either be empty or contain "unknown." If there is a response, the user's login name will be placed in the REMOTE_IDENT variable.

REMOTE_USER and AUTH_TYPE

Many servers provide a mechanism with which you can password-protect a document, a script, or even an entire directory of documents. This is called *access control*, and is in my opinion the safest way for protecting your documents, barring not having them on the Web in the first place. But this type of protection is far from foolproof. Sensitive information should never be accessible on your server, password-protected or not. It is your job to determine how sensitive your data is and, if an unauthorized user gains access, whether the results will be a simple nuisance or a major disaster.

Precisely how access control is accomplished for your server is completely at your server's discretion. Instead of spending several dozen pages explaining something which will only be applicable to those of you using only one type of server, I'd rather point you to your server's documentation, which I am sure will do more justice to the topic than I can. There is an excellent tutorial for NCSA's httpd server at *http://hoohoo.ncsa.uiuc.edu/docs/tutorials/user.html*. CERN also has online documentation at *http://www.w3.org/hypertext/WWW/AccessAuthorization/Overview.html*.

Server-Side Includes

Normally, when your server fills a browser's request for a document, it doesn't modify the document in any way, except perhaps tack on a few extra MIME headers to satisfy the requirements of the HTTP protocol. But other than that, your document's content is left untouched. On occasion, however, it may be beneficial to instruct your server to make some slight modifications to the document before serving it. For example, this might include a time stamp, appending another file to your document, or even inserting the output of a program or CGI script! The technique that makes this all possible is called the *server-side include (SSI)*.

SSIs are special instructions to your *server*, telling it to modify your document in some way before sending it to the user's browser. That is a key point, and the reason it is called a "server-side" include: The *browser* does not interpret these instructions, it is all done on the server's side of the conversation. Not all servers are capable of performing SSIs, so you will have to double-check with your server documentation and make sure your server *does* support them before spending fruitless hours trying to convince your server that it does. (Don't laugh. It's been done.) NCSA httpd most certainly does support SSIs, and since it's one of the more popular free servers on the Web, I'll be using NCSA httpd, version 1.3, as the basis for my examples. This is not to say that if you're using another server this section won't help you, but you may want to double-check your server's documentation if things don't seem to work correctly at first.

Configuring NCSA HTTPD 1.3 for SSIs

If you are running your server "straight out of the box," you will find SSIs disabled by default. To enable them, you need to edit two configuration files, SRM.CONF and ACCESS.CONF, both located in your server's conf directory along with all the other server configuration files. Don't panic, it's not as tough as it sounds. The first step is to load up your SRM.CONF file into a text editor and go to the very bottom of the file. You should see two lines commented out, with a "#" in front of them. You will want to delete the hash sign from the beginning of the following line:

```
#AddType text/x-server-parsed-html .shtml
```

If you don't see this line in the file, just enter it at the bottom of the file *without* the "#." The line shown tells your server that any documents with the .SHTML extention may contain SSIs and should be processed before sending them to the user's browser. Technically, you *could* change .SHTML to .HTML instead, but I would strongly recommend against it! This would tell your server that *all* your documents should be scanned for SSIs, and besides being a potential security risk (as I mentioned briefly in an earlier chapter), it will also make your server work a *lot* harder. More on that later.

After you've saved your changes to the SRM.CONF file, you should load the ACCESS.CONF file into your editor. Be *very* careful in this file, because all your server's security functions are handled here! Once again, go to the very bottom of the file. The last couple of lines should be comments informing you that you can add your own directories to the file beyond that point. Go ahead and insert the following lines beneath those comments, where *name* is the name of the directory you want to enable server-side includes (for example, */home/http/htdocs/ssi*).

```
<Directory name>
Options Includes
</Directory>
```

These three lines will tell our server that it is okay to parse documents with SSIs in the directory *name*. The keyword "Options" means that the keywords to its right on the line will define the allowable actions within this directory. The "Includes" keyword shown here enables SSIs in that directory.

Now you're almost done! If your server is currently running, you will need to restart it for the configuration change to take effect, because the server only reads the configuration files at startup. *Don't forget that!* More than once I've spent an hour or two trying to figure out why something wasn't working, and it turned out that I simply forgot to restart the server.

Now let's test it out!

SSI Syntax

Server-side includes aren't part of HTML. There is no "draft" or "specification" defining them, so their implementation is largely server-specific. (I suspect that most servers that can handle SSIs use the syntax I'm describing, or something very similiar.) What I can say for certain is that this is exactly how NCSA httpd 1.3 handles SSIs, and any information here will work using that server. Once you understand how SSIs work, you can figure out the details of their use from your specific server's documentation.

The syntax for SSIs is based on SGML comments, which I described earlier, back in Chapter 8. Why use comments? The main reason is most likely this: If a document managed to slip by without being parsed, the SSIs would simply be invisible to the user. A sample SSI might look like this:

```
<!--#command tag="value"-->
```

The "#" in front of "command" differentiates an SSI from a normal comment. It is important to note that the "command" and "tag" strings are both case-sensitive *and must be lowercase*. (So much for my suggestion about capitalizing all element names.) There are six commands, each of which I will describe below: **include**, **echo**, **flastmod**, **fsize**, **config**, and **exec**.

Including Documents

The command **include** instructs the server to include another document into your current document at that point. The **include** command can take two possible tags to specify the location of the inserted document: **virtual** and **file**. The **file** tag allows you to give the document's name and location relative to the current document's directory. Note: You cannot use ".." to travel up the directory tree! The **virtual** tag, by contrast, works relative to the DocumentRoot, thus allowing you to access any of the documents in your htdocs directory, or wherever you told your server to store them. These are *not* URLs, by the way, and you cannot include a document from another server outside your system's path.

This will gel a lot better once we create a test document and experiment a little bit. It doesn't matter what you call the document; however, it must end with an .SHTML extension, not .HTML, because of the way you configured the server in the SRM.CONF file mentioned earlier. If you use .HTML instead, SSIs simply won't work. Also, be sure to create the document in the directory for which you enabled SSIs! I'll call my document /ssi/test.shtml, since I enabled SSIs for my directory named /ssi.

Listing 11.4   LST11-4.HTM

```
<HTML>
<HEAD>
<TITLE>A Simple SSI Example</TITLE>
</HEAD>
<BODY>
<P>An included document is below.
<HR>
<!--#include virtual="/ssi/addme.html"-->
<HR>
<P>An included document is above.
</BODY>
</HTML>
```

The SSI in Listing 11.4 directs the server to insert the HTML document /ssi/addme.html into the current document. Had I wanted to, I could have used the following SSI instead:

```
<!--#include file="addme.html"-->
```

But if addme.html were really located one directory level higher, I could *not* use either of the following, because in both cases the file is in a directory above the current document, and going up in the path is not allowed:

```
<!--#include file="../addme.html"-->
<!--#include file="/addme.html"-->
```

In this case, I would have no choice but to use **virtual** instead.

Let's create the document /ssi/addme.html now, and then see what the original document will look like when it gets to the user's browser. Take a look at Listing 11.5, which is the file that will be included by the SSI line given earlier:

Listing 11.5   LST11-5.HTM

```
<HTML>
<HEAD>
<TITLE>An Included Document</TITLE>
</HEAD>
<BODY>
<H1>I am an included document!</H1>
<P>I will, in essence, &quot;Become One&quot; with the
original document.
</BODY>
</HTML>
```

When someone finally requests my document, /ssi/test.shtml, the server will realize that since the file's extension is .SHTML, it may contain SSIs. It will then double-check to make sure that SSIs are enabled for the directory /ssi, and if so, my SSI line will be replaced by the second document, with the results given in Listing 11.6:

Listing 11.6   LST11-6.HTM

```
<HTML>
<HEAD>
<TITLE>A Simple SSI Example</TITLE>
</HEAD>
<BODY>
<P>An included document is below.
<HR>
<HTML>
<HEAD>
<TITLE>An Included Document</TITLE>
</HEAD>
<BODY>
<H1>I am an included document!</H1>*
<P>I will, in essence, &quot;Become One&quot; with the
original document.
</BODY>
<Lis</HTML>
<HR>
<P>An included document is above.
</BODY>
</HTML>
```

Hmmmm. That did exactly what you expected, but perhaps not quite what you had hoped. It would have been wonderful if the head of the included document had been stripped out, or somehow combined with the head of the original document, with only the body inserted. What will this new, two-headed, and somewhat mangled HTML document do in the hands of a browser? Since it has become invalid HTML, that's impossible to predict—it's all up to the browser. Netscape displays the document itself correctly, but uses the *second* title instead of the original title. That's odd behaviour; you would think it would discard the second title instead. Regardless, my point is that the second document is inserted into the first document, lock, stock, and barrel. So if you're going to do this, make sure that the second document makes sense to be included in its entirety, HTML-wise. In other words, leave out the <HTML>...</HTML> tags, the head and title, and the <BODY>...</BODY> tags from the second document. That will ensure that the resulting document is indeed valid HTML.

Besides other HTML documents, with the **include** command you can also include plain text documents, and even other .SHTML documents! However, a special warning when including .SHTML documents within other .SHTML documents: Beware of creating "infinite" loops! For example, if you include a document that includes itself, the server will go into a loop, including the same document within itself over and over again, like holding up two mirrors facing each other. Eventually, the server will figure things out and stop, but you will still look pretty silly to your users.

One final note: SSIs and the **include** command are *not* meant to include inline images. Use the HTML element <IMG> instead. If you try to include an inline image with an SSI, you will simply get garbage.

Tell Me About My Document!

You can also use server-side includes to report on the current document, for example, to extract the document's name or its last modification date. This data is stored in various environment variables, and you can read them using the **echo** command. **Echo** only has one tag, **var**. There are six environment variables that are set specifically for the **echo** command; you can use many of the variables which are valid in CGI scripts as well. Table 11.2 contains a list of all six SSI-specific variables, plus a few of the more useful CGI-related variables.

Let's look at a quick example of **echo**, including all the variables from Table 11.2. The document's name is ECHO-TEST.SHTML, located in my SSI-enabled directory /ssi. To get to the document, I use an anchor from another document I created, TEST.HTML, which will help illustrate the operation of the HTTP_REFERER variable. Note that the value of QUERY_STRING_UNESCAPED is "(none)." Any environment variables which do not exist or are not set will return this same keyword.

Figure 11.4 shows Netscape Navigator's display of the HTML from Listing 11.7. Note that I edited the output to change my machine name and IP address.

Table 11.2   Environment variables for use with SSIs

Environment Variable	Purpose
DOCUMENT_NAME	The document's filename. Note: This is not the document's title!
DOCUMENT_URI	The document's URI (Universal Resource Identifier). Note: It should really be called "pathname" because that is what it essentially returns.
DATE_LOCAL	The current local date/time.
DATE_GMT	The current date/time, GMT.
LAST_MODIFIED	Date and time the document was last modified (or created).
QUERY_STRING_UNESCAPED	An unescaped query string sent to the document. Note: If you can get this to work for SSIs, you're a better webmaster than I!
SERVER_SOFTWARE	Name and version of your server's software.
SERVER_NAME	The machine name where your server is running.
REMOTE_HOST	The user's machine name. Note: This information may not always be available, but REMOTE_ADDR, below, will always be defined.
REMOTE_ADDR	Same as REMOTE_HOST but returns the IP address instead.
HTTP_REFERER	The document the user just came from. Note: Not all browsers send this information.
HTTP_USER_AGENT	The name and version of the user's browser.

Listing 11.7   LST11-7.HTM

```
<HTML>
<HEAD>
<TITLE>Example of the ECHO Server-Side Include</TITLE>
</HEAD>
<BODY>
<PRE>
DOCUMENT_NAME          : <!--#echo var="DOCUMENT_NAME"-->
DOCUMENT_URI           : <!--#echo var="DOCUMENT_URI"-->
DATE_LOCAL             : <!--#echo var="DATE_LOCAL"-->
DATE_GMT               : <!--#echo var="DATE_GMT"-->
LAST_MODIFIED          : <!--#echo var="LAST_MODIFIED"-->
QUERY_STRING_UNESCAPED: <!--#echo var="QUERY_STRING_UNESCAPED"-->

SERVER_SOFTWARE        : <!--#echo var="SERVER_SOFTWARE"-->
SERVER_NAME            : <!--#echo var="SERVER_NAME"-->
REMOTE_HOST            : <!--#echo var="REMOTE_HOST"-->
```

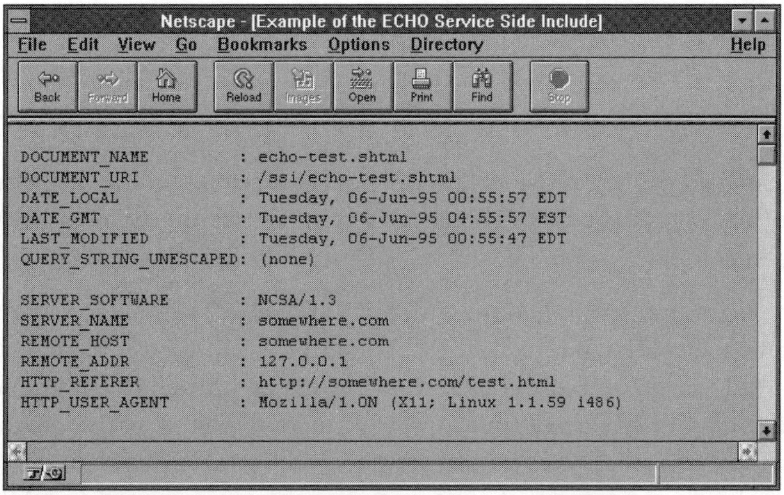

Figure 11.4   SSI return values from Listing 11.7

```
REMOTE_ADDR            : <!--#echo var="REMOTE_ADDR"-->
HTTP_REFERER           : <!--#echo var="HTTP_REFERER"-->
HTTP_USER_AGENT        : <!--#echo var="HTTP_USER_AGENT"-->
</PRE>
</BODY>
</HTML>
```

Finding a Document's Size or Modification Date

You may have noticed the LAST_MODIFIED variable for the **echo** command and thought that it would be a wonderful way to timestamp your documents for your users, but there is a special command just for that purpose. The **flastmod** (file last modified) command will allow you to not only retrieve the timestamp for the current document, but also to have the ability to find the date and modification times of other documents than itself. There are two tags that go along with this command, **file** and **virtual**, which work just like the tags from the **include** command.

A good use for **flastmod** is to timestamp your anchors to frequently updated documents. For example, if you have an automatically generated weather report, updated every hour or so, you could have an anchor like this, pointing to that document:

```
Take a look at the <A HREF="weather.html">weather report</A> (Updated:
<!--#flastmod file="weather.html"-->)
```

When served and interpreted by a browser, it would look something like this:

```
Take a look at the weather report (Updated: Tuesday, 06-Jun-95 06:00:00 PDT)
```

Now the user can see if the weather report is current, and decide whether or not to follow that link. The date is returned as the time local to the server machine.

There is another special command, **fsize** (file size), which works just like **flastmod** except that it returns the document's size instead of its timestamp. This would be great if the weather report were an automatically generated weather map in GIF form (perhaps downloaded from a weather satellite) so that you can warn users having slow connections how large the image is before they try to retrieve it. The document size is returned in kilobytes. The following HTML snippet:

```
Take a look at the <A HREF="weather-map.gif">weather map</A>, which is
<!--#fsize file="weather-map.gif"--> in size and was last updated at
<!--#flastmod file="weather-map.gif"-->.
```

might come up on the browser screen looking like this:

```
Take a look at the weather map, which is 274k in size and was last updated at
Tuesday, 06-Jun-95 06:00:00 PDT.
```

Changing the Date or File Size Format

If the format of the date returned by **flastmod** or the size returned by **fsize** is too cryptic or "unfriendly" for you, there is another command, **config**, that you can use to change either or both formats. The **config** command takes two tags, **sizefmt** and **timefmt**.

The **sizefmt** tag is used to change the format used by the **fsize** command. There are only two valid values for this tag, either "abbrev," which displays the size in kilobytes, and "bytes," which simply displays the size in bytes. The default is "abbrev." To set the size format to bytes, you would use this syntax:

```
<!--#config sizefmt="bytes"-->
```

The **timefmt** tag, used to change the timestamp format, is slightly more complex, but with a bit of experimentation you should be able to get the idea fairly quickly. The key to the whole system is the use of a series of special formatting symbols called *field descriptors* in Unix-speak, which are replaced by the appropriate value when the timestamp is output. For example, the field descriptors "%a," "%b," and "%y" are used for the day of the week, month, and year, respectively. To set the format to output "Tue 06-Jun-95" you would use the following:

```
<!--#config timefmt="%a %e-%b-%y"-->
```

A complete list of field descriptors is in Table 11.3. Experiment with them so you can get a better idea of how they work together.

Be sure to use the **config** command *before* the **fsize** or **flastmod** commands you want to customize. All occurences of **fsize** or **flastmod** coming after the **config** command will then use your new formats, but any above **config** will still be displayed using their defaults, or an earlier configuration set with a previous instance of **config**. You can use as many **config** commands as you would like in a document.

One more quick point about **timefmt**: It does not affect the format of environment variables, like LAST_MODIFIED, which are displayed with the **echo** command. It only affects dates displayed using **flastmod**. You may want to keep this in mind when deciding whether to use **flastmod** as opposed to LAST_MODIFIED, because you have no control over the formating of the data within the LAST_MODIFIED variable.

By the way, an SSI command can have more than one tag, which is great if you want to save some space and typing. I didn't mention it before because it doesn't make sense with the other commands, but **config** is very well suited to taking advantage of this feature. If you would like to change the **fsize** format to "bytes," and modify the **flastmod** format a bit as well, you can do it in one compact line:

```
<!--#config sizefmt="bytes" timefmt="%a %e-%b-%y"-->
```

This would have the same effect as two separate **config** commands.

Occasionally, when you're first getting used to the concept of SSIs, you may make a mistake or two. Some famous examples are trying to include a document that does not exist, or using an invalid tag. In these cases, instead of the response you're expecting, the server will send a terse and

Table 11.3   Time and date field descriptors

Field Descriptor	Description	Example using Monday, 05-June-1995 at 10:21:14 PM
%%	Display a percent sign (%)	%
%a	Abbreviated weekday name	Mon
%A	Weekday name	Monday
%b or %h	Abbreviated month name	Jun
%B	Month name	June
%c	Date and time like %x %X	Mon Jun 05 22:21:14 1995
%d	Day of month from 01 through 31	05
%D	Date in MM/DD/YY format	06/05/95
%e	Same as %d but single digits are not padded with 0	5
%H	Hour in military time from 00 through 23	22
%I	Hour in civilian time from 00 through 12	10
%j	Day of year	156
%k	Same as %H but single digits are not padded with 0	22
%l	Same as %I but single digits are not padded with 0	10
%m	Month from 01 through 12	06
%M	Minute from 00 through 59	21
%n	A newline, works like the tag	
%p	AM or PM	PM
%r	Time of day as %I:%M:%S %p	10:21:14 PM
%R	Time of day as %H:%M	22:21
%S	Seconds from 00 through 59	14
%t	A horizontal tab	
%w	Day of week if Sunday is day 0	01
%x	Date, using your country's regular date format	06/05/95
%X	Time, using your country's regular time format	22:21:14
%y	Year from 00 through 99	95
%Y	Year in a four digit format	1995
%Z	Timezone	PDT

Note: Characters which are not in the table above will be printed as-is, for example, dashes "-" and slashes "/".

very unfriendly error message. If you would like to customize the error message that the server transmits, **config** supports the **errmsg** tag, which does just that. An example of **errmsg** and all the other **config** tags in use is shown in Listing 11.8, with the browser display given in Figure 11.5.

Listing 11.8 LST11-8.HTM

```
<HTML>
<HEAD>
<TITLE>Examples of the config command</TITLE>
</HEAD>
<BODY>
<PRE>
SIZE, DEFAULT    : <!--#fsize file="sample.gif"-->
DATE, DEFAULT    : <!--#flastmod file="sample.gif"-->
ERROR, DEFAULT   : <!--#include file="bogus.gif"-->
<!--#config sizefmt="bytes" timefmt="%a %d-%b-%y" errmsg="[Oops!]"-->
SIZE, BYTES      : <!--#fsize file="sample.gif"-->
DATE, %a %d-%b-%y: <!--#flastmod file="sample.gif"-->
ERROR, CUSTOMIZED: <!--#include file="bogus.gif"-->
</PRE>
</BODY>
</HTML>
```

Executing Commands and CGI Scripts

Yes, server-side includes can also execute CGI scripts, as well as other programs that are not in your CGI directory! The **exec** command, with its two tags, **cmd** and **cgi**, makes this possible. As you may have guessed, the **cgi** tag is used to execute CGI scripts. The path to the script is the same as for

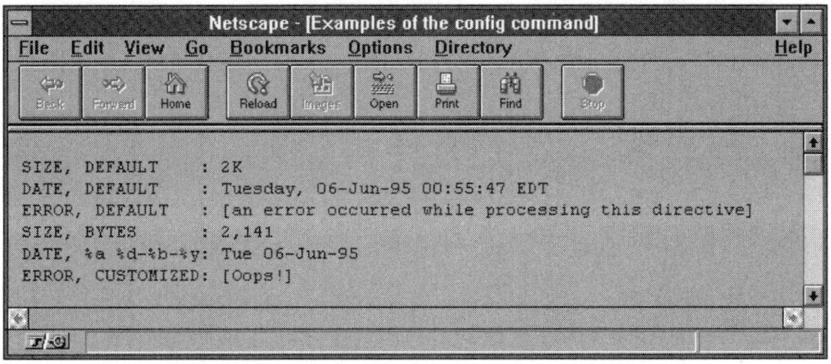

Figure 11.5   The config tags errmsg, timefmt, and sizefmt in action

regular CGI scripts, for example, /cgi-bin/myscript.pl. The **cmd** tag executes ordinary programs, such as the Unix date program. Unlike CGI scripts, the path is the absolute path, from your machine's root directory.

Executing CGI Scripts

CGI scripts are executed using the GET method. The script's output is then inserted in the document, with the exception of any headers, like "Content-type:." The following SSI will execute a CGI script called MYSCRIPT.PL located in my /cgi-bin directory:

```
<!--#exec cgi="/cgi-bin/myscript.pl"-->
```

One frustrating thing about executing CGI scripts this way is that it is difficult to pass the CGI script any information. For example, NCSA httpd 1.3 will *not* allow you to pass information to the CGI script on the command line, like this:

```
<!--#exec cgi="/cgi-bin/myscript.pl?NAME=value"-->
```

Why? I really don't know. It may be because the "?NAME=value" extension is a feature of URLs, and the "/cgi-bin/myscript.pl?NAME=value" is not a URL, but really a filename.

You *can* use a form to get information to your CGI script. Put the form in a separate document, and write it just as you would write any other form going to any other CGI script. Then, to pass the information to the SSI's CGI script, use the following <FORM> line:

```
<FORM METHOD="GET" ACTION="document.shtml">
```

Here, *document.shtml* is the name of the document including the **exec** SSI, and *not* the name of the script. One of the really neat things about this is that you can have several **exec** SSIs in the same document, and the form information will be passed to each of them!

Another way to get information to a CGI script is by using the <ISINDEX> element, but I'll talk about that a bit later in the chapter when I cover the <ISINDEX> element in general. The way scripts process information from <ISINDEX> is a little bit different from CGI scripts as well, so I would like to give it a small section of its own.

Executing "Regular" Non-CGI Programs

You can use **exec**'s **cmd** tag to execute a regular, non-CGI program as well. This is useful to include any other information that the other SSI commands don't cover, such as a command that displays the server's current load or a listing of who is currently logged in. Since programs which weren't explicitly written for your Web server probably won't use any HTML markup, you will have to use <PRE>...</PRE> or the program's output will look a bit strange. The following line will run a special Unix program that displays how long the machine has been up and running, as well as the machine's load and a few other interesting tidbits:

```
<PRE><!--#exec cmd="/usr/sbin/uptime"--></PRE>
```

Since **cmd** is intended to run programs not normally associated with your Web server, you will have to specify the full path to the command, which may be slightly different on your Unix system from the way it is on mine, but the concept is still the same. Be sure you get the pathname correct, or the server will completely ignore it, without even giving you an error message.

You can pass arguments to the program, just as you would normally on the command line of your system. For example, to "finger" someone on your machine (*finger* is a Unix command that tells you if someone is connected, if they've read their email, and a few other things) you will need to pass the **finger** command an argument, which is the user name. The SSI below will do the trick:

```
<PRE><!--#exec cmd="/usr/ucb/finger robertm"--></PRE>
```

Once again, the full pathname to the **finger** command on my system may be slightly different than on yours, so check the path on your system before you blindly use this SSI.

Security Risks and Performance Issues with SSIs

Are there security risks involved with enabling and using Service Side Includes? Yes—but the seriousness and extent of those risks are still hotly debated. On one end of the spectrum, there is the "SSIs are the biggest security risks on the Web" crowd. They refuse to use a server that even has the *capability* to use SSIs, let alone enable them. At the other extreme are those who believe that SSIs are completely safe, and that there is no reason not to enable them on every directory, without restrictions. I take a more balanced view of the situation: SSIs can be dangerous if used with impunity and ignorance, but when used properly and sparingly, they can be a valuable tool.

The biggest security risk is the **exec** command's **cmd** tag. With this SSI, you can run most of the programs on your system. In particular, you are asking for trouble if you allow your users' directories access to SSIs, since, either out of ignorance or malice, they can grant *anyone* anonymous access to your machine's full resources. Not a good thing. If anyone besides you, the webmaster, can create or edit a document in an SSI-enabled directory, *you have a security problem.* The solution, of course, is to enable SSIs in only a select few directories that only *you* control.

If you have one or two more trusted users, you can allow them access to a limited set of SSIs, typically everything except that dangerous **exec** command. To do this, instead of setting a directory's options (in the ACCESS.CONF file) to *Includes,* use the keyword *IncludesNoExec.* Here's an example:

```
<Directory name>
Options IncludesNoExec
</Directory>
```

This will enable all SSIs in the directory *name* except **exec**. For a more authoritative description of security issues involving server-side includes, and information on NCSA httpd in general, check out NCSA's official documentation at *http://hoohoo.ncsa.uiuc.edu/docs/tutorials/security.html.*

I think a more pressing issue with SSIs is not necessarily security, but server performance. Every time you use an SSI, your server has to work that much harder, since every .SHTML document must first be scanned for SSIs, and then each SSI that is found must be acted on. Yes, for a single user or two, that extra work isn't a big deal, but imagine a thousand. Or ten thousand. Maybe even a hundred thousand users, all scrambling to visit your nifty new pages. The burden adds up fast. Even worse, if you set SSIs for .HTML documents, instead of .SHTML documents, almost every document you serve will have to be checked for SSIs. That can put a real strain on your server, and if you have enough users scrambling to your pages, your server may not be up to the task.

Besides the extra overhead for processing SSIs, there is another indirect problem which can result in an even more dramatic increase in server load. Every time someone accesses a document on your server, their browser double-checks to see if they've already retrieved that URL at some previous point in time. If so, the server is first queried as to the last update of that URL. Only if the copy the browser has is older than the copy on the server is that document actually retrieved. This is called *caching* and trust me, it is your friend. But SSIs defeat caching, since every document with an SSI is essentially new *each and every time it is retrieved.* This forces the browser to continuously reload and re-serve the document to the user, irrespective of whether or not the information has *really* changed or not since the last time the user fetched the document. The extra stress this can put on your server can be dramatic, particularly if you enable SSIs for your home page.

Using <ISINDEX>

Before HTML allowed the use of forms, there was only one way to send a user's input to a script, and that was the <ISINDEX> element. It was originally intended as an interface to receive a search key from the user to search a document or entire Web server for a keyword or words, and is still in use today, though less frequently. The benefit of using <ISINDEX> instead of forms is portability. Every Web browser out there *should* support it, even browsers that don't support forms, as rare as they are coming to be.

There are a few odd things about <ISINDEX> which makes it a little tricky. It's not that it is difficult to use, but the differences between it and forms may throw you a bit at first. Physically, <ISINDEX> will create a simple text entry box, preceeded by a brief declaration that this is a "searchable index" or some such copy. The browser may surround this by horizontal rules or other decoration at its discretion. Unfortunately, you have no control over the size of the text entry box, whether or not it will be surrounded by horizontal rules, or even what the message is that will identify the text entry box as a "searchable index." All of that is strictly up to the browser. Anyway, the theory is that the user will see this text entry box, enter a keyword or two to search for, and a script of some sort will magically return a list of documents that match the search criteria. Let's look at a quick example and everything should make a lot more sense.

Listing 11.9 LST11-9.PL

```perl
#!/usr/local/bin/perl

print "Content-type: text/html\n\n";

if ($ENV{'QUERY_STRING'} eq "") {
        print "<HTML>\n";
        print "<HEAD>\n";
        print "<TITLE>An ISINDEX Example</TITLE>\n";
        print "<ISINDEX>\n";
        print "</HEAD>\n";
        print "<BODY>\n";
        print "<H1>An ISINDEX Example</H1>\n";
        print "</BODY>\n";
        print "</HTML>\n";
} else {
        print "<HTML>\n";
        print "<HEAD>\n";
        print "<TITLE>An ISINDEX Example</TITLE>\n";
        print "</HEAD>\n";
        print "<BODY>\n";
        print "<H1>An ISINDEX Example</H1>\n";
        print "<B>The user entered:</B> $ENV{'QUERY_STRING'}\n";
        print "</BODY>\n";
        print "</HTML>\n";
}
```

Listing 11.9 shows a Perl script which illustrates how <ISINDEX> works. It's nothing fancy, just simple code that takes some input from <ISINDEX> and displays it. Go ahead and enter this program, putting it in your CGI directory, and create an anchor in one of your HTML documents that points to it, like this:

```
<A HREF="/cgi-bin/script.pl">Test ISINDEX script</A>
```

Of course you should replace */cgi-bin/script.pl* with the name of your new script. Now click on the link and you should be taken to your ISINDEX script, as shown in Figure 11.6. Be sure your server is running, since <ISINDEX> relies on your server to execute the script, just like any other CGI script.

Notice in Listing 11.9 that the <ISINDEX> element is in the generated document's *head*. This tells the browser that this document is a "searchable index" and that it should prompt the user for a search string.

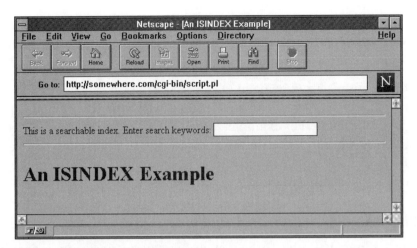

Figure 11.6   The <ISINDEX> text entry box

Here's what's happening: The script prints out our old friend, the "Content-type:" header, and then checks the value of the QUERY_STRING variable. It doesn't check REQUEST_METHOD because the method will always be GET. If QUERY_STRING is empty, you know that this script was called by an anchor, and not by entering a value in an <ISINDEX> query, so it displays a short document containing the <ISINDEX> element. If QUERY_STRING is not empty, you know that the script has been called by itself from a user entering a value in the <ISINDEX> query, and another document is displayed, this time telling the user what keyword he or she entered.

A little strange, isn't it? Unlike the operation of forms, the user is only prompted to enter his or her query *after* the script is called. When the user enters a query, the <ISINDEX> element tells the browser to call the *same script once again*, this time sending the query in the QUERY_STRING variable. This is what threw me for a long time, when I was first trying to figure out how all this stuff worked. You call the script first, then the user's query is entered, and the same script is called again, this time with the data.

Once your script has the data from QUERY_STRING, you will of course have to figure out what to do with that data. The first thing you will notice is that there are no NAME=VALUE pairs. Since there is only one text entry box, there is no need to name it, so only a single value is returned. This makes the script a *lot* simpler. All you need to do is unescape the value (from QUERY_STRING) and you can get on with the business of performing your searches, etc. Very shortly I'll go into how to search your documents, and what exactly a "searchable index" is. But for now, there are a few more interesting points you should know about <ISINDEX>.

Besides the user's input being in QUERY_STRING, it can also be found in the script's *argument list.* Each individual space-delimited word in the query is a single argument. For example, if the QUERY_STRING were "This Is A Test," $ARG[0] would contain "This," $ARG[1] would contain "Is," and so on. For searching applications, which is what <ISINDEX> was intended for, this is a very convenient way to retrieve the data.

<ISINDEX> and Server-Side Includes

You may remember a bit earlier, when I was discussing getting data into CGI scripts called from **exec** SSIs, that you could also use <ISINDEX>, but I didn't go into much detail. Now that you know a little more about <ISINDEX>, let's take a look at an example on how this is done.

For the previous <ISINDEX> example, we were calling the script by pointing an anchor to it from another document. With SSIs, however, you set your anchor to point to an .SHTML document, instead of to your script. If you include an **exec** SSI calling the <ISINDEX> script, it will have the same effect as if your anchor pointed directly to the script itself. The HTML document in listing 11.10 will call the script automatically. I've also rewritten the script a little bit. Since it is now being called from an SSI, I can eliminate all those extra HTML elements.

Listing 11.10   LST11-10.HTM

```
<HTML>
<HEAD>
<TITLE>SSI and ISINDEX Example</TITLE>
</HEAD>
<BODY>
<P>An SSI which calls my ISINDEX script is below:
<!--#exec cgi="/cgi-bin/script.pl"-->
</BODY>
</HTML>
```

Listing 11.11   LST11-11.PL

```
#!/usr/local/bin/perl

print "Content-type: text/html\n\n";
```

```
if ($ENV{'QUERY_STRING'} eq "") {
        print "<ISINDEX>\n";
} else {
        print "<P><B>The user entered:</B> $ENV{'QUERY_STRING'}\n";
}
```

Wow! That Perl script in Listing 11.11 ended up pretty simple, didn't it! Remember, since the output from the script will end up right in the middle of the document, you don't need to output most of elements you did before. Now, here's a point to ponder: The output from the script will end up in the document's body, and hence the <ISINDEX> element will end up there as well. Before, it was in the document's head. Will this be a problem? No—the <ISINDEX> element is valid in both the head and the body. As a matter of a fact, in Figure 11.7 the <ISINDEX> element ended up after a paragraph, and that is just where *most* browsers will put the text entry box as well!

How about some ACTION?

It appears as though some browsers, contrary to the HTML 2.0 draft, allow <ISINDEX> to take one attribute, ACTION. This is *not* valid HTML, so I discourage its use, shown here:

```
<ISINDEX ACTION="/cgi-bin/ascript.pl">
```

This would, when used with browsers that support this syntax, tell <ISINDEX> to use the script named in the ACTION attribute. Like I said,

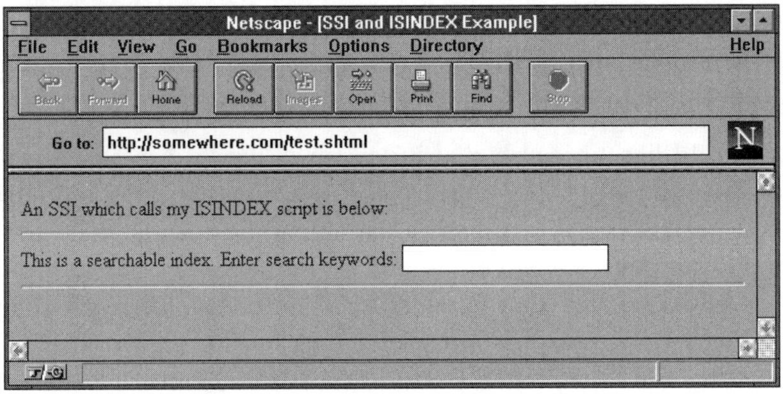

Figure 11.7   An <ISINDEX> script executed via an SSI

this is not valid HTML and not supported by many broswers, so use it at your own risk.

Indexing and Searching Your Web Pages

As your Web server grows in size and you add more and more documents, you may want to provide some sort of search mechanism to allow your users to quickly locate the exact information they're looking for. If you only have 10 or 20 documents, the need for such a mechanism isn't very high, but as your size approaches 100, 200, or more documents, your users will be grateful for some sort of searching apparatus. As luck would have it, quite a few webmasters before you have run into the same dilemma, and tools to do just that have been devised and widely tested.

You need to take two steps to implement a system that allows users to search your documents: First, create a *searchable index* of your documents, and second, install a script that interfaces to the index. The first step, creating the index, can be accomplished by using one of several freely available packages. The most popular is FreeWAIS-sf, based on a system written by WAIS, Inc. called, simply, WAIS (pronounced "wayz"). More on this later. First, some background on WAIS as an *idea*.

WAIS, which stands for *Wide Area Information Servers*, is actually a suite of software and protocols for indexing, searching, and serving documents. WAIS is a powerful system for indexing and searching many different kinds of documents, including HTML. Essentially, the system works like this: You tell a special program which documents you would like indexed. The program then looks at each of documents and creates a large index of all the keywords found in each document.

If you would like to search that index for a keyword or words, you run another program that takes your request, searches the index, and presents you with a list of every document it was able to find which fits your search criteria to any degree. Each document is given a numeric rating, based on how closely it matches your search criteria, so you can judge which hits are "close matches" to information you're hunting for. If you would like to make your index searchable from other machines, you have to use another program, a WAIS server, which listens and fills search requests from other, remote machines. A WAIS client is used to talk to the WAIS server using a special protocol called Z39.50 query protocol. Whew!

Sounds a lot like the World Wide Web paradigm, doesn't it? You have a searchable index, analogous to Web documents; a WAIS client, the equivalent of a Web browser; a WAIS server, which could be thought of as the Web server for WAIS searches; and the Z39.50 query protocol, which is to WAIS what HTTP is to the Web. In essence, the WAIS is to document indexing and searching as the World Wide Web is to hypertext information retrieval.

If you are under the impression that WAIS is really a separate client-server system, designed to solve the same problem as the Web, that is, organizing and retrieving massive amounts of information, you're right. WAIS just took a different approach from the Web's. As you know, the Web's approach is linking documents physically, with an emphasis on presentation once the document is found. WAIS, on the other hand, took the approach that presentation is meaningless if you can't find exactly what you're looking for quickly and easily. So is WAIS really a competitor of the Web? Not at all! When used together, WAIS can compliment the Web, each system providing features the other lacks, as shown in Figure 11.8. The Web connects documents and displays them very attractively, but finding the correct documents can be a hassle. WAIS indexes documents, making finding

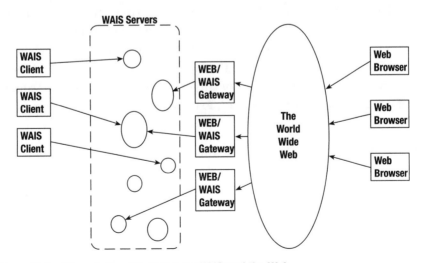

Figure 11.8 The relationship between WAIS and the Web

what you are looking for easy, but it falls flat on its face when it comes to connecting documents together, because WAIS servers are like islands, sprinkled throughout the Internet ocean.

Alas, WAIS and the Web weren't designed to work with one another. Z39.50 is not in the least compatable with HTTP, so the only way to access WAIS from the Web is to open a *gateway* between them. A gateway, in Web terms, is a script that bridges the gaps between different protocols. So, in addition to the WAIS software, you also need a gateway script to tie your Web pages to your WAIS index. If you would like more information on WAIS gateways, FreeWAIS-sf, or WAIS in general, I've included a table with pointers to further reading at the end of this chapter.

But is all the power of WAIS overkill, just to index a few hundred documents on your Web server? I think so, so instead of showing you how to set up a WAIS index and gateway, I've decided to introduce you to another piece of software, which is much simplier and designed specifically for Web pages. The software is a package called *SWISH*.

SWISH- "Simple Web Indexing System for Humans"

SWISH, the "Simple Web Indexing System for Humans" was written by Kevin Hughes of EIT as a simpler alternative to other, more complex document indexing systems, such as WAIS. Installation is easy, but it does require a C compiler (SWISH is available in source code form only) and it will only run on Unix machines. If you are using another operating system, your only option is to either try to "port" the code over to your system, which I am sure Mr. Hughes and the rest of the Web would be quite grateful for, or you can check the table at the end of this chapter for some further suggestions. If you are using Unix, however, I strongly recommend taking a look at SWISH.

SWISH is, as its full title says, an indexing system. There is no fancy server and thus no special protocol. SWISH does provide a simple program with which to access and search the index; however, it cannot access indexes on remote machines, like the WAIS client can. What makes SWISH my choice over WAIS for indexing small to medium sized Web servers is that it is simple to install and use, and specifically designed for use with HTML documents. It is for that reason that I find it strange that you still need a gateway to access SWISH indexes; the program that accesses your index is not a CGI script and does not output the results in HTML. This is a valid gripe, but a minor one. There is a gateway you can use, which I'll talk about later, and it is not too difficult to write your own if you don't like that one.

Interested? Then grab a copy of SWISH, and take a look at the installation instructions, at *http://www.eit.com/software/swish/swish.html*. The documentation is pretty good and you should be up and running with SWISH in no time, but to summarize the procedure, here's what is required of you: Fetch the software, compile it, set up the configuration file, and finally index your documents.

Sample SWISH Session: Configuration and Indexing

After you compile SWISH (it compiled fine on my Linux system; you can ignore any warnings the compiler gives you), you need to create a configuration file to tell it what documents you want indexed, what you don't want indexed, and a few other configuration variables. It's not too terribly difficult, and the SWISH documentation gives an excellent description of the process. The configuration file I used to index a few test documents is in Listing 11.12. I named the file index.swish, and put it in the same directory as the SWISH executable, /home/http. I like keeping all my Web-related files in one spot.

Listing 11.12   LST11-12.TXT

```
# Test SWISH Configuration File
# Robert Jon Mudry, robert@somewhere.com, 06/1/95


IndexDir /home/http/htdocs
# This is a space-separated list of files and
# directories you want indexed. You can specify
# more than one of these directives.


IndexFile /home/http/swish/index.swish
# This is what the generated index file will be.


IndexName "A Test Index"
IndexDescription "Nothing special, just some tests."
IndexPointer "http://somewhere.com/"
IndexAdmin "Robert Jon Mudry (robert@somewhere.com)"
# Extra information you can include in the index file.


IndexOnly .html .htm .txt .gif .xbm .au .mov .mpg
# Only files with these suffixes will be indexed.
```

```
IndexReport 3
# This is how detailed you want reporting. You can specify numbers
# 0 to 3 - 0 is totally silent, 3 is the most verbose.

FollowSymLinks yes
# Put "yes" to follow symbolic links in indexing, else "no".

NoContents .gif .xbm .au .mov .mpg
# Files with these suffixes will not have their contents indexed -
# only their file names will be indexed.

ReplaceRules replace "/home/http/htdocs" "http://somewhere.com"
# ReplaceRules allow you to make changes to file pathnames
# before they're indexed.

FileRules pathname contains admin testing demo trash construction confidential
FileRules filename is index.html
FileRules filename contains # % ~ .bak .orig .old old.
FileRules title contains construction example pointers
FileRules directory contains .htaccess
# Files matching the above criteria will *not* be indexed.

IgnoreLimit 50 100
# This automatically omits words that appear too often in the files
# (these words are called stopwords). Specify a whole percentage
# and a number, such as "80 256". This omits words that occur in
# over 80% of the files and appear in over 256 files. Comment out
# to turn of auto-stopwording.

IgnoreWords SwishDefault
# The IgnoreWords option allows you to specify words to ignore.
# Comment out for no stopwords; the word "SwishDefault" will
# include a list of default stopwords. Words should be separated by spaces
# and may span multiple directives.
```

My configuration file is based directly on the sample configuration included with the SWISH software. If you use this same approach, you will have to modify the configuration file slightly, before indexing, to remove the references specific to EIT's index. The file is commented like crazy, so it shouldn't be too difficult to figure out what's going on; however, if you're having trouble, the help files that come with SWISH do an excellent job explaining the process.

Once you've set up your configuration file, it's time to index. The procedure couldn't be simpler: Just execute **swish -c /home/http/swish/ swish.conf**, replacing the path with your path and "swish.conf" with the filename of your configuration file, and in a few seconds (or minutes depending on how many documents you need to index), SWISH will generate a single index file for all of your specified documents.

To test the index file, use the SWISH program to try a simple search. Complete instructions are in the SWISH documentation, but in a nutshell the command would look something like this:

```
swish -f /home/http/swish/index.swish -w apples and oranges
```

This will search your newly created index (assuming you used my configuration filename and path) for documents with the words "apples" and "oranges." If you wanted documents that contained *either* of those words, you would search for "apples or oranges." Pretty slick, right?

A SWISH Gateway (WWWWAIS): Tying it to Your Web

Before you can use the index created by SWISH (or even WAIS, for that matter), you will need another program, called a *gateway*. I mentioned gateways briefly before, and now I would like to give a specific example. The WWWWAIS gateway, written once again by Kevin Hughes, is designed to directly access the indexes generated by both SWISH and WAIS. It is a CGI script (remember, CGI stands for Common *Gateway* Interface—now you see exactly why) written in C. It can be found at *ftp://ftp.eit.com/pub/web.software/wwwwais/*. You'll need the retrieve the following files:

- WWWWAIS.25.C. This is the C source code for WWWWAIS.

- WWWWAIS.CONF. A sample configuration file. You'll want this too.

- ICONS.TAR. Some icons which WWWWAIS will display next to matching files, to describe, graphically, their file types.

- WWWWAIS.GIF. An optional GIF image with the WWWWAIS symbol. Personally, I don't like it, but I'm not exactly scrambling to design my own, either.

The documentation says the WWWWAIS.25.C file compiles fine using the gcc compiler. That's what I used, and it worked fine. You can ignore any warnings gcc gives you. The compile may work using regular cc as well. To compile, just type the following line at your shell prompt:

```
gcc -ansi wwwwais.25.c -o wwwwais
```

This will create the executable, naming it *wwwwais*. Since it is a CGI script, I put it in the same directory as my other CGI scripts: /cgi-bin.

Next, you'll want to unarchive the icons into an icon directory. I put them in the same directory with the rest of my Web icons: /icons, but you can put them wherever you want that is accessible by your HTTP server. Move the ICONS.TAR file to your icon directory and then type:

```
tar xvf icons.tar
```

This should work on most Unix systems. After it's done, you can delete the ICONS.TAR file. If you need some more help, the official documentation is at *http://www.eit.com/software/wwwwais/wwwwais.html*; however, I didn't find it as good as the SWISH documentation. Nonetheless, it should still get you going in the right direction if you have any trouble.

Your next task is modifying the WWWWAIS.CONF file to your liking. Put it in your /conf directory, with the rest of your Web configuration files, or you can also place it in the same directory as your SWISH configuration. Mine is shown in Listing 11.13.

Listing 11.13 LST11-13.TXT

```
# WWWWAIS configuration file
# 6/02/95
# Robert Jon Mudry
# Documentation at http://www.eit.com/software/wwwwais/wwwwais.html

# If this is a string, it will be a title only.
# If it specifies an HTML file, this file will be prepended to wwwwais
results.

PageTitle "A Test of the WWWWAIS Gateway for WAIS and SWISH"

# The self-referencing URL for wwwwais.

SelfURL "http://somewhere.com/cgi-bin/wwwwais"

# The maximum number of results to return.

MaxHits 40

# How results are sorted. This can be "score", "lines", "bytes",
# "title", or "type".
```

```
SortType score

# Only addresses specified here will be allowed to use the gateway.
# For the above mask option, these rules apply:
# 1) You can use asterisks in specifying the string, at either
#    ends of the string:
#    "192.100.*", "*100*", "*2.100.2"
# 2) You can make lists of masks:
#    "*192.58.2,*.2", "*.100,*171.128*", ".58.2,*100"
# 3) A mask without asterisks will match EXACTLY:
#    "192.100.58.2"
# 4) Define as "all" to allow all sites.

AddrMask all

# The full path to your waisq program.

WaisqBin /home/http/wais/waisq

# The full path to your waissearch program.

WaissearchBin /home/http/wais/waissearch

# The full path to your swish program.

SwishBin /home/http/swish/swish

# SWISH Index of my test pages

SwishSource /home/http/swish/index.swish "Search our Pages"

# WAIS Index on remote machine of the WAIS directory

WaisSource quake.think.com 210 directory-of-servers "WAIS directory of servers"

#Don't use icons

UseIcons no

# Where all your icons are kept.

IconUrl http://somewhere.com/icons/

# Information for figuring out file types based on suffix.
# Suffix matching is case insensitive.
#    TypeDef .suffix "description" file://url.to.icon.for.this.type/ MIME-type
# You can use $ICONURL in the icon URL to substitute the root icon directory.
```

```
TypeDef .html "HTML file" $ICONURL/text.xbm text/html
TypeDef .htm "HTML file" $ICONURL/text.xbm text/html
TypeDef .shtml "HTML file" $ICONURL/text.xbm text/html
TypeDef .sht "HTML file" $ICONURL/text.xbm text/html
TypeDef .txt "text file" $ICONURL/text.xbm text/plain
TypeDef .ps "PostScript file" $ICONURL/image.xbm application/postscript
TypeDef .eps "PostScript file" $ICONURL/image.xbm application/postscript
TypeDef .man "man page" $ICONURL/text.xbm application/x-troff-man
TypeDef .gif "GIF image" $ICONURL/image.xbm image/gif
TypeDef .jpg "JPEG image" $ICONURL/image.xbm image/jpeg
TypeDef .pict "PICT image" $ICONURL/image.xbm image/x-pict
TypeDef .xbm "X bitmap image" $ICONURL/image.xbm image/x-xbitmap
TypeDef .au "Sun audio file" $ICONURL/sound.xbm audio/basic
TypeDef .snd "Mac audio file" $ICONURL/sound.xbm audio/basic
TypeDef .mpg "MPEG movie" $ICONURL/movie.xbm video/mpeg
TypeDef .mov "QuickTime movie" $ICONURL/movie.xbm video/quicktime
TypeDef .Z "compressed file" $ICONURL/compressed.xbm application/compress
TypeDef .gz "compressed file" $ICONURL/compressed.xbm application/gnuzip
TypeDef .zip "zipped file" $ICONURL/compressed.xbm application/zip
TypeDef .uu "uuencoded file" $ICONURL/uu.xbm application/uudecode
TypeDef .hqx "Binhex file" $ICONURL/binhex.xbm application/mac-binhex40
TypeDef .tar "tar'red file" $ICONURL/tar.xbm application/x-tar
TypeDef .c "C source" $ICONURL/text.xbm text/plain
TypeDef .pl "Perl source" $ICONURL/text.xbm text/plain
TypeDef .py "Python source" $ICONURL/text.xbm text/plain
TypeDef .tcl "TCL source" $ICONURL/text.xbm text/plain
TypeDef .src "WAIS index" $ICONURL/index.xbm text/plain
TypeDef .?? "unknown" $ICONURL/unknown.xbm text/plain
```

One of the really neat things about WWWWAIS is that you can use it to search multiple indexes. If you give it more than one SwishSource or WaisSource in the configuration, it will prompt your users for which directory to search. To show off that feature, I've set up my configuration to allow searching of my test SWISH index, as well as a WAIS index on a remote machine. Unfortunately, if you would like to do this yourself, you will have to get a copy of FreeWAIS-sf. Pointers to where to find this program are at the end of the chapter. For now, you can simply ignore the WaisqBin, WaissearchBin, and WaisSource options in the configuration file.

Once you've set everything up, it is time to test things out! Put an anchor on one of your documents which points to the WWWWAIS CGI script, like this:

```
<A HREF="/cgi-bin/wwwwais">Do a search</A>
```

Now if all goes well, and everything is set up correctly, selecting that anchor should bring up the WWWWAIS query screen. Figures 11.9 and 11.10 show some sample searches. Figure 11.9 shows search results for a search on the keyword "oranges" of files on my local machine. Figure 11.10 shows search results for the keyword "food" using WWWWAIS as a WAIS gateway. The results are a list of further WAIS indexes on remote machines which may contain information on food.

The Uncommon Gateway Interface

I crammed a *lot* into this chapter. First I talked about *keeping state*, a technique used to pass information from one HTML form to another by a means transparent to the user, as well as some additional environment

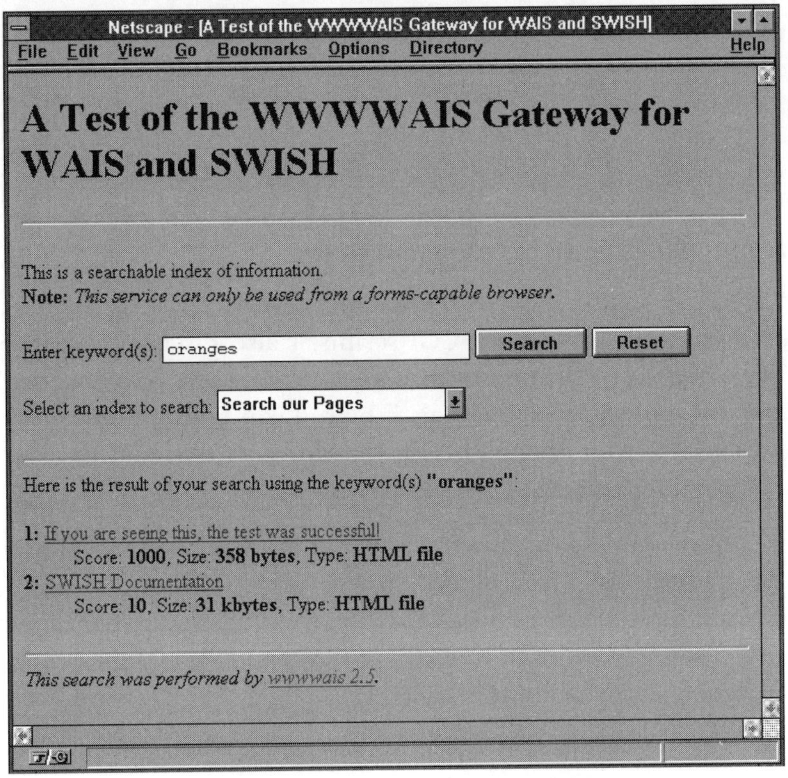

Figure 11.9   Sample search results using my test SWISH index and searching for the keyword "oranges," showing two potential matches

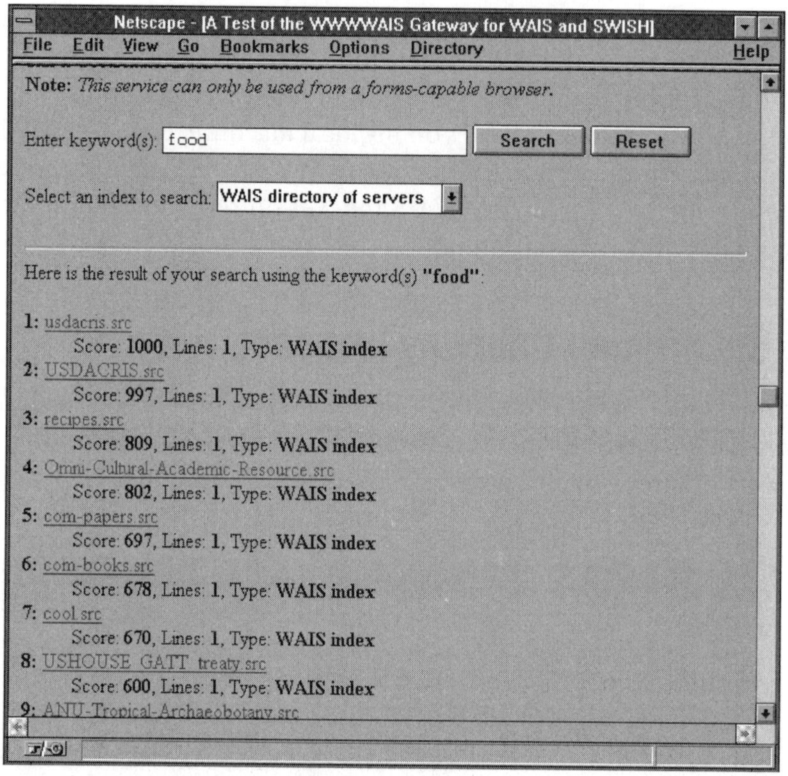

Figure 11.10   Search results on remote WAIS servers

variables you can use in your CGI scripts. I also discussed <ISINDEX>, another way a user can send information to your server. A thorough description of server-side includes also showed you how you can force your server to modify your documents before sending them to your users, and gave you yet another way to call CGI scripts.

Finally, I spoke of ways (excuse the pun!) of indexing your documents for searching. I gave some background on WAIS, the Wide Area Information Servers, and showed you a simpler method using a software package called SWISH. I also showed you how to search WAIS and SWISH indexes using a WAIS gateway script called WWWWAIS.

If you would like some pointers to more information on indexing your documents, check out some of the URLs given in Table 11.4.

Table 11.4   Pointers to WAIS and WAIS gateway-related items

Name of Resource	Location
Index of WAIS Databases	http://www.wais.com/wais-dbs/
FreeWAIS-sf FAQ (Frequently Asked Questions)	http://www.cis.ohio-state.edu/hypertext/faq/usenet/wais-faq/freeWAIS-sf/faq.html
FreeWAIS-sf Pages	http://ls6-www.informatik.uni-dortmund.de/freeWAIS-sf/README-sf
The Center for Networked Information Discovery and Retrieval (CNIDR)	http://kudzu.cnidr.org/
SFGate FreeWAIS-sf Gateway	http://ls6-www.informatik.uni-dortmund.de/SFgate/SFgate
Wais USENET Newsgroup	comp.infosystems.wais
Waistool (Windows NT)	ftp://emwac.ed.ac.uk/pub/waistool
WinWAIS (Windows 3.1 client)	ftp://ftp.einet.net/einet/pc/README.HTM
MacWAIS (Macintosh client)	ftp://ftp.einet.net/einet/mac/
Various WAIS Clients	ftp://ftp.wais.com/pub/freeware/
Yahoo	http://www.yahoo.com/Computers/World_Wide_Web/Databases_and_Searching/WAIS/
comp.infosystems.wais FAQ	http://www.cis.ohio-state.edu/hypertext/faq/usenet/wais-faq/getting-started/faq-doc-6.html
FTP site at Sunsite for WAIS Servers (Unix, Windows NT, VMS, and MVS)	ftp://sunsite.unc.edu/pub/packages/infosystems/wais/servers/
SWISH (WAIS "replacement")	http://www.eit.com/software/swish/swish.html
WWWWAIS (WAIS and SWISH gateway)	http://www.eit.com/software/wwwwais/

12

The Mozilla Extensions and Things Netscape

The HTML 2.0 draft, as it stands, works under the philosophy that it's not the layout that counts, but the content. HTML purists will pound that point into your head, over and over again. Now, I wouldn't exactly label myself an HTML purist, but in general I find myself very comfortable with the "content is everything" philosophy. A good portion of the Web community, particularly the newcomers, might on the other hand find the whole concept of leaving everything to the browser absurd. I can imagine marketing departments and a whole generation of graphic artists shuddering at the thought that they really don't have any control over how things will ultimately look. Clearly a new draft of HTML must be drawn up, giving webmasters a little more control.

So the IETF started work on a new version of HTML, the HTML 3.0 draft. And they worked. And they labored. And they argued. And they still haven't made up their minds about what the draft will ultimately look like. Meanwhile, a little company called Netscape Communications Corporation, fed up with waiting for the HTML 3.0 draft to be completed, released their browser, the Netscape Navigator. And the Web community rejoiced. (Most of us, at least.) Anyway, with Netscape came a "new version" of HTML. All of the HTML 2.0 draft is implemented, and a bit of HTML 3.0, and even a little more which they felt was cool. This hybrid HTML goes by the name of the "Mozilla extensions." Mozilla was the code name of the Netscape Navigator while it was under development, and is currently the name of Netscape's toothy cartoon dinosaur mascot who appears all over the Netscape Web site.

The Mozilla Extensions

Before telling you about "all things Netscape," I feel it is my duty to present you with a warning and my feelings on the whole situation. If you decide to use any of the Mozilla extensions (with the single exception of tables), what your users will see if they use any browser except Netscape Navigator is guaranteed to be radically different from what *you* think they'll see. So different, in fact, that the results could be unusable. I've warned about writing your HTML for a specific browser earlier in this book, and when you begin confronting the Mozilla extensions, that warning goes double. So basically what it comes down to is this: Do you want to limit yourself to users who browse with Netscape only, or do you want 99% of the Web community to be able to use your Web pages as intended?

My philosophy, as you might have guessed, is for the time being to avoid the Mozilla extensions like the plague, unless you are religious about double-checking to see whether your documents format reasonably, using a variety of browsers other than Netscape's. Don't get me wrong on this— I have nothing against Netscape. I actually like their browser, and it is what I normally use. But in spite of the claim that over 70% of the browsers in current use today are Netscape's, that other 30% is a significant number of users to alienate. On the other hand, most of the extensions are useful and make sense, and will probably become part of HTML in time. Some of the Mozilla extensions are unique to Netscape right now, whereas others are attempts at implementing some of the more stable features from the HTML 3.0 draft.

So let's begin our tour of Mozilla's improvements on HTML.

Improving on Inline Images

One of my favorite changes is the addition of a few more values for the <IMG> element's ALIGN attribute. Under Mozilla, when you want text to be aligned with the top of your image, it will behave logically, wrapping itself around the image. Before, if you aligned your text with the top of your image, the first line would indeed start at the top of the image, but subsequent lines would begin directly beneath. In addition, Mozilla gives a few more attributes to further control how your inline images are displayed.

ALIGN attribute

There are six new values for the ALIGN attribute, in addition to the three from the HTML 2.0 draft. They are **top**, **texttop**, **middle**, **absmiddle**, **baseline**, **bottom**, **absbottom**, **left**, and **right**. The left and right alignments are the most intriguing. Aligning an image left causes the image to lie flush with the left margin of the browser window, while the text flows around the image's right edge. Aligning an image to the right causes the image to lie flush with the right margin of the browser window, while the text flows around the image's left edge. These images are called *floating images*, since they seem to float through your text to the left or right margin. See Figure 12.1 for an example.

Another improvement is the addition of the **absmiddle** alignment. Unlike the old **middle**, which aligns the *baseline* of the text with the middle of the image, **absmiddle** does what should have happened in the first place: align the *middle* of the text with the middle of the image. It's a subtle difference, but an important one. Figure 12.2 shows this behavior in action. You may no-

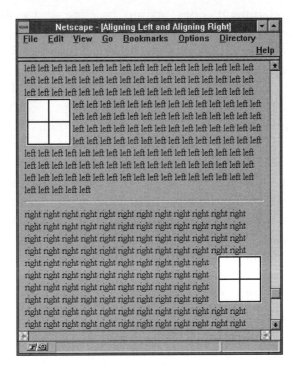

Figure 12.1   Images aligned to the left and right

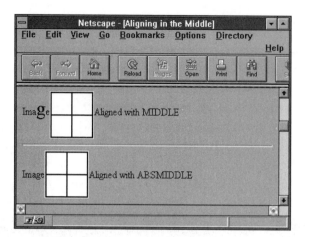

Figure 12.2   The use of middle versus absmiddle

tice that the "g" in the word "Image" is a bit bigger than normal. I did this to illustrate how the loop in the "g" dips below the baseline of the text. I'll show you how to change the font size a little later in this chapter.

The remaining alignment codes, **texttop**, **baseline**, and **absbottom**, are a little odd, probably because they were devised to correct some mistakes made when they first attempted to implement images in Netscape. Figure 12.3 shows them in action. Let's start from the bottom up: **baseline** and **bottom** work the same way, they're just different names. They both align the baseline of the text with the bottom of the image. If you would like the very bottom of the text (the loop in the "g" which dips below the text's baseline in Figure 12.3) to be aligned with the bottom of the image, use **absbottom** instead. If you would like to align text with the top of the image, **top** will usually work. However, there are some slight semantic problems: Instead of aligning the top of the image with the top of the tallest text, it aligns the top of the image with the top of the tallest object in that line. I know, it doesn't make much sense to me either, and looking at the top of Figure 12.3 you can see that things are *almost* aligned with the top of the image—but not quite. I think that is because of the presence of the large "g;" when I used a normal sized "g" there it lines up correctly, as with **texttop. Texttop** will align the tallest text on the line with the top of the image; notice how the top of the large "g" is aligned correctly with the top edge of the image.

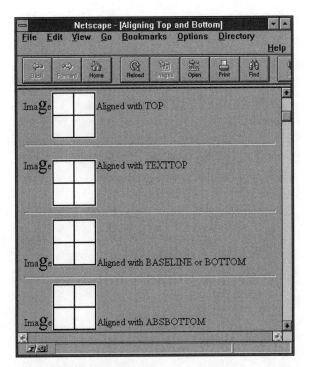

Figure 12.3   Top and bottom alignment

VSPACE and HSPACE Attributes: "Keep your distance!"

VSPACE and HSPACE were introduced to add a little more flexibility to the new **left** and **right** alignments, by allowing you to specify how close text may be to the image before wrapping around the image. As you may have guessed, VSPACE controls the vertical and HSPACE controls the horizontal. The upper portion of Figure 12.4 shows how text wraps around an image with the default VSPACE and HSPACE:

```
<IMG SRC="grid.gif" ALIGN="left">
```

The lower portion of Figure 12.4 shows alignment with VSPACE and HSPACE both set to 15:

```
<IMG SRC="grid.gif" ALIGN="left" VSPACE="15" HSPACE="15">
```

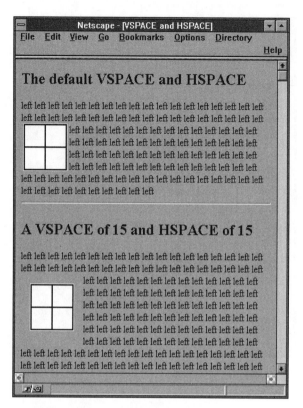

Figure 12.4   The use of VSPACE and HSPACE with ALIGN

The BORDER Attribute

The BORDER attribute is used to either add a solid border around an image, or control the thickness of the border around images that are inside of anchors. Now you can get rid of that hideous blue box drawn around your buttons and icons when they are inside anchors. I really do like this feature, since that ugly blue "anchor box" around images has always annoyed me, but you need to keep one thing in mind before using it: Your users are probably used to seeing those blue anchor boxes around images, and if they see an image without one, they may not assume that it's a link unless you make it painfully obvious some other way. For example, you could make the button actually look like a raised button with some sort of clear message on it, like "click me."

Figure 12.5 shows three images. The first is not in an anchor, and has the border set to 10:

```
<IMG SRC="grid.gif" ALIGN="absmiddle" BORDER="10">
```

The second image also has a border of 10, but this one is inside an anchor:

```
<A HREF="nowhere"><IMG SRC="grid.gif" ALIGN="absmiddle" BORDER="10">
```

And the last image is inside an anchor with the border set to 0:

```
<A HREF="nowhere"><IMG SRC="grid.gif" ALIGN="absmiddle" BORDER="0">
```

You will probably use the last example, an image inside an anchor with a border of 0, most often.

The WIDTH and HEIGHT Attributes

Netscape Navigator has the neat feature by which it attempts to load all the text of your document first, and load the images last. This allows you to scan through the text of a document while the images finish loading. In order

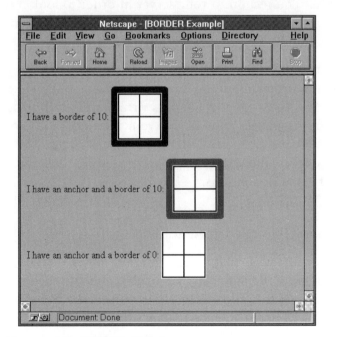

Figure 12.5   The use of the BORDER attribute

to do this properly (which Netscape *usually* does) Netscape must first determine the size of each image in your document, and set aside a bit of space for each image by dropping a properly sized *bounding box* where the image will eventually go. The only way Netscape can do this is by opening a new connection for each image, requesting its dimensions. This can be very time consuming; Wouldn't it be nice if Netscape could figure out the size without querying your server for it? It would indeed, and that is the purpose of the WIDTH and HEIGHT attributes.

Logically, the WIDTH attribute is used to specify the image's width, in pixels, and the HEIGHT attribute tells the browser the image's size. For example, let's say that you have an image that is 72 pixels wide by 74 pixels high. To clue Netscape in before it loads your image, you might call your image something like this:

```
<IMG SRC="grid.gif" WIDTH="72" HEIGHT="74">
```

Now, when Netscape loads the text part of your document, it will automatically know the image's size and can reserve space for it without having to open another connection to your server in order to look it up for itself. This can truly be a timesaver, particularly for large images and for documents containing a lot of images.

Automatic Image Scaling/Resizing

What if you're wrong about the image size in your WIDTH and HEIGHT attributes? Will Netscape throw up its virtual arms and mangle your image? Certainly not! Netscape will *scale* your image to fit in the dimensions you specify! For example, my GRID.GIF image is 72 pixels wide by 74 pixels high. But if I set the WIDTH to be twice as wide, Netscape will scale the GIF to fit the new dimensions, 144 by 74 pixels:

```
<IMG SRC="grid.gif" WIDTH="144" HEIGHT="74">
```

This behavior is illustrated in Figure 12.6.

Another nice feature is that if you leave out either HEIGHT or WIDTH and only set one of them, the image will be scaled with the image's original *aspect ratio* (that is, the ratio of height to width) intact. For example, if your image is 72 by 74 pixels and you scale it using this IMG tag:

```
<IMG SRC="grid.gif" WIDTH="144">
```

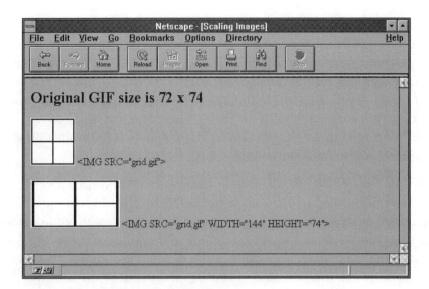

Figure 12.6   Image scaling in one dimension

the actual scaled dimensions will be 144 by 148, or double the original image size, because 144 is twice 72, which was the original image width. But the original proportions of the image are retained.

Percentage Scaling/Resizing

Sometimes it is more useful to be able to use percentage values to scale your images, instead of absolute pixel values, and Netscape provides that option. The really nice thing about the way that Netscape has implemented this feature is that your percentage is given as what percentage of the browser's window the image should subtend, and is not related to the original size of the image at all. This is wonderful, because even though you may never know the size of the browser's window, you can still ensure that your image will fit exactly the way you want. If you want your image to be the full width of the browser's window, specify a width of 100% and a height, in pixels, equal to the image's original size:

```
<IMG SRC="grid.gif" WIDTH="100%" HEIGHT="74">
```

This will stretch (or shrink) your image to the perfect size to fit the browser's window. If you want your image to be half the width of the window, specify the width as 50%:

```
<IMG SRC="grid.gif" WIDTH="50%" HEIGHT="74">
```

If you leave out the height attribute, the image will maintain its aspect ratio, so you will probably want to specify the HEIGHT manually, in pixels or a percentage. Speaking of which, giving HEIGHT a percentage doesn't seem to work very well. It does scale the image vertically, but for the life of me I can't tell you what it is basing the percentage on. It seems as though it is using the entire height of the user's *screen*, and not the browser's window. This is not quite as useful as WIDTH, which does faithfully follow the dimensions of the browser's window.

Figure 12.7 shows four rows of example images, scaled to various percentages. The first row is scaled so that each image is 25% of the width of the window, and the second is scaled so that each image is 50% of the width of the window. The third line shows one image set to 75% of the width of the window, and beside it the same image set to 25% of the width of the window. Finally, the last line shows an image scaled to 100% of the width of the window.

Since specifying a WIDTH as a percentage value relies on the width of the browser's window to make its calculations, resizing the window also resizes

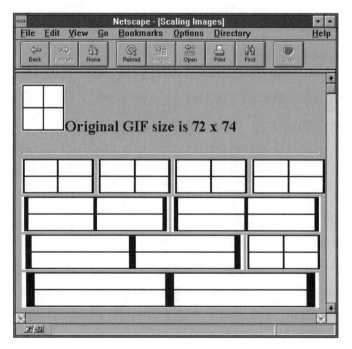

Figure 12.7   Images scaled to various percentages of the window width

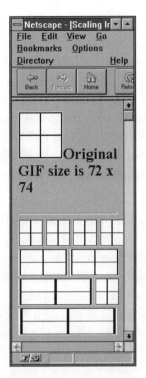

Figure 12.8   Images rescaled after the window is resized

the images! Figure 12.8 demonstrates this by showing the same screen as in Figure 12.7 after the browser's window is resized to be very narrow vertically.

Inline JPEGs

The de facto standard for inline images is the GIF format. If a browser can display inline images, it can display GIFs. But for a while now the Web community has been mulling around the idea of adopting a new graphics format for inline images, with JPEG as the primary choice. There are a few reasons, the most important of which is that JPEG images tend to be much smaller than the same GIF images, and therefore are faster to transmit over the Internet. A political issue also exists in that the mechanisms for handling the compression within GIF images are patented, and the patent holder has recently become militant about controlling the patent and charging vendors for its use. Moving away from GIF over time seems to be a good idea.

There is a bit of debate as to the quality of JPEGs compared to GIFs. JPEG uses what they call *lossy* compression to achieve its very compact size, which means that some of the image data is irretrievably lost in the JPEG compression. This accounts for an image that isn't quite as sharp as a GIF, and some people find that any loss of image quality is too high a price to pay for a smaller file size. On the other hand, some people claim that for "natural" images (photographs of real-life scenes like people, landscapes, etc.), the slight loss of clarity is not a problem. The important point here is that Netscape felt it was time that a browser became able to display inline JPEG images, so that capability was added.

I have no strong opinions, either way, regarding the inline GIF versus inline JPEG argument. I find the quality of JPEGs more than sufficient, and the faster transfer time is a good bonus. What does concern me is that including inline JPEGs in your documents will exclude non-Netscape browsers from viewing any of your inline images. This is disturbing because using the other Mozilla extensions will at worst make your documents look less than ideal on other browsers, but the content will remain the same and, for the most part, accessible. But with the use of inline JPEGs, the content of your document may be lost, since most other browsers simply can't display inline JPEGs.

The LOWSRC Attribute

It is a shame that inline JPEGs are not implemented in many browsers yet; their small size really is handy for transfer on limited bandwidth connections, such as a typical user's 14.4 Kbps modem. Acknowledging this, Netscape has implemented an additional <IMG> attribute, LOWSRC. The theory behind LOWSRC is that for any image, you can specify a smaller, low-resolution image to be displayed *first*. Once the entire document is loaded, and all the LOWSRC images are loaded into place, Netscape can then go back over the document and load the primary, higher-resolution images, specified by the SRC attribute. If the user thinks the low-resolution images are sufficient, he or she can stop the higher-resolution images from loading.

```
<IMG SRC="hires.gif" LOWSRC="lowres.gif">
```

An interesting side benefit of the LOWRSC attribute is that with its use it is safe to include inline JPEGs into your documents. Have one high-resolution

GIF as your primary image, specified by the SRC attribute, and the same image translated to a smaller JPEG image in your LOWSRC attribute. When Netscape sees the LOWSRC attribute, the small JPEG image will be loaded first. Once the JPEG is done loading, the high-resolution GIF can then be loaded. But when non-Netscape browsers see the LOWRSC attribute, they won't know what it means, so they will ignore it and go straight to the GIF image instead. An excellent solution, for the time being.

Specifying two images in one <IMG> element does cause at least one problem. There is no rule that says both images must have the same physical dimensions, pixel-wise, or even that they should display the same image at all. The LOWSRC image could be a 144 by 148 picture of your Aunt Carol, while the primary image in SRC could be a 72 by 74 image of your Uncle Jim. So how much physical space on your document is reserved for the image before it is loaded? The answer is that the LOWSRC image takes priority, as the first to be loaded, and only enough physical space is reserved on your document to accommodate this image. When it comes time to load the image in SRC, the new image is scaled to fit into that space. So, if the LOWSRC image is 144 by 148, and the image in SRC is 72 by 74, the SRC image must be scaled up to 144 by 148. This is, of course, done automatically. If you decide to specify a WIDTH and HEIGHT manually, however, both images are scaled to fit your specifications instead, regardless of their original sizes.

Interlaced Inline Images

Regular inline GIF images are stored with each scanline beneath the previous one, sequentially. But a special kind of GIF, called an *interlaced GIF*, is arranged a little differently. Instead of storing its lines one beneath the other, interlaced GIFs store two or more groups of lines together, and in each group you have every other line or every third line from the image as a whole. For example, imagine a GIF consisting of eight scan lines. A regular non-interlaced GIF would store those lines in order: 1, 2, 3, 4, 5, and so on. But an interlaced GIF would store those same lines in this order: 1, 3, 5, 7, 2, 4, 6, 8. If these lines are laid down in the space allotted to the GIF, it will look like the whole image comes in quickly, if sparsely, in the form of lines 1, 3, 5, and 7. Then the image "fills in" with the addition of lines 2, 4, 6, and 8. The desired effect is a "fade in" of the image rather than a more traditional "scroll down." Imagine that your GIF is drawn on your venetian blinds, and the blinds are completely open so you can't see any of the picture. Now, as you slowly close the blinds, the picture will slowly fade into view. This is roughly the idea behind interlaced GIFs.

Since Netscape displays inline images as it transfers them over the network, interlaced GIFs seem to slowly fade into view. Besides being a very nice effect, for those of us on slow networks, you are given a rough idea of what the GIF will look like before it is fully loaded, unlike non-interlaced GIFs which appear slowly and completely from top to bottom. Whenever possible, create interlaced GIFs, instead of normal GIFs, for your documents. Netscape displays them very nicely, and though other browsers may not display them as they are transfered, they will still look just fine on almost all browsers.

There are a number of graphics programs for Windows, Macs, and Unix which can create interlaced GIFs. If your paint program isn't capable of saving interlaced GIFs, take a quite visit to the "Transparent/Interlaced GIF Resource Page" at *http://dragon.jpl.nasa.gov/~adam/transparent.html*. Netscape also has some documentation on their "Creating High-Impact Documents Page": *http://home.netscape.com/assist/net_sites/impact_docs/index.html*.

New Attributes for the
 Element

One minor problem with floating images, that is, images aligned to the left or right, is that a normal <BR> or <P> will not stop the wrapping behavior of surrounding text. Your text will be broken, but the next line will continue wrapped along the edge of the image, amd not directly underneath the image, as you probably want. To correct this problem, a new attribute was added to the line break, <BR>, called CLEAR. The CLEAR attribute tells your text to break the current line, and then continue after you've cleared the bottom edge of the image. Oops! Which image? You can have an image floating on the left *and* right margins, with your text flowing between the two, and you may want to clear to the bottom of one image, but continue wrapping along the other, if one image is taller than the other. CLEAR has three values: **left**, which clears until it reaches the bottom edge of the image floating on the left margin; **right**, which clears until

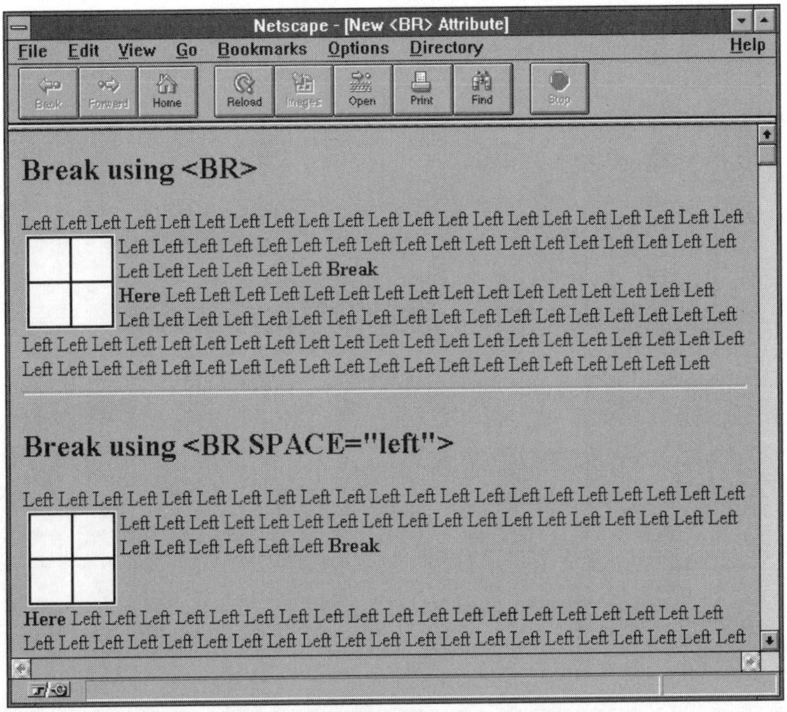

**Figure 12.9
 versus <BR CLEAR="left">**

the bottom edge of the image floating on the right margin; and **all**, which clears until both margins are free. Figure 12.9 should make this clear.

If you're wondering whether horizontal rules or paragraphs clear also, the answer is no. If you want to begin a new paragraph with the <P> element, or place a horizontal rule under your image, you will have to break until the margin is clear. See Figure 12.10.

New Attributes for Horizontal Rules

Netscape felt that horizontal rules needed to be spiffed up a little as well, so they added a few new attributes to give you better control over how your horizontal rules appear. You can control the thickness with SIZE, how wide the rule is with WIDTH, which margin of the document the rule is aligned with ALIGN, and whether the rule should appear shaded or not with NOSHADE.

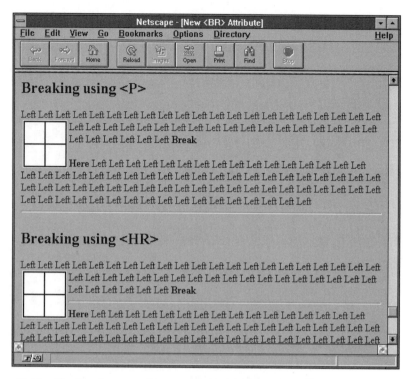

Figure 12.10   Floating images with paragraphs and horizontal rules

Setting Horizontal Rule Thickness

If you didn't think that Netscape's default horizontal rule was thick enough, the SIZE attribute lets you change the thickness to anything you want, in pixels. The modified <HR> tag looks like this:

```
<HR SIZE="thickness">
```

Here, *thickness* is replaced by the numeric value indicating the relative width of the rule. Try not to make your horizontal rules *too* thick, and don't change the thickness "just because you can." Anything thicker than 100 looks pretty ugly to me. The default size is 2. Anything less than 1 defaults to 1. For several examples of how the various sizes of horizontal rules come across, see Figure 12.11.

Setting Horizontal Rule Width

Since you control the thickness, you should be able to control how far across the browser's window the horizontal rule stretches, too. The WIDTH

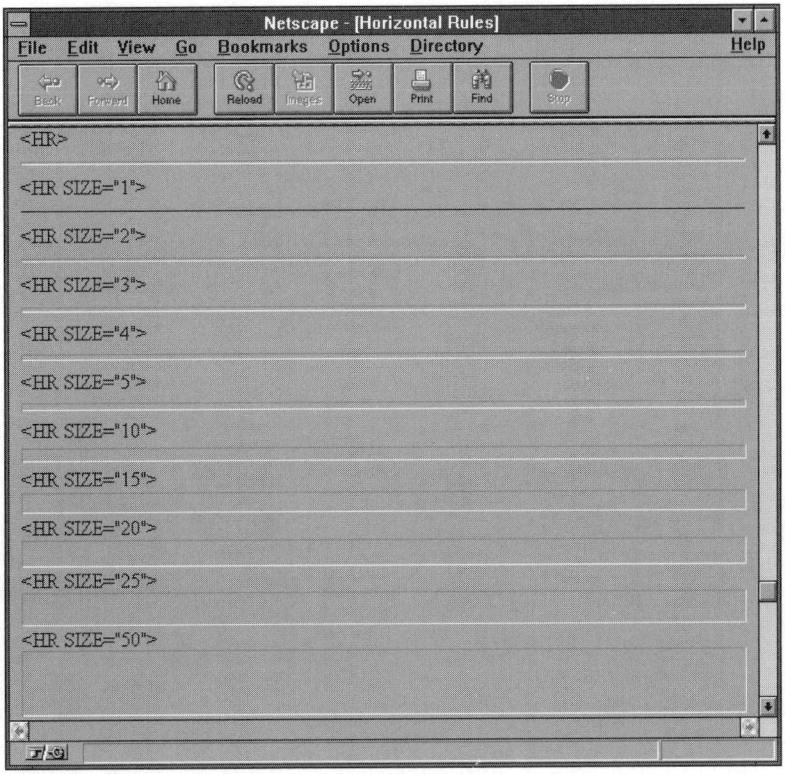

Figure 12.11   Horizontal rules with sizes from 1 to 50

attribute does this, and works just like the attribute of the same name for
<IMG>. You can specify the number of pixels wide the horizontal rule should
be, or give a percentage based on the width of the browser's window. If the
value given for WIDTH contains a percentage symbol "%", the value is a
percent of the browser screen's width; otherwise, it's the length of the rule
in pixels:

```
<HR WIDTH="225"
<HR WIDTH="75%">
```

Just as with images using percentage scaling, when the window is resized,
so is the width of the horizontal rule. The default value is 100%. Anything
less than 1 defaults to 1, and anything less than 1% defaults to 1%. Horizontal rules that are not as wide as the browser's window are centered. See
Figure 12.12 for examples of horizontal rules with widths set by both pixel
values and percentages.

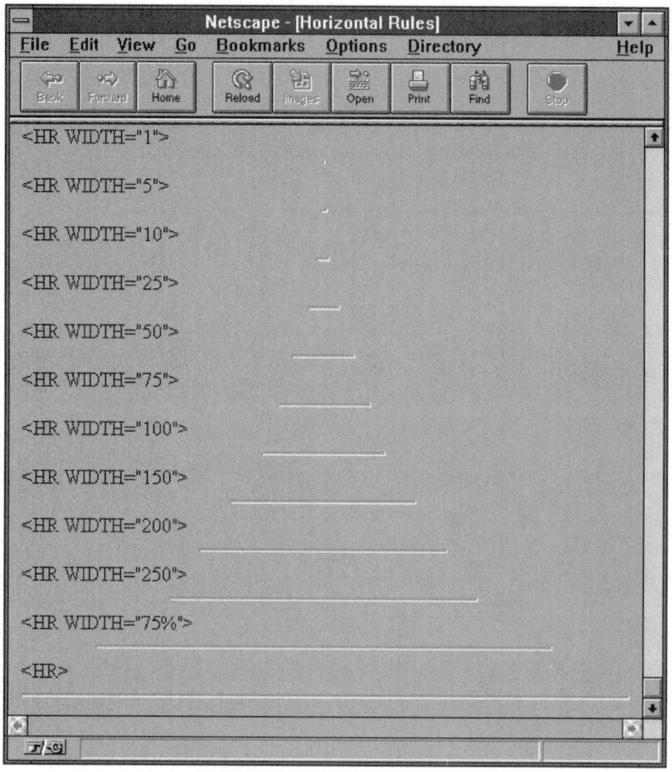

Figure 12.12   Setting the width of horizontal rules

I'm going to give the same advice with WIDTH as I did with SIZE: don't change the width simply because you can; rather, change it because you think it will add some value to your document.

Aligning Rules Left, Center, or Right

If you like, you can align your newly shrunk horizontal rules with the left or right margins, or with the center of the browser's window. Simply provide the values **left**, **center**, or **right** to the ALIGN attribute:

```
<HR ALIGN="left">
<HR ALIGN="center">
<HR ALIGN="right">
```

The default is **center**.

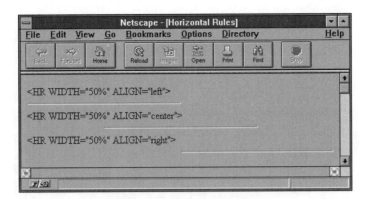

Figure 12.13   Horizontal rules aligned left, center, and right

Solid Rather than Shaded Rules

If Netscape's default "shading" of the horizontal rule bothers you, the NOSHADE attribute allows you to turn it off. Here's how to specify a horizontal rule as a simple solid line:

```
<HR NOSHADE>
```

NOSHADE accepts no values. If you change the thickness of the horizontal rule with SIZE, you will begin to notice that NOSHADE will round the ends of the rule as the rule becomes thicker and thicker. See Figure 12.14 for some examples of various horizontal rules rendered as both shaded lines and solid lines.

Changes to Lists: New Attributes for <UL>, <OL>, and <LI>

Netscape also decided it was time to make lists a little more flexible. You can explicitly set which bullet to use with unordered lists, either for an individual item or for an entire level. With ordered lists, you can specify which numbering system to use, for example, Arabic numerals, Roman numerals, or letters; as well as control where the numbering begins, again for an entire level, or for an individual item. I have noticed some strange behaviour (that is, bugs) with Netscape 1.1N for Windows, and I will point those out as well, including one "undocumented feature."

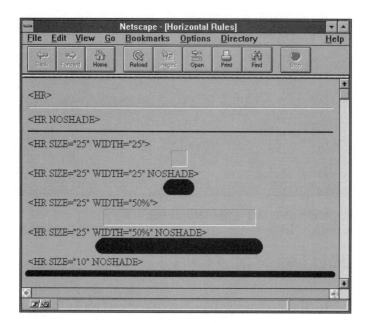

Figure 12.14   Shaded and unshaded horizontal rules

Unordered Lists

The new TYPE attribute allows you to change the bullet type for an entire level of your list. Valid and documented attribute values are **disc**, **circle**, and **square**. Use the TYPE attribute to override the default values for each level. For example, if you want a list that uses solid square bullets, instead of the default solid disc, use this:

```
<UL TYPE="square">
```

After tinkering with this for awhile, however, I noticed things that don't quite work as advertised. Both **disc** and **circle** produce the same, solid disc, and **square** produces a solid square, but there is no way to produce a hollow square, which is supposedly the default for the second level of an embedded list. Or is there? Well, I tinkered. And tested. And made a few phone calls. What I found was that **round** will generate a hollow square, but this behavior is undocumented (not to mention broken!) and will with any luck be fixed in an upcoming version. If you decide to use **round**, or any of the new unordered list types for that matter, double-check how your documents look in each new version of Netscape as soon as it becomes available, or you may be in for a surprise!

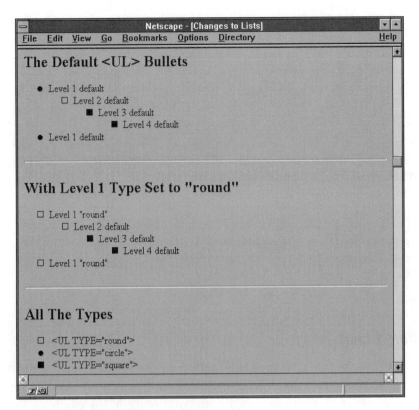

Figure 12.15   Netscape bullets for unordered lists

Controlling the bullet types for a whole level of your lists is interesting, but sometimes you may want to mix bullet types on the same level. To this end, Netscape also added the TYPE attribute to the <LI> element. If you change the TYPE attribute in an <LI>, that item's type, plus the types for all subsequent items in that level, will be changed to the specified type. The attribute values are the same as for the <UL> element.

Listing 12.1 shows how this is handled from a coding perspective, with the display for the code presented in Figure 12.16.

Listing 12.1   LST12-1.HTM

```
<HTML>
<HEAD>
<TITLE>Mixing Bullets</TITLE>
</HEAD>
<BODY>
```

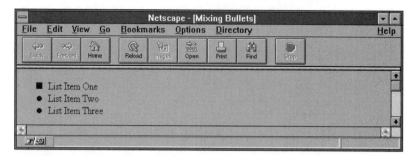

Figure 12.16 Mixing bullet types within a single level

```
<UL TYPE="square">
<LI>List Item One
<LI TYPE="circle">List Item Two
<LI>List Item Three
</UL>
</BODY>
</HTML>
```

Ordered Lists

The TYPE attribute can be applied to ordered lists as well, to control the numbering system used for that level of the list. Valid types are: "1" for the default, Arabic numbers; "I" for uppercase Roman numerals; "i" for lowercase Roman numerals; "A" for uppercase letters; and "a" for lowercase letters. If you would like to start your numbering at some point other than "1" (or that type's equivalent), you can use the new START attribute. Here's an example of both the TYPE and START attributes used within the <OL> (ordered list) element:

```
<OL TYPE="i" START="5">
```

The line above would begin an ordered list using lowercase Roman numerals starting at the number "5;" that is, "v." This is a great feature if your list is very large and you would like to split it among different, subsequent documents, but you want to pick up the numbering where you left off and not begin from scratch. The value for START is always given in Arabic numerals, regardless of the numbering type you specify. If you try to start at a number less than 1, the list will default to start at 1 anyway.

Just as with unordered lists, the <LI> element in ordered lists can accept a TYPE as well, so you can change numbering systems right in the middle of your lists. In addition, Netscape provides a VALUE attribute, which behaves like <OL>'s START attribute, allowing you to skip ahead (or back) to a new number. All subsequent items will follow. As with START, use Arabic numerals regardless of the current list's numbering type.

Listing 12.2 demonstrates just about anytyhing you'd want to do with an ordered list, with the results shown in Figure 12.17.

Listing 12.2 LST12-2.HTM

```
<HTML>
<HEAD>
<TITLE>A Wacky Ordered List</TITLE>
</HEAD>
<BODY>
<OL TYPE="I">
<LI>Introduction
        <OL TYPE="A">
        <LI>Why use cement?
        <LI>The evils of shredded plastic
        <LI>Who am I?
        </OL>
<LI>Power Tools Are Our Friends
        <OL TYPE="A">
        <LI>I Broke My Watch
        <LI>You did what?
                <OL TYPE="a">
                <LI>I said I broke my watch!
                <LI>Oh OK!
                </OL>
        </OL>
<LI>Music To Write By
        <OL TYPE="A">
        <LI>David Bowie
        <LI>White Zombies
                <OL TYPE="a">
                <LI>It's a weakness of mine
                        <OL TYPE="i" START="999">
                        <LI>Really now, is it?
                        <LI>Yes. It is
                        </OL>
                </OL>
        </OL>
<LI TYPE="i" VALUE="101">The 101
<LI>Number 102
<LI VALUE="408">The 408 Area Code?
<LI VALUE="405">The 405
</OL>
</BODY>
</HTML>
```

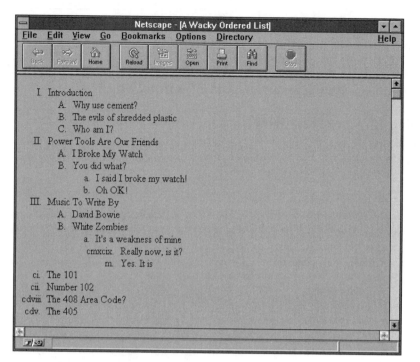

Figure 12.17   The diversity of ordered lists

Warning on the Use of These Extensions for Lists

Please be careful when you use the extensions for ordered and unordered lists. Specifically, Netscape is the only browser that recognizes these special extensions right now, so if you refer to the way the list appears, such as "Item number V, in Roman numerals, is..." you are begging for trouble. If the user isn't using Netscape, they will not see Roman numerals, and if you changed the count (using START or VALUE), they won't even see the same number you're referring to. At worst they'll think you're nuts, and at best they won't have a clue as to what you're talking about!

Also be careful if you use the **round** type for unordered lists. It's likely to change some time in the near future, and you will never know when instead of being a hollow square, it will suddenly turn into a solid disc, or even a hollow circle. Use these extensions to *enhance* your documents, but don't make them the basis for the information you are providing.

In other words, don't count on any of this stuff working the way you expect it to, or even the way it did yesterday. In a year or two it may all settle down, but until then...beware.

Changes to <ISINDEX>

The <ISINDEX> element also has a new addition, the PROMPT attribute. For Netscape, the default prompt is, "This is a searchable index. Enter search keywords:." If you want to specify something more creative, you can use the PROMPT attribute to set the message to anything you want. Remember, only Netscape recognizes the PROMPT attribute, so other browsers will still see their default messages. Don't base information or (especially) instructions based on a prompt you set via PROMPT! The syntax is this:

```
<ISINDEX PROMPT="Hey, my own custom prompt! Enter your data, please: ">
```

Figure 12.18 shows how the line above would be rendered. By the way, you cannot place any additional HTML markup inside the PROMPT attribute. For example, don't try to put a word in italics or make something bold in the prompt; it simply can't be done.

Brand New Elements

The elements I'll discuss in the next several pages are completely new, added to Netscape to make up for some deficiencies with the current HTML 2.0 draft. Using any of these elements is guaranteed not do a darn thing on most browsers, (except Netscape, obviously), so keep that in mind as you design your documents.

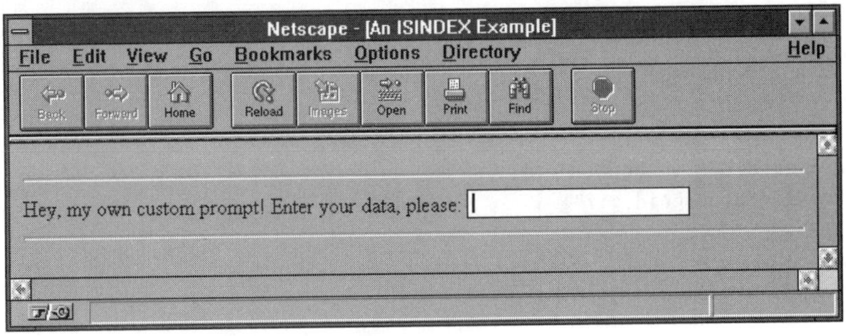

Figure 12.18   A customized <ISINDEX> prompt

Centering Your Text

The <CENTER> element allows you to center text and images in your browser's window. This is one of the most overused Mozilla extensions, although a few of the newer ones I will talk about later are gaining on it. As always, just keep in mind that even though your document may look nice and neat centered in Netscape, everyone else will see your document left justified, which will probably completely destroy the feel of your document. If you center a lot of text, take a look at things in a non-Netscape browser that doesn't support centering, to see how bad things look.

You can center *almost* everything, except floating inline images that have been aligned to the left or the right, and "partial" horizontal rules. The code in Listing 12.3 shows you how, and Figure 12.19 shows you what it will look like.

Listing 12.3   LST12-3.HTM

```
<HTML>
<HEAD>
<TITLE>Centering Your Document</TITLE>
</HEAD>
<BODY>
<CENTER>
This is centered text.
</CENTER>

<CENTER>
<H2>A Centered Heading</H2>
And this is more centered text. Whee!
<HR WIDTH="25%" ALIGN="left">
A &quot;partial&quot; horizontal rule is above, but it is aligned
to the left so it won't center.
</CENTER>

<P>I am not centered!

<CENTER>
<P>A Centered GIF is here:
<P><IMG SRC="book/grid.gif">
</CENTER>
</BODY>
</HTML>
```

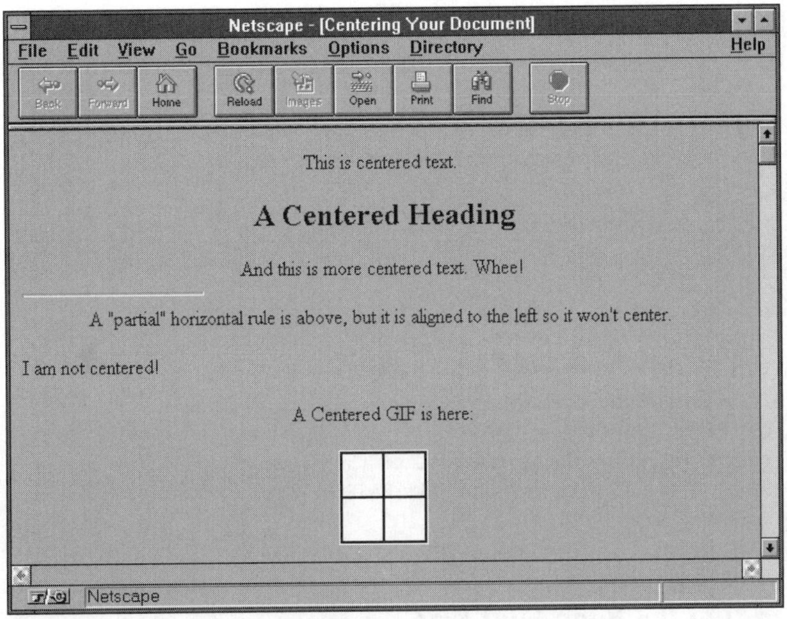

Figure 12.19   Centering text and images

Changing Your Font Sizes

Want something emphasized, and simple italics or bold won't do? Now, with Netscape, you can change the size of your fonts from 1, the smallest size, to 7, which is really large. This is different from headings in that headings are not specifically designed to change the size of your fonts. Though they often do, this is just coincidence; your browser can choose to display headings any way it wants, from changing the font size, to changing the color or alignment of the text. Besides, a heading implies a paragraph break, so you can't change the font size of just a single word or letter, but with Netscape's special <FONT> and <BASEFONT> elements, you can.

Changing the Base Font

The <BASEFONT> element allows you to change the base font size for your entire document, or until the next <BASEFONT> element is encountered. The default is size 3. There is one attribute, SIZE, used to give <BASEFONT> the size of the font you desire. There is no end tag; the size change affects all text until either the end of the document or a new

<BASEFONT> element. Heading sizes are *not* affected by <BASEFONT>. Listing 12.4 shows how it's done, and Figure 12.20 shows how it looks.

Listing 12.4   LST12-4.HTM

```
<HTML>
<HEAD>
<TITLE>Using BASEFONT</TITLE>
</HEAD>
<BODY>
<P>This is the default font size of 3.
<BASEFONT SIZE="5">
<P>This is a larger font size. I will maintain this size until the
next &lt;BASEFONT&gt; element.
<BASEFONT SIZE="1">
<P>This is a very tiny font. The rest of the document will stay this
size, since I do not have any more &lt;BASEFONT&gt; elements.
</BODY>
</HTML>
```

Overriding the Base Font Size

You can override the base font size for a single letter, word, or any arbitrary chunk of text in your document using the <FONT> element. It supports the same SIZE attribute as <BASEFONT>, and has an end tag </FONT>. For example, if your base font size is the default size (3), but you want the first letter of your first paragraph to be twice as large as the default, you would use this code:

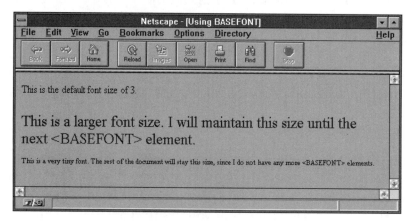

Figure 12.20   Using BASEFONT to change font sizes

```
<P><FONT SIZE="6">T</FONT>his is my first paragraph.
```

In this example, the font size of the first letter "T" is 6, and the rest of the paragraph, after the </FONT> end tag, remains the default size of 3. This is called an *absolute* font size, since you are specifically choosing a value of 6 for the font size.

Sometimes you might want to change your font a size or two up or down relative to the size of the base font, but you don't want to have to remember what the absolute size value of the base font is throughout your document. Or perhaps you decide to change the size of the entire document just one size larger, or one size smaller, and don't want to go back and change all the individual <FONT> elements, but rather one or two <BASEFONT> elements instead. You can do this using *relative* font size. Instead of saying "I want font size 6" as in the example above, you could have said, in essence, "Make this three sizes larger than the base font." Here's how:

```
<FONT SIZE="+3">T</FONT>his is my first paragraph.
```

Since the base font size is 3, the size of the letter "T" will be three sizes larger, 6. If you wanted to make the font size smaller, the reverse is true: Asking for a font size "-2" would give you a size 1, since the base font size was 3. Now, if you changed the base font size to, say 4, and asked for size "+3," you would get a size of 7. If you ask for a relative size that would end up larger than the maximum of 7, the size would be increased to 7 but no further. Conversely, if you request a size that would end up smaller than the minimum of 1, the size would decrease to 1 but no smaller.

Listing 12.5 demonstrates absolute and relative font size changes, and Figure 12.21 shows what they look like on the browser screen.

Listing 12.5   LST12-5.HTM

```
<HTML>
<HEAD>
<TITLE>Relative and Absolute Font Sizes</TITLE>
</HEAD>
<BODY>
<BASEFONT SIZE="4">
<P>I am a base font of four.
<P>I can specifically change a single <FONT SIZE="7">word</FONT> to size
seven using an absolute font size, or with a relative font size
```

```
of <FONT SIZE="+3">+3</FONT> I can do the same.
<P>I can also reduce the font size to <FONT SIZE="2">size 2</FONT> with
an absolute size change, or use <FONT SIZE="-2">a relative size of -2
</FONT> to do the same.

<P>The absolute sizes range from 1 to 7:
<P>
<FONT SIZE="1">Size One</FONT><BR>
<FONT SIZE="2">Size Two</FONT><BR>
<FONT SIZE="3">Size Three</FONT><BR>
<FONT SIZE="4">Size Four</FONT><BR>
<FONT SIZE="5">Size Five</FONT><BR>
<FONT SIZE="6">Size Six</FONT><BR>
<FONT SIZE="7">Size Seven</FONT><BR>

</BODY>
</HTML>
```

You can also use <FONT> to change the physical font size of headings; however, this behavior is not specifically documented, so I would avoid it

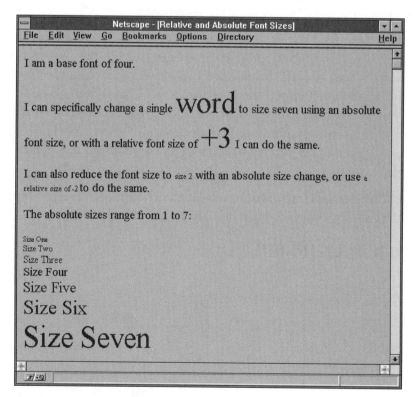

Figure 12.21   Font sizes: relative and absolute

whenever possible—at least until Netscape produces some sort of documentation that confirms that this behavior is intended and will continue to be supported in future releases.

To Break or Not to Break

A slightly less dramatic element than <CENTER> or <FONT> is <NOBR>...</NOBR>. Text inside this element will *not* be wrapped (broken) when it reaches the end of the browser's window, but instead will scroll off into infinity. Useful? Perhaps. For example, I used it in the inline image scaling demonstration. When I attempted to show you that four inline images scaled 25%, two scaled at 50%, and so on, would neatly fit in the browser's window, I had to cheat a little and use <NOBR> to keep the image on the very end from breaking onto the line beneath.

A better example might be a person's name. It can be frustrating when the name "Dr. Claire Widget" is broken off between the "Dr." and the "Claire." <NOBR> would prevent this from happening:

```
<NOBR>Dr. Claire Widget</NOBR>
```

The example glues the three words "Dr.," "Claire," and "Widget," together. Now, if you are near the right edge of the browser's window, instead of her name being broken at the "Dr.," all three words would begin at a new line, with her whole name treated as a single word.

The <NOBR> element prompted Netscape to create the <WBR> element. In the "very rare case" that you know *exactly* where a group of words inside a <NOBR> element should be broken, you can use <WBR> to clue Netscape in. This is not the same as <BR>, since a line break is not forced, just a hint to Netscape where a word can be broken if Netscape needs to:

```
<NOBR>Dr. Claire <WBR>Widget</NOBR>
```

Now "Dr. Claire Widget" is considered one big word by Netscape, but if it does need to be broken, the <WBR> element gives Netscape permission to break between "Dr. Claire" and "Widget". This is analogous to the "soft hyphen" supported by some word processors and page layout programs. Listing 12.6 shows you how, and Figure 12.22 shows you how it looks.

Listing 12.6   LST12-6.HTM

```
<HTML>
<HEAD>
<TITLE>Breaking Up Is Hard To...</TITLE>
</HEAD>
<BODY>
<H3>No &lt;NOBR&gt;...&lt;/NOBR&gt;</H3>
<P>Blah blah blah blah blah blah blah blah blah blah blah blah blah blah blah
blah
Dr. Claire Widget

<H3>Using &lt;NOBR&gt;Dr. Claire Widget&lt;/NOBR&gt;</H3>
<P>Blah blah blah blah blah blah blah blah blah blah blah blah blah blah blah
<NOBR>Dr. Claire Widget</NOBR>

<H3>Using &lt;NOBR&gt;Dr. Claire &lt;WBR&gt;Widget&lt;/NOBR&gt;</H3>
<P>Blah blah blah blah blah blah blah blah blah blah blah blah blah blah blah
<NOBR>Dr. Claire <WBR>Widget</NOBR>

</BODY>
</HTML>
```

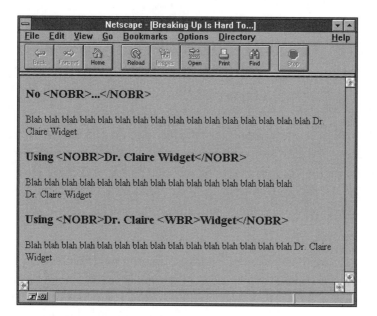

Figure 12.22   <NOBR> and <WBR> in action

The Dreaded "Blink"

The most infamous Mozilla feature is the <BLINK>...</BLINK> element. Any text, including headers, within the <BLINK> element, will...blink. I find it annoying. Really. Furthermore, it's undocumented, and support for blinking text is likely to removed at any moment. For my money, the Web will be a far better place when it's gone.

Tables

The table is a special new feature, proposed for the HTML 3.0 draft, that Netscape has attempted to faithfully implement in line with the 3.0 draft. It has been difficult, I am sure, because the draft seems to be changing almost every day, but what they have so far is quite workable. Since this is a proposed feature of HTML 3.0, it is one of the few Mozilla extensions that other browsers have attempted to implement as well—particularly Arena and the latest version of NCSA Mosaic. There are some slight incompatibilities between Netscape's interpretation of tables and that of other browsers, but with the exception of a few enhancements, the tables that Netscape has implemented are the same as described in the HTML 3.0 draft.

A Simple Table

There are five elements that can be used in creating tables. The <TABLE>...</TABLE> element serves a function similiar to the <FORM>...</FORM> element for forms; it's a sort of container for the rest of the table elements. If any of the four remaining table elements are found *outside* of the <TABLE>...</TABLE> start and end tags, they will be ignored. The <TR>...</TR> element defines a single *table row*. You can have as many rows as you would like inside one table. Inside a table row, you use the <TD>...</TD> element to define an individual "cell." These are the only three elements you absolutely need to know to make a table, so let's pause here for a demonstration. I'll talk about the other two elements later.

Listing 12.7   LST12-7.HTM

```
<HTML>
<HEAD>
<TITLE>A Simple Table Example</TITLE>
</HEAD>
<BODY>
```

```
<TABLE BORDER>
<TR>    <!-- Row One -->
        <TD>Cell 1,1</TD> <TD>Cell 2,1</TD> <TD>Cell 3,1</TD>
</TR>

<TR>    <!-- Row Two -->
        <TD>Cell 1,2</TD> <TD>Cell 2,2</TD> <TD>Cell 3,2</TD>
</TR>

<TR>    <!-- Row Three -->
        <TD>Cell 1,3</TD> <TD>Cell 2,3</TD> <TD>Cell 3,3</TD>
</TR>
</TABLE>

</BODY>
</HTML>
```

Listing 12.7 is the HTML for a simple three-row, three-column table shown in Figure 12.23. The first relevant tag is of course <TABLE>, which tells Netscape that you are defining a table. The attribute BORDER tells Netscape to turn on those nifty raised borders shown in Figure 12.23. If you leave out the BORDER attribute, there would be no raised borders and the table would look pretty plain.

The very next tag is <TR>, which begins the definition of a table row. I put a comment on the same line to help you remember which row each <TR> is defining, but don't let that throw you; the comment is not required. After the <TR> tag come the cells, defined by the three sets of <TD>...</TD> elements. Finally, the first row is closed with the </TR> end tag and the next row begins. After all three rows have been defined, the whole table is closed with the </TABLE> end tag. Three rows,

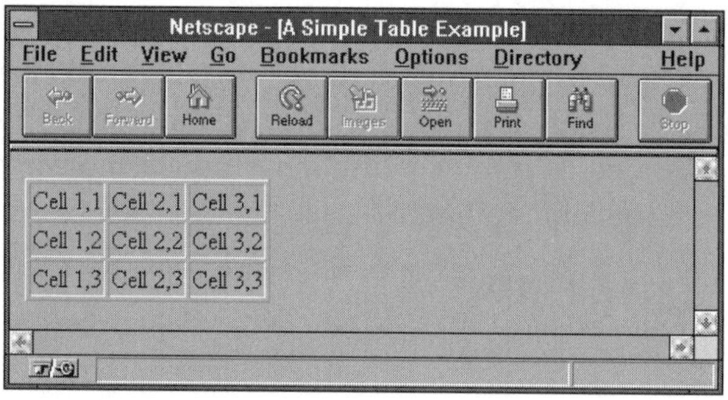

Figure 12.23   A simple 3x3 table

three cells in each row (hence three columns), and that's it. A simple table.

You may have noticed that I laid out my rows and cells in a nice neat fashion in my HTML file. (See Listing 12.7.) This is mostly for my own clarification, to help me see which rows are where and what cells go with what; it's like "prettyprinting" a source code file in C or Pascal. The browser doesn't care how your markup looks, but you may want to adopt a style of your own so that you can see how your table will look at a glance. As I introduce more features, you will notice that the HTML for tables can get fairly cluttered, and you will have an easier time of it if you lay out your rows and cells neatly.

My first table was a nice and simple 3 by 3 grid, but what if you make your table lopsided? In other words, do all your rows need to have the exact same number of cells? No; as you can see from Listing 12.8 and its display in Figure 12.24, each row can have a different number of cells. If one or more of your rows are "short," the table will be padded to the right with empty "raised" space.

Listing 12.8   LST12-8.HTM

```
<HTML>
<HEAD>
<TITLE>A Simple Table Example</TITLE>
</HEAD>
<BODY>

<TABLE BORDER>
<TR>    <!-- Row One -->
        <TD>Cell 1,1</TD> <TD>Cell 2,1</TD> <TD>Cell 3,1</TD>
        <TD>Cell 4,1</TD>
</TR>

<TR>    <!-- Row Two -->
        <TD>Cell 1,2</TD> <TD>Cell 2,2</TD> <TD>Cell 3,2</TD>
</TR>

<TR>    <!-- Row Three -->
        <TD>Cell 1,3</TD> <TD>Cell 2,3</TD> <TD>Cell 3,3</TD>
</TR>
</TABLE>

</BODY>
</HTML>
```

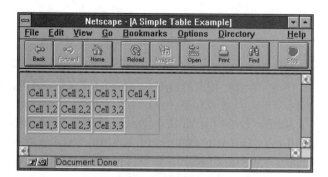

Figure 12.24 Table rows with differing numbers of cells

Cells that Span Rows and Columns

The <TR>...</TR> element takes several attributes that control each row's behavior. Two of these attributes, ROWSPAN and COLSPAN, allow your cells to span row and column boundaries. In other words, you can stretch a single cell horizontally to take up more than one column's worth of space, or vertically such that the cell spans more than one row. This is far easier to show than to describe, so look carefully at the HTML in Listing 12.9, and its browser display in Figure 12.25.

Listing 12.9 LST12-9.HTM

```
<HTML>
<HEAD>
<TITLE>A Simple Table Example</TITLE>
</HEAD>
<BODY>

<P>A table with the upper right cell set to span to the bottom of the table:
<TABLE BORDER>
<TR>    <!-- Row One -->
        <TD>Cell 1,1</TD> <TD>Cell 2,1</TD> <TD>Cell 3,1</TD>
        <TD ROWSPAN="3">Cell 4,1</TD>
</TR>

<TR>    <!-- Row Two -->
        <TD>Cell 1,2</TD> <TD>Cell 2,2</TD> <TD>Cell 3,2</TD>
</TR>

<TR>    <!-- Row Three -->
        <TD>Cell 1,3</TD> <TD>Cell 2,3</TD> <TD>Cell 3,3</TD>
</TR>
</TABLE>
```

```
<P>A table with the upper right cell set to span two rows, and the
middle left cell set to span to the bottom of the table:
<TABLE BORDER>
<TR>    <!-- Row One -->
        <TD>Cell 1,1</TD> <TD>Cell 2,1</TD> <TD>Cell 3,1</TD>
        <TD ROWSPAN="2">Cell 4,1</TD>
</TR>

<TR>    <!-- Row Two -->
        <TD ROWSPAN="2">Cell 1,2</TD> <TD>Cell 2,2</TD> <TD>Cell 3,2</TD>
</TR>

<TR>    <!-- Row Three -->
        <TD>Cell 1,3</TD> <TD>Cell 2,3</TD> <TD>Cell 3,3</TD>
</TR>
</TABLE>

</BODY>
</HTML>
```

The ROWSPAN attribute's value is the number of rows the cell should span in a vertical direction, toward the bottom of the table. If you ask for a row span that will continue beyond the last row in the table, it will be truncated. In the first table implemented in Listing 12.9 and shown in Figure 12.25, the far right cell of the first row has been set to span all three rows, filling up the blank space left when I added this extra, fourth cell.

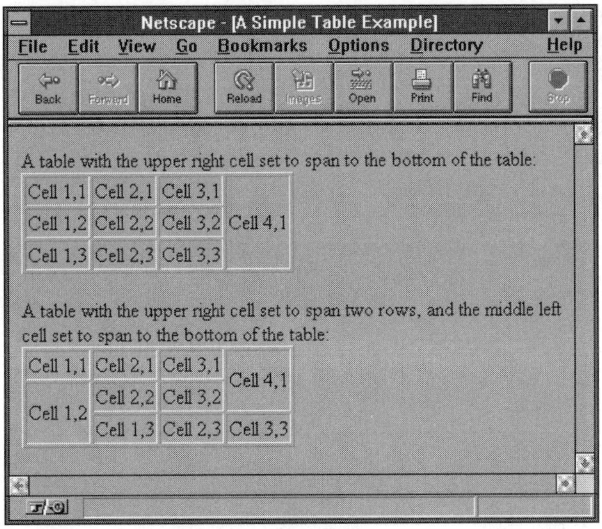

Figure 12.25   Cells that span rows and columns

The second table is a little more complicated. The last cell in the topmost row has been set to only span two cells, and the first cell in the second row has also been set to span two cells. Since this is now taking up the space the first cell in the third row would have used, the cells in the third row are all pushed over to the right by one column. If I had left the fourth cell in the first row spanning all three rows, there would have been yet another clash, and the third cell in the third row would have been forced over into yet another column, to the right of the overzealous cell, as shown in Figure 12.26.

The COLSPAN attribute does for columns what ROWSPAN does for rows, forcing a cell to span across neighboring columns and pushing cells over to the right. If you ask for a COLSPAN that extends off the right edge of the table, it will be truncated to span only the maximum number of columns already present in the table; however, any cells to its right will be pushed off the right edge of the table. Listing 12.10 and Figure 12.27 provide an example of COLSPAN in use:

Listing 12.10   LST12-10.HTM

```
<HTML>
<HEAD>
<TITLE>A Simple Table Example</TITLE>
</HEAD>
<BODY>

<P>Cell three in row two spans two columns and cell two in row three spans
three columns:
<TABLE BORDER>
<TR>    <!-- Row One -->
        <TD>Cell 1,1</TD> <TD>Cell 2,1</TD> <TD>Cell 3,1</TD>
        <TD>Cell 4,1</TD>
</TR>
```

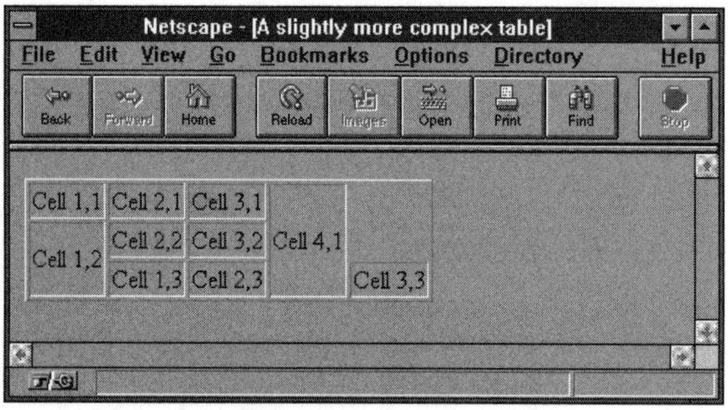

Figure 12.26   A more complex table where cells span rows

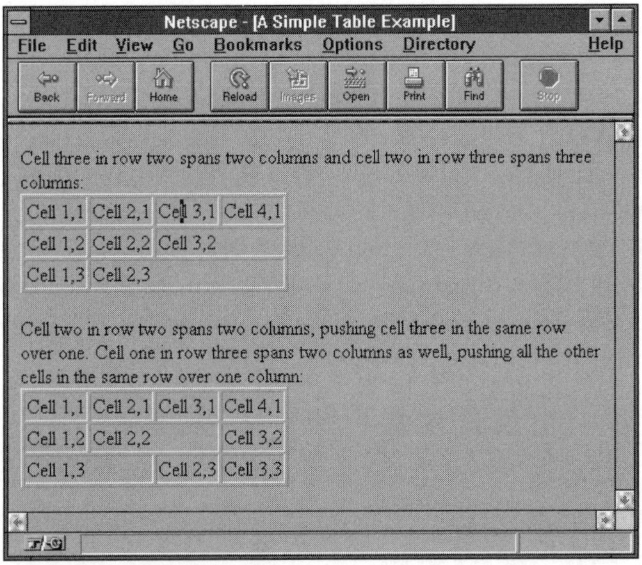

Figure 12.27   Two examples of COLSPAN

```
<TR>    <!-- Row Two -->
        <TD>Cell 1,2</TD> <TD>Cell 2,2</TD> <TD COLSPAN="2">Cell 3,2</TD>
</TR>

<TR>    <!-- Row Three -->
        <TD>Cell 1,3</TD> <TD COLSPAN="3">Cell 2,3</TD>
</TR>
</TABLE>

<P>Cell two in row two spans two columns, pushing cell three in the same
row over one. Cell one in row three spans two columns as well, pushing
all the other cells in the same row over one column:
<TABLE BORDER>
<TR>    <!-- Row One -->
        <TD>Cell 1,1</TD> <TD>Cell 2,1</TD> <TD>Cell 3,1</TD>
        <TD>Cell 4,1</TD>
</TR>

<TR>    <!-- Row Two -->
        <TD>Cell 1,2</TD> <TD COLSPAN="2">Cell 2,2</TD> <TD>Cell 3,2</TD>
</TR>

<TR>    <!-- Row Three -->
        <TD COLSPAN="2">Cell 1,3</TD> <TD>Cell 2,3</TD> <TD>Cell 3,3</TD>
</TR>
</TABLE>
```

```
</BODY>
</HTML>
```

Combining ROWSPAN and COLSPAN can be pretty tricky, since it's easy to accidentally overlap cells—and that looks *real* ugly. For example, if cell 2 in row 1 spans three rows down, and cell 1 in row 2 spans three rows across, the two cells will intersect. But if you plan on making complex but still useful tables, you will have to learn to deal with these difficulties. I suggest planning your tables on graph paper first. You're job will become a lot easier. In the meantime, take a look at the examples in Listing 12.11 and Figure 12.28 that combine ROWSPAN and COLSPAN.

Listing 12.11 LST12-11.HTM

```
<HTML>
<HEAD>
<TITLE>Some Complex Tables</TITLE>
</HEAD>
<BODY>

<P>Combining COLSPAN and ROWSPAN:
<TABLE BORDER>
<TR>
        <TD COLSPAN="2">Two Columns</TD> <TD COLSPAN="2">Two Columns</TD>
</TR>
<TR>
        <TD ROWSPAN="2">Two Rows</TD> <TD>Cell A</TD> <TD>Cell B</TD> <TD>Cell
C</TD>
</TR>
<TR>
        <TD>Cell D</TD> <TD>Cell E</TD> <TD>Cell F</TD>
</TR>
</TABLE>

<P>You can also assign a single cell both a ROWSPAN and a COLSPAN:
<TABLE BORDER>
<TR>
        <TD>Cell A</TD> <TD ROWSPAN="2" COLSPAN="2">Cell B</TD> <TD>Cell C</
TD>
</TR>
<TR>
        <TD>Cell D</TD> <TD>Cell E</TD>
</TR>
<TR>
        <TD>Cell F</TD> <TD>Cell G</TD> <TD>Cell H</TD> <TD>Cell I</TD>
</TR>
</TABLE>
```

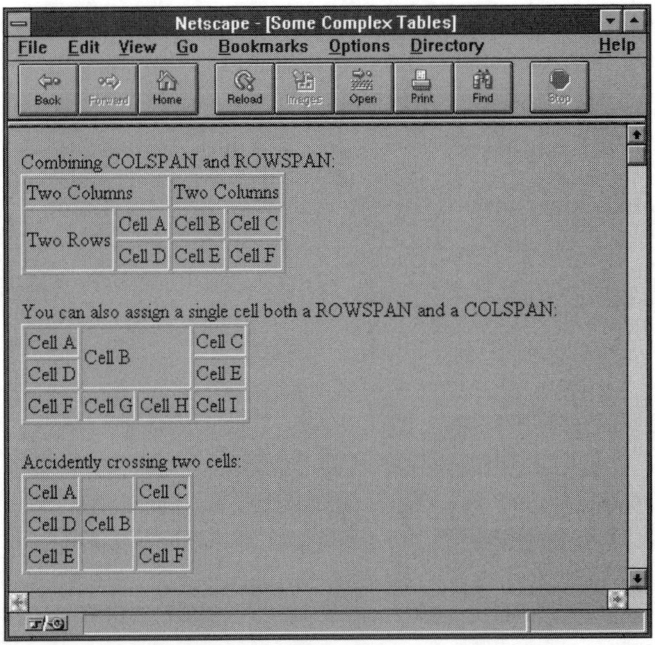

Figure 12.28 Combining COLSPAN and ROWSPAN

```
<P>Accidently crossing two cells:
<TABLE BORDER>
<TR>
        <TD>Cell A</TD> <TD ROWSPAN="3">Cell B</TD> <TD>Cell C</TD>
</TR>
<TR>
        <TD COLSPAN="3">Cell D</TD>
</TR>
<TR>
        <TD>Cell E</TD> <TD>Cell F</TD>
</TR>
</TABLE>

</BODY>
</HTML>
```

Header Cells

A *header cell* is just a cell where the text is in boldface and is centered in the cell. Header cells are created with the <TH>...</TH> element, and the rules for their use are identical to those of regular cells using the <TD>...</TD>

element. Note that you *can* use any HTML markup in a cell that you would normally use in your HTML document's body. A picture is worth a thousand words; take a look at Figure 12.29 to see an expression of the HTML in Listing 12.12.

Listing 12.12   LST12-12.HTM

```
<HTML>
<HEAD>
<TITLE>Headers and Such in Tables</TITLE>
</HEAD>
<BODY>

<P>Headers as column labels:
<TABLE BORDER>
<TR>
        <TH>Column A</TH> <TH>Column B</TH> <TH>Column C</TH>
</TR>
<TR>
        <TD>Cell 1</TD> <TD>Cell 2</TD> <TD>Cell 3</TD>
</TR>
</TABLE>

<P>Headers as row labels:
<TABLE BORDER>
<TR>
        <TH>Row A</TH> <TD>Cell 1</TD> <TD>Cell 2</TD>
</TR>
<TR>
        <TH>Row B</TH> <TD>Cell 3</TD> <TD>Cell 4</TD>
</TR>
</TABLE>

<P>A calendar using headers for the month name, and days of the week:
<TABLE BORDER>
<TR>
        <TH COLSPAN="7">June</TH>
</TR>
<TR>
        <TH>Sun</TH> <TH>Mon</TH> <TH>Tue</TH> <TH>Wed</TH>
        <TH>Thu</TH> <TH>Fri</TH> <TH>Sat</TH>
</TR>
<TR>
        <TD COLSPAN="4"></TD> <TD>1</TD> <TD>2</TD> <TD>3</TD>
</TR>
<TR>
        <TD>4</TD> <TD>5</TD> <TD>6</TD> <TD>7</TD> <TD>8</TD>
        <TD>9</TD> <TD>10</TD>
```

```
</TR>
<TR>
        <TD>11</TD> <TD>12</TD> <TD>13</TD> <TD>14</TD> <TD>15</TD>
        <TD>16</TD> <TD>17</TD>
</TR>
<TR>
        <TD>18</TD> <TD>19</TD> <TD>20</TD> <TD>21</TD> <TD>22</TD>
        <TD>23</TD> <TD>24</TD>
</TR>
<TR>
        <TD>25</TD> <TD>26</TD> <TD>27</TD> <TD>28</TD> <TD>29</TD>
        <TD>30</TD>
</TR>
</TABLE>

</BODY>
</HTML>
```

Of the three examples in Listing 12.12, I think the most interesting is the calendar. Notice how the first week is indented in Figure 12.29. It's done

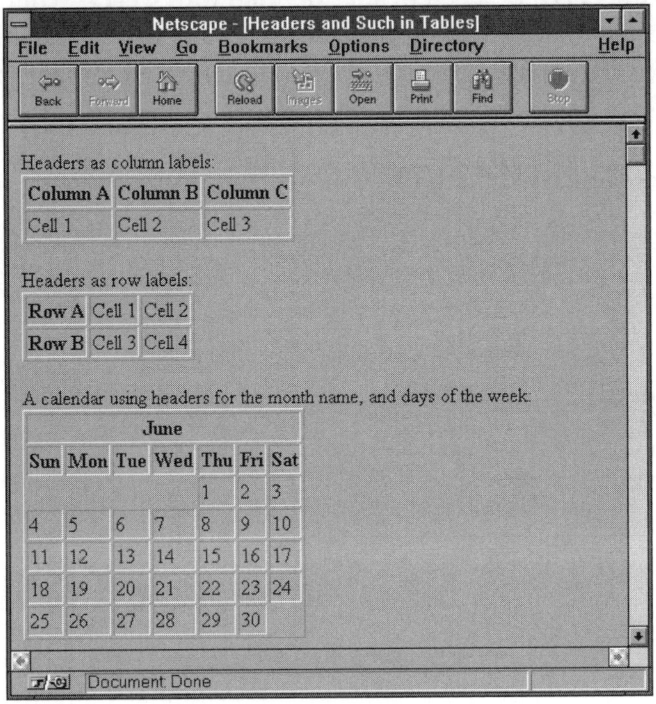

Figure 12.29   Header cells and an HTML calendar

not with four empty cells, but rather with four cells' worth of blank space. Glance back to the HTML in Listing 12.12 and take a look at the third row in the calendar table. In order to get that four columns' worth of empty space, so that the remaining three cells would be in the correct columns, I was forced to created a bogus cell with a COLSPAN of 4 and no content at all. Normally, a cell with content is surrounded by a border, which is not the effect I was looking for here. Instead, I wanted a completely blank area, with no cell boundaries at all. If, on the other hand, you *do* want a border around your empty cell, put a <BR> line break in the cell. This will force the browser to add a border.

Aligning Text within Cells

The ALIGN and VALIGN attributes can be used to align the text within each cell. ALIGN accepts three values: **left**, **center**, and **right**. VALIGN accepts four values: **top**, **middle**, **bottom**, and **baseline**. Both attributes may be applied to an entire table row defined with <TR>, an individual cell defined with <TD>, or a cell header defined with <TH>. When applied to <TR>, the alignment attributes affect every cell in that row. If an individual cell has the alignment attributes applied to it, the alignment specified for the row as a whole is overridden. See Listing 12.13 and Figure 12.30.

Listing 12.13   LST12-13.HTM

```
<HTML>
<HEAD>
<TITLE>Aligning Text in Your Cells</TITLE>
</HEAD>
<BODY>

<TABLE BORDER>
<TR>
        <TH></TH> <TH ALIGN="left">Left</TH> <TH>Center</TH> <TH
ALIGN="right">Right</TH>
</TR>
<TR>
        <TH>Row 1</TH> <TD ROWSPAN="2" VALIGN="top">Aligned to the Top</TD>
                        <TD ROWSPAN="2" VALIGN="middle">Aligned in the Middle</
TD>
                        <TD ROWSPAN="2" VALIGN="bottom">Aligned at the Bottom</
TD>
</TR>
<TR>
        <TH>Row 2</TH>
```

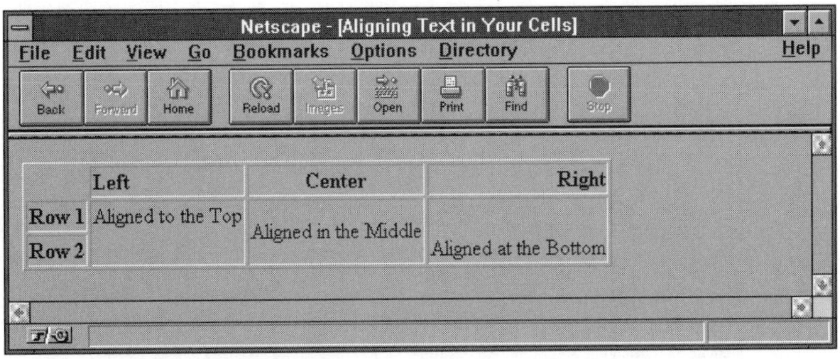

Figure 12.30   Aligning text inside cells

```
</TR>
</TABLE>

</BODY>
</HTML>
```

Text Wrapping inside Cells

All the tables I've shown you so far have had very small cells, since I haven't been including very much text. But if your table contains a lot of text, your cells may get pretty large, and once the table is as wide as the browser's window, the table must either wrap the text in each cell, or continue making the cells longer and longer until they scroll off the edge of the window. The default action is (thankfully, I think) to wrap the text in each cell when the cells become too wide to fit horizontally in the window.

If allowing the browser to choose where to wrap your cells is disturbing, the <TR> and <TH> elements will accept a special attribute, NOWRAP. Any text in a cell with the NOWRAP attribute will *not* wrap unless you specifically request a "hard wrap" with the <BR> line break. But be careful, because by taking control away from the browser, you may have cells so large that the table is forced to scroll off the edge of the browser's window. See Listing 12.14 for an example of text wrapping and the use of NOWRAP. Figure 12.31 shows how it all looks.

Listing12.14   LST12-14.HTM

```
<HTML>
<HEAD>
<TITLE>Wrapping Text</TITLE>
</HEAD>
```

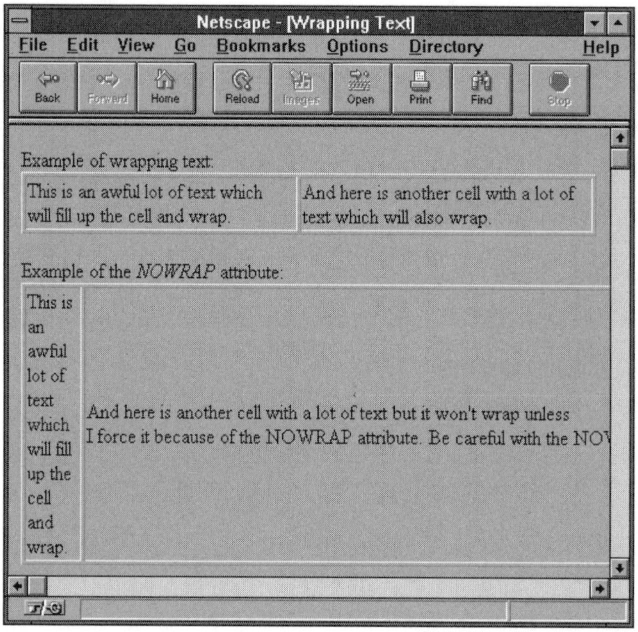

Figure 12.31   Text wrapping and NOWRAP

```
<BODY>

<P>Example of wrapping text:
<TABLE BORDER>
<TR>
        <TD>This is an awful lot of text which will fill up the cell and
wrap.</TD>
        <TD>And here is another cell with a lot of text which will also
wrap.</TD>
</TR>
</TABLE>

<P>Example of the <I>NOWRAP</I> attribute:
<TABLE BORDER>
<TR>
        <TD>This is an awful lot of text which will fill up the cell and
wrap.</TD>
        <TD NOWRAP>And here is another cell with a lot of text but it won't
wrap unless<BR>
                I force it because of the NOWRAP attribute. Be careful with
the NOWRAP
                attribute or your cells could get very long</TD>
</TR>
</TABLE>
```

```
</BODY>
</HTML>
```

Normally, when you think of a table, you think of spreadsheets, charts full of scientific data, and other information that usually doesn't take up much space inside any single cell. So, unless your table is completely stuffed with cells, you won't likely run into very much text wrapping. There is, however, another creative use for tables: formatting your documents into columns, as with newspaper or magazine articles. Listing 12.15 and Figure 12.32 implement a simple example of this type of table. To give things more of a newspaper-article feel, I've removed the BORDER attribute from the <TABLE> element, so that borders are no longer visible.

Listing 12.15 LST12-15.HTM

```
<HTML>
<HEAD>
<TITLE>Press Release: The Widget Company Creates New Widget</TITLE>
</HEAD>
<BODY>

<H1>Press Release!</H1>
<H2>The Widget Company's New Line of Widgets</H2>

<TABLE>
<TR VALIGN="top">
        <TD><CITE>12 October 94, Chicago- </CITE> <FONT SIZE="+2">T</FONT>he
Widget Company,
        leading manufacturer of Widgets and Gizmos, announced today its new
line of widgets.
        Company spokesperson Tracy Roberts says &quot;This new line of
widgets, the TX-100 series,
        will revolutionize the widget community. Dr. Claire Widget would be
proud of this new
        concept in widget design.&quot; When asked about their marketing
plans, Ms. Roberts stated
        &quot;We're really excited about this new product line, and plan on a
nationwide campaign
        to get the word out.&quot;
        </TD>
        <TD>The new line of widgets will be available for retail sale by the
end of this
        quarter, according to Ms. Roberts. Expected sales are in the tens of
thousand, but
        don't expect to see one of these fancy new widgets in your home any
time soon. They
```

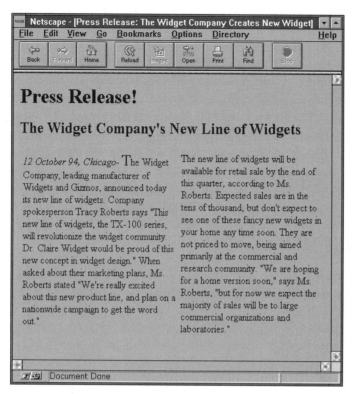

Figure 12.32   A table with a newspaper-article feel

```
        are not priced to move, being aimed primarily at the commercial and
research community.
        &quot;We are hoping for a home version soon,&quot; says Ms. Roberts,
&quot;but for now we expect the
        majority of sales will be to large commercial organizations and
laboratories.&quot;
        </TD>
</TR>
</TABLE>

</BODY>
</HTML>
```

Adding Captions

What's a table without a caption? The <CAPTION>...</CAPTION> element allows you to add captions to your tables. The caption can be aligned to appear at the very top of the table, or at the very bottom. If you have a particularly long caption, it will automatically wrap at the edge of the table. The <CAPTION>...</CAPTION> element is only appropriate inside a table, but outside of all other table elements. Its one attribute, ALIGN, specifies whether the caption should appear at the top of the table or at the bottom, with the default being the top. Captions are always centered.

Listing 12.16   LST12-16.HTM

```
<HTML>
<HEAD>
<TITLE>A Demonstration of Captions</TITLE>
</HEAD>
<BODY>

<TABLE BORDER>
<TR>
        <TH></TH> <TH>Peanuts</TH> <TH>Pretzels</TH> <TH>Cheese</TH>
</TR>
<TR>
        <TH>Jan</TH> <TD>$125</TD> <TD>$532</TD> <TD>$23</TD>
</TR>
<TR>
        <TH>Feb</TH> <TD>$75</TD> <TD>$473</TD> <TD>$97</TD>
</TR>
<TR>
        <TH>Mar</TH> <TD>$43</TD> <TD>$600</TD> <TD>$156</TD>
</TR>
<CAPTION ALIGN="bottom">Sales Figures for First Quarter 1991 in Millions</CAPTION>
</TABLE>

</BODY>
</HTML>
```

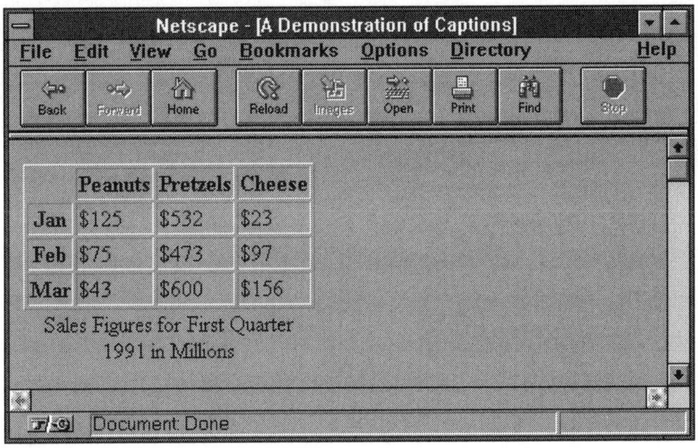

Figure 12.33   A table with a caption

None of the documentation I've seen so far specifically excludes the use of multiple captions; however, when I tried it, things didn't quite work as I expected. The second caption was always displayed at the top of the table, and it was not centered. Unless you see information stating otherwise, don't include more than one caption for each table. Remember, the HTML 3.0 draft is in a constant state of flux, and although the sections on tables seem to be a bit more stable than the rest of the draft, the details are bound to change.

Things about Tables that Are Netscape-Specific

Everything I have described about tables so far is as faithful to the HTML 3.0 draft as possible. After playing with tables for a while, Netscape decided that a few more features were in order to give everyone a little more control over table appearance. The following material applies to tables for Netscape only, and can be considered part of the Mozilla extensions. On the bright side, Netscape is trying to get this additional material into the HTML 3.0 draft, so it may do you some good to learn it regardless.

Cell Spacing
You can change the spacing between your cells using <TABLE> element's CELLSPACING attribute. Cell spacing is the amount of space between each cell in your table. The default value is 2. A value of 0 does not completely eliminate spacing between cells, but it does produce a very fine border if you have borders enabled on your table. Figure 12.34 shows a few examples of cell spacing.

Cell Padding
You can also change the spacing between the contents of each cell and the cell wall interior, using the <TABLE> element's CELLPADDING attribute. The default value is 1, and a value of 0 completely removes all padding. Figure 12.35 shows a few examples of cell padding.

Changing Border Thickness
If you really want your table to stand out, you can give the BORDER attribute a value, to change the thickness of your table's *outside* border, and give it a more pronounced 3-D appearance. The first example in Figure 12.36 shows a table with the border, cell padding, and cell spacing values all set to 0. This is about as compact as your tables are going to get—and

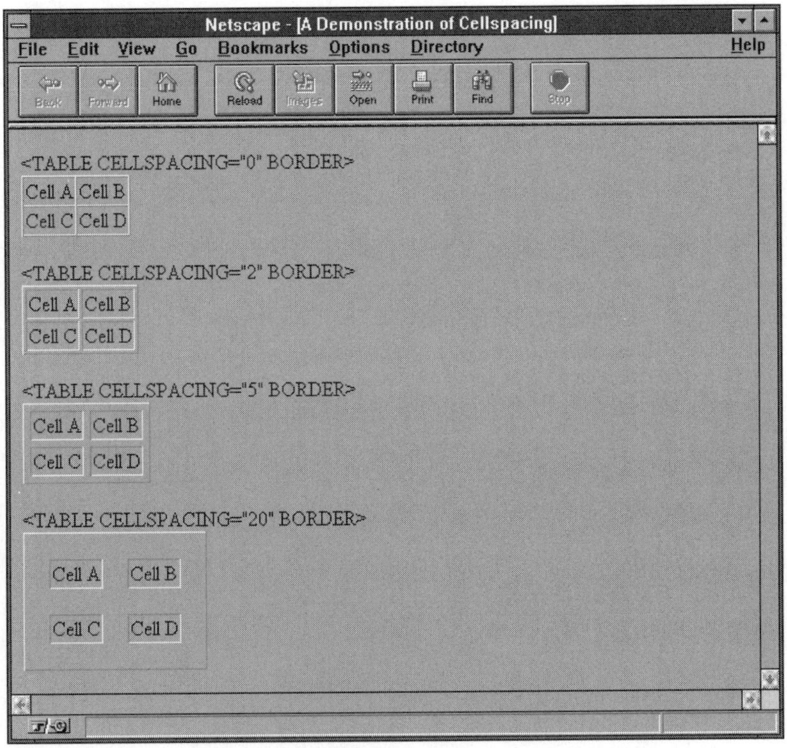

Figure 12.34   Examples of the CELLSPACING attribute in use

some people will not look at it and think "table" at all. The default border thickness is 1, as shown in the next example table in the figure. A border of 5 and cell spacing of 10 gives your table a slightly raised look, with extra-thick cell separators. The last example table has a border of ten, and the default cell spacing, providing a much more 3-D look. Take special note that border thickness does not affect the cell separators inside your tables, only the outside border. You will have to use CELLSPACING to change the thickness of the cell separators.

Forcing Tables and Cells to a Set Width

In general, it's best to let your browser figure out the best way to present your table, but sometimes you want a little more control over the width of the table or of the individual cells. Normally, a column will be as large as its largest cell, and the table will be as large as the sum of the width of its columns. You can, however, take full control, setting table and cell widths as you see fit.

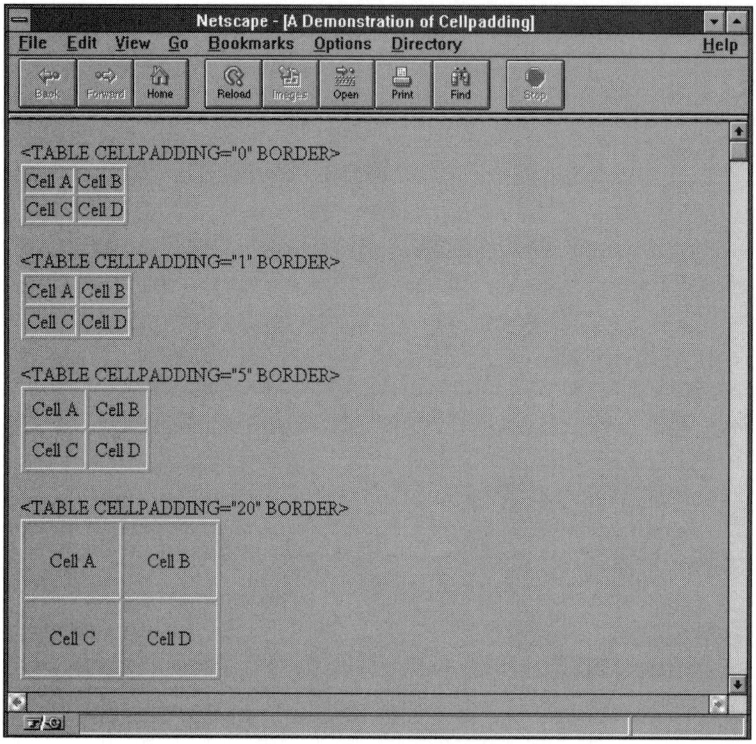

Figure 12.35   Examples of the CELLPADDING attribute in use

The WIDTH attribute allows you to specify the width of a single cell, or of your entire table, expressed as either pixels or a percentage value. When used as an attribute in the <TABLE> element, WIDTH controls the width of your entire table. If you specify a value in pixels, Netscape will attempt to fit all your cells in a table that many pixels wide. A better approach is to give the width as a percentage, which will force the table to assume a width equal to the specified percentage of the browser's window at any given time. If you set the width value to something too small to fit all your cells, Netscape will do the best it can to fit the cells into your table.

If WIDTH is applied to an individual cell, defined with either <TD> or <TH>, that cell will become the specified number of pixels wide, or the requested percentage *of the total width of the table*, depending on whether you give an absolute value in pixels or a percentage. If the cell is too large, because you specified a size larger than the table itself, Netscape will do its best to fit the cell into your table, but there may be some serious distortion.

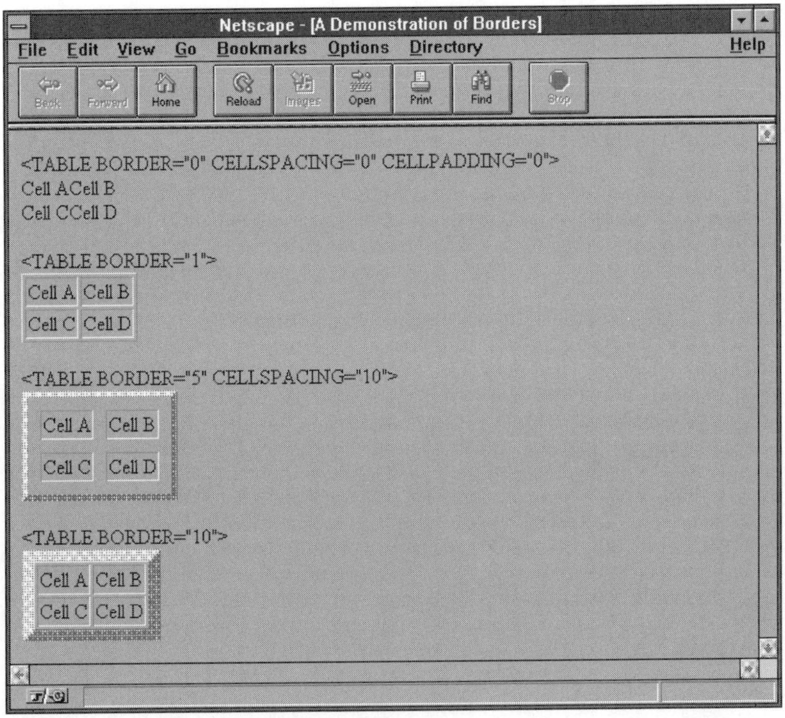

Figure 12.36   Examples of border thickness

Listing 12.17   LST12-17.HTM

```
<HTML>
<HEAD>
<TITLE>A Demonstration of WIDTH</TITLE>
</HEAD>
<BODY>

<TABLE BORDER>
<TR>
        <TH>Column A</TH> <TH>Column B</TH> <TH>Column C</TH>
</TR>
<TR>
        <TD>Cell 1</TD> <TD>Cell 2</TD> <TD>Cell 3</TD>
</TR>
<TR>
        <TD>Cell 4</TD> <TD>Cell 5</TD> <TD>Cell 6</TD>
</TR>
</TABLE>

<P>
<TABLE BORDER WIDTH="100%">
```

```
<TR>
        <TH>Column A</TH> <TH>Column B</TH> <TH>Column C</TH>
</TR>
<TR>
        <TD>Cell 1</TD> <TD>Cell 2</TD> <TD>Cell 3</TD>
</TR>
<TR>
        <TD>Cell 4</TD> <TD>Cell 5</TD> <TD>Cell 6</TD>
</TR>
</TABLE>

<P>
<TABLE BORDER>
<TR>
        <TH WIDTH="10%">Column A</TH> <TH WIDTH="45%">Column B</TH>
        <TH WIDTH="45%">Column C</TH>
</TR>
<TR>
        <TD>Cell 1</TD> <TD>Cell 2</TD> <TD>Cell 3</TD>
</TR>
</TABLE>

<P>
<TABLE BORDER WIDTH="75%">
<TR>
        <TH WIDTH="10%">Column A</TH> <TH WIDTH="45%">Column B</TH>
        <TH WIDTH="45%">Column C</TH>
</TR>
<TR>
        <TD>Cell 1</TD> <TD>Cell 2</TD> <TD>Cell 3</TD>
</TR>
</TABLE>

<P>
<TABLE WIDTH="400" BORDER>
<TR>
        <TD WIDTH="20">Tiny</TD> <TD WIDTH="80">Bigger</TD>
        <TD WIDTH="200">Even bigger</TD>
</TR>
<TR>
        <TD WIDTH="40">Wow A Really Tiny Cell!</TD> <TD WIDTH="10">Teeny</TD>
        <TD WIDTH="300">Oops!</TD>
</TR>
</TABLE>

</BODY>
</HTML>
```

Figure 12.37 shows a few examples of tables and cells resized using the WIDTH attribute. The HTML is in Listing 12.17. The first table does not use WIDTH, and allows the browser to pick the size for you. The second table is identical, except the table has been sized to fit the full width of the browser's window. Each column in the third table is set for a different width, and the fourth table is identical to the third except the entire table has been set to a width of 75% of the browser's window. The final table uses absolute widths to set the table and cell sizes. Notice how the sizes as set in the HTML just don't add up. Even cells in the same columns are defined to be of different widths. In this case, Netscape's only recourse is to figure out the best way to represent this table. The widest cell in each column takes precedence and defines the width of the column as a whole.

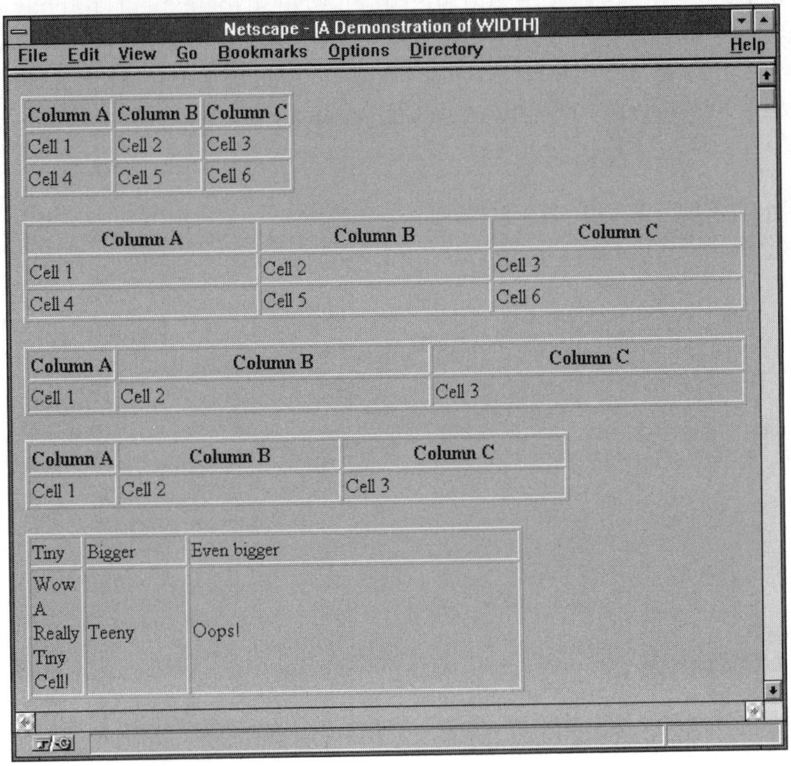

Figure 12.37   Table and cell widths

How about Images, Horizontal Rules, Forms, and Other Stuff?

You can have images, as well as text, in any of your table's cells. Horizontal rules, regular headings, and anchors are also allowed in tables. Generally, if it is allowed in an HTML document's body, it is allowed in a table. You can even put a form in a table, using the table to help lay out the form, for example, lining up buttons in neat ways, ensuring that text entry boxes are aligned correctly, and so on.

Here's a non-obvious troubleshooting tip: If your image is not centered within its cell, you may have added extra whitespace to the <TR>...</TR> or <TH>...</TH> elements that contain your image. Be careful not to have any spaces between the tags. Listing 12.18 and Figure 12.38 will show you what I mean. Speaking of whitespace, right now the <TABLE>...</TABLE> element implies a line break before and after it, but Netscape expects to change this behavior soon. The advantage of *not* implying line breaks is that you will then be able to treat tables just like inline images. For now, your only options for table placement are against the left margin or centered with the <CENTER>...</CENTER> element.

Listing 12.18   LST12-18.HTM

```
<HTML>
<HEAD>
<TITLE>Miscellaneous Tables</TITLE>
</HEAD>
<BODY>

<P>Image which is nice and centered:
<TABLE BORDER="5">
<TR>
        <TD><IMG SRC="book/grid.gif"></TD>
</TR>
</TABLE>

<P>Image with a little extra space to the right and bottom:
<TABLE BORDER="5">
<TR>
        <TD>
        <IMG SRC="book/grid.gif">
        </TD>
</TR>
</TABLE>
```

```
<P>Horizontal Rules, Headings, Anchors, and Forms!
<FORM>
<TABLE BORDER="10">
<TR>
        <TD>This is<HR>A Test</TD> <TD>This<P>Is a test</TD>
</TR>
<TR>
        <TD><H1>Test!</H1></TD> <TD><A HREF="/">Testing!</TD>
</TR>
<TR>
        <TD><INPUT TYPE="text" NAME="TEST"></TD>
        <TD><INPUT TYPE="submit"></TD>
</TR>
</TABLE>
</FORM>

</BODY>
</HTML>
```

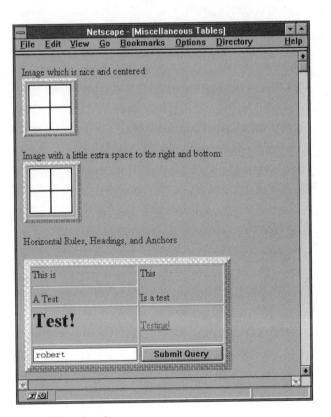

Figure 12.38   Table odds and ends

Of course, you can also embed tables into other tables. Your HTML is going to start to look *real* messy at this point, so I'd like to reassert my previous suggestion: Buy some graph paper! You will save a lot of time if you plan your tables out on paper first, especially if you start embedding tables within tables within tables and so on. Listing 12.19 shows a quick example; two tables are embedded within another, larger table. The results are shown in Figure 12.39.

Listing 12.19 LST12-19.HTM

```
<HTML>
<HEAD>
<TITLE>Embedded Tables Within Tables</TITLE>
</HEAD>
<BODY>

<CENTER>
<TABLE BORDER="8" CELLPADDING="4">
<TR>
        <TH COLSPAN="2">Table A</TH>
</TR>
<TR>
        <TD>
        <TABLE BORDER="4">
        <TR>
                <TH COLSPAN="2">Table B</TH>
        </TR>
        <TR>
                <TD>Cell B-1</TD> <TD>Cell B-2</TD>
        </TR>
        </TABLE>
        </TD>

        <TD>
        <TABLE BORDER="4">
        <TR>
                <TH ROWSPAN="2">Table C</TH> <TD>Cell C-1</TD>
        </TR>
        <TR>
                <TD>Cell C-2</TD>
        </TR>
        </TABLE>
        </TD>
</TR>
<CAPTION ALIGN="bottom">Two Tables Within A Table</CAPTION>
</TABLE>
</CENTER>
```

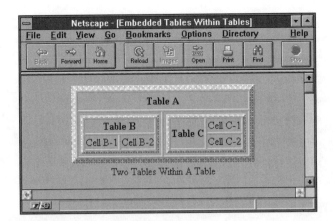

Figure 12.39   Two tables inside another table

```
</BODY>
</HTML>
```

How NCSA Mosaic Handles Tables

Most of the table features in the HTML 3.0 draft work in the latest version of NCSA Mosaic, with the exception of those attributes I have labeled as belonging to Netscape only. The <CAPTION>...</CAPTION> element is not implemented in NCSA Mosaic, and Mosaic will completely mangle your table if you try to include it. If you want your tables to work with NCSA Mosaic, be sure to leave out values for the BORDER attribute, CELLSPACING, CELLPADDING, and WIDTH. Embedding tables within tables also causes NCSA Mosaic to completely melt down. At some time in the near future, we can hope that these bugs will be fixed and tables will be more reliable and robust in NCSA Mosaic—and best of all, work consistently between both NCSA Mosaic and the Netscape Navigator, which between them own the loyalties of the vast majority of Web users.

"Things Netscape"

In this chapter you learned about "things Netscape," including Netscape's interpretation of HTML 3.0 tables, and its extensions thereto. Netscape really is a nice browser, capable of rendering some visually stunning documents, but you should always remember that Netscape isn't the only browser your users will be using to view your documents. If you want the widest

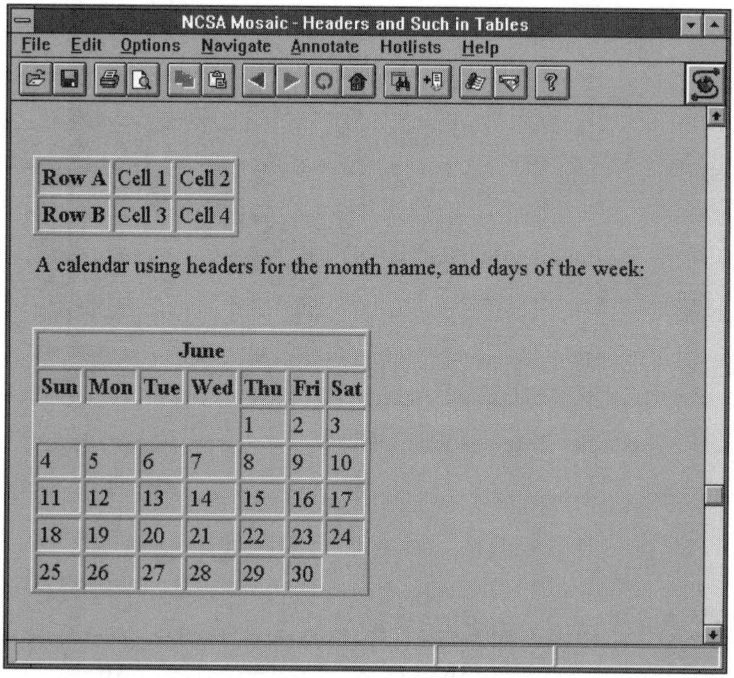

Figure 12.40   NCSA Mosaic's rendering of Listing 12.12

possible audience, it's wise (for now at least) to keep your use of the Mozilla extensions to a minimum.

In the next chapter, I'll show you even more Netscape extensions. It's possible to change the background color, foreground color, and even add bitmapped background textures to your documents with Netcape, and I'll show you how. Netscape has also implemented a couple of neat new features called *client pull* and *server push*, which I do hope other browsers will begin to implement. Client pull is a way of instructing the user's browser to fetch another URL, automatically, after a certain period of time, without any user intervention. Slide shows and tradeshow demonstrations are two uses that immediately pop to mind. Server push allows your server to keep the connection with the user's browser open, continually "pushing" new information to it as it becomes available. Live stock quotes, real-time interactive "chatting," and a myriad of other applications become possible.

If you want to be on the cutting edge of Web technology, don't skip the next chapter!

13

More From Mozilla

Need even more control over your documents? How about the background and foreground colors? Or maybe a custom background *image* would help spruce up your documents. Netscape has extensions to control these functions, as well as a few more advanced features to add even more character to your pages. For example, a feature called *client pull* can be used to force Netscape, and perhaps other browsers in the future as well, to automatically redirect itself to another URL after a certain period of time that you specify. How does a slide show sound? An unattended walkthrough of your Web server at tradeshows? An automated kiosk? These applications and countless others are perfect for client pull.

Later in the chapter, I will also tell you about client pull's evil twin, *server push*. With server push, and a bit of fancy CGI scripting, you can force your server to keep its connection to Netscape open, piping new data to it as it becomes available. For example, live stock quotes updated minute-by-minute, real time chatting, and even simple animations can be done using server push. It's a little tricky, and absolutely bleeding edge, but well worth the effort to explore. The applications are endless.

Changing Colors

With the addition of a few new attributes for the <BODY>...</BODY> element, Netscape has made it possible to change the color of the browser's background field, foreground (text), and hyperlinks. Right now, these attributes all fall under the "Mozilla Extensions" umbrella, supported primarily by

Netscape and not in any "official" draft or specification. But Netscape hopes this will change soon, and they are trying to get their enhancements included in the HTML 3.0 draft. For now, however, only the Netscape Navigator will honor background and foreground color changes.

How Computers See Color

One way to represent colors in a computer is by the "amount" of red, green, and blue that are used to make up that color. The amount of a color is represented by a number from 0, meaning the complete absence of that color, to 255, meaning "the most," or "brightest." For example, if you want a bright red color, you would say you have "255" red, "0" blue, and "0" green. Purple is a mixture of red and blue, so a bright purple would be "255" red, "0" green, and "255" blue. If you want a little more "bluish-purple" you could "take away" some of the red: "222" red, "0" green, and "255" blue. Taken together, these three numbers are called an *RGB triple*. The acronym RGB stands for red-green-blue, which is the order of the colors in an RGB triple.

If you are a programmer, you know that hexadecimal is a numbering system using *base 16*. Basically, instead of each "place" being a multiple of ten, like decimal, it is a multiple of sixteen. For example, the decimal number "29" is "9 ones" and "2 tens." That is: $(2 \times 10) + (9 \times 1) = 29$. In hexadecimal, the same number would be represented as "1D." The letter "D" is the "13th" digit, so "1D" is "13 ones" and "1 sixteens." Or: $(1 \times 16) + (13 \times 1) = 29$. Hexadecimal digits range from 1 through F, with "A" being "10," and so on. Here is another one: the hexadecimal number "5A" is the same as the decimal number "106." Or: $(5 \times 16) + (10 \times 1)$. For those of us who can't convert from decimal to hexadecimal in our heads, Table 13.1 lists the decimal numbers from 0 to 255, and their hexadecimal equivalents.

Background Colors

Combining the two concepts of hexadecimal and RGB triples, you will come up with an *RGB hexidecimal triple*, which is simply an RGB triple using hexadecimal notation instead of decimal. Background colors are controlled with the <BODY> tag's BGCOLOR attribute, whose value is an RGB hexadecimal triple, corresponding to the desired background color:

```
<BODY BGCOLOR="#RRGGBB">
```

Table 13.1   Hexadecimal numbers and their decimal equivalents

Dec	Hex	Dec	Hex	Dec	Hex	Dec	Hex	Dec	Hex	Dec	Hex
0	00	43	2B	86	56	129	81	172	AC	215	D7
1	01	44	2C	87	57	130	82	173	AD	216	D8
2	02	45	2D	88	58	131	83	174	AE	217	D9
3	03	46	2E	89	59	132	84	175	AF	218	DA
4	04	47	2F	90	5A	133	85	176	B0	219	DB
5	05	48	30	91	5B	134	86	177	B1	220	DC
6	06	49	31	92	5C	135	87	178	B2	221	DD
7	07	50	32	93	5D	136	88	179	B3	222	DE
8	08	51	33	94	5E	137	89	180	B4	223	DF
9	09	52	34	95	5F	138	8A	181	B5	224	E0
10	0A	53	35	96	60	139	8B	182	B6	225	E1
11	0B	54	36	97	61	140	8C	183	B7	226	E2
12	0C	55	37	98	62	141	8D	184	B8	227	E3
13	0D	56	38	99	63	142	8E	185	B9	228	E4
14	0E	57	39	100	64	143	8F	186	BA	229	E5
15	0F	58	3A	101	65	144	90	187	BB	230	E6
16	10	59	3B	102	66	145	91	188	BC	231	E7
17	11	60	3C	103	67	146	92	189	BD	232	E8
18	12	61	3D	104	68	147	93	190	BE	233	E9
19	13	62	3E	105	69	148	94	191	BF	234	EA
20	14	63	3F	106	6A	149	95	192	C0	235	EB
21	15	64	40	107	6B	150	96	193	C1	236	EC
22	16	65	41	108	6C	151	97	194	C2	237	ED
23	17	66	42	109	6D	152	98	195	C3	238	EE
24	18	67	43	110	6E	153	99	196	C4	239	EF
25	19	68	44	111	6F	154	9A	197	C5	240	F0
26	1A	69	45	112	70	155	9B	198	C6	241	F1
27	1B	70	46	113	71	156	9C	199	C7	242	F2
28	1C	71	47	114	72	157	9D	200	C8	243	F3
29	1D	72	48	115	73	158	9E	201	C9	244	F4
30	1E	73	49	116	74	159	9F	202	CA	245	F5
31	1F	74	4A	117	75	160	A0	203	CB	246	F6
32	20	75	4B	118	76	161	A1	204	CC	247	F7
33	21	76	4C	119	77	162	A2	205	CD	248	F8
34	22	77	4D	120	78	163	A3	206	CE	249	F9
35	23	78	4E	121	79	164	A4	207	CF	250	FA
36	24	79	4F	122	7A	165	A5	208	D0	251	FB
37	25	80	50	123	7B	166	A6	209	D1	252	FC
38	26	81	51	124	7C	167	A7	210	D2	253	FD
39	27	82	52	125	7D	168	A8	211	D3	254	FE
40	28	83	53	126	7E	169	A9	212	D4	255	FF
41	29	84	54	127	7F	170	AA	213	D5		
42	2A	85	55	128	80	171	AB	214	D6		

where "RRGGBB" is the RGB hexadecimal triple. Constructing this number can be a little tricky, so I've provided Table 13.2 with the values for a little over a dozen common colors. For example, if you want your background color to be a dark blue, Table 13.2 tells you the value to use would be "000080," so you would use the following line to change the background to dark blue:

```
<BODY BGCOLOR="#000080">
```

If you don't see the exact color you are looking for in Table 13.2, most paint programs should be able to give you the proper RGB triple for any color. Even better, you should also be able to create your own colors, using simple "slide bars" to easily find the perfect shade. If your favorite paint program only gives you RGB triples with decimal values, use Table 13.1 to convert it to hexadecimal.

Table 13.2   Some RGB hexadecimal triples for popular colors

Color	Red	Green	Blue
White	FF	FF	FF
Light Gray	C0	C0	C0
Medium Gray	A0	A0	A4
Dark Gray	80	80	80
Black	00	00	00
Red	FF	00	00
Dark Red	80	00	00
Green	00	FF	00
Dark Green	00	80	00
Blue	00	00	FF
Dark Blue	00	00	80
Yellow	FF	FF	00
Brown	80	80	00
Purple	FF	00	FF
Dark Purple	80	00	80
Cyan	00	FF	FF
Dark Cyan	00	80	80

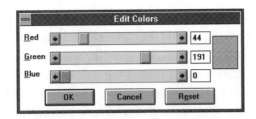

Figure 13.1   The color editor from Microsoft Windows Paintbrush

The Dithering Blues

As you can see, an RGB triple uses three bytes, or 24 bits, to represent a single color. This is called *24-bit color* and, unfortunately, most people's computers can't display 24 bits worth of color. A little quick math tells us that using 24 bits, we can create over 16 million colors. That's a wee bit high of the 256 colors my copy of MS Windows is currently set to display *at once*. The key word here is "at once." Those remaining 16 million colors don't just disappear, and are still there. But if you can only display 256 colors at once, your computer will have to pick *which* 256 colors it is going to be able to display. This is called your *palette*, and it is the current set of colors you have to choose from. You can change your palette whenever you want, but you are locked into set maximum number of colors you can display at once. My computer is currently set up to display 256. Yours may display only 16, or (as is increasingly common) many more.

If you request a color that is not in your palette, you have three choices of how to display it. You can pick the color that is closest to it in your palette, you can throw away one of your other colors and use the desired color instead, or you can approximate your desired color with what is called *dithering*. Dithering takes advantage of the fact that your eyes can only see so much detail, and they can take two adjacent pixels on your monitor and merge them into yielding the impression of color different from that of either of the two adjacent pixels. So let's say you want a color that is somewhere between color A and color B. With dithering, the computer will take two adjacent pixels and set one for color A and one for color B. Over a large area, your eyes will merge those pixels together, and you will see something that is roughly the target color.

As good as this sounds, dithering isn't perfect. You can't quite fool your eyes that easily, and the color will look grainy. And depending on how many colors are in your palette, the result may look awful. If you don't have two colors in your palette that are close enough to the color you want, the resulting dither may look more like a fine checkerboard instead of a new color. Now this wouldn't be as big a deal if it weren't for the effect it can have on your text. If your background is heavily dithered, your text will look very washed out and nearly impossible to read, depending on the size of your text and its color. But even a foreground and background color that are highly contrasted can still look awful with a heavily dithered background.

There really is no solution to the dithering blues. If your palette doesn't match someone else's, which is a problem even from MS Windows machine to MS Windows machine and an even bigger problem across differing platforms, you are going to have to deal with dithering. Sometimes it won't be too bad, but sometimes it will be nearly lethal—and just because a color looks fine on your computer it doesn't necessarily mean it will look fine on someone else's. The lesson here may be "don't change background colors at all," but I know that isn't an acceptable solution. Try not to make too "complex" a color, and make sure that your colors at least don't dither on your machine. It isn't much of an answer, but it will have to do. The colors in Table 13.2 should work fine on most machines, but I offer no guarantees.

More Than One Background Color
Since the background color is specified as an attribute in the <BODY>... </BODY> element, and an HTML document may only have one body, background colors are all or nothing. You can't change the background halfway through your document. Being the curious type, I decided to play around with this a bit and here is what I discovered. It seems as though if you place several <BODY> start tags one above the other, you can force the background color to change rapidly before it settles on the final color, which is taken from the last <BODY> tag. With enough of these tags, you can force the background color to flash, change, and pulsate for as long as you want.

There are a few problems with this. One, it is illegal HTML. For another, it is really, really annoying. Your document won't display until the background finally finishes flashing, so while your user's head is swimming from the rapidly flashing background, he or she will also be frustrated at the delayed loading time. Also, you can't just stick a new <BODY> tag in the middle of your document to change the color. It doesn't work. Furthermore, this behavior, being undefined, is not something you can count on to be supported in Netscape or any browser in the future.

Foreground Colors

After you have changed the background color, you will almost certainly want to change the foreground color, which is the color of your text. The default black text color will likely be unreadable on most of the darker backgrounds. The TEXT attribute accepts the same value as the BGCOLOR attribute, and is used in the same way to change the color of your text. One of my favorite combinations is white text on a dark blue background. Using the TEXT and BGCOLOR attributes, and looking up the RGB values for each color in Table 13.2, this line would give the desired effect:

```
<BODY TEXT="#FFFFFF" BGCOLOR="#000080">
```

And what about hyperlinks? The default blue color for unvisited links probably won't be very clear on this dark blue background, and neither will the default purple color for already visited links. Not a problem—the LINK and VLINK attributes handle that. LINK is used to set the color of unvisited links, and VLINK sets the color for visited links. Your links can also be in still another state, called *active*. I didn't know this myself until one day I noticed that while clicking on a link and holding the mouse button down for just a few extra seconds, the link had turned a red color, just for a moment. I also noticed that sometimes if you click on a link that your browser is already trying to access, the link will turn red as well, warning you that you are already trying to access that document and to be patient. If you want to change the color of active links, the ALINK attribute works just like the others. The example shown below is for a dark blue document, with white text. The unvisited links are yellow, visited links are brown, and active links are green for just a moment:

```
<BODY BGCOLOR="#000080" TEXT="#FFFFFF" LINK="#FFFF00" VLINK="#808000"
ALINK="#00FF00">
```

Background Patterns

Just changing colors isn't enough for you, is it? Netscape didn't think so either, so they decided to implement an interesting idea they got from the HTML 3.0 draft: *background patterns*. With the help of Netscape 1.1N, it is now possible to set a GIF image as a background for your documents. Just give your document the small GIF image you want for the background, and Netscape will happily "tile" your document with it.

Your background image is specified in the <BODY> tag, just like the foreground and background colors, using the BACKGROUND attribute. All you need is the URL of a GIF image suitable for a background, and before your document is displayed Netscape will paste together as many copies of the image as needed to fill your document. Note in the previous sentence the word "suitable." In my opinion, there are quite a few criteria that need to be met for an image to be suitable for a background.

For one, it must be small so it can load quickly. Netscape must transfer the background image first, before it can load and display your document. If your background image is too large, there might be a sizable delay before your document is displayed. The image also shouldn't be too "busy," or it will detract from the rest of your document, or worse, make your document's text unreadable.

The image should also paste together, from any side, seamlessly. In other words, when the image is "tiled" onto your document, you shouldn't be able to see any seams. The pattern should be regular enough so that its edges can join to one another without any visible discontinuities, which are what give the impression of "seams." Listing 13.1 shows how to include a background image in your documents. Since it is the home page of a fictitious rock climbing club, I thought a background with a rock-like texture would be cute. I also made a little transparent mountain range inline image to show how transparent GIFs are handled with backgrounds. Just as you would suspect, the background texture does show through. Nice. The results are shown in Figure 13.2.

Listing 13.1   LST13-1.HTM

```
<HTML>
<HEAD>
<TITLE>&quot;We Climb Rocks&quot; Home Page</TITLE>
</HEAD>
<BODY BACKGROUND="http://home.netscape.com/home/bg/rock/gray_rock.gif"
BGCOLOR="#808080" TEXT="#FFFFFF" LINK="#FFFF00" VLINK="#8080FF">

<CENTER>
<H1>The &quot;We Climb Rocks&quot; Club</H1>
```

```
<IMG SRC="book/rock.gif">
<BASEFONT SIZE="4">
<P>A home page dedicated to the sport of rock climbing. Written by
rock climbers, for rock climbers.
</CENTER>
<HR>

</BODY>
</HTML>
```

If your document has a background image, the *BGCOLOR* attribute is ignored; however, it is always a good idea to include a background color anyway. If Netscape has trouble displaying your background image, it will try to display your background color instead. If you don't specify one, it will ignore your foreground color changes. The theory is that without your background, your foreground colors may not be visible on Netscape's default gray background. In my sample home page, I set the background to a medium gray, roughly the color of my rock texture.

There are a number of reasons your background image may not be displayed. If your background image is on another server that is temporarily unavailable, your image won't be loaded. Another far more likely situation occurs if the user has "inline image loading" turned off.

The Netscape home page has a small archive of background images you can use in your own pages. You can either download your own copy, or as

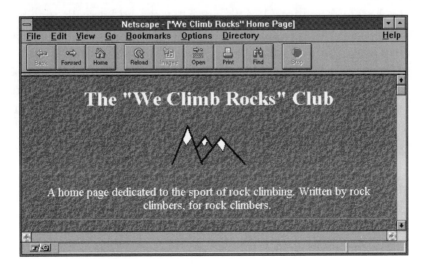

Figure 13.2   A rock-like texture background

they recommend, just make a link to it. I strongly recommend *against* linking to a background on Netscape's server, because that puts you at their mercy. If their server is overloaded, it will take that much longer for the background to be loaded, and if their server goes down your background won't be loaded at all. There is some logic to their recommendation, however. If everyone links to Netscape's backgrounds, then the odds of one of your users having run into it before and the image already being in their cache is much higher, which means that there will be practically no wait for the image to be loaded. If you copy it to your own server instead, Netscape has no way of knowing that it already has that image in its cache from a previous page, so it will have to be reloaded. You'll have to make your own decision. Their logic is sound; I just don't agree with it.

If you would like to take a look at Netscape's background archive, the URL is *http://home.netscape.com/assist/net_sites/bg/backgrounds.html*. I also found another site with even more backgrounds, called "Texture Land," you may want to check out. They are at *http://www.europa.com/~yyz/textures/textures.html*. There are some really nice backgrounds there. Well worth a quick visit. Yahoo also has a small index of background archives at *http://www.yahoo.com/Computers/World_Wide_Web/Browsers/* listed under "Netscape." There isn't much on backgrounds there yet, but you may want to check back every so often for new listings, as they're added.

Evil Lurks...

I like background textures, I really do. They can add a really nice feel to your pages. But evil lurks here as well! Let's just say that I've seen some really bad background textures in my travels. A poorly picked background, with the wrong foreground colors, can render a page almost impossible to read, so exercise a bit of caution. How do you know you have a bad background? One indication is if it causes physical pain to the viewer, headaches, dizziness, crossed eyes, and maybe even nosebleeds. Really, I've seen them this bad.

If your background is a little busy, and your text is hard to read, barring changing or removing your background you might want to try increasing the size of your font and picking a foreground color with a bit more contrast to the background's predominant color. A larger font can help a lot, particularly for very busy or complex background textures. You also might want to try lightening (or darkening) your background image so your text stands out a bit more. When you think you've finally got it right, ask a friend or coworker for their advice. The more bluntly honest they are, the better.

Client Pull

Client pull and its companion *server push* (which I'll talk about later) are foremost among the most innovative new features on the Web. Client pull gives you the means to tell the user's browser to access a new URL after a certain time value that you specify. In other words, Netscape will load any URL you request after displaying the original document, with absolutely no user intervention. The applications are endless, and I'll show you a few of my ideas in just a moment. Unfortunately, right now only Netscape Navigator 1.1N is aware of client pull, but that is very likely to change in the near future.

Before you can understand client pull, you will need a little more background on how HTTP works. In particular, you need to understand what an *HTTP response header* is.

HTTP Response Headers: The Short Story

An HTTP response header is a list of *meta-information*, extra information about your document that the browser may be able to make use of, which the server sends to your browser just before sending the requested document itself. A typical response header may contain information about when the document was last modified, the length of the document, the type of information contained in the document (an HTML file, a plain text file, a GIF image, etc.) and when the information contained in the document expires. Some information about the server, the version of the HTTP protocol, and other useful data may also be returned. After the response header is sent, the requested document immediately follows, separated from the header with a blank line.

The form of the response header is based on the MIME format for Internet email. I spoke of MIME awhile back, in the CGI chapters. Listing 13.2 shows an actual HTTP response header.

Listing 13.2   LST13-2.TXT

```
HTTP/1.0 200 Document follows
MIME-Version: 1.0
```

```
Server: CERN/3.0pre6
Date: Sunday, 18-Jun-95 11:59:05 GMT
Content-Type: text/html
Content-Length: 2121
Last-Modified: Tuesday, 13-Jun-95 23:42:36 GMT
```

The first line of the header tells the browser that the server will be using version 1.0 of the HTTP protocol to send the document. The number "200" is called a *response code*, which essentially means "here comes the document." If there were an error, this number would tell the browser what error occurred. The rest of the header is self-explanatory.

The beauty of the HTTP protocol is that it is designed to be very simple, and very flexible. *Every* line in the header is optional. If the browser wants to use the information, it can. If it doesn't, it just ignores it.

The <META> Element

Sometimes your document may have additional information about itself that it wants the browser to know about, but it knows the server won't send it in the HTTP response header. For these occasions, a new HTML element, <META>, was developed. The <META> element goes in your document's head, with the <TITLE> and all those other "administrative" elements, and can communicate extra meta-information about itself to the browser. Here's how it works...

Suppose there is a special browser that has been designed specifically for young children to use for browsing the Web. There are some pretty "adult" places on the Web, and this particular browser is designed to filter out documents depending on a certain rating they may have, perhaps along the same lines as the ratings now given to movies. Anything that is rated "adult" gets blocked out, and anything rated "general audience" is allowed through. Through whatever mechanism is evolved for the purpose, a Web document is given an "Adult" rating. But there is no HTML markup specifically for rating a document's content, so what can you do? This is a perfect job for <META>!

You can use <META> to "inject" a little extra information into the HTTP response header, for example:

```
<META HTTP-EQUIV="Rating" CONTENT="adult">
```

The HTTP-EQUIV attribute is the name of the information type, and the CONTENT attribute contains the value. This information is then "placed" into the HTTP response header, with the rest of the meta-information, in the form of the following line, per our ratings example:

```
Rating: adult
```

Actually, this isn't exactly true. Technically, the information isn't injected in the header itself, but the browser *thinks* it was, so it has the same effect. There's a bit more to <META> than this, but as far as client pull is concerned, that's all you need to know.

The Response Header and Client Pull

Now that all of that is out of the way, here is how the response header relates to client pull. Netscape understands a special response header called "Refresh." This is where the real magic happens. If Netscape sees a line in the HTTP response header like this

```
Refresh: 5
```

it knows that it should reload the same document in five seconds. So, if you want your document to reload itself in five seconds, perhaps because you know that the document will contain new information at that time, you need to convince the browser that the "Refresh: 5" header was received with the document. For this, you can use the <META> element, and here's the way:

Listing 13.3   LST13-3.HTM

```
<HTML>
<HEAD>
<META HTTP-EQUIV="Refresh" CONTENT="10">
<TITLE>The Incredible Reloading Document</TITLE>
</HEAD>
<BODY>

The current date and time is: <!--#echo var="DATE_LOCAL"-->

</BODY>
</HTML>
```

Listing 13.3 is a simple document that will reload itself every ten seconds. A server side include inserts the current date and time into the document, which will be updated every time the document is reloaded. If you have a server that supports server side includes, go ahead and try this out. Remember, you will need Netscape Navigator 1.1N, or later, for this to work.

After awhile I'm sure you'll get pretty bored watching your browser continuously reload the same document over and over and you will want it to stop. Yikes! How *do* you turn this thing off? Short of exiting from Netscape, the only way to stop the document from reloading is to go to another document—any other document that doesn't have a "Refresh" header pointing back to this one. Once you tell Netscape to load any other document, the looping will immediately stop.

So far so good. The question now arises: Can I use this mechanism to load a *different* document instead of the original one? Certainly, but the syntax is slightly different. Specifically, you need to add a little extra data to the value of the CONTENT attribute: the destination URL. Here is how you would tell Netscape to load a document at a different URL fifteen seconds after finishing the current document:

```
<META HTTP-EQUIV="Refresh" CONTENT="15; URL=http://www.yahoo.com/">
```

Now look carefully, because this line may seem just a little bit goofy. Is URL a new attribute for <META> and if so, why is it stuck inside the value for CONTENT? The answer is, URL is *not* another attribute for <META>, but instead contains additional information for the "Refresh" header. What you are trying to do is create an HTTP response header that looks like this:

```
Refresh: 15; URL=http://www.yahoo.com/
```

So, "15; URL=http://www.yahoo.com/" is the full value of the CONTENT attribute. Try the example in Listing 13.4 below for a quick example of how this works.

Listing 13.4   LST13-4.HTM

```
<HTML>
<HEAD>
<META HTTP-EQUIV="Refresh" CONTENT="15; URL=http://www.yahoo.com/">
<TITLE>My Super Mega Index of Internet Stuff</TITLE>
</HEAD>
<BODY>

<H1>Super Mega Index of Internet Stuff</H1>
```

```
Due to the popularity of Yahoo, I have decided to remove all trace of
my own Mega Index. Much more information is available at Yahoo.
Go ahead and <A HREF="http://www.yahoo.com">take a look</A> for
yourself!

</BODY>
</HTML>
```

The example shown involves the ex-home of an Internet resource list that has "gone out of business" because of Yahoo's unprecedented thoroughness. A short note is displayed telling the disappointed visitor that the list is no longer here, and to try using Yahoo instead. For users not using Netscape, there is a link to Yahoo's home page, but for Netscape users, Yahoo will *automatically* load in fifteen seconds.

And fifteen seconds after Yahoo loads, Netscape will do...nothing! The "Refresh" header is a one-shot deal. It doesn't say "Keep on reloading this document every fifteen seconds," but "In fifteen seconds, go here" instead. In the previous examples, the original document was reloaded, and since there was a "Refresh" on it, an endless loop resulted. But Yahoo has no such header, so there is no loop. The user is back in control.

Client Pull in CGI

There are two ways in which you can create a CGI script that uses client pull. Obviously one method is to have your CGI script emit an appropriate <META> element along with the rest of its HTML output. But what if your CGI script is not outputting HTML? Remember, with a CGI script you have full control over the type of document served, from HTML to plain text and even graphics or audio, simply by changing the value of the "Content-type" header. The <META> element is only valid in an HTML document since it is, after all, an HTML element. What then?

The second solution is easy to see once you've made the connection between what the "Content-type" header is, and the HTTP response header. The truth is, when your script outputs the "Content-type" header it is actually sending part of an HTTP response header, and there is nothing to stop your script from sending other parts of the header as well, including a "Refresh."

Listing 13.5   LST13-5.PL

```perl
#!/usr/local/bin/perl

print "Content-type: text/html\n";
print "Refresh: 30; URL=http://www.yahoo.com/\n\n";

print "<HTML>\n";
print "<HEAD>\n";
print "<TITLE>I Am A Client Pull CGI Script</TITLE>\n";
print "</HEAD>\n";
print "<BODY>\n";
print "<P>I am a client pull CGI script. I will redirect your browser\n";
print "to Yahoo in thirty seconds.\n";
print "</BODY>\n";
print "</HTML>\n";
```

Listing 13.5 is a simple CGI script in Perl that employs client push to redirect your browser to Yahoo in 30 seconds. There are only two things I'd like to point out. One, notice that there is only *one* newline after "Content-type." If I were to put two, the browser would think that the header ended there and would interpret the second line, the "Refresh," as part of your HTML document. Not very refreshing. The second thing to notice is that there *are* two newlines after the "Refresh," so that the browser knows the header ends there. Got it? Incidentally, you could have put the "Refresh" before the "Content-type" if you had wanted to, since the HTTP draft says that the order does not matter, but always remember that the last line in the header must have two newlines: One to end the line, and the other to insert a blank line between the header and the document itself.

If you are doing client pull in a CGI script, it just makes more sense to put the "Refresh" in by hand, instead of using <META>. Remember, <META> is a way of tricking the browser into thinking that it received an HTTP response header when it didn't. Why trick the browser when you have the power to simply add the "Refresh" by hand and bypass <META> altogether?

Things Not To Do With Client Pull

I know I'm beginning to sound like a broken record, but please don't use client pull, or any of the Mozilla Extensions for that matter, "just because you can." Like a hammer, client pull is a tool. If you need to drive in a nail, by all means use it. But if you're just pounding away at nothing in particular, at the very least you're going to annoy your neighbors. In other words, use client pull if you have a task for which client pull is suitable. Here is a list of some all-too-common uses of client pull that just irritate me no end:

- Loading a series of pages, one after the other, every second or two, each of which contains a single word: "Thank"... "You"... "For"... "Visiting"... "My"... "Home"... "Page!"... It is only cute once, which is the maximum number of times I'll visit a place that does this!

- A series of two or three pages are set in an endless loop, each displaying a silly message similar to the one above: "You were just at XYZ's Home Page!"... "Thank you! Come back again!"... "You were just at XYZ's Home Page!"... Thank you! Come back again!"... Trust me, I won't.

- A two or three page "slide show" that you have to go through to get to the home page proper. The difference between this and the previous two "pet peeves" is that the other two are usually displayed *after* the home page is loaded. This one comes before: "You're about to enter"... (5 second pause) "The XYZ Home Page!"... (5 second pause) "Enjoy your visit!"... (5 second pause and finally the home page) Unless you're giving away free money, I'll probably quit and go somewhere else before even reaching your home page.

  On the other hand, I do have a few recommendations for ways of making your client pull documents a little more polite.

- On every client pull page, give the user a link he or she can use to get "straight to the punchline;" in other words, back to your real home page.

- Whenever possible, warn the user that this page will reload itself/fetch a new URL in X seconds.

- Use client pull where most appropriate—for example, fetching new stock quotes every thirty seconds, updating "gaming" scores every few minutes, etc.

- I like "show off" documents, which implement these techniques in new and unusual ways. *Once.* If you want to show off, do so in a separate document that the user visits under the pretense that this is "neat and new," *not* on the necessary path to your home page.

Server Push

Server push is the companion feature to client pull. Like client pull, additional information can be sent to the browser, beyond the initial document. But whereas client pull relies on the browser actively loading a new document, server push is used to force the server to "push" new documents to the browser as they become available. On the surface, this may seem like mere semantics, but soon you will discover that the differences are more than superficial. First a little review on MIME.

Oh No! More MIME!

Way back in Chapter 9, I spoke very briefly of MIME, and how it relates to HTTP. It's time to pull all the pieces together. The HTTP protocol uses the conventions set forth in the MIME specification to describe the documents that the server sends to the browser, and the queries that the browser sends to the server. MIME's relationship to HTTP is similar to SGML's relationship to HTML. MIME is a set of guidelines for describing the content of an arbitrary "message," and HTTP is designed to follow those guidelines when sending a message from a Web server to a Web browser, or vice versa. So, in essence, an HTTP response header is really a MIME header insofar as HTTP uses MIME as the basis for forming its headers.

A "message" is a little different from a "document." Usually, it refers to just the header and the single document you are sending. However, and this is an important point, one of MIME's strongest features is the ability to send *multiple* documents within a single message. It is this feature of MIME that Netscape exploits, and it is the basis for server push.

The special MIME content-type "multipart/mixed" is used to tell the browser that what follows is a message containing multiple documents, which may be of many different types. In other words, the server will be sending more than one document, one of which may be an HTML document, another plaintext, maybe another a GIF image, and so on. On the same line as the content-type, the server defines the "boundary" used to separate the documents. The boundary is just a random text string that will be inserted between each document, so the browser knows where one document ends and another begins.

Listing13.6   LST13-6.TXT

```
Content-type: multipart/mixed;boundary=IAmTheBoundary

--IAmTheBoundary
Content-type: text/plain

I am the first document!

--IAmTheBoundary
Content-type: text/plain

I am the second document!

--IAmTheBoundary--
```

Listing 13.6 is a simple multipart MIME message. The first line is the content-type, which describes the entire message. This example of a multipart message could have several different document types mixed together in one message. The boundary string that will separate each document is set to the phrase "IAmTheBoundary." Just as we have been doing all along for our CGI scripts, the next line is blank, which means that the header is finished and the rest of the message may begin.

On a line by itself, preceded by two dashes, is our first boundary. It is an important distinction to note that boundaries mark the *start* of a new document, not the end. Notice a content-type specifier in the middle of Listing 13.6. Since there can be many different document types in a single MIME message, you must specify a new content-type directly beneath each boundary. Skip a line, and the first document begins.

Every time you reach a new boundary, the previous document ends and a new document begins. The content-type for the new document is specified, a line is skipped, and the new document begins. Eventually, your message will run out of documents, in which case one final boundary is given, this time with two dashes before *and* after. You're done.

Applying Multipart MIME Messages to Server Push

Server push uses the MIME multipart message technique to send any number of documents, of any type, to the browser. Before you run off thinking "Oh, that looks easy!" and try implementing your own server push scripts, read through this section completely. Server push has a few quirks, as you will see shortly. Like client pull, Netscape 1.1N is the only browser that can handle this technique right now, but it is expected that more browsers will support it soon.

The MIME type "multipart/mixed" was intended to allow several documents of potentially different types to be sent in one message. You know, all that "multimedia email" hype: the text, a sixty-second audio recording, a moving picture of the sender as he "speaks" the message, and so on. Each document contributes to the message as a whole, and when extracted from the message and "played/displayed," you have a complete message. Server push has a slightly different philosophy. Each document stands on its own. When a new document is extracted from the message, that document is meant to *replace* the previous document, not be displayed in addition to it. In other words, when the first document is pushed to the browser, it is displayed. When the next document is pushed to the browser, the old document is discarded and the new one takes its place.

Netscape felt this difference required a new MIME type, similar to "multipart/mixed" but more specific to the "display, discard, and replace" method. The new type is "multipart/x-mixed-replace." The "x" reflects that this is an experimental MIME type, "mixed" is because documents of all different types may be mixed into the same message, and "replace" because this is what each new document extracted from the message does to the last one—replaces it.

How Not to Write a Server Push Script

By now you're probably getting a bit impatient and just want to dive in. But before I show you how to write a server push script, I'd like to show you how *not* to write one.

Listing 13.7   LST13-7.PL

```perl
#!/usr/local/bin/perl

# Tell Netscape that this is a server push script and I will be
# separating my document's with the boundary "ThisIsMyBoundary"
# Don't forget the second newline!

print "Content-type: multipart/x-mixed-replace;boundary=ThisIsMyBoundary\n\n";

# I am starting the first document so here is the first boundary
```

```
# Only one newline

print "--ThisIsMyBoundary\n";

# Now declare the content-type of the first document. Once again, don't
# forget the second newline!

print "Content-type: text/html\n\n";

print "<H1>Document One</H1>\n";
print "This is my first document. It will be replaced with another in\n";
print "just a few seconds.\n\n";

# OK. The first document is done. Start the second document.

print "--ThisIsMyBoundary\n";

# Go to sleep for five seconds, so the next document doesn't replace
# the first document too fast! Sleep AFTER displaying the boundary,
# or the first document won't be displayed correctly.

sleep(5);

print "Content-type: text/html\n\n";

print "<H1>Document Two</H1>\n";
print "This is my second document. I'm done.\n\n";

# OK. We're done.

print "--ThisIsMyBoundary--\n";
```

Listing 13.7 was my first attempt at a server push script, complete with extensive comments. Don't bother typing it in—it doesn't actually work, although according to the documentation at Netscape's home page it should. I'd like to go through it with you line by line anyway, because I intend on building on this script shortly so that it *does* work. The key to understanding why server push is done the way it is lies in understanding why it doesn't work the way you would *think* it should.

The script starts off innocently enough:

```
print "Content-type: multipart/x-mixed-replace;boundary=ThisIsMyBoundary\n\n";
```

This is the first thing your script should output, just as a normal CGI script outputs something like "Content-type: text/html." In this case, I've told the browser that this is a server push script and the boundary between documents will be "ThisIsMyBoundary." There is nothing magical about what you set the boundary to. It should be one continuous word, or some sort of random string. I could have used "XyZzY123AbC" had I wanted to. The most important thing is that this string won't appear somewhere in the midst of one of your actual documents; otherwise, the browser will get confused. You also want to make sure there are no spaces in your content-type, except after the first colon, or some servers (NCSA httpd in particular) won't send any part of the content-type after the extra space. Also, don't forget that you need *two* newlines. One ends the line, and the other adds a blank line.

The next thing your script should print is the first boundary—that is, the string you specified earlier plus two dashes before it. This tells the browser that the first document is about to begin.

```
print "--ThisIsMyBoundary\n";
```

Don't add any spaces between the dashes and your boundary string. End the line with a *single* newline.

Now comes the content-type for the first document:

```
print "Content-type: text/html\n\n";
```

Remember, since the *entire message's* content-type is "multipart/x-mixed-replace," you can have many different types of documents inside the message. Each individual document in the message needs its own content-type, or the browser won't know what kind of document it is. Don't forget, you will need two newlines here.

Now you can start with the actual document:

```
print "<H1>Document One</H1>\n";
print "This is my first document. It will be replaced with another in\n";
print "just a few seconds.\n\n";
```

The last line in your document outputs two newlines. I like to have a blank line between the document and the next boundary.

Since this document is done and you need to start the next one, you must output a new boundary, just like before. But this time I tell the script to "sleep" for five seconds before going on:

```
print "--ThisIsMyBoundary\n";
sleep(5);
```

If I don't do this, both documents would flash up on the screen, one after the other, the second replacing the first so fast you would only see it for a fraction of a second. I sleep *after* printing the next document's boundary. This is important, because if you don't output the boundary before telling the script to pause for a few seconds, the browser won't know that the first document is over and won't display *anything*. But after the five seconds are up, the boundary would be displayed, the browser would end the document, and then the next document would immediately be displayed. This defeats the whole purpose of sleeping in the first place. Worse, it would be five seconds before even the first document was displayed.

After the script is done sleeping, the next document's content-type is immediately sent, followed by the second document. Seeing this second document, the browser will immediately replace the first document, showing this one in its place:

```
print "Content-type: text/html\n\n";
print "<H1>Document Two</H1>\n";
print "This is my second document. I'm done.\n\n";
```

Finally, the last boundary is displayed to end the message. Note the two dashes at the end, as well as the beginning of this boundary. That tells the browser you're done:

```
print "--ThisIsMyBoundary--\n";
```

Actually, this last line isn't really necessary. If you leave it out, the browser will end the message when the script is finished anyway.

Ok. All of this *should* work, but it doesn't. (At least not very well.) It turns out that a little detail called *I/O buffering* is fouling the whole thing up. I/O (Input/Output) buffering is a method used to speed up communications between your computer and another device, such as your hard drive, by storing (buffering) away a large group of characters and, when you have enough, sending them in large batches. Sending or reading a group of characters is a lot more efficient than doing it one character at a time. This is particularly true of reading or writing to a network connection. And this buffering is what is hurting us.

If you ran the script in Listing 13.7, it would pause for five seconds, and then the browser would receive both documents one after the other in rapid succession, the second document overwriting the first almost instantly. What is happening is that when your script sends its output to your server, the data is automatically *buffered* until enough is accumulated to send in a nice big chunk. The script never even comes close to filling up the buffer, so nothing is actually sent to your server until the script is finished.

The solution? Force your script to *flush* the contents of the buffer to the server after each document. In other words, you need to tell your script to send whatever is currently in the buffer onto its final destination even though the buffer isn't full yet. This is called *flushing* the buffer. Listing 13.8 shows the modified script. I removed some of the old comments and added a few new ones to save space.

Listing 13.8   LST13-8.PL

```perl
#!/usr/local/bin/perl

# Tell Perl that you want to use the following Perl library, which can be found in the
# standard Perl distribution.

require "flush.pl";

print "Content-type: multipart/x-mixed-replace;boundary=ThisIsMyBoundary\n\n";

print "--ThisIsMyBoundary\n";
print "Content-type: text/html\n\n";

print "<H1>Document One</H1>\n";
print "This is my first document. It will be replaced with another in\n";
print "just a few seconds.\n\n";

print "--ThisIsMyBoundary\n";

# I know the buffer isn't full yet, but send it on its way anyway!

&flush(STDOUT);

# Now that the data I just sent to the buffer is on its way to the
# server (where it is then processed and sent to the browser) I can
# sleep.

sleep(5);
```

```
print "Content-type: text/html\n\n";

print "<H1>Document Two</H1>\n";
print "This is my second document. I'm done.\n\n";

print "--ThisIsMyBoundary--\n";
```

Listing 13.8 only adds two new lines, and a couple of comments. The command that allows you to flush your buffers is not built into the Perl language itself. Instead, it's found in a separate file called a *library*. Before you can use the flush command, you must first tell Perl where the library can be found:

```
require "flush.pl";
```

When Perl sees this line, it hunts down the library called FLUSH.PL and slurps it into your program. Now you can use the flush command. The FLUSH.PL library is included in the standard Perl distribution and if Perl is installed properly on your machine, your script won't have any problem finding the library.

From this point on, the script works the same as before, until it runs into my second addition, the command to flush the buffers:

```
print "--ThisIsMyBoundary\n";
&flush(STDOUT);
sleep(5);
```

Right after you output your second boundary, which indicates that a new document is about to begin, and just before you go to sleep, the command is issued to flush the buffers. More specifically, the buffer is flushed for standard output, which is where all the data destined for your server is sitting. Once this command is received, the buffer is flushed and everything you just output is sent to your server for processing, where it is then forwarded to the browser.

Once the browser receives the first document, and the boundary to tell it that a new document is on the way so it had better display the first document *right now*, your document is displayed and the browser starts waiting for the next document. Time to sleep. Five seconds later, your script wakes up and sends the second document. No need to flush again, as the buffers automatically flush when your script finishes. The browser receives the second document, throws away the first, and displays the second one in its place. Life is good.

Or is it? This doesn't seem to work correctly either, and it behaves exactly the same way as it did the first time. What in the world could be wrong? The buffers were flushed at the right times, sending the data you just output straight to the server to be processed and sent on to the browser. Oops! What was that? "The buffers were flushed...*sending the data you just output straight to the server to be processed and sent on to the browser.*" Your output doesn't go straight to the browser. *It has to wait for the server to process it first.*

What Does the Server Have to Do with It?

In previous chapters I have alluded several times that the output from all your CGI scripts goes from the script to the server and then from the server to the browser, with vague mention of some sort of "processing" that is done somewhere along the way. It's time to shed some light on this mystery, as the solution to our dilemma lies here.

A little earlier in this chapter, I rambled on at some length about HTTP response headers, and how the "Content-type" line we're forced to send before anything else in our CGI scripts is really part of the HTTP response header, which is sent to the user's browser with the rest of your document. What I didn't make clear was that the output from your script, content-type and all, is sent to your server *first*, and that some additional headers are also added to your script's output. Only after this extra information is prepended to your output are the results sent, by the server and *not* your script, to the user's browser. This is the *processing* I've been talking about. Listing 13-9 is a sample of the type of data that the server adds.

Listing 13.9 LST13-9.TXT

```
HTTP/1.0 200 Document follows
MIME-Version: 1.0
Server: CERN/3.0pre6
Date: Tuesday, 20-Jun-95 09:20:24 GMT
Content-Type: text/html
Content-Length: 1505
```

This is an actual HTTP response header, sent in reply to a query I made to one of my own CGI scripts. I chopped off the rest of the reply (the document it returned) for brevity's sake. The only part of this HTTP response header that my CGI script actually generated is the "Content-type: text/html" line. The rest of the header was generated by the server. CGI is designed to shield you from all this extra work; all you need to provide is the one piece of information that the server cannot guess, which is the content-type of your document. All the rest the server figures out for you.

I'm sure you can see the problem, now that you know what's really going on. For example, take a look at the "Content-Length" header. The only way the server knows the actual content length is by counting the number of characters in your document, after it has received *all* of your script's output. That's a fundamental flaw with the server push model right there! Server push is explicitly designed so that you can send many documents in one message, as they become available, without the browser having to wait for all of them to be received before displaying them. But the server has to receive the entire message first, before it can form a proper HTTP response header. Yikes! Thankfully, there is a solution for this problem as well.

No-Parse-Header (NPH) Scripts— Bypassing the Server

Now that I've crisply described the problem, the solution is clear. The only way that you will be able to make server push work is, ironically, to take the server out of the loop. Not completely, of course—the server is still needed to relay the output from your server push script to the browser, but you have to stop the server from trying to process your script's output. Your script should create its output, hand it to the server, and the server should immediately hand it off to the browser. This *is* possible, but it requires a special kind of CGI script, called a *No-Parse-Header (NPH)* script.

An NPH script is really just a fancy name for a CGI script that generates output that the server passes directly to the browser, without the server trying to parse the header information present in the script output. On the upside, this now takes the server mostly out of the loop. Everything your script outputs is passed on to the browser without question or delay. The downside is that your script is now responsible for creating the full HTTP response headers itself.

It turns out that, thanks to the flexibility built into the HTTP protocol, this isn't as difficult as it sounds. I mentioned earlier, while chatting about client pull and HTTP, that almost all of the headers are optional. Some of them, like the date and content-length, are nice to have, but if they are missing the browser will just have to deal with it and usually can without disruption. As a matter of fact, there is only one additional piece of the response header you absolutely *must* have for an NPH script to generate a valid header, in addition to the content-type. It is that very first line in Listing 13.9, "HTTP/1.0 200 Document follows." The first part, "HTTP/1.0" identifies the following message as conforming to the HTTP 1.0 protocol, and the "200" is a special code that tells the browser that the status of its request is "Life is great, here is your requested document!" Strictly speaking, you can even leave out the "Document follows" part. It is only there to translate the numeric 200 code into something human readable so that nosy people like me who like to watch HTTP transactions in progress don't have to remember what those cryptic numbers mean.

Turning a CGI Script into an NPH Script

There are two steps involved in transforming a normal CGI script into an NPH script: Informing the server that the script is in fact an NPH script, and generating a full HTTP response header. As luck would have it, both are easy.

The server recognizes an NPH script by how the script is named. If the script's file name begins with "NPH-" it is treated as an NPH script. For example, a script named "NPH-DOIT.PL" will be treated as an NPH script, because its name begins with the "NPH-" prefix. Why a prefix and not a suffix like ".NPH"? If there is a reason, I am not aware of it. Traditionally, this is just the way it is done. It may be possible that your server recognizes NPH scripts in some other way, so if your NPH scripts don't seem to be recgnized as such, you may want to double check your server's documentation under "NPH" or "No-Parse-Headers." As far as I am aware, however, naming your NPH scripts using the "NPH-" prefix is generally the standard.

The second step in NPH-izing a CGI script is to output a complete HTTP response header, instead of just the content-type. The absolute simplest HTTP response header you can get away with is shown in Listing 13.10, and this is as far as I would like to go right now, since it is all you really need for server push to work.

Listing 13.10   NPH-1310.PL

```
#!/usr/local/bin/perl

print "HTTP/1.0 200\n";
print "Content-type: text/html\n\n";
```

```
print "<H1>An NPH Script!</H1>\n";
print "I am an NPH script. Exciting, isn't it?\n";
```

This is undoubtedly the simplest NPH script you will ever see. The only difference between the NPH script in Listing 13.10 and a normal CGI script is that the NPH script is outputting the line "HTTP/1.0 200" immediately before the content-type, so that the browser knows what's going on. There is nothing else to it. It would be nice to add a few extra headers in there, like the name of the server, the date, the content-length, etc. But you don't *need* to—so don't worry about it. Perhaps later on, as your scripts become more advanced, you'll want to add those headers in, but by the time you get to that point, all this will seem second nature. If you know you need to do it, you'll know how to do it.

And that, in a nutshell, is the No-Parse-Header script. Let's turn your server push script into an NPH script and see what happens.

Implementing an Effective Server Push Script

It seems that all I need to do now is rename the script to begin with the "NPH-" prefix so that the server knows not to bother parsing the header, and add that one little "HTTP/1.0 200" line above the first content-type. That done, the task is finished. To test it, I just call it like any other CGI script directly from my browser's "go to URL" option. Of course, you can also call it in an anchor or as the action in a form:

```
<A HREF="/cgi-bin/nph-doit.pl">My NPH Script</A>
```

Now comes the moment of truth. Immediately, the first document pops into the browser. If you look at the progress indicator, you'll notice that it keeps moving as the script sleeps. Remember, the HTTP connection is still open, and the browser knows that something should be "coming down the pipe" any second now. Five seconds later, the hard drive clatters briefly, and...the second document is loaded, replacing the first. Netscape proudly announces that the document is finished loading. Success! I'll spare you the screen shots this time. They aren't very exciting and it is impossible to demonstrate this dynamic behavior on a static printed page. Just try it for yourself.

Listing13.11   NPH-1311.PL

```
#!/usr/local/bin/perl

require "flush.pl";
```

```
print "HTTP/1.0 200\n";
print "Content-type: multipart/x-mixed-replace;boundary=ThisIsMyBoundary\n\n";

print "--ThisIsMyBoundary\n";
print "Content-type: text/html\n\n";

print "<H1>Document One</H1>\n";
print "This is my first document. It will be replaced with another in\n";
print "just a few seconds.\n\n";

print "--ThisIsMyBoundary\n";

&flush(STDOUT);

sleep(5);

print "Content-type: text/html\n\n";

print "<H1>Document Two</H1>\n";
print "This is my second document. I'm done.\n\n";

print "--ThisIsMyBoundary--\n";
```

How Many Documents Can I Send in One Script?

The answer to this question? As many as you want. Or, at least, as many as the user is willing to accept. As long as you keep on sending new documents, the browser will happily accept them. There is no time limit involved (except, of course, the user's patience!) and the only way to stop it is for either the script to stop sending documents by exiting, and thus severing the connection, or for the user to specifically ask the browser to close the connection itself, by clicking on the "stop" button or loading a new URL. You can wait for as much or as little time as you want between sending documents, and you can send as many as the user is willing to receive.

The Drawbacks

The most important drawback to server push is that a connection is held open for as long as your script wants it to be open. This can be a big problem if your machine can only accept a certain number of connections at once. Normally, simultaneous connections are not a problem since a typical HTTP access only takes a few seconds, but if you're holding open the connection with server push—for example, sending a continuous feed of stock quotes—the connection can be open for hours, tying that port to a single user, when over a period of time that one port could serve hundreds or perhaps even thousands of users.

At the same time, one could also argue that keeping the connection open for multiple documents is a good thing, efficiency-wise. The most expensive part of sending a document to a user is opening the connection in the first place. If you know you will be sending multiple documents, keeping the connection open might be preferable to using client pull, where a new connection must be open for each document. After all is said and done, both methods of forcing multiple documents onto the browser, server push and client pull, have benefits and drawbacks. It all comes down to a judgment call as to whether one would be better than the other for any given application.

Server Push and the "Poor Man's Animation"

Remember inline images and the <IMG> element? The SRC attribute accepts the URL of an image, typically a GIF image, which is then displayed on your document. Old news. But think about it for a second: The SRC attribute accepts a URL, *any* URL. The only requirement is that accessing this URL will return an image suitable for displaying inline on your document. Hey, I've been saying all along that "Content-type" specifies what type of document is being sent: HTML, plain text, *an image...* Maybe you can see where I'm leading you? *The URL in an <IMG> tag does not have to point to an actual image file.* There is nothing to stop you from giving <IMG> a URL pointing to a CGI (or NPH) script that outputs an image, instead of text, and it will be displayed by <IMG> just fine, as long as you get the "Content-type" correct and the data you send is in fact a valid image.

What does all this have to do with server push? You will love this: If the URL you hand to an <IMG> tag happens to point to a server push script that sends a series of images, one after the other, *each image will be replaced by each new image sent by the server.* The document itself stays in place; only the images are replaced. Poor man's animation! Obviously, it's not too terribly fast, and if your images are larger than 1 K or so each, most of your users connected through typical dialup modems will see a *very* slow-moving animation, but it is a pretty neat technical demonstration of the machinery behind server push.

I wrote a quick demonstration script, which is presented Listing 13.12. It's a simple animation of an arrow twirling around clockwise: up, right, down, and left. The script is in an endless loop, so the arrow will twirl forever, at least until the user breaks the connection.

Listing 13.12   NPH-1312.PL

```perl
#!/usr/local/bin/perl

require "flush.pl";

print "HTTP/1.0 200\n";
print "Content-type: multipart/x-mixed-replace;boundary=ARandomString\n\n";

print "--ARandomString\n";

while (1) {
        print "Content-type: image/gif\n\n";
        open(IMAGE, "</home/http/icons/a_up.gif");
        while (read(IMAGE, $buf, 1024)) {
                print $buf;
        }
        close (IMAGE);
        print "\n--ARandomString\n";
        &flush(STDOUT);
        sleep(1);

        print "Content-type: image/gif\n\n";
        open(IMAGE, "</home/http/icons/a_right.gif");
        while (read(IMAGE, $buf, 1024)) {
                print $buf;
        }
        close (IMAGE);
        print "\n--ARandomString\n";
        &flush(STDOUT);
        sleep(1);

        print "Content-type: image/gif\n\n";
        open(IMAGE, "</home/http/icons/a_down.gif");
        while (read(IMAGE, $buf, 1024)) {
                print $buf;
        }
        close (IMAGE);
        print "\n--ARandomString\n";
        &flush(STDOUT);
        sleep(1);
```

```
print "Content-type: image/gif\n\n";
open(IMAGE, "</home/http/icons/a_left.gif");
while (read(IMAGE, $buf, 1024)) {
        print $buf;
}
close (IMAGE);
print "\n--ARandomString\n";
&flush(STDOUT);
sleep(1);
}
```

There really isn't much here you haven't already seen. I would like to point out two things, however. Notice the content-type for each document is "image/gif". The browser knows when it sees this that it should prepare for a GIF image. After sending the content-type, the script opens a GIF, reads 1024 bytes of it at a time, and then sends that data to the server. The decision to read only 1024 bytes at a time was arbitrary on my part. The GIFs are pretty small, all under 1024 bytes each. I just picked a "round" number that in many cases would be able to get the entire image at once. If the images were larger than 1024 bytes, this would still work, but would simply take an extra couple of passes to read the whole thing.

After I send an image, the file is closed and I send the boundary, then flush the buffer and sleep for a second before sending the next image. Don't forget to close the file after you're done reading it! If you don't close it, your script will reopen the image over and over again, eventually running out of file handles, with predictably dire consequences. You also don't want to forget to place a newline before the boundary as well as after. If you don't, the boundary won't start on a line of its own, but will be included as part of the image data instead, and the browser won't know when this image ends and the new one begins.

After going through each image, the script starts over, sending each image over and over again, until the user finally gets tired of watching it. And there you have it—real-time (sort of) animation on the Web!

Mozilla Swings!

Background and foreground colors can add a little personality to your documents, and background patterns can spruce things up even more, but they can also render your documents unreadable if used carelessly and without a certain sense for effective graphics design. Also, these features are also only supported by the Netscape Explorer 1.1N for the time being, so people with other browsers will be left out.

Server push and client pull are two far more useful Mozilla contributions to the Web community, but once again, they are Netscape 1.1N specific and won't be available to non-Netscape users of your Web content. As with most advanced features, there is also plenty of potential for abuse. The rule of thumb is to use them if you need them, not simply because you can.

Obviously, Netscape hopes to have its enhancements to Web technology "mainstreamed" and adopted by other technology vendors, and even incorporated into the HTML 3.0 spec, but you must remember that until that happens, using the Mozilla extensions described in this and the previous chapter can at best be ignored by non-Netscape Web browsers, and at worst will scramble your Web presentation beyond usefulness.

So be a pioneer if you want—but watch out for arrows!

14

After Your Documents Are Written

Your job as webmaster doesn't end after your documents are written and your Web server starts accepting connections. If no one knows about your Web server, all your work will be wasted. And even after you've told people where to find all your wonderful documents, your Web server will always be in a state of flux and change. Adding new documents, removing and updating old ones, changing style, layout, and design, and so on—all of these things will happen, and the burden will be on you to do them. Then there are access and error logs to read and analyze, statistics to gather, and user problem reports to answer. You'll need to fix occasional problems, and deal with network and other hardware failures.

Have you thought about legal issues? Copyright problems? Royalties? Digital signatures? Trademarks and servicemarks? Software piracy issues? Local, federal, and international laws relating to the distribution of your information? Credit card fraud? If not, you may want to check with a lawyer or read up on any legal issue you think may even remotely apply to you. The Internet and the World Wide Web have up to this point been largely unpoliced, but as they attract the attention of the world at large, the politicians and busybodies will be close behind. The *last* thing you want is to be a test case for new and unproven Internet laws.

Your job as webmaster is varied and time consuming, and you may end up wearing many hats: a marketing expert, graphics designer, publisher, copy-writer, programmer, quality control expert, systems and network administrator, customer service representative, and more often than I like to think about, data entry clerk. And if you want your Web server to succeed, you must be at least mildly good at *all* of these! Don't let yourself be caught off guard!

Marketing and Promoting Your Web Pages

The webmaster-as-marketing-expert has a two-fold job: promoting your Web server, and promoting your organization. How easy or difficult either of these jobs is depends on a number of things:

- Is your Web server for the needs of your organization, or is it strictly a hobby?

- Does your organization have a marketing department? What is their level of technical expertise?

- How's your budget looking after footing all the expense of simply getting the system up and running?

If all this is a hobby, you can market your Web server as much or as little as you like and accept whatever comes back. But if the installatrion is for an organization, particularly if you are trying to sell something, you will have to pay special attention to marketing your Web server.

There are four basic outlets you can use in promoting your Web server: Internet newsgroups, Internet directories, for-pay Internet marketing groups, and "trading links" with other webmasters. Most of these methods are free, with the obvious exception of "for-pay Internet marketing groups." At the very least, you will want to take advantage of two: Internet newsgroups and registering with an Internet directory.

Internet Newsgroups

Announcing your Web server using Internet newsgroups is free and easy, but it can be the source of some grief if you don't go about things correctly. If your Web server is for an organization, particularly a commercial organization, going about this wrong could be "bad for business" as well. Thankfully, the rules are few and easy: Don't "spam," and avoid marketing copy.

Spamming

Spamming is the worst "crime" anyone can possibly commit on Internet news. The word itself is rumored to have come from the old Monty Python "Spam" skit. Essentially, spamming is the posting of many identical (or very similar) articles to the same or (more often) multiple newsgroups. It is hard to quantify what is meant by "many," but the general consensus is more than twenty-five. I tend to be a little less lenient personally, and think the number should be closer to ten or fifteen. The severity of the "crime" is even worse if your article is posted to a newsgroup for an unrelated topic. For example, announcing a Web server about motorcycle repair on a *rec.pets.cats* would be considered off-topic. Do that to eight or ten other off-topic newsgroups, and people are going to start thinking "Spam" when they see your name.

The "punishment" for spamming varies, depending on the severity of your "spam," however it usually involves receiving lots of hate mail, "email bombs" (hundreds or thousands of copies of your article or any large file sent straight back into your mailbox), and complaints to your ISP. Hate mail can be unsettling but ignored, however email bombs can render your own mailbox unusable, and maybe even "break" your company or organization's mail system. A complaint to your ISP could result in a suspension, or cancellation, of your Internet access!

Spamming will almost certainly result in alienating your customer base if you are a commercial organization, especially one trying to sell a product over the Internet. At the very least, it will definitely not get you any new customers or visitors to your Web server.

So be careful where you post any sort of announcement. Do your best to tie any kind of announcement to the newsgroup topic. And in any event, keep the nature of the announcement reasonably low-key. Which brings us to...

Marketing Copy
Traditionally, the Internet has been considered a non-commercial entity. This is changing, but many people, Internet old-timers in particular, are still very resentful of any commercial presence on the Internet. This stems from the old days when the Internet was very much fueled by government funds and was the exclusive turf of researchers, academics, and government types. The government funding is now gone, for the most part, and the old legalities about commercial copy have evaporated. Still, any sort of commercial advertisement is going to get under some people's skin, and there is nothing you can do to avoid it. However, even for people who don't mind the commercial presence on the Internet, *nobody* likes to run

into "commercials" while reading their favorite newsgroups. Your company's history, a complete product catalog, and forty pages of marketing copy won't cost you a cent to send, but is definitely going to irritate a lot of people.

"Marketing copy" is a pretty broad term, and tough to define crisply. Definitely avoid what most people would point to and say, "Ad copy." The idea is to sound like you're pointing to a resource that some readers of the newsgroup would find useful. Don't try to pump up enthusiasm by describing how great your Web site is. Stick to describing it in ordinary, objective terms. Don't go on at length. Don't use superlatives. Above all, don't run down anyone or anything, especially an entity perceivable as your competition.

Keep the whole thing to ten or fifteen lines, tops. Such a self-imposed limitation is excellent discipline, and good practice in keeping your ego down to size. Never forget this: *What you're doing is pointing the way, not selling a product!*

Where and How to Post

The first place you should post your product announcement is in *comp.infosystems.www.announce*, a moderated newsgroup specifically for this purpose. Before you post, be sure to read the FAQ (Frequently Asked Questions) file describing how your message should be formatted and what sorts of posts are accepted. The FAQ can be found at *http://www.halcyon.com/grant/charter.html*.

After posting to the *comp.infosystems.www.announce* newsgroup, you may also want to announce your new Web server in any newsgroups that *directly* (read that word again!) relate to the topic of your Web server. In other words, if your Web server is on the joys of being a cat owner, you may post an announcement to *rec.pets.cats* with a clear conscience. Before doing so, however, it might be worth your time scanning the newsgroup to determine if your announcement is really appropriate there. Do you see other announcements for Web servers? Does the newsgroup's FAQ say anything about being allowed, or not allowed, to post such an announcement? A little research will help ensure that your announcement reaches your intended audience.

Get in a FAQ

Most Internet newsgroups have at least one FAQ, and sometimes several, with pointers to other sources of information related to the newsgroup's topic. Many FAQs now list Web servers that contain information pertaining to the newsgroup. By emailing the maintainer of a FAQ that you think would benefit from listing a pointer to your Web server, you may well be listed as one of the places that the readers of that newsgroup can go to for additional information. It never hurts to ask, and many times the maintainers of these FAQs would be delighted to add a pointer to your Web server, with the belief that the more information their FAQ can offer, the more value the FAQ has to the newsgroup.

Internet Directories

If you're even slightly interested in the Web you're probably familiar with Internet directories like Yahoo and Lycos by now. They're a great ally for the webmaster looking for tips, tools, and information on designing Web documents, and now they'll be a great help in "getting the word out" about your Web server. There are generally two types of these services: Internet directories, which get their information from Web citizens like yourself; and automated Internet indexing services, like Lycos, which get their information from "robots" that wander the Web looking for new information to index. More on these robots later; it's a fascinating subject.

Directories like Yahoo

It is very important that your Web server be listed in as many of these directories as possible. Perhaps the most important is Yahoo, and that is the first place you will want to be registered with. There are also other directories, some of which may specialize in certain categories, which you may want to register with as well. Registering with these directories is almost always free. A list of some of the general directories can be found in Table 14.1.

Automated Indexing Services like Lycos

Eventually, your Web server will probably be discovered by one of these automated indexing services, and even without any intervention from you, your Web server will end up listed. But if you'd like to speed things along, and go to the indexer before the indexer comes to you, most allow you to manually submit an entry. Like directories, being listed should be free, and it is in your best interest to be listed with as many as possible. Being registered with Lycos, one of the most popular indexers, is an absolute must.

Table 14.1　Popular indexing services and directories

Index Or Directory Name	URL	Type
ALIWEB	http://web.nexor.co.uk/public/aliweb/aliweb.html	Gen
BizWeb	http://www.bizweb.com/InfoForm/infoform.html	Bus
Commercial Sites Index	http://www.directory.net/dir/submit.cgi	Bus
EINet Galaxy	http://www.einet.net/cgi-bin/annotate	Gen
Harvest Gatherers	http://rd.cs.colorado.edu/Harvest/brokers/ register-with-CU-gatherers.html	Gen
Internet Mall	http://www.mecklerweb.com/imall/howto.htm	Bus
Internet YellowPages	http://www.yellow.com/cgi-bin/online	Bus
Lycos	http://fuzine.mt.cs.cmu.edu/mlm/lycos-register.html	Gen
Mother-Of-All-BBS	http://www.cs.colorado.edu/homes/mcbryan/ public_html/bb/summary.html	Gen
NCSA's What's-New Page	http://www.ncsa.uiuc.edu/SDG/Software/Mosaic/ Docs/submit-to-whats-new.html	Gen
Nikos	http://www.rns.com/www_index/new_site.html	Gen
Online Whole Internet Catalog	http://nearnet.gnn.com/wic/about.rescat.html	Gen
Otis	http://www.interlog.com/~gordo/otis_index.html	Gen
Submit It!	http://www.cen.uiuc.edu/~banister/submit-it/	*
Webcrawler	http://webcrawler.cs.washington.edu/WebCrawler/ SubmitURLS.html	Gen
White NetPages	http://www.aldea.com/whitepages/addform.html	Gen
WWW Business Yellow Pages	http://www.cba.uh.edu/ylowpges/ypform.html	Bus
Yahoo	http://www.yahoo.com/	Gen

* Submit It! is not an actual index, but a service that allows you to easily register with many different indices and directories, including many of the indices listed above.

For-Pay Internet Marketing

If you would like someone else to do your Web marketing for you, there are quite a few for-pay marketing services springing up, which specialize in promoting Web services. The services they offer range from finding other Web servers, directories, and indices on which to list your Web server, to providing "advertising space" on their own server, and offering advice or advertising campaigns. Prices vary greatly, so shop around and be careful when approached by one of these services. In general, if you feel like you're being ripped off, you probably are.

A special type of service, called *electronic malls* by their promoters, are also becoming very popular now. You are charged some fee to have a "store-front" in their electronic mall, perhaps grouped with other vendors or Web servers offering similar information as yourself. Such a mall is very much like a home page for commercially-oriented home pages. Some Internet people favor them because they "concentrate" commercial activity behind one link, although that's really a specious point if you think about it. Those who rent storefronts in such malls favor them because mall shoppers often linger in the mall and sample other sites, just like the psychology at work in physical shopping malls. This is definitely true, and may be the only significant reason to take part in such a program. Some—but by no means all—electronic malls also offer assistance in setting up and maintaining your Web presence there. These services tend to be expensive, and if you're reading this book you can probably handle such things yourself.

I'm definitely lukewarm about electronic malls, and therefore I haven't gone too far out of my way to list a large number of these services. After all, if you don't run into them all by yourself without any help from me, they aren't doing a very good job, now, are they? However, I have listed some of the more interesting ones below. The list in Table 14.2 is in no way comprehensive, as indicated by a quick search for the keyword "mall" on the WebCrawler Index—which returned *1888* URLs!

Trading Links

The entire basis for the Web is documents linking to other related documents, so it should come as no surprise to find your Web server listed on other people's Web servers. Someone may have found your Web server

Table 14.2 Internet "malls"

Name of Mall	URL
The Branch Mall	http://florist.com:1080/
The Internet Plaza	http://plaza.xor.com/
The Internet Mall	http://www.mecklerweb.com/imall/imall.htm
NetMall	http://www.ais.net:80/netmall/
CommerceNet	http://www.commerce.net/

interesting and decided to place a link to it on their "public hotlist," or maybe someone uses your site in a reference to places where people can find more information on a particular subject. Either way, this is how many of your visitors will find you.

If you find a Web server with information related to what your own Web server provides, you may want to approach its webmaster and point out your Web server to them. Quick, free advertising. But be ready to make a link from your Web server back to theirs; I scratch your back and you scratch mine, if you know what I mean. Try to keep your competitive urges at bay here; the Internet is primarily a collaborative environment.

Working With Your Marketing Department

If your organization has a marketing department, you will want to be sure to interact with them extensively before and after your Web site comes on line. You are their bridge to the Web community; their guide and translator. Keep in constant contact, and make sure that they know what you're doing. Even if your official position is that of system administrator or programmer, your responsibilities as webmaster have cast you head first into the marketing department's domain, and a clear communication channel is essential. If you don't talk to Marketing, you risk miscommunications, misunderstandings, and potential public relations disasters. The last thing you want to hear from your manager is "But that promotion was over *weeks* ago!"

Internet marketing is a brand new discipline, and it is likely that your marketing department knows little if anything about it or the technology that makes it possible. Schedule some time with some of your marketing people at your workstation to show them the Web, what others are doing, and most importantly, what *you* are currently doing. Show them what is possible, and let them know what isn't. Explain why you can't format that flier exactly as they want it. Above all, be patient and open, and never sound condescending or arrogant. You want Marketing to feel as though they can ask you any question, and not get barked at or talked down to. As they learn how things work, you'll get fewer impossible requests and perhaps even some helpful suggestions or comments.

Make sure your marketing department sees every important document or press release that you place on the Web server. The extra proofreading doesn't hurt, and they can point out misunderstandings before you announce a canceled project or withdrawn promotion to all your Internet customers. If people in Marketing have access to a browser and a Net connection, even better. Properly managed, they can even be led to do much of your work for you—and there's always that possibility that they can do certain things (construct sentences, spell, design sales materials) *better* than you can!

Helping Marketing Promote Your Web Server

If your marketing department wants to promote your Web server in some printed form (remember paper?) you will definitely be involved in the process. Questions that seem completely obvious to you, like what is the Web server's URL (or what a URL *is*, for that matter!) and how should it be printed in brochures and fliers, may leave Marketing baffled. Make sure they don't make bizarre or outrageous claims about what your Web server can do. Proper use of the terminology is also a big thing to look out for. Beware of copy such as "Visit our Mosaic!" or "Call us at Httb: / / Www. Somewhere. Comm/!" It's your job to proofread *everything* they generate about your Web site, at least until your marketing department figures out the unwritten conventions of Internet parlance, and how all the technology works.

It may seem at times that people in Marketing are all technology-bankrupt salespeople, but if you look closely you'll often find one or two individuals who are truly sharp and have investigated the Internet on their own—perhaps even to the lengths of surfing the Web and having their own home page with their ISP. Deputize them, and see if you can set up a formal liaison relationship between your department and theirs. Much more will happen, and that which happens will be better, if you have knowledgable allies in Marketing.

Making Sense of Your Logs

Your server software will assiduously log every access to your Web server in a special log file for later analysis. Every document downloaded, every image delivered, every script executed...everything. With this log file, typically named *access_log* or some other equally obvious name, you will be able to generate any report imaginable to satisfy your own curiosity, and the quiet, incessant prodding from whoever put up the money for this project. Marketing will want demographics, management will want proof that customers are actually using it, and you yourself will want the cheap jolt to your self esteem that only a fat log file can generate. It's all in there: when who accessed what from where and how.

The Common Log Format

Most Web server software is capable of storing log file information in a standard format, called the *common log format*. This is of course a good thing, as it makes analyzing the logs quite a bit easier. A common set of tools and report generators can be used on almost any server's log files, many of which are freely available. I'll be spending a little bit of time later talking about one of my favorites, called Getstats, by Kevin Hughes, which works on just about any Unix (or VMS) system, and can analyze the logs from any server using the common log format. But first, here's a quick look what at the common log format is.

The common log format is extremely simple and designed to be easily readable by humans, as well as by report generating programs, such as *getstats*. For every access to your Web server, a single line is added to the log file. If you want to find the number of accesses, or (as we say in Web lingo) *hits* your Web server has received, simply count the number of lines in the log file. The format for each entry in the log file is as follows:

```
hostname identd authuser [date] "request" status length
```

The *hostname* is the name of the machine from which this request was received. If your server could not determine the hostname, its numeric IP address will be used instead. If you have remote user identification enabled, *identd* will contain the login name of the user who accessed this document. If your server is not set to check remote identification, a "-" will appear instead. If your server could not get this information but remote identification *is* enabled, the keyword *unknown* will be used. If your document is protected with file access control, then *authuser* will be the name of the authenticated user. Remember the AUTH_USER environment variable? This is it. If there is no file access control enabled for this document, a "-" will be used. Next is the time and date the connection took place, in the format "DD/MMM/YYYY:HH:MM:SS GGGG" where

"HH" is the hour in military time (00-23) and "GGGG" is the number of time zones away from GMT.

The "request" specifies which method was used to request the document, what document was requested, and the HTTP protocol version. In essence, it is the HTTP "command" used to access the document. For "normal" documents, the method will generally be "GET." If you have any scripts that use the post method, the method will be "POST" instead for those scripts. Following the request method is the HTTP response code (*status*) this access generated. You may recall that I spoke briefly about HTTP response codes. The status "200" means "everything went fine." Occasionally you will see another number here, which may indicate an invalid document, a redirection, or some other error condition. A listing of all these codes can be found in Table 14.3. The last number in the entry record, *length*, is how many bytes were transferred as a result of this access.

Lines from a Sample Log File

Here are a few lines from a typical access log file using the common log format, with descriptions of what each line means. Don't try too hard to memorize the details, however. There are numerous free programs available that will read and analyze your log files for you.

```
user.machine.com - - [21/Jun/1995:21:09:51 -0400] "GET /test.html HTTP/1.0"
200 6431
```

This typical log file entry is from a machine named "user.machine.com." Your server is not doing remote identification and the document does not have access control enabled. The document was retrieved using the "GET" method, which is the standard way any normal document would be accessed. The document's name was "/test.html" and HTTP version 1.0 was used. The status "200" indicates that everything went well, and a total of 6431 bytes were transferred.

```
127.0.0.1 - - [21/Jun/1995:21:10:02 -0400] "POST /cgi-bin/myscript.pl HTTP/
1.0" 200 8753
```

Here, the server couldn't find the name of the accessing machine, so it used the IP address instead. The document that was accessed was really a CGI script called "/cgi-bin/myscript.pl" that used the "POST" method.

```
somewhere.com joe - [21/Jun/1995:22:12:34 -0400] "GET /oops.html HTTP/1.0" 404 -
```

Here, I turned on remote user identification. Now I know that the user named "joe" from "somewhere.com" tried to access a document "/oops.html." This time, the status "404" came back, indicating that the server couldn't find the document. The length is thus a "-", because no document was actually transmitted.

Table 14.3   HTTP response codes

Code	Keyword	Short Description
200	OK	The request was fulfilled.
201	CREATED	Successful POST.
202	ACCEPTED	Request accepted for processing, but processing not completed.
203	PARTIAL INFORMATION	Information returned may not be complete.
204	NO RESPONSE	Don't display any data, and stay in the same document..
301	MOVED	The document requested has moved.
302	FOUND	The document was moved but the server found it (Redirection).
303	METHOD	Go try another URL with this new method instead.
304	NOT MODIFIED	The requested document has not changed since you last saw it.
400	BAD REQUEST	Client gave improper request.
401	UNAUTHORIZED	Client tried to access a protected document without authority.
402	PAYMENTREQUIRED	Client needs to send a suitable "ChargeTo:" header.
403	FORBIDDEN	Document cannot ever be accessed, regardless of authorization.
404	NOT FOUND	Client requested a URL which was not found.
500	INTERNAL ERROR	Server had a melt down.
501	NOT IMPLEMENTED	Server does not implement the feature the client is requesting.
502	SERVICE TEMPORARILY OVERLOADED	Things are awfully busy! Come back later... OK?
503	GATEWAY TIMEOUT	A CGI script or other gateway isn't responding.

Analyzing Your Logs with "getstats"

Scanning through a potentially *huge* log file by hand isn't a very appealing task. Besides being grueling, it is impossible to get a full picture of what is really going on. Do you receive more hits on the weekends or weekdays? What documents are accessed most frequently? Are most of your visitors from commercial or from educational computers? These types of statistics are crucial for determining the direction you should take your Web server, not to mention feedback for the marketing folks. If there are any doubts about the benefit of your Web server, statistics like these will put management at ease. You are not, however, going to impress anyone with a raw log file.

Kevin Hughes' Getstats will run on just about any Unix system (it compiles fine using Linux) and with a little tinkering, I am certain you will be able to convince it to compile on other operating systems as well. There is a version for VMS too. What Getstats will do for you is take any log file in the common log format and produce any of a dozen different reports of your choosing:

- A concise report listing the server's major statistics
- A monthly report
- A weekly report
- A daily summary of accesses, or a more detailed daily report
- An hourly summary, or a more detailed hourly report
- A full report of all accesses
- A report of all the requests made, sorted by type
- A "domain report," analyzing where your hits are coming from
- A "directory tree report," for pinpointing the sections of your Web server that are more popular than others
- A report of any errors your users may have encountered

Getstats has helped me find the "weak" areas of my Web server that are in need of improvement. It has helped confirm when I am doing something right. It has pointed out problems, and even alerted me of problems before they became serious. Marketing loves it. Management loves it. And if Marketing and Management are happy, so am I!

Getstats is freely available from EIT's Web server. If you would like more information about the types of reports it generates, and how to retrieve, compile, and use getstats, go visit *http://www.eit.com/software/getstats/ getstats.html.* Like Mr. Hughes' other programs, Getstats is "no-frills" as far as installation goes, but if you have an ANSI C compiler like gcc, you shouldn't have any problems. Fetch the programs from *ftp://ftp.eit.com/ pub/web.software/getstats/* or their Web site listed above, and compile it. Instructions for modifying and installing the program are available from the Web URL cited above, in the README file at the ftp URL, and in the C source code itself. You shouldn't run into any serious problems. The files you will want to retrieve are as follows:

- **README** Installation information
- **README.vms** If you are using VMS instead of Unix
- **domain.codes.txt** A list of *top level domains* and english descriptions
- **getstats.12.c** The getstats source code, version 1.2

If Getstats doesn't suit you, or if you can't get it to run on your computer, a list of several other popular log file analyzers can be found in Table 14.4. Personally, I find that Getstats offers everything I need in a log file analyzer; however there is no harm in trying out several others until you find which suits your style.

Table 14.4 Log file analyzer utilities

Name	Location	Description
GetStats	http://www.eit.com/software/getstats/getstats.html	Unix/VMS
MacHTTP Logger	http://arpp1.carleton.ca/machttp/doc/util/stats/machttplogger.html	HyperCard
Multi Server WebCharts	http://engelberg.dmu.ac.uk/webtools/mw3s/mw3s.html	Perl
VBStat	http://www.city.net/win-httpd/#vbstat	MS Windows
WAMP	http://rowlf.cc.wwu.edu:8080/~n9146070/wamp.html	Perl
WebStat	http://arpp1.carleton.ca/machttp/doc/util/stats/webstat.html	Mac
wusage	http://siva.cshl.org/wusage.html	Unix/VMS
wwwstat	http://www.ics.uci.edu/WebSoft/wwwstat/	Unix

Back To Reality: The Dazzling Stats Syndrome

After you have announced your Web server to the world and have been running along nicely for a few weeks, you will notice your log file start to swell. It'll happen slowly at first, as word trickles out, but soon, if all goes as planned, you may start seeing some absolutely startling statistics. It's hard to put a finger on the "average" number of hits per month that you should see, but it's not unheard of to get figures like 10,000, 50,000, or even 100,000 hits a month. Some of the largest Web servers claim to serve more than a million hits a month! While that is an unusually high number, reserved for places like Yahoo and the Netscape home page, you personally may see a solid 10,000 or 20,000 hits a month, depending on what type of information you are distributing and what the demand for that information is.

When you start seeing your log files grow to 10,000 or 20,000 hits a month, you're probably going to start feeling pretty good about yourself, and so (with any luck at all) will your management. But what do these figures really *mean*? 20,000 is a pretty big number, but how many people are *really* using your Web server? I can guarantee that it's quite a bit less than 20,000!

Here's why: Let's say a user, we'll call her Tracy, visits your Web server for the first time. She points her browser at your home page, and your server happily sends it her way. Hit number one. But Tracy's Web browser soon discovers that your home page has a masthead, five icons, and a little inline image of your smiling little mug sitting at the bottom of the document, next to your copyright notice. Her browser requests them from your server. Seven more hits. That is eight hits total and Tracy has only visited your home page once. Next, Tracy sees something of interest and selects one of your links. Your server gets her request for the new document, which itself has a small masthead and another three icons. Four more hits. Oops— Tracy's lunch hour is now over and it's back to work for her, and away with Netscape. So for one user who visited only two of your documents, your logs will now record a total of *twelve* hits.

Obviously, the log files are a little misleading, once your realize that a user who is simply "passing through" can generate twelve hits simply by looking at two documents. If all your users were like Tracy, with 20,000 hits you would have only seen around 1667 visitors to your Web server in that month. This is certainly nothing to sneeze at—but it's nowhere near the 20,000 the logs originally implied. Vince Emery summed up the situation very nicely in his book *How to Grow Your Business on the Internet*: "Reality slowly settled in. We sobered up. Hits are misleading."

Hits are misleading. *Very* misleading—but certainly not useless. As a quick gauge of growth, they can't be beat. If you received 2,000 hits in January, 5,000 in February, and 15,000 in March, you may not know precisely how many people are using your Web server, but you certainly know the number is increasing rapidly. A better gauge of success is the number of hits on your home page specifically, *not* including images. A logfile analyzer will be able to give you this information. If you are receiving 10,000 hits a month, but only 250 home page hits, you either have an awful lot of inline images, or your users are sticking around for awhile, exploring your Web server thoroughly. Of course the latter is the better scenario!

What all this means is that it's not the quantity of your hits, but the *quality*. A lot of home page hits and a diverse range of accessed documents is your goal. Speaking of home page hits, these can be misleading too, but in this case they can be an understatement rather than an overstatement of your Web server's popularity. Your home page isn't the only way into your Web server; a user can come in through a link to any of your documents. So even with a rigorous analysis of your log files, at best you will only have an estimate of how many visitors you've really had.

Making Your Statistics Publicly Available

If you are really excited about how much attention your Web server has been getting, you may be tempted to show off by publicizing your Web server's statistics. There is nothing wrong with this in itself, and if you are one of those "Web malls" I talked about earlier, you will want to advertise your statistics to help attract potential new "storefronts." But before you make any of this information available, remember to check with your management first. Some companies feel that this information is proprietary, something which would be harmful in a competitor's hands. I'm not suggesting that this *should* be your organization's attitude towards making logs publicly available. Just warning you to think twice, and ask, before releasing them.

Archiving Your Logs

As your Web server becomes more and more popular, your log files are going to become more and more massive—so massive that you may even run out of space to keep them. Your logs can quickly grow to 10 or 20 megabytes just over a months time. What do you do? If you don't care about your Web server's statistics after you've glanced over them, then just delete them. But I like to keep things around for awhile, particularly anything that can document the growth of my Web server and prove its usefulness to my management, as well as to myself. But if you're like me, you probably don't have a gigabyte or two worth of disk space on which to archive your log files.

After several months of struggling to keep my log files under control, I finally came up with a great solution. First I tried compressing and archiving each month's logs. That quickly became overwhelming. Still reluctant to delete anything, I tried archiving the logs off to tape, which was a serious nuisance—and an ever-growing pile of tapes. Finally, it dawned on me: Don't archive the log files themselves, archive the statistics and reports from the log analyzer!

I use the Getstats program with the "-a" option to create the most complete record of that month's statistics without having to keep the log file itself. If you then compress the report, using any of several popular file compresion utilities, it will take relatively little space; perhaps 50 Kb for a 100,000-hit log.

There Be Robots A'roaming

Eventually, if you check your logs often enough, you will find an entry that may puzzle you. There will be a request for a file named */robots.txt*, which obviously does not exist. Why would anyone request this file, and how do I know that you'll someday see a request for it? The answer to that question lies in a phenomenon few Web users really understand, but all webmasters must become familiar with.

A Web robot is a sort of automated Web browser program that reads Web pages, indexing as it goes. The robot's operator hands the robot program a list of URLs to start with, and turns it loose. The robot starts with the top

URL and starts traversing links, visiting Web sites and logging each document, its title, and in some cases (like Web Crawler) a keyword index of its entire contents. The resulting index is then made available to users of the Web, to help people navigate through the global tangle that the Web has become. Most robots don't simply visit the lists of URLs that they start with; they also travel links encountered in Web pages to discover other pages, and so on. So a Web robot may visit your Web site even if you have no idea what a Web robot is, because some other Web site known to a Web robot contains a pointer to yours.

The Web robot issue is slightly controversial, because there is some necessary duplication of access that some people view as a waste of bandwidth. But because the service they provide is so valuable and necessary, few have gotten worked up about it, and a consensus policy (which I'll return to shortly) on robot operation is emerging to address potential problems. One of these is that sometimes Web robots can end up someplace where you don't want them, like a directory containing temporary documents or a CGI script that might "trap" the robot, causing it to continually access your Web server without getting anywhere.

That's where this consensus policy on robot operation comes in. To prevent robot problems, you can create a special file called */robot.txt,* which contains instructions on what documents or directories robots are allowed to access, and which ones they should stay out of. Before a robot tries to access your Web server, it will check and see if this file exists. If it doesn't, it will happily index away, but if it does exist and the instructions tell it to go away, it will. (Or at least it should—depending on whether its creator is aware of emerging robot standards.) For more details on how to create this special */robot.txt* file, and what to put in it if you want one, go to *http://web.nexor.co.uk/mak/doc/robots/norobots.html.* All your questions will be answered there.

General Web Server Maintenance

Your job isn't finished after you've gathered together all your documents and have your Web server running nice and smoothly. If you want things to continue running smoothly, you will have to spend some time maintaining your Web server. Maintenance usually means adding new documents as they become available, removing or replacing old documents with updated information, and correcting errors like typos, spelling, and obsolescence. (Your January sale notice should probably be pulled from your server before June.) You may also need to write new CGI scripts and update old or broken scripts. At some point you may decide to redesign or reorganize your documents. Periodical publications like magazines are redesigned every so often. Web sites should work the same way.

Maintenance also means double checking that all your links work. Sometimes you may move a document and forget to change any links to it from other documents, or you may have links to documents on other people's servers which may move or change without your knowledge. Nothing is more frustrating for a user than to stumble across a link that seems like it should lead to exactly what you are looking for, but ends up being broken and returning an error. And even if the target of the link was at fault for stealing away in the night, it's *your* Web site, which contains the bad pointer, that will usually be handed the blame. Table 14.5 lists a few utilities to help determine if your server's links are at least internally consistent.

Other maintenance issues include checking, archiving, and removing log files, monitoring the load on your Web server for possible network connection or hardware upgrades, and making sure your Web server hasn't crashed or locked up and is still serving requests from the outside. All this can be an awful lot of work, particularly if you're trying to maintain a very large Web server, but it is absolutely essential. Lack of maintenance can lead to your Web server's sudden death, as documents become out of date, links are broken, and software or hardware fails to work properly.

Robert's Eight Rules of Web Server Maintenance

I've distilled what I have learned about Web server maintenance down to eight useful rules, in the hope that your eyes won't glaze over completely when confronting this necessary issue.

Table 14.5   Tools to verify your Web server's links

Name	Location	Description
<htmlchek>	http://uts.cc.utexas.edu/~churchh/htmlchek.html	Perl
lvrfy	http://www.cs.dartmouth.edu/~crow/lvrfy.html	Unix

- **Always check your links.** Links to documents on your own server should be checked whenever you move or delete a document. Links to documents on other people's servers should be checked at least weekly. This doesn't mean reading what's at the other end of all those links. Just make sure that they work.

- **Check your CGI scripts periodically.** Configuration files become corrupted. Data files are sometimes moved or deleted inadvertently. Any number of things can go wrong. For example, I just "fixed" a script on my own server that had been broken for at least a week, but had been working for months previously.

- **Update stale information.** Don't let the information in your documents go stale. Old price lists, catalogs, and promotions will cause friction between you and your customers. Outdated technical papers or research can frustrate researchers. Always date documents that contain time-sensitive information. If the only information available is stale, at least place a time stamp and warning on the document so people can place it in its proper "historical" context.

- **Don't move important documents without dire need.** Moving important documents can frustrate your users and other webmasters who may have links directly to that information without passing through your home page first. See Rule #1! If you must move your documents, put a document in its prior place warning of the change and providing a link to the new location for at least a month, and longer if possible.

- **Check your server for proper operation.** At least once a day you should check your server software to make sure it's running properly. Like all software, your server can crash or lock up, denying all users access to your documents. Experienced users familiar with your site will likely try again later, but new users may get the wrong impression and never come back.

- **Check your network's connectivity.** Networks go down and network equipment can fail, locking users out of your server. Checking from the same workstation that runs your server won't catch this problem. You have to either try to access your server from outside your own network, or try contacting someone else's server from yours, by way of the network in question. I very recently had this problem with my own server, and it would have been down for an entire weekend if I hadn't checked our network that Saturday morning. **Corollary:** Always have a backup plan if your network does go down due to equipment failure. A spare 28.8 K modem can act as a temporary fix until new equipment is purchased.

- **Keep an eye on network and server response time.** As your Web server attracts more and more hits, your network will become more and more loaded. Your server's hardware may also suffer lags and slowdowns, particularly if you use the equipment for other things such as your organization's email gateway or Usenet news processing. Check from outside your own network, or ask a friend not on your network to check. I have several accounts on the Internet for this purpose alone. If things seem sluggish, you may want to consider upgrading your network connection or hardware.

- **Don't forget your log files.** Archive, compress, or delete your log files when they start getting too large. Logs can grow out of hand very rapidly and can fill up your disk space, dragging your machine to its knees or even locking it up.

Dealing with Problem Reports and Suggestions

You will have problems. Rarely will things completely melt down, but little problems here and there are an inescapable fact of webmastering. In spite of your vigilance, a broken link will slip through the cracks, a CGI script will temporarily stop working for some mysterious reason, or someone at a distant ISP back room will spill a cup of coffee on a router, cutting off a major chunk of the Internet for an hour or two. Some of these things you can control and fix, and others are simply beyond your control. But you can rest assured that your users will point out any little thing that goes wrong, and how you deal with these problem reports is the real defining factor of yourself as a webmaster. This is a question of "customer service," and as with everything in life, how you react to criticism is the real definition of success or failure.

Your users are your life's blood, and their comments are definitely gold. The user who takes a moment of precious time to inform you of a problem, make a complaint, or give a suggestion, is a rare and special treasure. It is a sign that they care, and are interested in your service and concerned about your Web server's well-being. Even a complaint that sounds angry or belligerent should be treated as you would a compliment: with gratitude. They wouldn't write at all if they didn't care. They would simply go away. These are your best users, and the ones you should be most concerned with making happy.

I reply to every letter I receive, good or bad, compliment or complaint, suggestion or criticism. I may not be able to respond immediately, but eventually I will respond, either with a thank you or an explanation. This is important. It tells your users that you care about what they have to say just as much as they care about your Web server.

Solutions to Common Problem Reports

In this section I'll present five common problem reports that you may receive, along with some possible solutions. It should go without saying that you should attempt to track down and fix any problems that are reported to you. If you can't find the problem in a day or two, write the user back and ask for more specific details, and perhaps even a screen shot of the strange behavior in question. If you can't reproduce the problem, try using the same browser they use. If that doesn't help, ask them to try again; it may have been a temporary glitch. I *hate* those, but we all must expect to run into them. The Internet is still an inexact science.

1. **Your Web server is responding very slowly.** Of course the obvious conclusion is that either your Web server's machine is overloaded, or more likely your network connection can't handle all the traffic. But there may be a few other less obvious reasons:

   • **Temporary Internet problems.** The path from their computer to yours may be overloaded or down. There's nothing you can do about this except wait it out and try again later. This type of problem is a fact of life on the Internet.

   • **DNS lookups.** DNS stands for Domain Name Server, and it is the mechanism used to convert a domain name like *host.somewhere.com* into an IP address like 127.0.0.1 and vice versa. Occasionally this system can break down, causing huge delays. You may have noticed it yourself while browsing, and not even know it. If you have ever tried to go somewhere but your browser just seemed to hang there forever "transferring data," this may be a DNS problem. The Web server at the other end of the link is trying to figure out who the heck you are, and it won't fill your request until it finds out. Fortunately, better and better Web servers are being designed all the time, and this may not be a problem on your particular server. The fix? Since DNS lookups are really only used by your Web server for logging, you may be able to disable them. On both CERN and NCSA httpd you can specify the "-nodns" flag on the command line, when you launch the server. Your log files will be filled with IP addresses instead of domain names, but your users shouldn't have a problem getting through anymore.

2. **Your documents look ugly.** This may seem like something that is purely subjective, but in reality they may be right. Did you specify invalid HTML, which *your* browser handled fine, but their browser handles strangely? Find out what they mean and maybe even ask for a screen shot. You may find that your documents look a lot different on an unfamiliar browser than you think. This is yet another reason to become familiar with the major Web browsers and test your Web pages with *all* of them.

3. **You mention a table/image/color, but I can't see it.** You're using the Mozilla extensions, aren't you? Remember, not everyone has the good taste in browsers that you do, and other people may not be using the Netscape Explorer. Even differing versions of Netscape may render your documents very differently. If you want to use the Mozilla extensions, you're going to have to get used to this type of problem report. One way to minimize your problems is to not refer to a part of your document by physical its appearance, but instead by its content. Instead of "the information in the green table" say "the information about miniature poodles."

4. **Regarding fill out forms: You say enter the information here, but there is no place for me to type.** They must be using a browser that does not support forms. Ask them if they have ever been able to use fill-out forms before, and find out what browser they are using so you can try it yourself. It is amazing how often I get this complaint, considering that nearly all browsers can handle fill-out forms by now.

5. **I selected the link that said it pointed at documents on genetic reengineering of wildflowers, but all I got was the same document again.**

I see this a lot on other people's Web servers, so I have become very sensitive about double checking that my links don't do this. It is a typo in your HTML. You left out a double-quote in your anchor, like so:

```
<A HREF="http://somewhere.com>
```

Some browsers will handle this error correctly, but most will choke and reload the same document, and not the intended one. It's easy to fix, but not easy to spot.

"mailto:" is Your Friend

With all the little problems that can go undetected, your own users are your best allies for finding and fixing these pesky little problems. They are also your best source of suggestions, as well as a big confidence builder. A few "good job" emails, and you'll be on cloud nine. Also, it doesn't look too bad to have a few in hand during your salary review! Regardless, it is in your best interest to make it as easy as possible for your users to contact you with problems, suggestions, complaints, and compliments.

Every important Web document, and some would argue every document of any importance at all, should have your contact email address at the bottom, with a mailto anchor to make it even easier for your users to reach you. A typical mailto anchor might look like this:

```
<A HREF="mailto:webmaster@somewhere.com">webmaster@somewhere.com</A>
```

The easier it is for your users to contact you, the more you will hear from them. As long as you keep receiving comments, both good and bad, you are in good shape. It's when you stop hearing from your users that you should start to worry! Make it easy: Use mailto anchors wherever possible.

Some Concerns About the Law

The Internet and the World Wide Web are the last, great, uncharted legal frontier. For years now, 'Net citizens have been going about their business with little regard to how real-world laws might affect them, and for the most part this has worked. But the Internet has grown to include more then the educators, scientists, and researchers of its early years. The sheer volume of humanity squeezing itself through our thin network cabling has seen a much more diverse group of people, pushing and shoving their way online. And as with any large community, people start stepping on each others' toes.

How do real-world laws apply to this new Internet community? This is the question now being asked by organizations and government. Since I'm not a lawyer, I am in no way qualified to answer this question. But be aware (especially if you employ or retain a lawyer) that even if I were, I probably couldn't answer that question anyway, at least not with 100% certainty. Much of this law does not yet exist, in the reliable sense of the word "law." So instead of attempting to answer your legal questions, I have decided to simply point out some questions that you and your management way want to consider as you begin to settle into your new, electronic home. If you begin to think that one of these questions may apply to you, talk to a lawyer first. No one wants to be a legal test-case, and in today's legal climate a touch of paranoia and caution may be healthy.

- **How are your copyrights protected?** It's a very simple matter to make copyrighted materials available for the Internet community, and an even simpler matter for someone to copy this material and distribute it without your knowledge or approval. What kind of copyright notices and legal disclaimers do you need to ensure your copyrighted materials are protected? By all means make sure you have some kind of copyright notice, even if you aren't clear on what makes a good one or not. *If you do not put some kind of copyright notice on a document, you are unlikely to win an infringement case.*

- **Are you violating someone else's copyright?** That icon you've swiped off a Web server in some far corner of the world may well be considered copyrighted material. So too may that article on wombat mating rituals. Are you violating any copyrights by copying or making this material available on your own Web server?

- **Have you paid for your software?** Shareware software is available all over the Internet. It's a great way for programmers to distribute their work without bothering with a middleman, but it can also be an open invitation for theft. You may be using unregistered (that is, not yet paid for) shareware without even knowing it. For that matter, you may have discovered some commercial, pirated software on an ftp site somewhere, and begun using it under the assumption that it is free. Most shareware is labeled as such; if a software product does not encourage you to "spread it around" you are probably using commercial software, to which you must have a valid license.

- **Are your service marks and trademarks valid on the Internet, and how do you protect them?** There are procedures to be followed in registering trademarks, and the presence of a trademark on a Web site changes nothing. See your lawyer about registering trademarks. As with copyrights, it's difficult to defend against trademark infringement if you haven't "done the paperwork."

- **If you accept credit card numbers over the Internet, what are your legal responsibilities?** How much protection do you need to provide? Should you be required by law to use encryption? What if someone does intercept these credit card numbers? What are your responsibilities to your customers and the credit card companies? These are still largely unanswered questions, yet to be tested in a court of law.

- **What is the definition of libel on the Internet?** It is extremely easy to make a libelous document available for millions of readers. How are you protected from libel? Slander and libel have established definitions, and precedents have been applied to electronic media. Your lawyer must advise you in detail and about specific cases, but a good overview can be found in *The Associated Press Stylebook and Libel Manual* (Addison-Wesley, 1992.)

- **Pornography. Can you distribute it?** What kind of protections are you required, by law, to keep minors from retrieving this material? What are the international laws involved? If someone from out of your state or region accesses this material, are any laws being violated and by whom? For that matter, do you know the legal definition of pornography? This is one area that appears to be changing fast, and I don't think I need to be a lawyer to advise you that distributing sexually explicit photos these days is asking for trouble. The situation for textual material is much more tangled; if you have any doubts as to whether any of your Web material legally qualifies as obscene or indecent, consult your lawyer at length. Pornography on the Internet is, as I write this, the cover story in *Time Magazine*, and pending legislation in Congress will almost certainly change the whole sexual landscape of the Net. Some cynically suggest that a witch hunt is brewing, so this is *not* a good time to be wearing a pointed hat.

Conclusion

Okay. Your server is up and running—but don't let yourself become lax in your duties as webmaster. There is a lot of work to be done. Log files must be analyzed and archived. Marketing must be made aware of what you're doing and what materials are being made available to the Web surfing public. Links must be checked regularly, documents must be updated as they wobble toward obsolescence. All problems, be they software, network, or hardware-related, must be addressed as they come up.

Treat your user feedback like gold. Never ignore a complaint or suggestion, and always email back your appreciation for "job well done" letters. Don't let complaints or criticism get you down or make you angry! A complaint or a harsh letter is the most flattering kind of feedback, because it comes from users who care enough to take their precious time to tell you what they feel. Work with your users to resolve problems. A problem report is a user's way of offering a helping hand to get things working, and many times they will be thrilled to help further by providing screen shots or further testing.

The legal situation on the Internet is still in its infancy. As new laws are being considered and old laws are being reinterpreted to apply to this new medium, you will want to protect yourself from becoming a test case in this newly evolving area. Ask yourself tough questions about what your legal risks might be, and talk to a lawyer if there is even a shred of doubt. It is better to be cautious than caught!

15

Future Directions

The World Wide Web has a bright and exciting future. The new HTML 3.0 draft should prove much more robust then the current HTML 2.0 draft. For virtual reality buffs, the *Virtual Reality Modeling Language (VRML)* promises to transform the Web into a fully interactive 3-D environment, where Web servers are navigated by moving through simulated worlds. Something like a more serious Doom, without all the blood and dismemberment. There have also been talks about allowing external programs to communicate directly with your browser. From within your browser you could call an external program that will take over your browser, feeding it information and instructing it to retrieve and display new documents. There have even been advances in "real-time" audio over the Internet.

And then there is the matter of electronic cash and secure financial transactions. These are two things the Web will need to realize its full potential as a viable medium for commerce. But will allowing financial transactions freely over the Web turn it into a world of micro-tolls and pay-per-visit areas? Only time will tell, both whether or not it will happen, and whether or not it will be a good thing.

The rest of this chapter is my view of things to come: the good, the potentially good, and the God I hope it's good. All these things are happening now, and are at various levels of development. All are inevitable, but it remains to be seen which will thrive and prosper.

HTML 3.0

The next generation of HTML, the HTML 3.0 draft, attempts to make up for all the shortcomings of the current HTML 2.0 draft. You've already seen one of HTML 3.0's new features, tables (as implemented by Netscape) but there are quite a few others: inline figures, support for proper display of mathematical formulas and equations, customized lists, better control over text and graphic positioning, static banners that stay at the top or bottom of the document regardless of scrolling, and style sheets.

The problem that I see with HTML 3.0 is that it is attempting to make up for all, and I mean *all* of HTML 2.0's shortcomings, to the point of tossing in a virtual kitchen sink. The draft evolves, is debated, mutates a bit, and then evolves some more, with no end in sight. One has to wonder if the draft is ever going to be completed. With all the uncertainty surrounding the stability of the HTML 3.0 draft at any particular time, browser authors are understandably very hesitant to adopt any of the draft, with perhaps the exception of much-needed tables. Meanwhile, the Web community is growing more and more impatient, and browsers like Netscape are attempting to make up for the void that HTML 3.0 has been promising to fill for so long. I think a much less ambitious approach should have been taken. However, the fact still remains that HTML 3.0 is a long way from being completed, and any attempts at implementing already existing features have been thwarted by the draft's legendary instability.

Since the HTML 3.0 draft is so unstable, attempting to write about it with any sort of authority would be ridiculous, and writing HTML 3.0-compliant documents at this time would be futile. However if you are interested in a complete look at the draft's current status, and would maybe like to try your hand at writing a few documents, you can retrieve the draft's full text at *ftp://ds.internic.net/internet-drafts/draft-ietf-html-specv3-00.txt*. There is even an X Windows-based browser, Arena, which you can use to view your newly created HTML 3.0 documents. The browser's home page is at *http://www.w3.org/hypertext/WWW/Arena*.

It is recommended that HTML 3.0 "compliant" documents use the ".html3" or ".ht3" extensions, instead of the normal ".html" or ".htm" extensions for HTML 2.0 documents, so browsers that are not HTML 3.0 capable do not attempt to display these documents. The MIME type "text/html; version=3.0" should be used for HTML 3.0 documents. It is also recommended that HTML 3.0 documents start with the SGML prologue:

```
<!DOCTYPE HTML public "-//W3O//DTD W3 HTML 3.0//EN">
```

This should go at the very top of your document, before any HTML markup, including the <HTML> start tag. Is HTML 3.0 really so different from HTML 2.0 that it requires all these precautions to prevent non-HTML 3.0 browsers from being confused, and for HTML 3.0 browsers to be sure that it is displaying an HTML 3.0 document? Apparently so.

I had wanted to give examples of some of the new elements, attributes, and features of HTML 3.0 but there is just so much new material that I had no idea where to start. The draft as of March 28, 1995, is 190 pages long. I would have to write a whole new book to give the topic any justice at all.

All in all, I think HTML 3.0 is going to be a big step forward for the Web, if the draft is ever finished. It's a lot more robust than HTML 2.0, but also more involved, and I think the learning curve will be a lot higher, at least if you want to understand the whole thing. But before running out and trying to author your own HTML 3.0 documents, it is probably wise to sit back and wait for things to calm down a bit, or you may end up doing a lot of work that comes to nothing, due to the speed of your rapidly moving target.

VRML—Virtual Reality on the Internet

Virtual reality (VR) has finally come to the Internet universe. In fact, VR has been implemented as a layer over the Web, through VRML, the *Virtual Reality Modeling Language*. With VRML, you can encode your data into a 3-D scene of peaks and troughs, towers and arcs, and fly through it as though it were some kind of alien landscape. Other uses of VRML include the creation of Internet shopping malls that really look like malls, right down to photorealistic depictions of products that you can pick up, rotate, and even re-render in X-ray view. Looking for house plans? With a house plan encoded via VRML, you can literally approach the front door, open it, and move through the house, seeing it as you would were you actually living there.

In the view of many, VRML is the next manifestation of the *idea* of the World Wide Web, and the pioneers who are experimenting with the technology have made incredible progress in an extremely short time. VRML has gone from a dream to experimental reality in only about a year, and at this rate, in just a few years nearly all your Web browsing may be done in a fully 3-D environment. The World Wide Web could become a virtual city, with each Web site a building. You will be able to travel from building to building by flying over the landscape with your mouse. In these buildings, the home page will be the foyer, and hallways will connect various "rooms" which will be your documents. Hyperlinks are doorways, and traveling through a door can bring you to another document.

Can you experiment with this technology now? Yes, you can. A number of special VRML browsers have been released for testing for a number of platforms, including MS Windows, Windows NT, the Macintosh, and some flavors of Unix. VRML browsers for other platforms are in development. You can download and install one of these browsers, and configure it as a helper application for your favorite HTML browser, Netscape being the most popular at this time. This combination will allow you to enter some of the experimental virtual "worlds" currently in development and available for visiting.

You can identify a world by the document's .WRL file extension. Select a link that leads to such a world, and Netscape will launch your VRML browser, much as clicking on a link to an image might load up a paint program. Now the VRML browser has control. As you explore the virtual world, you may come to an object that acts as a link to another world. Click on that object and your VRML browser will retrieve the new world so that you can continuing browsing. Or maybe you will run into a link to a regular HTML document, in which case the VRML browser will return control to Netscape, which will load and present the HTML document in the usual way.

I should warn you: The first generation of browsers are still in the testing phase. They are clunky, not especially stable, and may not be able to view all available worlds properly, but still they represent a giant leap forward. It's not exactly "The Lawnmower Man" yet, but we're getting there.

The VRML specification resembles HTML in that it is implemented as regular ASCII text files. VRML is based on SGI's *Open Inventor* format for rendering 3-D environments; however, several other specifications are also being considered. Open Inventor is currently leading the pack. One of the biggest benefits of Open Inventor is that you are not forced to transfer large quantities of bitmapped graphics, but instead instructions that your VRML browser uses to reconstruct the world on the client machine. A typical VRML document is very small, often as little as 5 K for a small object, or 400 K for a more complex environment. This is certainly within the reach of current networking technology, with a 400 K document taking less than two minutes to transfer with a 28.8 K modem connection. Inline objects can be embedded in a world, much as inline images can be embedded in a regular HTML document, so worlds can be split among many servers.

If you would like to jump right in and see what all this is about, the number one VRML resource page seems to be at *http://www.utirc.utoronto.ca/ AdTech/rd/vrml/main.html.* You will want to go there first. Of course, Yahoo also has a list of pointers at *http://www.yahoo.com/Entertainment/ Virtual_Reality/.* Go to the "Virtual Reality Modeling Language (VRML)" link. Once you've stopped drooling, go get a VRML browser and try it out. The first MS Windows 3.1 browser is WorldView, which you can get at *http:/ /www.webmaster.com/vrml/wvwin/.* It's still a little clunky and perhaps a bit buggy, but it is in the alpha stage, after all.

If you are lucky enough to have a high powered Unix workstation on your desk (SGI, Sun, or IBM's AIX) or you are using Windows NT, WebSpace is

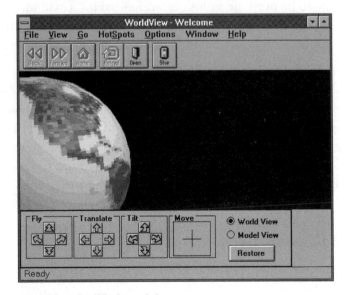

Figure 15.1 WorldView for Windows 3.1

what you will want to get. They can be found at *http://www.sgi.com/Products/WebFORCE/WebSpace/* or more directly at *http://www.sd.tgs.com/~template/WebSpace/monday.html.* I've seen a previous version of WebSpace on an SGI Indigo and it is *hot*!

VRML is not intended to be written by hand, although if you're so inclined, make sure you have lots of graph paper handy and a whole bunch of free time to devote to it. The latest VRML specification can be found at *http://www.hyperreal.com/~dagobert/.* (HTML has been around for "years" and is still a draft, but VRML is just an infant and is claiming to be nearly a specification. Go figure.) These links should be enough to start out with. Check them often—this stuff is evolving *very* quickly!

Helper Apps That Control Your Browser

The Web is a pretty diverse place. You frequently run across documents that your Web browser is unable to display directly as inline content. These might be external images, audio files, movies, and even those VRML worlds I spoke of earlier. Your Web browser handles documents it cannot display itself by calling an external program, a *helper application* in Web lingo, which does the work for it. After the helper application is called, and the browser gives it the file to be presented plus any additional information, the application is on its own, running independent of the browser. In other words, the helper application is incapable of talking back to the browser.

Wouldn't it be nice if your helper apps could send information back to the Web browser? For example, an audio player helper application could send an HTML document back to the browser describing the name, size, description, and playing time for the sound it is playing. Or perhaps an image viewer could tell the browser where you clicked on the image it is displaying, acting as a sort of external imagemap. Quite a few people think so as well, and there are currently two proposals to address this issue: NCSA's Common Client Interface (CCI), and Sun Microsystem's JAVA.

CCI—The Common Client Interface

CCI is an experimental protocol for facilitating communication between a Web browser and an external program such as a helper application. Currently, the only browser that supports CCI is NCSA Mosaic for X Windows. Here's how it works:

The Web browser turns itself into a mini-server, listening for requested connections from an external program, much as your Web server listens for requested connections from Web browsers. Once a connection is made, the external program will be able to request the Web browser to perform any number of tasks. These include:

- Request the Web browser to retrieve a document for it from the Web
- Force the Web browser to display a document
- Ask the Web browser to forward some information to a Web server
- Tell the browser to shut itself down

The CCI protocol itself looks quite a bit like HTTP, and is in fact based on the MIME specification, just as HTTP is. Information on the current CCI specification is available at *http://www.ncsa.uiuc.edu/SDG/Software/XMosaic/ CCI/cci-spec.html*. This information is really of interest only to programmers who would like to write helper applications that can communicate with Web browsers, or programmers currently writing a Web browser who wish to incorporate CCI support. Sample code and an API layer are available in C at the site above.

NCSA Mosaic was once *the* Web browser, but recently its position has slipped dramatically, so I'm a little unsure of the future of CCI. The designers still haven't worked out how to handle some severe security risks (would you like a Web browser that will accept a TCP/IP connection and blindly follow the calling program's instructions?) and Netscape, the current "browser to have" has decided to adopt an entirely different means (JAVA, see below) of addressing the same issue.

JAVA

JAVA (an acronym for "coffee" as its creators say with a grin) is a full-fledged programming language developed by Sun Microsystems. In a typical scenario, a JAVA program (called an *applet*) is stored on the Web server. When your Web browser finds a document with a JAVA applet embedded in it, *the applet is transferred over the Internet to your computer*. The connection to the server is then severed, and the applet begins to run, communicating its wishes to the Web browser. Essentially, a JAVA applet is an inline *program* rather than an inline image or an inline sound. The is entirely different from the CCI approach, which is simply a means for your already installed helper applications to communicate with your browser. JAVA applets *are* the helper applications, which are assumed *not* to be installed on your computer.

JAVA has built-in security, ensuring that the JAVA applet you receive is the JAVA applet you requested. There is no concern that some alien program will all of a sudden take control over your browser; you must specifically perform some action that causes a JAVA applet to be transferred to your computer and executed. The only drawback I can see is that it does scare me a little to execute a program which I've received automatically off the Web.

Netscape recently announced that they will be supporting JAVA in a future version of their Netscape Navigator, so I'll put my money on JAVA to be the defacto standard in this area. Besides, feature for feature, it beats CCI hands down. For more information on JAVA, visit Sun's JAVA home page at *http://java.sun.com/*.

RealAudio

When I first saw RealAudio, a neat new product from Progressive Networks in Seattle, Washington, I was quite impressed. RealAudio is a sound player for MS Windows and the Mac, with a twist. When you select a link to a normal sound file, like the Web's ubiquitous ".au" format, you probably have a long wait in store before you can hear it, due to a sound file's generally large size and the fact that you usually must complete downloading the sound before a player will begin playing it. But a RealAudio file (the extension is ".ram" or ".ra") begins playing within just a few seconds of your initiating the transfer. It doesn't matter whether it's ten seconds of sound or ten hours—playing begins almost immediately, and the sound is played directly as it comes over the network.

The truly amazing thing about RealAudio is the amount of bandwidth you need to play a RealAudio sound "live" over the Internet. The bandwidth requirement is only about 10 Kbps, just within range of a tiny 14.4 K modem. Even better, you can go off and do other things while the sound is playing. RealAudio accomplishes this by massively compressing the audio.

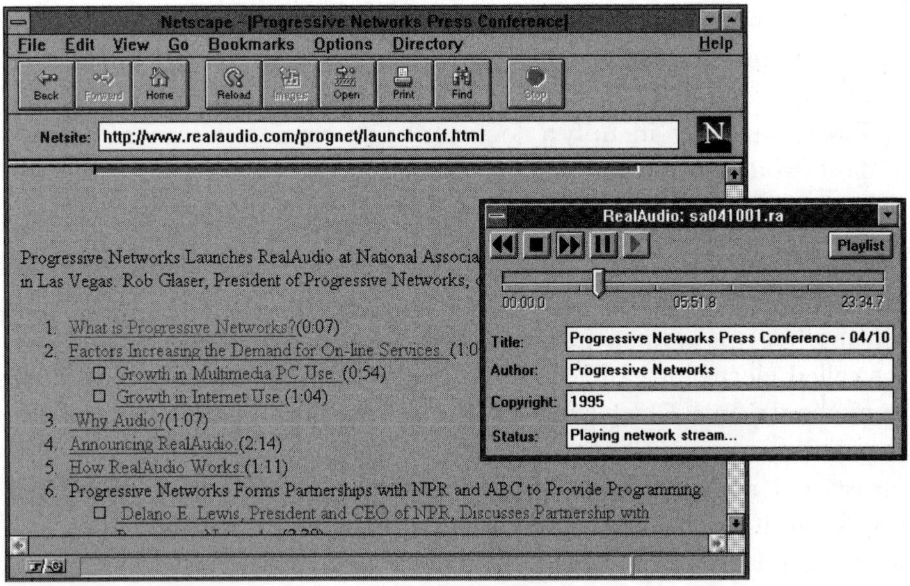

Figure 15.1   RealAudio

For example, a 14.0 MB .au file in RealAudio format would take only 1.8 MB of space. That is a little over 30 minutes of audio.

The only drawback of RealAudio right now is the quality of the sound. It's okay, probably better than you'd expect, but it's not exactly CD quality either. For speech, it's wonderful; for music, well, it lacks a certain something. But RealAudio is currently working to improve the sound quality, and I'm sure they'll get way better results as their product matures. They have also managed to drum up quite a bit of interest, and more than a few sites currently feature RealAudio. I expect you will be hearing a lot more about this product real soon now.

More information on RealAudio is available from their home page: *http:// www.realaudio.com/*.

Cash and Security

Two areas where you should expect some improvement shortly are in the electronic cash arena, secure credit card transactions, and general Internet security. With the development of Secure Socket Layers (SSL) and Secure-HTTP

(SHTTP), more servers will be able to accept credit card numbers and other sensitive information without fear of being overheard or the data intercepted. A side effect of this technology is the ability to create a *digital signature*, which can identify a document or message as coming from you and only you. As these technologies become more widespread, expect the number of financial transactions and other confidential business transactions over the Web to skyrocket.

Most of the discussion of Web security has involved credit card numbers, but another type of financial transaction involves no credit card data at all. It's called electronic cash, or e-cash, and may revolutionize the way you think about money. E-cash exists only in electronic form. You download e-cash to your hard drive, you "deposit" it in the "bank," and you spend it as you please. The mechanism is complex and difficult to describe in only a few words, but it involves encrypted bit patterns stored as a disk file or transferred as a data stream. E-cash will make Internet-based "micropayments" possible; that is, very small electronic funds transfer (EFT) payments for services, for example, a 25 cent charge to access a weather map or weather report. Is this a good thing? Will the Web end up as a network of millions of tiny toll-booths? I don't know, but for a hint at where to look for the answer, try *http://www.digicash.com/ecash/ecash-home.html*. Another source of information, and a slightly different view on the electronic cash solution is *http://firstvirtual.com/*, First Virtual Holdings, Inc.

Spinning the Future

The Web came out of nowhere only a couple of years ago. Nobody expected it, and it took a little while for people to really understand what it could do. And although it's definitely become the Internet's "killer application," and cast much of the rest of the Net (like the estimable Gopher system) into its shadow, few people realize just how much of a work-in-progress the Web really is, and how much work remains to be done.

HTML is a good start, but it's still very much a *document* specification, and perhaps the single greatest lesson to be learned from the nature of the Web is that it's about a lot more than documents. It's about the global presentation of information, and to do justice to that concept, HTML will have to do some growing. The HTML 3.0 spec is just the thing—and if it ever sits still enough to be called a standard, we'll be in fine shape. Mechanisms like RealAudio and JAVA will mutate the Web away from documents as electronic paper even further, and upcoming technologies like Internet Radio (which I did not have room to discuss in this book) and real-time videoconferencing will put real pressure on existing information delivery services.

Many people complain at the high noise level and the erratic quality of the material to be found on the Web. In an all-volunteer system, that's only to be expected. Once mechanisms are in place to charge for information transferred over the Web, this will change radically. The quantity of Web traffic will likely drop...but the quality should go through the roof, and funds will be generated that can support the creation of high-quality content specifically for the Internet, content that can earn its keep.

How well VRML does depends heavily on the future distribution of bandwidth in the world. Far more than HTML, VRML requires bandwidth, and lots of it. If high-speed fiber optics links do not become commonplace, VRML may remain a laboratory curiosity. But if high-speed links through fiber optic and cable TV networks become common and cheap, not only the Web but the Internet itself will be transformed in ways I find difficult to even speculate about.

May you live in interesting times, goes the old Chinese proverb.

We're here. This is about as interesting as it gets. I'll take my chances.

16

Using the CD-ROM

The companion CD-ROM contains over 600 MB of the best programs and clips to help you get the most out of the Web, especially if you're interested in creating and administering your own Web server. A few of these shareware and freeware programs and resources are described here, but make sure you look at the CD-ROM directory for the complete list. And don't be afraid to experiment!

You've probably heard shareware described as "software on the honor system." Basically, if you try a program and decide to keep and use it, you should register and pay for it. Basic registration instructions are given for each of the shareware programs discussed here, but more details can be found in the programs themselves, usually in the form of a "readme" file or screen.

Freeware is fully functional software that the author has generously made available to whomever wants it, no strings attached (although commercial versions, with more features, are sometimes available). Note, however, that the author almost always retains full rights to the program, and distribution policies vary, so read any copyright information carefully before you distribute your favorite freeware program to a hundred friends and business associates.

The audio and visual clips and art, images, and icons on the CD-ROM are in the public domain, which means that no single person or organization claims copyright. That means you can do whatever you want with them and to them—except, of course, claim copyright.

Enjoy!

Audio, Video, Animation, and Clip Art

What: Hundreds of audio and visual clips to dress up your Web pages.
Where on the CD-ROM: \clips
Where on the Net: Various sites

You'll find over 40 MB worth of audio, video, animation, and image files on the CD. All the clips can be run directly from the CD as long as the appropriate player or viewer program is installed on your PC. They provide examples, inspirations, and the beginnings for your own collection of multimedia goodies to add to your Web pages.

Audio

The audio files in WAV format provide sound effects for every conceivable situation, while the MIDI files provide pieces of music in styles ranging from classical to country. One especially nice feature of the MIDI files here: They're not tiny pieces that seem to be over before they've begun—some play for as long as 10 minutes! You can play the audio files with Windows' own Sound Recorder and Media Player accessories, or, for cooler-looking control panels and more playback options, use the Wham and Wplay programs in the \helper branch of the CD.

Images

If you've been looking longingly at all the nifty buttons, bullets, lines, and icons on other people's Web pages, check out the files in \clips\images and \clips\art. They're public domain and ready to use in GIF, BMP, and PCX formats. If one of these clips is almost, but not quite, right for your purpose, just install Paint Shop Pro from the CD (discussed later in this chapter) and change it!

Video and Animation

The animation and video files in \clips\animatio and \clips\video will provide examples and inspiration when you're ready to add movement to your Web site. To run the FLC and FLI files, use the AAplayer program in \helpers\waaplay. You can run the player from the CD, or, if you prefer, copy it to the hard disk. In either case, run aawin.exe, choose File|Open

Animation, select the clip you want to watch, click the >> (play) button, and watch it go. You can even add WAV or MIDI sound effects if you like, using File|Get Sound. The Truespace animations can be run by the ViewSpace program, discussed later in this chapter.

Two types of video clips are included on the CD: AVI and MPEG. AVI videos can be run by Windows' Media Player accessory, but MPEG requires the MPEGplayer program discussed later in this chapter.

Slackware 2.2.0

What: PC based version of the Unix operating system.
Where on the CD-ROM: \linux
Where on the Net: ftp://tsx-11.mit.edu/pub/linux
 ftp://sunsite.unc.edu/pub/Linux

I could write an entire book about how to set up and use Linux. Fortunately, the Slackware distribution of Linux that comes on the CD-ROM is one of the easiest to install. Plus, there is quite a bit of documentation already on the CD-ROM. Look in the /linux/howto directory for some really good help files that will walk you through just about every step of the process, not to mention all the customization that can be done.

If you choose to install Linux, you have a tremendous number of options. You can go for the minimal install, or add support for networking, or throw in the Xwindows shell, and so on. Another nice feature of the Linux OS: It is constantly evolving. Just about every hour of every day, someone, somewhere is working on a new Linux program, updating a patch, or fixing a bug. Because the OS is free, it is widely used by creative people around the world who still need to watch their pennies.

Another bonus is that Linux is a resource miser—you only need 4 MB of RAM to run it. So, why don't more people use Linux? It's not the type of system that a weekend hacker can install in a few hours. You should be very familiar with your hardware and have at least a basic understanding of how Linux and Unix systems work. Don't be put off by this warning: The documentation provided on the CD-ROM offers enough to get most people up and runnning in a matter of days. There are also several books available that help walk you through the installation process.

Internet Chameleon with Instant Internet

What: Suite of applications to aid you in getting set up on the Net.
Where on the CD-ROM: \connect\instinet\disk1

Internet Chameleon is a complete Windows-based Internet connection suite. You can use it to get connected to just about every corner of the Internet. Supported protocols include FTP, Telnet, e-mail, ping, and the World Wide Web. If you haven't set yourself up with an access provider yet, then this package or the NetCom package is a good way to start.

Before you run the install program, it's best to close all other running programs, because the program will make some minor changes to your AUTOEXEC.BAT file and will need to restart the computer for those changes to take effect.

To begin the installation, run the file setup.exe in the \connect\instinet\disk1 directory. Then, when the install program asks for the next two disks, simply enter the path name that points to the appropriate disks.

I recommend registering the software to get the full benefit of the package, but do try it out first to see whether you like it.

Internet Documentation

What: Internet STDs, Request for Comments (RFCs), and FYIs.
Where on the CD-ROM: \docs

These are some pretty impressive documents. Basically what you get is all the notes, memos, and specifications that have been used to document the growth and development of the Internet. This might sound too good to be true, but it's not! If you want to learn more about a certain Internet protocol or standard, the information is here. Since 1969, these memos have been written up and passed between colleagues so that everyone would have a common point of reference for developing new protocols or building applications that worked with older ones.

For instance, if you want to know exactly how the FTP protocol should be implemented, just look it up here! If you want to find out who was involved with a certain committee or project, that's here too.

Three different types of documents are listed. First, in the \docs\rfc directory, you'll find the Requests For Comments (RFCs). These documents contain the information about a new protocol so that it can get approved (or killed). These are the working notes of the committees that develop the protocols and standards for the Internet. Next are the FYIs (For Your Information). They're a subset of the RFCs and tend to be more informational and less technical. Finally, the STDs (Internet Activities Board standards) are what RFCs grow up to be. When an RFC becomes fully accepted and serves as a standard, it's designated as an STD—much like a bill becoming law.

In each of these directories, you'll find indexes to help you locate the specific document you need.

HomePage Creator

What: Visual home page designer tool.
Where on the CD-ROM: \tools\html\hpc

HomePage Creator is a new tool designed to help you automatically create your own Web pages. It's not just another HTML editor, though. It allows you to insert a picture, text, and links to your favorite sites on the Web and then does the dirty work of generating HTML tags for you.

The installation procedure for HomePage Creator is easy: Just run the setup.exe program in the directory \tools\hpc. You'll need to specify the directory where you want to install the HomePage Creator program. The developer of this program, Demetris Kafas, is currently developing a more feature-rich version of HomePage Creator that you'll be able to purchase in the future.

Microsoft Internet Assistant for Word 6.0

What: Word 6.0 based HTML editor.
Where on the CD-ROM: \tools\html\ia

Internet Assistant is both a powerful HTML document creator and an easy-to-use Web browser. The creation of documents is very easy, although a little slow. You simply type in your code, and format it by using styles and the extra toolbar that it creates while you are editing or browsing Web pages. You can move from document creating, to editing, to browsing with the click of a button.

The downside of this package is speed—or the lack of it. Because of the inherent overhead of the Word 6.0 environment, processing tends to be a little slow. However, if you're patient, the rewards are gratifying. Many of the Word tools still work with the Assistant, including spell-checking and grammar-checking. You won't find those features in very many standalone products.

HotMetal

What: HTML editor.
Where on the CD-ROM: \tools\html\hotmetal
Where on the Net: ftp://ftp.ncsa.uiuc.edu/Web/html/hotmetal/

HotMetal is a Windows-based freeware HTML editor from SoftQuad. An HTML editor is a standalone program; it's used to write Web pages, and isn't something you add onto a word processor or other program.

HotMetal has several elements that make it a good choice for beginning HTML publishers. It sticks to the basic, standard features of HTML, so you won't be overwhelmed by dozens of different tags. In fact, selecting Hide Tags from the View menu lets you ignore the tags altogether, so you can read just the text on the page that, for example, you saved to disk from someone else's Web site. Also, from the View menu, the Structure function creates an "outline" of your document, so you can keep track of its links without driving yourself crazy.

Best of all, HotMetal comes with 14 templates for typical documents like home pages, customer registration forms, and hotlists. Just choose File|Open Template, pick the appropriate one from the list, type your text between the tags, save your work as an HTM file, and *voila!*—instant HTML. Be sure to start with readme3.htm—a template that describes the other templates.

It's possible to run HotMetal straight from the CD, but installing it on your hard disk is more practical. It's not self-installing, so you'll have to copy the entire \hotmetal branch from the CD to the root directory of your hard drive, and then make an icon for it. Here are the steps to follow:

1. In Program Manager, open (or create) the group in which you want HotMetal to be placed.

2. Choose File|New. The Program Item option should be selected. Click OK to display the Program Item Properties dialog box.

3. Type Hot Metal in the Description box.

4. Click Browse and navigate through your hard disk until you find sqhm.exe. Click on that file to select it, then click OK.

5. Click OK again, and the HotMetal icon should appear in your group.

HotMetal takes up only about 5 MB of hard disk space, but is fairly greedy in its memory consumption. So, unless you have plenty of RAM to spare, it's a good idea to shut down other programs when you run HotMetal.

HTML Assistant

What: HTML editor.
Where on the CD-ROM: \tools\html\htmlasst
Where on the Net: http://fox.nstn.ca/~harawitz/htmlpro1.html

HTML Assistant is an extremely popular freeware HTML editor for Windows. Like HotMetal, it's a standalone program for creating Web pages. The two differ, however, in their approach and specific feature sets. HTML doesn't come with a wide variety of pre-written templates like HotMetal does, but makes up for that with an elegant interface and, especially, an easy-to-use Test function that lets you see how your page will actually look on the Web.

The installation procedure for HTML Assistant is basically the same as for Hot Metal: Copy the directory and create a program icon. The file that runs HTML Assistant (step 4 in the installation instructions listed for HotMetal) is different from the one for HotMetal, of course; the one to browse for here is htmlasst.exe.

To create a page with HTML Assistant, start by choosing Command|Display Standard Document Template. This will bring up a skeleton Web page with basic codes. Add your text, and then add other elements by clicking on them from the toolbars or selecting them from the menus. When your page looks ready, choose Save and type in the filename, including the HTM extension. Important: You have to explicitly type **.htm**; it won't be added for you, and without it, your pages won't display properly.

The real fun starts after you've saved a document. Click the Test button. The first time you do this, you'll be asked for the test program name—the file name of the browser program you use. HTML Assistant will then run the browser, and your pages will appear just as they would on the Web! Note, however, that you have to close the browser yourself so HTML Assistant can restart it the next time you want to test a page. Once you've gotten the hang of basic HTML, dive into HTML Assistant's extensive support for URLs and start creating lots o' links.

HTMLed

What: Another HTML editor — very easy to use.
Where on the CD-ROM: \tools\html\htmled

This powerful HTML editor features a very well-laid-out interface. All the often-used tags are right here, ready to use. The menus are also clear and intuitive. Unfortunately, HTMLed does not support any of the HTML3 tags (yet), but the author tells us that omission will soon be corrected.

No installation instructions are provided, but you won't miss them. Just create a directory somewhere on your hard drive and copy all of the files to that directory. Or, you can just run the program off the CD. If you're already familiar with HTML, I highly recommend this program for its great interface and intuitive use of function keys and shortcuts.

HTML Writer

What: Another HTML editor—try not to fall asleep.
Where on the CD-ROM: \tools\html\htmlwrit

If you've tried all the other HTML editors included on the CD, this one might not seem special. But HTML Writer has a very nice interface—with extensive menus, a nice toolbar, and good shortcut keys. One advantage to this standalone application is its use of templates. You can use the ones that come with it, or develop your own for speedy Web page creation.

Installation is easy too. Just copy all of the files from the \tools\html\htmlwrit directory into the directory of your choice. This program may not run well from the CD, because it will try to write an INI file to the executable directory. If the program does not run from the directory you created, move the DLL and VBX files to your \windows\system directory and try again.

RTF2HTML

What: Converts file from RTF to HTML.
Where on the CD-ROM: \tools\html\rtf2html

Here's a neat little utility for converting documents from RTF to HTML. RTF (Rich Text Format) is a common text format that most word processing programs, including Word for Windows, can import and export. The package also includes a Word 2 for Windows template for writing HTML.

To install RTF2HTML, just copy all of the files in the \tools\html\rtf2html directory into a directory of your choice on your hard drive. Then, move the file RTFTOHTM.DLL to your \windows\system directory. You should also move the HTML.DOT file to the template directory of your word processor, if it is available (try \winword\template).

You can then open a new document in your word processor, using HTML.DOT as a template. The template works by giving you a preset list of styles that you use to signify different types of text, formatting, size, and so on. When you've finished composing your pages, you can then save them as RTF documents. In turn, you can use the converter to turn the RTF documents into HTML documents.

MPEGplay version 1.65

What: Player for MPEG videos.
Where on the CD-ROM: \helpers\mpegwin
Where on the Net: ftp://ftp.cica.indiana.edu
ftp://gatekeeper.dec.com/pub/micro/msdos/win3/
desktop/

MPEGplay is a fast MPEG animation player that uses Win32s and WinG. If you don't already have either of these Windows extensions, they're both available on the CD-ROM. Install them on your hard disk by running \tools\win32s\disk1\setup.exe before installing MPEGplay.

MPEGplay's interface looks like a VCR, with the standard rewind, stop, and play buttons, plus a button that allows a video clip to be played frame-by-frame. To get the most out of any machine, MPEGplay gives the user control over the number of colors displayed in the clip and the size of the window. If you have a fast machine, you can set these options high for the best detail; if you have a slower machine, you can sacrifice a little detail for less jerky motion. You can even choose Movie|Time Play to find out how fast your PC is playing the video, in frames per second.

MPEGplay is shareware. If you find it useful, support the author by sending $25 (U.S.) for a single-user license to:

Michael Simmons
P.O. Box 506
Nedlands WA 6009
Australia

The included register.txt file has more details about registration and distribution conditions.

Paint Shop Pro version 3.0

What: Image conversion and enhancement program.
Where on the CD-ROM: \helpers\psp3
Where on the Net: ftp://oak.oakland.edu/SimTel/win3/graphics/
psp30.zip

Paint Shop Pro, from JASC Corporation, is a shareware program that gives you much control over your graphics. You might use it, for example, to open a PCX file, copy a small part of it to a new window, resize and flip the new image, put a red border around it, and save it as a GIF file. It would then be ready to use as an icon for your Web pages.

Paint Shop Pro has several features that have helped it to become the standard shareware graphics-conversion program for Windows:

- Screen capture

- Multiple document windows

- Filters for special effects

- Support for over 20 file formats

- TWAIN scanner support

- Batch conversion so that you can, for example, turn ten WMF images into GIFs with a single click

Paint Shop Pro is self-installing; just run setup.exe from the CD. If you use the program for more than 30 days, buy it by sending $69 to:

JASC, Inc.
10901 Red Circle Drive, Suite 340
Minnetonka, MN 55343

ViewSpace

What: 3-D animation program.
Where on the CD-ROM: \helpers\viewspace\disk1

ViewSpace is a freeware 3-D animation and rendering program from Caligari Corporation. You can use it with objects that have been created separately by a CAD program or with Truespace animations. ViewSpace is relatively easy to use, but at first you'll probably want to make use of its online help. (You might need to resize the program window to see the Help menu. Unlike most Windows programs, ViewSpace's menu bar is at the bottom of the window.)

To run an animation, you simply choose File|Animation. To create an animation, you first position your wireframe objects in the 3-D space by choosing File|Load Object. Then, using the tools at the bottom of the window, you can move, rotate, render (add surfaces and depth), and ultimately animate your objects.

ViewSpace is self-installing; just run vsetup.exe. Note, however, that ViewSpace is not for slow computers. To really exploit its features, you'll need a fast 486 or a Pentium with plenty of RAM and a fast video card.

Web Spinner

What: HTML editor (yes, another one).
Where on the CD-ROM: \tools\html\webspin

Web Spinner is the new kid on the block of HTML editors. It's a very powerful but easy-to-use editor for creating HTML documents. Web Spinner is a snap to install and to use. Just make sure you have Win32s installed on your computer if you're running Windows 3.1. If you're running Windows 95, you won't need Win32s to run Web Spinner.

This simple application uses multiple child windows to speed up page creation. The toolbars are some of the best designed that I've seen anywhere. Adding images, horizontal ruiles, and special characters is simple to do. Web Spinner also lets you customize image placement to allow for formatted alignments.

Setting up links and anchors is painless also. Just highlight and click—Web Spinner displays a dialog box with all the available options. Even though this is a newer product, it does not support HTML3. Look for a slew of new editors that will make it a snap to create HTML3-compliant pages.

DOSPERL

What: DOS implementaion of the Perl language.
Where on the CD-ROM: \systems\dos\dosperl

If you're thinking about setting up a Web server under a DOS or Windows environment, you'll definitely find this software to be handy. This is the code used to interpret the scripts used in the book. Perl is a fairly simple scripting language that, if used wisely, can yield some pretty powerful and interesting results.

Tasks such as file management, database searches, and imagemapping can all be handled with Perl. I've included version 4.0 with this CD, but new version are always in the works. Run NetSeeker to see if it offers you a newer version. See the section *Running Netseeker* near the end of this chapter.

Web4ham

What: Windows-based Web server.
Where on the CD-ROM: \systems\windows\web4ham
Where on the Net: ftp://ftp.informatik.unihamburg.de/pub/net/
winsock/web4ham.zip

The documentation that comes with this simple Web server tells you all you need to get started. Web4ham can be run under any Windows environment, even Windows 3.1. This version of the server is pretty limited. It was written mostly as an exercise by the author, who wanted to learn more about asynchronous file transfer over the Internet. The author took it a few steps further, though, and has created a simple, efficient Web server.

Windows httpd 1.4

What: Windows based Web server.
Where on the CD-ROM: \systems\windows\whttpd
Where on the Net: http://www.alisa.com/win-httpd/

This Windows-based Web server is much more powerful than Web4ham. It includes full support for CGI scripting, caching, up to 16 simultaneous connections, directory indexes, and password encryption—just to name-drop a few features.

Setting up the software is not difficult. Simply follow the directions supplied (in HTML format) with the software. The documentation is located in the \systems\windows\whttpd\httpddoc directory, and is named overview.htm. Take my advice and read through the supplied documentation carefully; you'll save a lot of time and avoid a lot of frustration if you go into the installation with a little knowledge.

Win32 and WinG

What: Windows enhancement APIs.
Where on the CD-ROM: \tools\win32s \tools\wing
Where on the Net: ftp://ftp.microsoft.com

These two Windows APIs (Application Programming Interfaces) are just about a prerequisite for modern Windows software. Win32 adds support for many 32-bit Windows calls, which many packages use to speed up programs—a huge difference when running complicated applications that perform a lot of file I/O (like Web browsers).

WinG is used less than Win32, but can supply some pretty amazing results. WinG is an add-on API whose sole purpose is to bring Windows up to speed in the gaming world. Previously, very few games were written for Windows, because the device-independence that makes Windows so powerful and easy-to-use also makes its graphics routines dreadfully slow. WinG provides game creators with a few key API calls that significantly increase the speed at which graphics can drawn to the screen.

Book Examples

What: CGI scripts and HTML files from the book.
Where on the CD-ROM: \docs\book

These are the Perl scripts and HTML files found within the book. The scripts include lessons on many different CGI concepts, including data manipulation, equations, and imagemaps. The HTML files provide a step-by-step illustration in getting started with the Hypertext Markup Language.

Microsoft Video for Windows 1.1e

What: Windows video player with 32-bit extensions.
Where on the CD-ROM: \helpers\vfw11e

This is the latest release of the Video for Windows standard. If you already think you have Video for Windows, you should upgrade anyway, because this release has a few minor tweaks that can really speed up playback, especially if you're running on a 32-bit operating system (Windows 95 or Windows 3.1 with Win32 extensions).

NetSeeker

NetSeeker™ is a product created by The Coriolis Group that downloads programs from the Internet, uncompresses them, and installs them. Before you can use NetSeeker, you must make sure that you are connected to the Internet.

Running NetSeeker

To use NetSeeker, follow these steps:

1. Install NetSeeker by running the setup.exe program located in the /netseek directory on the CD-ROM.
2. Run your Internet connection software to connect to the Internet.
3. Once you are connected to the Internet, run the NetSeeker program (netseek.exe) by double-clicking on its icon in the program group. Figure 16.1 shows the start up screen that is displayed.
4. To continue, click the Begin button. NetSeeker will then take over and access the Internet for you to obtain setup information. **This may take a few moments.**
5. While NetSeeker is accessing the Internet, status information will be displayed in a status box at the center of the screen and in the status panel at the bottom of the NetSeeker window as shown in Figure 16.2.
6. During these periods, NetSeeker will be automatically downloading files for you. The status bar tells you the percentage of the download that has been completed. You can cancel the process at any time by clicking the Cancel button.
7. When NetSeeker has finished its configuration, the message "NetSeeker Setup Complete! You may begin." is displayed at the bottom status panel, and the startup screen will change as shown in Figure 16.3.

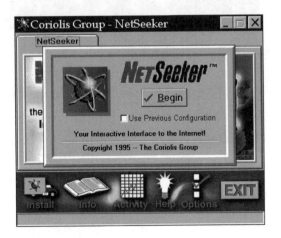

Figure 16.1   NetSeeker start up screen

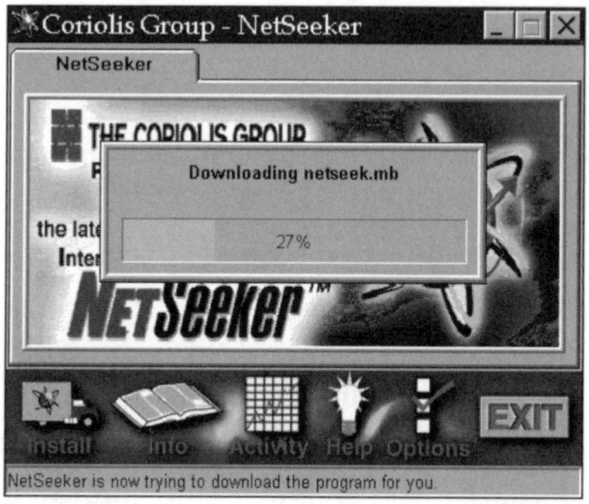

Figure 16.2   NetSeeker status

Figure 16.3   Completed NetSeeker installation

You are now ready to use NetSeeker to access new Internet applications, or to update your old ones.

If NetSeeker can't configure itself, you will receive a message indicating that you are either not currently connected to the Internet or that the NetSeeker database cannot be accessed. For more information on what to do if problems occur, see the section "Troubleshooting NetSeeker" in this guide.

Using the NetSeeker Interface

The main NetSeeker window provides two groups of selectable options: *clickable tabs* and *buttons*, shown in the figure on the next page. You click on one of the tabs to select a particular software program or a group of resources that you want to retrieve from the Internet. The buttons listed at the bottom of the window operate as follows:

Install Starts the downloading and installation process. When this button is clicked, only the programs and resources that you've previously selected will be downloaded and installed.

Info Displays information about NetSeeker including its version number.

Activity Displays a log of the programs and resources that you've previously downloaded and installed with NetSeeker.

Help Displays help information for using NetSeeker.

Options Displays an Options dialog so that you can select different installation options.

Exit Quits NetSeeker.

Using NetSeeker to Download Resources and Software

To download and install a particular software program or set of resources, follow these steps:

1. Click on the tab that represents the software or group of resources that you want to retrieve from the Internet. (Some of the options may include Netscape, Helper Programs, Web Publishing, NCSA, Mosaic, and so on.)

2. When the new section appears, select the different options you want to download by clicking the appropriate checkboxes.

3. Click on the Install button.

4. If you are downloading new content, NetSeeker will bring up a dialog box showing approximately how long it will take to download the requested data. If you are downloading anything other than content, NetSeeker will then display a dialog box so that you can create a diretory to store the file(s) that NetSeeker will download. After you've selected or created a directory, click the OK button.

NetSeeker will then display the software you've selected from the Internet. As it downloads the file(s), a status indicator will be displayed at the center of the NetSeeker window. If you are downloading a large file or if you have a slow connection to the Internet, this process could take a few minutes.

After NetSeeker finishes retrieving the file(s) for you, it will automatically decompress and install all of the programs and files that it has retrieved, if necessary. To decompress some files, NetSeeker may need to run a DOS program. If you desire, you can turn off the automatic installation feature by clicking on the Options button and deselecting the appropriate check box.

Selecting Installation Options

If you are downloading an application, NetSeeker offers a few options. By default, NetSeeker will automatically uncompress files retrieved for you and install them on your hard drive. You can override any of these installation features at any time by clicking on the Options button. Figure 16.4 shows the dialog box that is displayed.

Here is a description of these options:

Automatic Uncompress When this option is selected, the files that are retrieved by NetSeeker will automatically be uncompressed for you. If you deselect this option, you'll need to uncompress the files that are retrieved manually.

Automatic Installation When this option is selected, NetSeeker will both uncompress and install the files and programs that it retrieves. Installing programs typically involves running a special setup program and updating Windows configuration files.

Figure 16.4   NetSeeker options dialog box

Getting More Help and Information

You can view help information for NetSeeker at any time by clicking on the Help button. If you want more information about the software and resources that NetSeeker can retrieve for you, you can use the Info feature. To get more information:

1. Click on the tab that corresponds with the software or resource group you are interested in. For example, Helpers, Netscape, Internet Tools, and so on.

2. Click the Info button.

Notice that the Information window (Figure 16.5) displays a description and file sizes for the software that is available for you to retrieve.

When you are done viewing this window, click its close button, the Exit menu command, or just click anywhere on the form to make it disappear.

Getting a Report of Your Activity

NetSeeker allows you to view or print a log of your installation activity so that you can keep track of what you've retrieved from the Internet (Figure 16.6). To use this feature, click on the **Activity** button.

Notice that each entry listed contains a date, time, description, and version number. You can print a report by clicking on the Print menu. You can also delete an entry in the log by selecting the item with the mouse and then clicking on the Clear menu. NetSeeker will then display a confirmation dialog, as shown in Figure 16.7, to verify that you really want to delete the item you've selected.

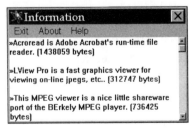

Figure 16.5   Information window

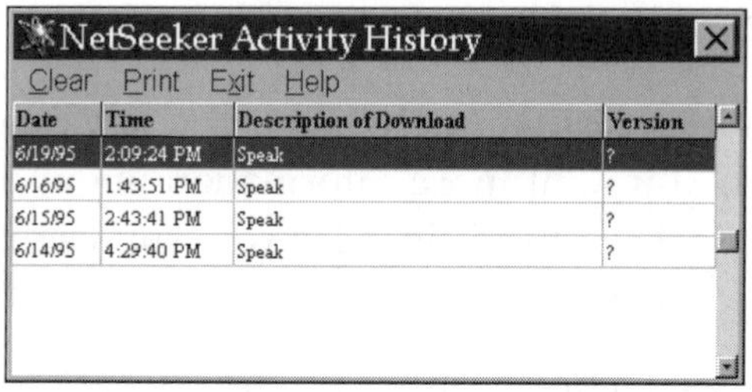

Figure 16.6 Activity report

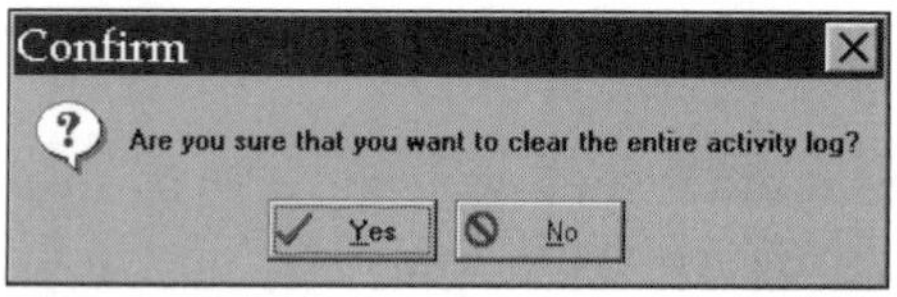

Figure 16.7 Confirmation dialog box

Quitting NetSeeker

To quit NetSeeker, click the Exit button. After NetSeeker shuts down, you may want to disconnect from the Internet if you no longer need to be connected.

Troubleshooting NetSeeker

Here are some problems that you may encounter while you are using NetSeeker and solutions to help you out.

When I first run NetSeeker nothing happens.
In order for NetSeeker to run properly, you must restart your computer after running the installation program. If restarting your computer doesn't help, try reinstalling NetSeeker and restarting your computer.

You must also have TCP/IP Internet connection software running on your computer before you can start NetSeeker.

After I click on the Begin button, nothing happens or I get a timeout error.
This indicates that your computer is not currently connected to the Internet. You must quit NetSeeker, connect to the Internet, and then restart NetSeeker.

After I click on the Begin button I get a "Busy-Try Again" warning.
This indicates that the NetSeeker Internet site is swamped with requests and that you should try again in a moment. If you continue to have problems logging in, you might want to wait a few minutes before trying again.

While I'm retrieving files with NetSeeker I receive a download error message.
NetSeeker may encounter a problem while retrieving a file for you, but it will do its best to keep trying. If after trying a number of times it can't retrieve the file for you, you may want to cancel and try again in a few minutes.

HTML Reference

The following reference covers the HTML 2.0 draft, including elements that are deprecated and proposed but as yet not in the draft. *Deprecated* elements are those found in previous versions of the HTML draft but have been replaced with newer elements, and are included here only for completeness. Many browsers still honor these deprecated elements, but their use is strongly discouraged. The Mozilla extensions are also covered, though again they should be used in full knowledge that most browsers do not yet support them.

Table A.1   Top-level HTML elements

Element Name	Mozilla Extension Attributes	Notes
<HTML>		
<HEAD>		
<BODY>	BACKGROUND	
	BGCOLOR	
	TEXT	
	LINK	
	VLINK	
	ALINK	
<!-- A Comment -->		Comments may be placed anywhere in your document.
<PLAINTEXT>		*Deprecated*

Table A.2   Elements contained in a document's head

Element Name	HTML 2.0 Attributes	Mozilla Extension	Notes
<BASE>	HREF		
<ISINDEX>		PROMPT ACTION	This element may also be placed in your document's body.
<LINK>	HREF METHODS REL REV TITLE URN		
<META>	CONTENT HTTP-EQUIV NAME		
<NEXTID>	N		
<TITLE>			

Table A.3   Physical and logical styles

Element Name	Attributes	Notes
<CITE>		
<CODE>		
<EM>		
<I>		
<KBD>		
<LISTING>		*Deprecated*
<PRE>	WIDTH	
<SAMP>		
<STRONG>		
<TT>		
<VAR>		
<XMP>		*Deprecated*
<DFN>		*Proposed*
<STRIKE>		*Proposed*
<U>		*Proposed*

Table A.4 General elements

Element Name	HTML 2.0 Attributes	Mozilla Extension Attributes	Notes
<A>	HREF METHODS NAME REL REV TITLE URN		
<ADDRESS>			
<BASEFONT>	*Mozilla only*	SIZE	Sizes are from 1 to 7 with the default 3.
<BLINK>	*Mozilla only*		
<BLOCKQUOTE>			
 		CLEAR	CLEAR's valid values are *left*, *right*, and *all*.
<CENTER>	*Mozilla only*		
<FONT>	*Mozilla only*	SIZE	Sizes are from 1 to 7 with the default 3.
<H1> ... <H6>			
<HR>		SIZE WIDTH ALIGN NOSHADE	ALIGN's valid values are *left*, *right*, and *center*.
<IMG>	ALIGN ALT ISMAP SRC	VSPACE HSPACE BORDER WIDTH	ALIGN's valid values are *top*, *middle*, and *bottom*. Mozilla has also added *absmiddle*, *baseline*, *bottom*, *absbottom*, *left*, and *right*.
<NOBR>	*Mozilla only*		
<P>			An end tag is optional, but I recommend one.
<WBR>	*Mozilla only*		Used in conjunction with <NOBR>.

Table A.5   Elements for creating lists

Element Name	HTML 2.0 Attributes	Mozilla Ext. Attributes	Notes
<DIR>	COMPACT*		
<DL>	COMPACT		
<DD>			For use in <DL>. Every <DD> must have one <DT> following it.
<DT>			For use in <DL>. Every <DT> must have one <DD> preceeding it.
<MENU>	COMPACT		
<OL>	COMPACT	TYPE START	TYPE's valid values are *1, I, i, A*, and *a*.
<UL>	COMPACT	TYPE	TYPE's valid values are *disc, circle*, and *square*.
<LI>		TYPE VALUE	TYPE's valid values are the same as if they were used in context of <OL> or <UL>, whichever is appropriate. VALUE is only appropriate in context of <OL>.

*   COMPACT is a rarely used attribute to create a more compact looking list. Most browsers decide automatically to use COMPACT, and ignore the use of this attribute. It is included here only for completeness.

Table A.6   Elements for use in forms creation

Element Name	Attributes	Notes
<FORM>	ACTION ENCTYPE METHOD	METHOD is usually GET or POST. ENCTYPE defaults to its only valid value, *application/x-www-form-urlencoded*.
<INPUT>	ALIGN CHECKED MAXLENGTH NAME SIZE SRC TYPE VALUE	TYPE's valid values are *text, password, checkbox, radio, submit, reset, image*, and *hidden*.

Table A.6 Elements for use in forms creation (continued)

<SELECT>	MULTIPLE NAME SIZE	
<OPTION>	SELECTED VALUE NAME ROWS	Only valid when used with <SELECT>.

Table A.7   Elements for Mozilla and HTML 3.0 tables

Element Name	HTML 3.0 Attributes	Notes
<TABLE>	BORDER CELLSPACING CELLPADDING WIDTH	
<CAPTION>	ALIGN	ALIGN's valid values are *top* and *bottom*.
<TR>	ALIGN	ALIGN's valid values are *left*, *center*, and *right*.
	VALIGN	VALIGN's valid values are *top*, *middle*, *bottom*, and *baseline*.
	NOWRAP	
<TD>	ROWSPAN COLSPAN	ALIGN's and VALIGN's valid values are the same as for <TR>.
	ALIGN	
	VALIGN	
	NOWRAP	
	WIDTH	
<TH>	ROWSPAN COLSPAN	ALIGN's and VALIGN's valid values are the same as for <TR>.
	ALIGN	
	VALIGN	
	NOWRAP	
	WIDTH	

The behavior of any or all of these elements and their attributes is subject to the interpretation of the individual browser. The HTML 2.0 draft is still in a state of flux, and some elements may be added, removed, or modified before it is frozen. This problem is even more pronounced with the Mozilla Extensions. Netscape is continually experimenting with and improving their specifications, so I would recommend you check the available documentation often. You can find more information on the Mozilla Extensions at *http://home.netscape.com/* and on the HTML 2.0 (and HTML 3.0) drafts at *http://www.w3.org/*.

ISO-Latin-1 Coded Character Set

HTML uses the ISO-Latin-1 Coded Character Set (ISO 8859-1:1987 Information Processing 8-bit single-byte coded graphic character sets — Part 1: Latin alphabet No. 1) to render your text. Most of the characters in the ISO-Latin-1 character set can be reproduced with simple keystrokes on your keyboard; however, a few are "special" characters that can be more difficult to generate. For these cases, you can use either the character's reference number or a mnemonic entity reference defined in HTML and recognized by browsers that fully support the HTML spec.

An example of the copyright symbol © using the mnemonic entity reference:

`&copy;`

An example of the copyright symbol © using its reference number:

`&#169;`

It is generally preferable to use the mnemonic entity reference when possible.

Table B.1   The ISO-Latin-1 Coded Character Set

Character	Char. Ref.	Entity Ref.	Description	Character	Char. Ref.	Entity Ref.	Description
Unused	0 - 8	*Unused*	Unused	Horiz. Tab	9		Horizontal Tab
Line Feed	10		Line Feed	*Unused*	11 - 31	*Unused*	Unused
Space	32		No-break Space	* !	33		Exclamation mark
"	34	&quot;	Quotation mark	#	35		Pound sign

459

Table B.1   The ISO-Latin-1 Coded Character Set (continued)

Character	Char. Ref.	Entity Ref.	Description	Character	Char. Ref.	Entity	Description
$	36		Dollar Sign	%	37		Percent sign
&	38	&	Ampersand	'	39		Apostrophe
(	40		Left parenthesis	)	41		Right parenthesis
*	42		Asterisk	+	43		Plus sign
,	44		Comma	-	45		Hyphen
.	46		Period	/	47		Slash
0	48			1	49		
2	50			3	51		
4	52			5	53		
6	54			7	55		
8	56			9	57		
:	58		Colon	;	59		Semicolon
<	60	<	Less than	=	61		Equals sign
>	62	>	Greater than	?	63		Question mark
@	64		Commercial at sign	A	65		
B	66			C	67		
D	68			E	69		
F	70			G	71		
H	72			I	73		
J	74			K	75		
L	76			M	77		
N	78			O	79		
P	80			Q	81		
R	82			S	83		
T	84			U	85		
V	86			W	87		
X	88			Y	89		
Z	90			[	91		Left square bracket
\	92		Backslash	]	93		Right square bracket
^	94		Caret	_	95		Underscore
´	96		Acute accent	a	97		

Table B.1   The ISO-Latin-1 Coded Character Set (continued)

Character	Char. Ref.	Entity Ref.	Description	Character	Char. Ref.	Entity Ref.	Description
b	98			c	99		
d	100			e	101		
f	102			g	103		
h	104			i	105		
j	106			k	107		
l	108			m	109		
n	110			o	111		
p	112			q	113		
r	114			s	115		
t	116			u	117		
v	118			w	119		
x	120			y	121		
z	122			{	123		Left curly brace
|	124		Vertical bar	}	125		Right curly brace
~	126		Tilde	¡	161		Inverted exclamation mark
¢	162		Cent sign	£	163		Pound sterling
¤	164		General currency	¥	165		Yen sign
¦	166		Broken vertical bar	§	167		Section sign
¨	168		Umlaut	©	169	&copy;	Copyright *
ª	170		Feminine ordinal	«	171		Left angle quote
¬	172		Not sign	–	173	&shy;	Soft hyphen *
®	174	&reg;	Rgstrd Trdmrk *	¯	175		Macron accent
°	176		Degree sign	±	177		Plus or minus
²	178		Superscript two	³	179		Superscript three
´	180		Acute accent	µ	181		Micro sign
¶	182		Paragraph sign	·	183		Middle dot
¸	184		Cedilla	¹	185		Superscript one
º	186		Masculine ordinal	»	187		Right angle quote
¼	188		One-fourth	½	189		One-half
¾	190		Three-quarters	¿	191		Inverted question mark

Table B.1   The ISO-Latin-1 Coded Character Set (continued)

Character	Char. Ref.	Entity Ref.	Description	Character	Char. Ref.	Entity	Description
À	192	&Agrave;	grave-A	Á	193	&Aacute;	acute-A
Â	194	&Acirc;	circumflex-A	Ã	195	&Atilde;	tilde-A
Ä	196	&Auml;	umlaut-A	Å	197	&Aring;	ring-A
Æ	198	&Aelig;	dipthong	Ç	199	&Ccedil;	cedilla
È	200	&Egrave;	grave-E	É	201	&Eacute;	acute-E
Ê	202	&Ecirc;	circumflex-E	Ë	203	&Euml;	umlaut-E
Ì	204	&Igrave;	grave-I	Í	205	&Iacute;	acute-I
Î	206	&Icirc;	circumflex-I	Ï	207	&Iuml;	umlaut-I
Ð	208		Icelandic Eth	Ñ	209	&Ntilde;	tilde-N
Ò	210	&Ograve;	grave-O	Ó	211	&Oacute;	acute-O
Ô	212	&Ocirc;	circumflex-O	Õ	213	&Otilde;	tilde-O
Ö	214	&Ouml;	umlaut-O	x	215		multiplication sign
Ø	216	&Oslash;	slash-O	Ù	217	&Ugrave;	grave-U
Ú	218	&Uacute;	acute-U	Û	219	&Ucirc;	circumflex-U
Ü	220	&Uuml;	umlaut-U	Ý	221	&Yacute;	acute-Y
Þ	222	&THORN;	Icelandic Thorn	ß	223	&szlig;	German sz-ligature
à	224	&agrave;	grave-a	á	225	&aacute;	acute-a
â	226	&acirc;	circumflex-a	ã	227	&atilde;	tilde-a
ä	228	&auml;	umlaut-a	å	229	&aring;	ring-a
æ	230	&aelig;	dipthong	ç	231	&ccedil;	cedilla
è	232	&egrave;	grave-e	é	233	&eacute;	acute-e
ê	234	&ecirc;	circumflex-e	ë	235	&euml;	umlaut-e
ì	236	&icirc;	circumflex-i	ï	239	&iuml;	umlaut-i
ð	240	&eth;	Icelandic eth	ñ	241	&ntilde;	tilde-n
ó	242	&ograve;	grave-o	ó	243	&oacute;	acute-o
ô	244	&ocirc;	circumflex-o	õ	245	&otilde;	tilde-o
ö	246	&ouml;	umlaut-o	÷	247		division sign
ø	248	&oslash;	slash-o	ù	249	&ugrave;	grave-u
ú	250	&uacute;	acute-u	û	251	&ucirc;	circumflex-u
ü	252	&uuml;	umlaut-u	ý	253	&yacute;	acute-y
þ	254	&thorn;	Icelandic thorn	ÿ	255	&yuml;	umlaut-y

* These entity references may or may not be supported in your browser since they are new to the HTML 2.0 draft. If the browser does support the full ISO-Latin-1 character set, however, the numerical character reference should produce the proper symbol.

The Common Gateway Interface and Server-Side Includes

CGI Environment Variables Reference

Table C.1   Environment variables for use in CGI scripts

Environment Variable	Brief Description	Sample Values
AUTH_TYPE	Authentication type (see REMOTE_USER)	Basic
CONTENT_LENGTH	Length of information sent to server	123456
CONTENT_TYPE	Type of information sent to server	application/x-www-form-urlencoded
GATEWAY_INTERFACE	The CGI version the server uses	CGI/1.1
HTTP_ACCEPT	MIME types browser can accept	*/*, image/gif, image/x-xbitmap, image/jpeg
HTTP_REFERER	The "referring" document	http://www.host.com/lastdoc.html
HTTP_USER_AGENT	Name and version of browser	Mozilla/1.0N (X11; Linux 1.1.59 I486)
PATH_INFO	The extra path information	/blah
PATH_TRANSLATED	Virtual to Physical path mapping	/home/http/htdocs/blah
QUERY_STRING	Information sent to a GET script	NAME1=VALUE1&NAME2=VALUE2
REMOTE_ADDR	Address of the requesting machine	127.0.0.1
REMOTE_HOST	Name of the requesting machine	users.machine.com
REMOTE_IDENT	RFC 931 remote user identification	robertm
REMOTE_USER	Authenticated username (see AUTH_TYPE)	username
REQUEST_METHOD	The request method	POST
SCRIPT_NAME	Virtual path to script	/cgi-bin/script.pl
SERVER_NAME	The server's machine name	www.host.com
SERVER_PORT	The port number used	80
SERVER_PROTOCOL	The HTTP version the request used	HTTP/1.0
SERVER_SOFTWARE	The name and version of the server	NCSA/1.3

Server Side Includes (SSIs) Reference

Table C.2 Server-side includes

Command	Tags	Notes
config	errmsg timefmt sizefmt	Configure format for displaying the time and file size. Also used to customize the SSI error message. Note: sizefmt's valid values are *bytes* and *abbrev*.
echo	var	Echo an environment variable.
exec	cmd cgi	Execute a command or a CGI script
flastmod	virtual file	File's last modification.
fsize	virtual file	File's size.
include	virtual file	Include another document.

Table C.3   Environment variables for use with the #echo var SSI

Environment Variable	Purpose
DOCUMENT_NAME	The document's filename. Note: This is not the document's title!
DOCUMENT_URI	The document's URI (Universal Resource Identifier). Note: It should really be called "pathname" because that is what it essentially returns.
DATE_LOCAL	The current local date/time.
DATE_GMT	The current date/time, GMT.
LAST_MODIFIED	Date and time the document was last modified (or created).
QUERY_STRING_UNESCAPED	An unescaped query string sent to the document. Note: If you can get this to work for SSIs, you're a better Webmaster than me!
SERVER_SOFTWARE	Name and version of your server's software.
SERVER_NAME	The machine name where your server is running.
REMOTE_HOST	The user's machine name. Note: This information may not always be available, but REMOTE_ADDR, shown next, will always be defined.
REMOTE_ADDR	Same as REMOTE_HOST but returns the IP address instead.
HTTP_REFERER	The document the user just came from. Note: Not all browsers send this information.
HTTP_USER_AGENT	The name and version of the user's browser.

Table C.4   Field descriptors for timefmt

Field Descriptor	Description	Example using Monday, 05-June-1995 at 10:21:14 PM
%%	Display a percent sign (%)	%
%a	Abbreviated weekday name	Mon
%A	Weekday name	Monday
%b or %h	Abberviated month name	Jun
%B	Month name	June
%c	Date and time like %x %X	Mon Jun 05 22:21:14 1995
%d	Day of month from 01 through 31	05
%D	Date in MM/DD/YY format	06/05/95
%e	Same as %d but single digits are not padded with 0	5
%H	Hour in military time from 00 through 23	22
%I	Hour in civilian time from 00 through 12	10
%j	Day of year	156
%k	Same as %H but single digits are not padded with 0	22
%l	Same as %I but single digits are not padded with 0	10
%m	Month from 01 through 12	06
%M	Minute from 00 through 59	21
%n	A newline, like 	
%p	AM or PM	PM
%r	Time of day as %I:%M:%S %p	10:21:14 PM
%R	Time of day as %H:%M	22:21
%S	Seconds from 00 through 59	14
%t	A horizontal tab	
%w	Day of week if Sunday is day 0	01
%x	Date, using your country's regular date format	06/05/95
%X	Time, using your country's regular time format	22:21:14
%y	Year from 00 through 99	95
%Y	Year in a four digit format	1995
%Z	Timezone	PDT

Note: Characters that are not listed in Table C.4 will be printed as-is. For example, dashes "-" and slashes "/".

Decimal to Hexadecimal Conversion

Table D.1 will allow you to easily convert from decimal to hexadecimal and back. Hexadecimal numbers are typically written with a leading "0x" to differentiate them from regular decimal numbers, when the difference may not be immediately apparent. For example, 0x3A is the same as the hexadecimal number "3A."

Table D.1   Decimal to Hexadecimal conversion chart

Dec	Hex	Dec	Hex	Dec	Hex	Dec	Hex	Dec	Hex	Dec	Hex	Dec	Hex	Dec	Hex
0	00	16	10	32	20	48	30	64	40	80	50	96	60	112	70
1	01	17	11	33	21	49	31	65	41	81	51	97	61	113	71
2	02	18	12	34	22	50	32	66	42	82	52	98	62	114	72
3	03	19	13	35	23	51	33	67	43	83	53	99	63	115	73
4	04	20	14	36	24	52	34	68	44	84	54	100	64	116	74
5	05	21	15	37	25	53	35	69	45	85	55	101	65	117	75
6	06	22	16	38	26	54	36	70	46	86	56	102	66	118	76
7	07	23	17	39	27	55	37	71	47	87	57	103	67	119	77
8	08	24	18	40	28	56	38	72	48	88	58	104	68	120	78
9	09	25	19	41	29	57	39	73	49	89	59	105	69	121	79
10	0A	26	1A	42	2A	58	3A	74	4A	90	5A	106	6A	122	7A
11	0B	27	1B	43	2B	59	3B	75	4B	91	5B	107	6B	123	7B
12	0C	28	1C	44	2C	60	3C	76	4C	92	5C	108	6C	124	7C
13	0D	29	1D	45	2D	61	3D	77	4D	93	5D	109	6D	125	7D
14	0E	30	1E	46	2E	62	3E	78	4E	94	5E	110	6E	126	7E
15	0F	31	1F	47	2F	63	3F	79	4F	95	5F	111	6F	127	7F

Table D.1 Decimal to Hexadecimal conversion chart (continued)

Dec	Hex	Dec	Hex	Dec	Hex	Dec	Hex	Dec	Hex	Dec	Hex	Dec	Hex	Dec	Hex
128	80	144	90	160	A0	176	B0	192	C0	208	D0	224	E0	240	F0
129	81	145	91	161	A1	177	B1	193	C1	209	D1	225	E1	241	F1
130	82	146	92	162	A2	178	B2	194	C2	210	D2	226	E2	242	F2
131	83	147	93	163	A3	179	B3	195	C3	211	D3	227	E3	243	F3
132	84	148	94	164	A4	180	B4	196	C4	212	D4	228	E4	244	F4
133	85	149	95	165	A5	181	B5	197	C5	213	D5	229	E5	245	F5
134	86	150	96	166	A6	182	B6	198	C6	214	D6	230	E6	246	F6
135	87	151	97	167	A7	183	B7	199	C7	215	D7	231	E7	247	F7
136	88	152	98	168	A8	184	B8	200	C8	216	D8	232	E8	248	F8
137	89	153	99	169	A9	185	B9	201	C9	217	D9	233	E9	249	F9
138	8A	154	9A	170	AA	186	BA	202	CA	218	DA	234	EA	250	FA
139	8B	155	9B	171	AB	187	BB	203	CB	219	DB	235	EB	251	FB
140	8C	156	9C	172	AC	188	BC	204	CC	220	DC	236	EC	252	FC
141	8D	157	9D	173	AD	189	BD	205	CD	221	DD	237	ED	253	FD
142	8E	158	9E	174	AE	190	BE	206	CE	222	DE	238	EE	254	FE
143	8F	159	9F	175	AF	191	BF	207	CF	223	DF	239	EF	255	FF

The RGB hex triples for some common colors are listed in Table D.2. Use these values when changing background and foreground colors using the Mozilla extensions.

Index

—A—

Access control, 79, 263
Access log, 399
Adding to a mailing list, 194
America Online, 18
Anchor
    attributes, 162
    description, 109
    name, 112
    with icon, 128
Animation, 432
Archiving logs, 407
Arena, 420
Associative array, 191, 211
Attribute value, 106
Audio files, 432
Authentication, 73
Authoring tools
    introduction, 133
    list of available, 135
    system requirements, 134
Automated indexing services, 395
Avoiding Mozilla extensions, 298
Avoiding physical styles, 94

—B—

Background colors, 358
Background patterns, 363
Bandwidth, 37, 54, 165
Base font, 323
Basic Rate Interface. *See* BRI
Be a Web user first, 17
Bearer channels, 44
Blink, 329
Bonding, 44

Book
    examples on CD-ROM, 444
    focus, 17
    network assumption, 2
    purpose, 1, 17
Borders, 302
Bottom alignment, 300
Bounding box, 304
BRI, 44-45, 59
Broken image icon, 121
Browser list, 25
BSDI, 69
Buffer flushing, 380
Bullet types, 317
Bullets, 102

—C—

C language, 178
Cabling
    10baseT, 40
    coaxial, 40
    twisted pair, 40
    UTP, 40
Caching, 279
Captions, 344
CCI, 424
CD-ROM
    animation, 432
    audio, 432
    book examples, 444
    DOSPERL, 442
    HomePage Creator, 435
    HotMetal, 436
    HTML Assistant, 437
    HTML Writer, 438
    HTMLed, 438

images, 432
Internet Assistant, 435
Internet Chameleon, 434
Internet documentation, 434
introduction, 431
MPEGplay, 439
NetSeeker, 444
Paint Shop Pro, 440
RTF2HTML, 439
Slackware, 433
video, 432
Video for Windows, 444
ViewSpace, 441
Web Spinner, 442
Web4ham, 443
Win32, 443
Windows httpd, 443
WinG, 444
Centering, 322
CERN, 27, 229
CERN httpd, 69
Certificate, 74, 76
Certificate-based validation, 74
Certification, 75
CGI
    as a protocol, 12
    client pull, 371
    concept, 178
    considerations, 15
    data stream definition, 178
    definition, 12
    environment variables
        CONTENT_LENGTH, 260
        CONTENT_TYPE, 260
        GATEWAY_INTERFACE, 259
        PATH_INFO, 260
        PATH_TRANSLATED, 261
        QUERY_STRING, 259
        REQUEST_METHOD, 259
        reference, 465-466
        SERVER_NAME
        SERVER_PORT
        SERVER_PROTOCOL, 259
        SERVER_SOFTWARE, 258
    example, 12

generating forms, 247
scripts, 4, 178
server push, 374
tested scripts, 217
troubleshooting, 198
when to use, 10
Changing colors, 357
Channel Service Unit/Data Service
    Unit. *See* CSU/DSU
Channels, 43-44
Check boxes, 184, 201
Chroot, 82
Circles, 229
Clicking action, 232
Client pull, 357, 367, 369
Client-server
    definition, 1
    WAIS approach, 285
    Web approach, 285
Clip art, 129
Color
    approximation, 361
    background, 358
    computer representation, 358
    current set, 361
    foreground, 363
    list to avoid most dithering, 362
    more than one background, 362
    palette, 361
    values, 359
Comments, 266
CommerceNet, 60
Commercial potential, 419
Common Client Interface. *See* CCI
Common Gateway Interface
    as a protocol, 12
    client pull, 371
    concept, 178
    considerations, 15
    data stream definition, 178
    definition, 12
    environment variables
        CONTENT_LENGTH, 260
        CONTENT_TYPE, 260

GATEWAY_INTERFACE, 259
PATH_INFO, 260
PATH_TRANSLATED, 261
QUERY_STRING, 259
REQUEST_METHOD, 259
reference, 465-466
SERVER_NAME
SERVER_PORT
SERVER_PROTOCOL, 259
SERVER_SOFTWARE, 258
example, 12
generating forms, 247
scripts, 4, 178
server push, 374
tested scripts, 217
troubleshooting, 198
when to use, 10
Common log format, 77, 400
Compact list. *See* menu list
Compressed SLIP. *See* CSLIP
Compression, 308
CompuServe, 18-19
Computer security consultant, 80
Configuration problems, 197
Connection
computer configuration, 53
equipment, buying your own, 53
frame relay, 41
high-speed, 8-9
importance to Web server, 54
ISDN, 43
leased lines, 38
low-speed, 37
medium-speed, 8
number of simultaneous, 10
operating system, 53
T1, 42-43
T3, 45
Content
subtype, 194
type, 194
Content is everything, 297
CONTENT_LENGTH, 260

Contention, 56-57
Conventions, 33
Converter
definition, 133
description, 149
Copyrights, 415
Creating a table, 329
Creating an HTML document with
image maps, 225
Creating image maps, 223
Credit card, 5, 64, 72, 416, 427
Cryptography
certificates, 74-75
public key, 73
RSA data security, 75
CSLIP, 37
CSU/DSU, 39
Custom messages, 249

Decimal to Hexidecimal
conversion, 469-470
Declaration, 87
Definition list. *See* glossary list
Designing an image map, 225
Designing Web pages, 163
Dialup shell account, 19, 30
Digital signature, 428
Directory list, 103
Dithering, 361
DNS, 412
Document
address formatting, 98
BASE element, 156
blockquotes, 98
body, 88, 90
comments, 154
digital signature, 428
dynamic, 175-176, 194
echo command, 269

formatting, 86
fragment, 113
head, 88, 155
heading guidelines, 96
heading levels, 95
horizontal rules, 97
image map, 225
implementing interactive
    HTML, 179
including in current
    document, 266
Internet, 434
line breaks, 100
LINK element, 158
linking, 109, 397
moving, 410
NEXTID element, 161
non-text, 116
number in script, 386
owner, 89
paragraph, 92
relationships, 158, 160
root, 266
searching, 284
section headings, 95
size, 117, 272
static, 175-176
style, 92
title, 89
title size, 90
wrapping, 91
Document instance, 87-88
Document type declaration. *See* DTD
Domain name, 263
Domain Name Server. *See* DNS
DOSPERL, 442
Downloading a program
    with NetSeeker, 447
DTD, 87-88, 107
Dumb terminal, 27
Dynamic document, 176, 194
Dynamic HTML document, 11
Dynamic IP, 37
Dynamic script, 12

—E—

E-cash, 428
Editing HTML, 135
Editor
    definition, 133
    learning curve, 142
    raw HTML, 137
    word processing templates, 142
    WYSIWYG, 136
Electronic cash. *See* E-cash
Electronic funds transfer
    cost, 11
    micropayments, 428
    regulations, 11
Electronic mall, 397
Element attribute, 105
Empty elements, 92
EMWAC HTTPS, 70
Encryption
    browser support, 72
    certificates, 74-75
    public keys, 73
    RSA data security, 75
    server, 72
    S-HTTP support, 67
    SSL support, 67
Environment variables
    CONTENT_LENGTH, 260
    GATEWAY_INTERFACE, 259
    HTTP_ACCEPT, 261
    HTTP_REFERER, 262
    PATH_INFO, 261
    PATH_TRANSLATED, 261
    QUERY_STRING, 259
    reference, 465-466
    REMOTE_ADDR, 262
    REMOTE_HOST, 262
    REMOTE_IDENT, 263
    REQUEST_METHOD, 259
    SERVER_NAME, 258
    SERVER_PORT, 258
    SERVER_PROTOCOL, 259
    SERVER_SOFTWARE, 258
    user agent, 262

Equipment
    buying your own, 53
    failure, 411
Error messages, 275
Escape character, 113
Ethernet, 39-40
Exploring the Web, 32
Extensions (Mozilla)
    ALIGN attribute, 299
    BORDER attribute, 302
    centering text, 322
    font size, changing, 323-324
    HEIGHT attribute, 303
    inline JPEGs, 307
    interlaced inline images, 309
    ISINDEX changes, 321
    HSPACE attribute, 301
    List attributes, 315-320
    LOWSRC attribute, 308
    tables, 329-355
    VSPACE attribute, 301
    WIDTH attribute, 303

—F—

FAQs, 4, 131, 394
Field descriptors, 273
File
    animation, 432
    archive, 407
    configuration, 264
    converter program, 149
    format assumptions, 118
    image, 116, 432
    index, 289
    library, 381
    log, 77, 399-400, 411
    log analyzers, 404
    log sample, 401
    log size, 403
    map, 229
    map configuration, 227, 230

    MIDI, 432
    movie clip, 116
    sound, 116
    space required, 10
    video, 432
    WAV, 432
Filter. *See* converter
Firewall, 31, 79, 80
Font
    fixed-width, 91
    proportional, 91
Font sizes, 323
Form
    check boxes, 184
    custom user-feedback, 199
    definition, 177
    design, 180
    drawback, 234
    environment variables, 188
    example, 180, 194
    image map, 235
    ISINDEX alternative, 279
    mailing list example, 186
    multiple, 247
    name attribute importance, 181
    popularity, 262
    resetting, 186
    sample with data, 214
    screen display, 182
    separator lines, 183
    size, 183
    storing data received, 215
    submitting, 185
    tags, 179
    uses, 177
Formatting extensions, 104
Formula for user access to a
    Web page, 54
For-pay Internet marketing, 396
Fractional T1, 43, 59
Fragment navigation, 113
Frame cloud, 41
Frame relay, 32, 41, 58
Free icons and art, 129
Free premade scripts, 217

FreeWAIS-sf. Pointers, 292
Freeware, 431
Frequently Asked Questions. *See* FAQs
Frog dissection page, 222
Full T1, 59

—G—

GATEWAY_INTERFACE, 259
Generalized markup language, 87
GEnie, 18
GET method, 186, 259
Getstats, 400, 403
Getting your Web pages on
    the Internet, 45
GIF, 118, 130, 224, 309, 363
Glossary list, 104
Gopher, 67
GoServe, 71
Graph paper, 354
Graphical setup and maintenance, 67
Graphics
    alternative to, 119
    file space required, 10
    interactivity, 219
    size, 166
    time required, 32
    using on a home page, 164

—H—

Halo Desktop Imager, 225
Header, 240, 259
Header cell, 337
Helper applications, 424
Helper program, 116
Hexadecimal equivalents, 358
Hidden boxes, 253
Hidden fields, 255
Home page

brevity, 166
color use, 165
conciseness, 166
contact information, 167
design, 163-164
example, 171, 220
graphics use, 164
hits, 406
layout, 166
links, 167
modification dates, 167
offering, 3
organization's image, 164
saving bandwidth, 165
simplicity, 168
sizing graphics, 166
uses, 4
what's new, 167
HomePage Creator, 435
Hoo's On First, 241
Horizontal rule, 97, 123, 311, 314
Hosting your Web site, 4
HoTMetaL, 137, 436
Hotspot
    CERN map format, 229
    coordinates, 225
    demo, 241
    identifying, 226
    NCSA map format, 229
HREF, 109
htimage, 230
HTML
    alignment, 119
    alternate text, 119
    authoring products, 133
    backward compatibility, 108
    command reference, 453
    comments, 154
    compact list, 102
    converter, 149
    creativity, 168
    customizing output, 196
    description, 85
    design purpose, 88
    directory list, 103

document parts, 88
dynamic, 176
dynamic document, 11
editors, 135
editor, raw, 137
editor, WYSIWYG, 136
embedding lists, 101
extensions, 105
file space required, 10
forms use, 175
glossary list, 104
image map, 231
inconsistencies, 107
levels, 108
lists, 101
manual, 133
markup, 88
menu list, 102
META element, 368
older method of text handling, 208
ordered list, 101
platform-independent, 88
preformatted text, 105
rapid changes, 154
section commenting, 155
source, 155
static, 176
static document, 11
style checking tools, 169
tags
    body, 90
    content, 87
    description, 85
    element, 87
    end, 87, 162
    form, 180
    input, 180
    pair, 89
    parameters, 178
    start, 87
    templates, 142
    unordered list, 102
HTML 1.0, 108
HTML 2.0, 108, 154, 159, 297

HTML 3.0, 108, 163, 297, 420
HTML Assistant, 437
HTML Validation Service, 168
HTML Writer, 438
HTMLed, 438
HTTP
    definition, 2
    protocol, 259
    response code, 401
    response header, 367, 374
    service, 63
HTTP_ACCEPT, 261
HTTP_REFERER, 262
httpd server, 225, 227
Hypertext, 85
HyperText Markup Language.
    See HTML
HyperText Transport Protocol.
    See HTTP

Icon, 119, 128
IETF, 107, 297
Illegal use of icons and images, 130
Image
    alignment with Netscape
        Navigator, 298
    automatic scaling, 304
    background, 357, 364
    border, 302
    centering, 322
    color, 131
    external, 116
    foreground, 357
    horizontal rule, 123
    icon, 123
    inline, 118, 121, 219
    low-resolution, 308
    maps, 180
    masthead, 121
    samples, 432

scaling, 305
text description, 119
Image map
    clicking action, 232
    coordinate name, 239
    creating, 223
    definition, 219
    design, 225
    form, 235
    HTML, 231
    INPUT method, 233
    ISMAP method, 231
    overuse, 226
    requirements, 223
    size, 226
    style, 232
    submit button, 235
IMAGEMAP.CONF, 230
index searching, 284
inline images, 118, 387
INPUT, 233
Integrated Services Digital Network.
    See ISDN
Interlaced GIF, 309
Internet
    backbones, 36
    business operation legalities, 5
    commercial presence, 393
    community, 415
    connection, 36
    dialup shell account, 18
    direct connection, 35
    directories, 395
    draft, 107
    email, 27
    firewall, 31
    future, 419
    how it works, 35
    legalities, 414
    mail specification, 193
    MIME, 193
    online service connection, 19
    packet, 40
    provider list, 60
    punishment, 393

spamming, 392
    text-only access, 26
    virtual reality, 421
Internet Assistant, 143, 435
Internet Chameleon, 434
Internet Club, 19
Internet documentation, 434
Internet Engineering Task Force.
    See IETF
Internet Protocol. *See* IP
Internet service provider. *See* ISP
inverse multiplexing, 44
IP
    address, 37
    dynamic, 37
    packets, 40
    static, 38
ISDN, 8, 43
ISINDEX, 279, 321
ISMAP, 231
ISO-Latin-1 character set, 459-464
ISP
    access, 50
    CGI script support, 50
    choosing, 47
    connection, using theirs, 5
    consulting services, 50
    cost, 51
    graphic artists, 51
    hosting your Web site, 4
    hourly charge, 37
    Internet layer, 36
    leased line, 38
    leasing space, 5
    local, 59
    network administrator, 49
    network connection type, 50
    other offerings, 48
    plans, 49
    question list, 48
    references, 49
    server security, 50
    size, 49
    space for Web pages, 46
    staff assignment, 49

technical support, 51
time in business, 48
using for home page, 4
Web page experience, 48

—J—

JAVA, 425
JPEG, 118, 307

—K—

Keeping state, 248, 251
Key encryption
    example, 74
    private, 73
    public, 73
    reference, 76
Keyword, 400
Kiosk, 24

—L—

Lack of maintenance, 409
LAN, 40
Laying out your home page, 166
Leased line, 38
Left alignment, 299
Libel, 416
Link
    active, 363
    checking, 409-410
    colors, 363
    description, 109
    documents, 109
    home page, 167
    nonstandard files, 118

sound file, 426
specific point, 111
trading, 397
utilities, 409
what's new, 167
Linux, 6, 54, 69, 433
List
    descriptive titles, 90
    flexibility, 315
    scrolled, 204
    scrolled with multiple options, 205
List of available servers, 65
List of providers, 60
List of questions for ISPs, 48
Log file, 77, 404
Log format
    common, 77
    description, 76
    side includes, 77
Logical style, 92-93
Lossy compression, 308
LVIEW, 116, 225
Lycos, 395
Lycos Search, 33
Lynx
    description, 26
    obtaining, 26
    text-only, 2
    trying out, 27

—M—

MacHTTP, 71
Macintosh server, 71
Mailing list project, 256
Mailto, 414
Map configuration file, 227
MapEdit, 225, 227
Marketing copy, 394
Marketing department, 398
Marketing your Web server, 392
Markup, 86, 331

Markup language, 86
Masthead, 121
Menu list, 103
Message, 374
Meta-information, 367
Micro-tolls, 419
Middle alignment, 299
MIME, 193, 239, 367, 374
Minimum computer configuration, 53
Modem
    14.4, 58
    28.8, 7, 58
    dialup, 35
    speed, 37
Mosaic
    CCI support, 425
    description, 22
    home page, 22
    kiosk, 24
    obtaining, 23
    popularity, 2
    presentation mode, 23
    tables, 355
Mouse clicks, 225
Mozilla, 20, 297-389
    extensions
        ALIGN attribute, 299
        BORDER attribute, 302
        centering text, 322
        font size, changing, 323-324
        HEIGHT attribute, 303
        inline JPEGs, 307
        interlaced inline images, 309
        ISINDEX changes, 321
        HSPACE attribute, 301
        List attributes, 315-320
        LOWSRC attribute, 308
        tables, 329-355
        VSPACE attribute, 301
        WIDTH attribute, 303
MPEG, 117
MPEGplay, 439
Multimedia email, 376
Multipart message, 375
Multipart/x-mixed-replace, 378

Multiple background colors, 362
Multiple submit buttons, 236
Multiple-option scrolled list, 205

Name=value pair, 190, 212, 249
NAP, 36
National Center for Supercomputer
    Applications. *See* NCSA
Navigator. *See* Netscape; Navigator
NCSA, 22
NCSA httpd, 69
NCSA Mosaic. *See* Mosaic
Netcruiser, 19
Netscape
    advantages, 21
    background images archive, 365
    borders, 302
    document size, 304
    Explorer, 358
    extensions, 357
    filling the void of HTML 2.0, 420
    home page, 20
    keeping an open connection, 357
    market leader, 2
    Mozilla extensions, 297
    Navigator, 20, 297
    obtaining, 21
    table-specific features, 346
    text alignment, 298
Netscape Communications, 20
NetSeeker
    activity log, 449
    downloading resources and
        software, 447
    help, 449
    installation options, 448
    interface, 447
    introduction, 444
    quitting, 450

running, 445
    troubleshooting, 450
NetSite Commerce Server, 64, 69-70
Netsite Communications Server, 69-70
Network connectivity, 410
Network Access Points. *See* NAP
Newline, 91, 193
Newsgroup
    posting announcements, 394
    promoting your Web server, 392
    provider feedback, 60
    using FAQs, 394
Nobreak, 327
Non-Parsing Headers. *See* NPH
Notepad, 3
NPH, 259, 383

—O—

Online services, 18
Open Inventor, 422
OPTION menu, 202
Optional end tags, 163
Ordered list, 101, 318
Organizational image, 164
OS/2
    servers, 71
OS2HTTPD, 72
overriding the base font size, 324

—P—

Page breaks, 310
Paint program, 224
Paint Shop Pro, 440
Paintbrush, 171
Palette, 361
Password, 256, 263
PATH_INFO, 261

PATH_TRANSLATED, 261
Patterns, 363
Peak hours on the Web, 32
Perl, 12, 178, 188-218
Permanent Virtual Circuit. *See* PVC
Phone line
    connected, 7
    dedicated, 8
    high-speed, 8, 9
    leased, 38
    regular, 37
Physical style, 94
Pitfalls of icons, 124
Plain Old Telephone Service. *See* POTS
Plaintext, 85, 269
Platform, 17
Platform independence, 88
Point to Point Protocol. *See* PPP
Polygons, 229
Poor man's animation, 387
Pornography, 416
Port 80-81 258
    default, 81
    privileged, 81
    unprivileged, 81
POST method, 200, 259
POTS, 38
PPP, 37
Preformatted text, 105
Prettyprinting, 331
PRI, 44
Primary Rate Interface. *See* PRI
Private key, 73
Private network, 37
Problems, potential
    background, 366
    background color, 365
    client pull, 372
    configuration, 197
    document appearance, 413
    fill-out forms, 413
    general webmaster, 411
    incorrect link pointers, 413
    infinite input, 208

Mozilla extensions, 299-355, 413
open connections, 386
programming, 197
radio buttons, 202
robot, 408
server push, 376
server response, 412
spamming, 392
T1 lines, 42
using icons, 130
VRML browsers, 422
Processing mouse clicks, 225
Prodigy, 18
Program
    CGI script, 179
    converter, 149
    downloading, 447
    execution, 277
    gateway, 289
    helper, 116
    paint, 129, 224, 360
    PERL example, 188
    robot, 90
    security risk, 216
Programming
    experience, 217
    problems, 197
Protocol definition, 2
Prototyping, 5
Providing 24-hour Web access, 7
Proxy server, 31
Public domain, 431
Public key, 73
Public key cryptography, 73
Publishing setup steps for the Web, 10
Purveyor, 70
PVC, 42

—Q—

QUERY_STRING, 259

—R—

Radio buttons, 199-201
Raw editor, 136
RealAudio, 426
Rectangles, 229
Red-green-blue triple. *See* RGB
Reference numbers, 211
REMOTE_ADDR, 262
REMOTE_HOST, 262
REMOTE_IDENT, 263
Request header, 261
REQUEST_METHOD, 259
Response code, 368, 401
Response header, 367, 369, 374
Response time, 411
Restricted characters, 113
RGB, 358
RGB hexadecimal triple, 358
Rich Text Format. *See* RTF
Right alignment, 299
Robot, 90, 407
Router, 39
RSA Data Security, 75
RTF, 85, 149, 439
RTF2HTML, 149, 439

—S—

Sample home page, 171
Scaling examples, 306
Script
    additional processing, 247
    and programming knowledge, 217
    buffering, 380
    checking, 410
    client pull, 371
    communicating to user's Web
      browser, 192
    converting special characters, 187
    converting to NPH, 384

definition, 11
displaying a new form, 252
dynamic, 12
dynamic behavior, 385
dynamic HTML, 177
example, 12, 212, 241
execution, 276
finding data returned from a form, 187
GET method, 188
hotspots, 220
input, 235
ISINDEX example, 280
keeping state, 248
languages, 12
mailing list, 248
MIME header, 194
name, 384
NCSA's imagemap, 230
NPH, 259, 383
one-dimensional, 247
operating systems, 15
parsing data, 187
POST method, 187-188
premade, 217, 234
process, 179
processing, 382
program, 179
query string, 259
redirection with Location, 239
security, 215
simple animation example, 388
SSI execution, 275
two-dimensional text box, 205
unique name problem, 209
with Web Crawler, 14
writing, 188
Scrolled list mode, 204
Searchable index, 284
Section heading, 95
Secure server, 64
Secure Socket Layer. *See* SSL
Secure-HTTP. *See* SHTTP. *See* S-HTTP
Security, 72, 215, 277, 428

Serial Line Internet Protocol.
    See SLIP
server
    access control, 63
    access control format, 79
    advanced concepts, 76
    business, 64
    CGI revision, 259
    choosing, 63-64
    common log format, 77
    configuration files, 264
    cost, 64, 68
    data stream, 178
    data stream length, 260
    editors, 150
    encryption, 72
    extra path information, 261
    firewall, 80
    free, 64
    gopher, 67
    graphical setup and
        maintenance, 67
    image maps, 63
    list, 65
    maintenance, 408-409
    matter of personal taste, 68
    name, 258
    path information, 261
    performance with SSIs, 278
    port, 258
    protocol, 259
    request method, 188, 259
    running scripts, 63
    scenarios, 3
    scripts, 175
    security, 72, 216
    setting up, 35
    side includes format, 78
    software name and version, 258
    SSI, 264
    summary, 69
    transaction logs, 63
    two-way conversation, 178
    Unix, 69

user directories, 68
VMS-ported, 69
server program
    availability, 64
    description, 2
    features, 63
server push, 357, 374
server-side includes, 77, 247, 264, 282,
    466-468
server software. *See* server program
SERVER_NAME, 258
SERVER_PORT, 258
SERVER_PROTOCOL, 259
SERVER_SOFTWARE, 258
serving content on the Web, 3
SGML
    declaration, 87
    description, 85
    document instance, 87
    document type declaration, 87
    sections, 87
SGML prologue, 421
Shareware, 64, 415, 431
S-HTTP, 67, 72, 427
Signing, 74
Simple Web Indexing System for
    Humans. *See* SWISH
Simultaneous connections, 10
Slackware, 433
SLIP
    cost, 37
    description, 30
SlipKnot, 30
Software
    checking, 410
    shareware, 415
Spaces in names, 114
Spamming, 392
Spanning rows and columns, 332
Special characters, 113, 187
Special formatting symbols, 273
SSL, 67, 72, 427
Standard Generalized Markup
    Language. *See* SGML

Standard HTTP port, 258
Standards, 169
static document, 176
static HTML document, 11
Static information, 175
stdin, 188
stdout, 193
Style guidelines, 163
Submit buttons, 235, 249
Suid nobody, 81
Summary
    accessing the Web overview, 33
    advanced HTML features, 173
    choosing a server, 82
    future of the Web, 428
    gateway interface, 293
    HTML editors, 150
    image maps, 245
    Mozilla features, 389
    Netscape, 355
    setting up a Web server, 61
    webmaster responsibilities, 417
SWISH, 286, 288

—T—

T1 line, 6, 32, 42
T3, 45
Table, 329, 336
Tags
    body, 90
    content, 87
    description, 85
    element, 87
    end, 87, 162
    form, 180
    input, 180
    pair, 89
    parameters, 178
    start, 87
Telnet, 27
Template, 133

Text
    alignment, 298
    alignment in tables, 340
    centering, 322
    content length, 210
    default, 206
    default color, 363
    height, 304
    horizontal spacing, 301
    vertical spacing, 301
    width, 304
    with dithered background, 362
    wrapping, 341
Text box, 183, 254
Texture Land, 366
The Internet Adapter. *See* TIA
TIA, 30
Timestamp, 271
Top alignment, 300
Trademarks, 416
Transparent GIFs, 130

—U—

Universal Resource Name. *See* URN
Unix
    learning, 5, 54
    security tips, 81
    servers, 69
    shell account, 19
    with high-speed connections, 9
Unordered list, 102, 316
Unwritten laws of the Web, 32
URL
    absolute, 109, 156
    alternative, 160
    context, 110
    double dot, 110
    examples, 111
    hash sign, 114
    hexadecimal notation, 114
    path, 231

    plus sign, 114
    pointing to image output script,
        387
    relative, 110
    slash, 110, 114
    source file, 119
    spaces, 114
    special characters, 113
URN, 160
User access formula, 54
User agent, 262
User directories, 68
User input, 177
Using several different browsers, 33

—V—

Variable (CGI)
    CONTENT_LENGTH, 260
    GATEWAY_INTERFACE, 259
    HTTP_ACCEPT, 261
    HTTP_REFERER, 262
    PATH_INFO, 261
    PATH_TRANSLATED, 261
    QUERY_STRING, 259
    reference, 465-466
    REMOTE_ADDR, 262
    REMOTE_HOST, 262
    REMOTE_IDENT, 263
    REQUEST_METHOD, 259
    SERVER_NAME, 258
    SERVER_PORT, 258
    SERVER_PROTOCOL, 259
    SERVER_SOFTWARE, 258
    user agent, 262
Video, 432
Video for Windows, 444
ViewSpace, 441
Virtual reality. *See* VR
Virtual Reality Modeling Language.
    See VRML
VLINK, 363

VR, 421
VRML, 419, 421

—W—

WAIS, 284
warnings, 117
Web
    access time calculation, 55
    "attitude", 33
    client description, 17
    conventions, 33
    creating content, 3
    emergence, 15
    forms, 177
    future, 419
    getting started, 17
    graphics size and resolution, 32
    hits, 406
    HTML editors, 150
    hypertext architecture, 86
    index, 90
    interactivity, 176, 178, 419
    ISP pointers, 60
    legalities of icons and images, 130
    linking documents approach, 285
    maintenance rules, 409
    marketing, 392
    online service access, 19
    page, 45
    page access example, 55-56
    page design, 163
    page feedback, 177
    page indexing, 284
    page searching, 284
    paid marketing services, 396
    pizza, 176
    practice research project, 33
    providing content continuously, 7
    publishing setup steps, 10
    robot, 90, 407

    security, 79
    server selection, 63
    server setup, 35
    server, fast start, 4
    serving content examples, 3
    statistics, 405
    surfing, 32
    traffic, 32, 57
    unwritten laws, 32
    user input, 177
    using a Web site agency, 9
Web browser
    applet, 425
    as a tool, 20
    choosing, 20
    communicating with a script, 192
    data stream, 178
    description, 17
    email, 27
    examples, 2
    focus, 17
    fonts, 91
    helper applications, 424
    hidden variables, 253
    hits, 400
    HTML conformance, 108
    image file type, 121
    image handling, 261
    image map support, 223
    inconsistencies, 168, 320
    line mode, 27
    list, 25
    Location handling, 240
    Lynx, 26
    Mosaic, 22
    Netscape Navigator, 20
    other "Mosaics", 23
    redirection, 219
    tags, 85
    trying several, 33
    wrapping, 100
Web Spinner, 442
Web4ham, 443

WebCrawler, 13, 33
WebMap, 225, 227
Webmaster, 168, 391
WebSite, 70
WebStar, 64, 71
Whitespace, 91
Wide Area Information Servers.
    See WAIS
Win32, 443
Windows
    3.1 servers, 71
    Internet access, 19
    NT servers, 70
Windows HTTPD, 71, 443
WinG, 444
Word HTML template, 143
WordPerfect HTML template, 142
World Wide Web. *See* Web

Writing a simple script, 188
Writing the HTML for an
    image map, 231
WWWWAIS, 293
WYSIWYG, 136

—Y—

Yahoo, 60, 135, 366, 395

—Z—

Z39.50, 286

THE INTERNET:

THE POTENTIAL:

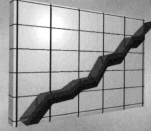

THE COMPANY:

INTERNET™ DIRECT

The Internet is an opportunity your business can't afford to ignore... that's why we've made it easy.

With our I-Site Internet Server, you can have a fully-functioning Root Web Server, an FTP Server, and e-mail host in one package.

Featuring 24-Hour Technical Support, turn-key solutions, and the most comprehensive experience, Internet Direct is your solution to total success on the Internet World Wide Web and beyond.

phone: 1 800 TRY-EMAIL e-mail: sales@direct.net web: http://www.direct.net

READ THE MAGAZINE OF TECHNICAL EXPERTISE!

Published by The Coriolis Group

For years, Jeff Duntemann has been known for his crystal-clear, slightly bemused explanations of programming technology. He's one of the few in computer publishing who has never forgotten that English is the one language we all have in common. Now he's teamed up with author Keith Weiskamp and created a magazine that brings you a selection of readable, practical technical articles six times a year, written by himself and a crew of the very best technical writers working today. Michael Abrash, Tom Swan, Jim Mischel, Keith Weiskamp, David Gerrold, Brett Glass, Michael Covington, Peter Aitken, Marty Franz, Jim Kyle, and many others will perform their magic before your eyes, and then explain how *you* can do it too, in language that you can understand.

If you program under DOS or Windows in C, C++, Pascal, Visual Basic, or assembly language, you'll find code you can use in every issue. You'll also find essential debugging and optimization techniques, programming tricks and tips, detailed product reviews, and practical advice on how to get your programming product finished, polished, and ready to roll.

Don't miss another issue—subscribe today!

- -

☐ 1 Year $21.95   ☐ 2 Years $37.95

☐ $29.95 Canada; $39.95 Foreign   ☐ $53.95 Canada; $73.95 Foreign

Total for subscription: _____
Arizona orders please add 6% sales tax: _____
Total due, in U.S. funds:_____

Send to:
PC TECHNIQUES
7339 E. Acoma Drive, Suite 7
Scottsdale, AZ 85260

Name _____

Company _____

Address _____

City/State/ZIP _____

Phone _____

Phone
(602) 483-0192
FAX
(602) 483-0193

VISA/MC # _____   Expires: _____

Signature for charge orders: _____

Great Deals Online!

Learn MOSAIC Today!

CORIOLIS GROUP BOOKS
Order Form

Name _____

Company _____

Address _____

City/State/ZIP _____

Phone _____

VISA/MC # _____ Expires: _____

Signature for charge orders: _____

Quantity	Description	Unit price	Extension
	FREE STUFF From the Internet	$19.99 U.S.	
	Shopping on the Internet and Beyond	$19.99 U.S.	
	Mosaic & Web Explorer	$34.99 U.S.	
		TOTAL	

FAX, phone, or
send this order form to:

The Coriolis Group
7339 E. Acoma Drive, Suite 7
Scottsdale, AZ 85260

FAX us your order at (602) 483-0193
Phone us your order at (800) 410-0192

Form: 30-6

What's on This CD-ROM

If you've been exploring the Internet and are ready to take the next step—building your own Web server—then the companion CD is your ticket to the next level. In fact, the software on the CD-ROM includes *everything* you need to get started as a Webmaster. Even if you have absolutely no Internet software, this CD will supply you with all the software you need to get connected! Here are just a few of the great tools and items you'll find on the disk:

- Web server software for multiple platforms

- NetSeeker™ software that gives you instant access to the latest Internet software

- Slackware distribution of Linux, a Unix operating system that runs on PCs

- The Perl language engine for running Perl-based CGI scripts on your Web server—for DOS and Windows NT

- Source code for sample applications and CGI scripts

- Connectivity software from NetCom and Chameleon

- Over 10 different HTML editors

- Sound applications for playback, recording, and editing

- Large collection of Web-usable clip art; includes sounds, images, and video

- HomePage Creator—a fast, simple way to make Web pages

- Complete listing of Internet RFCs, STDs, and FYIs

- Image editing tools for creating GIFs for your Web pages—includes capabilities to do transparencies and interlacing

- Clients for e-mail, FTP, Gopher, WWW, and newsreaders

- Win32s and WinG API extensions